AN ODE TO SALONIKA

INDIANA SERIES IN SEPHARDI AND MIZRAHI STUDIES

Harvey E. Goldberg and Matthias Lehmann, *editors*

AN ODE TO

Salonika

THE LADINO VERSES
OF BOUENA SARFATTY

RENÉE LEVINE MELAMMED

Indiana University Press
Bloomington and Indianapolis

Published with the generous support
of the Helen and Martin Schwartz Endowment.

This book is a publication of

Indiana University Press
601 North Morton Street
Bloomington, Indiana 47404-3797 USA

iupress.indiana.edu

Telephone orders   800-842-6796
Fax orders   812-855-7931

© 2013 by Renée Levine Melammed

Manufactured in the United States of America

Library of Congress Cataloging-in-Publication Data

Melammed, Renée Levine.
An ode to Salonika : the Ladino verses of Bouena Sarfatty /
Renée Levine Melammed.
p. cm. — (Indiana series in Sephardi and Mizrahi studies)
Includes bibliographical references and index.
ISBN 978-0-253-00681-3 (cl : alk. paper) — ISBN 978-0-253-00709-4 (eb)
1. Ladino poetry—20th century. 2. Coplas—Greece—Thessalonike. 3. Jews—
Greece—Thessalonike—Social life and customs—20th century. 4. Jewish women—
Greece—Thessalonike—Intellectual life—20th century. 5. Jews—Greece—
Thessalonike—Intellectual life—20th century. 6. Holocaust, Jewish (1939–1945)—
Greece—Thessalonike—Personal narratives. 7. Garfinkle, Bouena Sarfatty,
(1916–1995) 8. Greece—History—Occupation, 1941–1944.
9. Thessalonike (Greece)—Biography. I. Title.
PC4813.7.M45   2013
861'.62—dc23
2012032101

1   2   3   4   5   18   17   16   15   14   13

DEDICATED TO THE MEMORY OF

Bouena Sarfatty Garfinkle (1916–1995)
and Denah Levy Lida (1923–2007)
and to the health of Güler Orgun (1947–).

*Each woman transmitted the Sephardi heritage
in her own remarkable way.*

CONTENTS

It was purely due to chance that I happened to gain access to the writings of Bouena Sarfatty Garfinkle. In the 1970s, while researching the de Botons—an eminent family of rabbinic scholars, I corresponded with Sephardi communities worldwide. Bouena Sarfatty of Montreal wrote me a letter in French informing me that she knew many de Botons who had perished in Auschwitz. In the fall of 1989 I flew to Montreal to meet her. After recording her memories of this family, we talked about more general topics. When Bouena heard that I offered a course in the history of the Sephardi Jews during World War II, she told me she had written about the Nazi takeover of Salonika and offered me a large packet of photocopied verses comprising some two hundred pages. I must confess that I was not free at the time to address this material, but in 1995, I consulted with Moshe Shaul, a colleague active in the Ladino world, who was enthusiastic and encouraging. Slowly but surely, I worked my way through these *komplas* (coplas in Spanish). Having transcribed Inquisition documents, I was familiar with the travails of paleography—yet these pages presented a challenge of their own. Bouena's Ladino, as will be seen in the texts, is characterized by her sometimes-creative orthography; by French, Italian, Greek, and Turkish influences; and by the idiosyncrasies of her handwriting.

In order to understand Bouena's poetry, one needs to be acquainted with the history of Salonika as well as with the poet's personal history. Bouena Sarfatty was born November 15, 1916,[1] in Salonika, Greece, to an eminent family of Sephardi Jews that traced its origins to the expulsion from Spain in 1492. She passed away at age eighty on July 23, 1997. Although she was born into an established family of comfortable means, Bouena did not have an easy life. Her father died when she was two years old,[2] leaving her brother, Eliaou, to care for his five younger sisters, his mother (who died of cancer in 1940), and his aged maternal grandmother. Eliaou was a dedicated brother who ensured his sisters were well educated and fluent in a number of languages; he also arranged for their debutante presentations.

The Nazis invaded Greece in April 1941, when Bouena was not yet twenty-five years old and was engaged to be married to a fellow Salonikan. Bouena's brother, Eliaou; her younger sister, Regina; her centenarian grandmother; and her aunts would all be deported and perish in Auschwitz. An older sister, Marie, moved to Marseilles before the war and her two remaining sisters, Rachel and Daisy, immigrated to Palestine in the 1930s. Bouena remained in Greece and became active in the resistance. After the war, on July 14, 1946, Bouena married

Max Garfinkle, a Ukrainian-born Canadian active in the socialist youth movement Hashomer Hatsa'ir and a founder, in the mid-1930s, of Kibbutz Ein Ha-Shofet.

When Italy attacked Greece on October 28, 1940, Bouena's first cousin Samuel and her fiancé, Chaim, were drafted into the Greek army.[3] On April 6, 1941, with the Italians facing defeat, the Germans attacked Greece and the Greek army began its retreat. Bouena and her widowed aunt Donna were concerned that they had not received letters recently from their "boys." When they realized that the retreating Greek soldiers were entering the city, they glued themselves to the window, hoping to sight their loved ones among them. An entry in Bouena's memoirs exposes the delicacy of this moment:[4]

> Tia Donna and I were watching the retreating soldiers, and it was the most depressing sight of my life. Some of the soldiers in the ranks were crying. Others couldn't walk anymore. Others were wounded and in pain. It was a very dark tableau; there was silence in the house. Tia Donna broke the silence.
>
> "With this good deed that we will do tomorrow, God is going to help Samuel and Chaim," she said. She had not finished saying this when a soldier escaped from the ranks. He was heading for our door. I went down the stairs and spoke to him from afar.
>
> "Come in, come into my apartment."
>
> "It's me, Chaim, it's me!" I heard a very familiar voice say. He came upstairs. Tia Donna, a woman who never lost her courage, had the bathwater warming before we got upstairs. She took Chaim's uniform and he put on pajamas until the bath was ready. She put the khaki clothes in a laundry sack, made a parcel and tied it well, and threw it into the yard as far away as she could. . . . Two hours later, we could see only German tanks in the street. . . . When we got up the next morning, the yard was full of parcels with uniforms inside. Everyone had copied Tia Donna's idea: every apartment had soldiers hiding inside.[5]

The community suffered as a result of the German occupation and also faced a severe winter (1941–42) that was exacerbated by a food shortage. The Red Cross sought to alleviate the situation, as did the Jewish community itself.[6] Bouena, her sister Regina, her best friend Sarah, and other young women offered their services to this international agency. Bouena had previously worked for Matanot La-Evionim, so she essentially was following a similar path—once again distributing food to the hungry and, in this case, providing milk for children from the working districts. Mothers arrived at the Soupe Populaire with empty bottles and displayed the required cards indicating their daily quotas; volunteers prepared the condensed milk and filled the bottles accordingly.

On July 11, 1942, the Nazis began forced conscription of all Jewish males between the ages of nineteen and forty-five.[7] Bouena continued her volunteer work, which by then also included providing for the children of married soldiers in compulsory service. She devoted many verses of poetry to this experience.[8] Some months later, on March 15, 1943, the mothers from the Baron de Hirsch neighborhood did not appear at the regular distribution time and a great deal of condensed milk was left over.[9] The Red Cross representative volunteered his car and driver to take Bouena to that neighborhood in order to deliver the milk to these women. They were surprised and disconcerted to find the neighborhood under heavy guard. Because of its proximity to the train station, Baron de Hirsch had become the designated ghetto from which deportations were arranged. On this very day, Bouena had a traumatic encounter with Vital Hasson, the head of the Jewish police; this experience convinced her that it was no longer safe for her to remain in Salonika. Because of the imminent danger to Bouena as well as to her fiancé, Chaim proposed that they be wed the next day, presumably prior to a joint flight from the city. That night Bouena was warned by an anonymous non-Jew that it would be dangerous for her to sleep in the ghetto.[10] As a result, she stayed with friends who lived near what she referred to as the "Midrash," the synagogue (chapel) where the rabbi was scheduled to marry them.[11] The following morning, she arrived at the Midrash as planned only to find that Chaim had been shot by the Germans and lay dying as he waited for her at the wedding canopy.

Bouena was subsequently arrested and taken to the Pavlos Melas camp on the northern end of Salonika. This was the SS camp in which most of the inmates were political prisoners, and whose fate would be execution.[12] Bouena was subjected to numerous interrogations, apparently because she was suspected of having knowledge of the partisans. Ironically, it was only after her escape that she became affiliated with them. At any rate, she began to chat from time to time with her Greek-speaking female guard, although the latter had been ordered to refrain from conversing with the prisoners. Bouena, who had expertise in embroidery and knowledge of haute couture, began to make fashion suggestions to the guard, and recommended a certain shop where the guard could order a special blouse—and unwittingly provide a clue as to Bouena's whereabouts. This ploy succeeded, and salvation materialized: A German-speaking Greek partisan, masquerading as a senior officer, arrived at the prison. He drugged her guard, and Bouena wore her uniform during her escape. Her subsequent flight from Salonika itself is described in her poems: she was aided by the Italian consul and Daniel Modiano—an Italian Jew who was a family friend, and whom she also lauds numerous times in her writings.[13]

Bouena—bearing an Italian passport in the name of Flora Tivoli of Livorno—eventually managed to leave by train and arrived in Athens in the back of a truck; she immediately approached a friend of her father's who put her in contact with Greek partisans.[14] Her memoirs include accounts of numerous stressful situations in which she managed to avoid arrest as well as death. Known by her nom de guerre, Maritsa (Maria Serafamidou) of Comotini, Bouena served first with the loyalists;[15] after her first contact was killed, she aligned with the communists.[16] In Veria she was a courier who carried bags from partisan headquarters to a soup kitchen for children, where an unseen and unidentified contact would surreptitiously exchange bags with her by means of codes and signs. In Evvia she performed mostly menial tasks, but also threw grenades at German vehicles attempting to pass through mountain roads. One of her more challenging tasks in the underground was to pose as a cook in the kitchen of a camp for German officers in Crete and gather information about them. In this way she enabled her group to capture the German commandant and hold him prisoner until they rendezvoused with a British submarine. Bouena was assigned to be the lookout and informed the signalman of the submarine's approach; the officer was taken to England for interrogation.[17] Bouena also saved the lives of many children by smuggling them via Turkey and Syria to Palestine;[18] she helped wounded and pregnant women she found en route, risking her life time after time. Most of the children Bouena brought to Palestine had been stranded in Evvia after the boat in which they had originally been traveling was attacked.[19] Her mission to accompany them to safety was successful.

In June 1945, Bouena returned to Greece, ostensibly as a dietitian for the soup kitchens set up by the Palestinian Jewish Relief Unit of the UNRRA for refugees from the camps, but in reality she was an agent assigned to set up an underground railroad to Palestine for survivors.[20] The quartermaster who was sent on a similar mission was her future husband, Max Garfinkle. They were both stationed in a former army camp in Siderokastro, a small town near the Bulgarian border. While there, Bouena had many dealings with other members of the unit as well as with survivors of the camps; her poems describe of a number of these encounters.

After completing her mission, Bouena decided to remain in Greece and to return to her hometown in the hope of locating property, funds, belongings, and remnants of her past and her family.[21] As she roamed the streets of postwar Salonika, her sharp eye enabled her to recognize cloth embroidered in her own unique style, her mother's Passover Haggadah, as well as some gifts she had received. On one occasion, she recognized a man from whom she would unsuccessfully attempt to recover funds. She referred to him as

> a gentleman who was supposed to send Chaim and me to Athens after our wedding. He received me very well. Chaim had given him one thousand gold liras. He gave me ten. He took me back to my hotel. On

the way, I said, "I think Chaim gave you a little more money." "Oh, no," he said. "This is what he gave me." I had helped Chaim carry the valises full of money to him. I said to myself, "I have to take what they give me and not think of what we gave to them."[22]

When she saw this "gentleman" for a second time, she was slightly more successful at reclaiming her belongings:

> He introduced me to his wife. His wife was holding a silver handbag in her hand. My eyes stayed on the bag. It was mine. Chaim's grandmother had given it to me. It was very old. Very distinguished women carried bags like this. This bag was handed down from mother to daughter. I said to the gentleman, "For sure you forgot to return this bag to me." He emptied the bag and gave it to me right away.[23]

Precisely because her brother had scattered family possessions and funds among friends and neighbors, Bouena felt she might succeed in reclaiming some remnants of her lost life.[24] When she noticed a girl wearing a very familiar looking jacket she made great efforts to track down the girl's address, suspecting that more of her belongings might be found there. She, Max, and a driver went out to the farm, only to be greeted by a hostile farmer's wife:

> A lady came out. She said, "We don't know any Jewish people and we don't want to know them. If you don't leave immediately, I will untie the dogs." She approached the dogs. I was getting scared but I didn't budge. She said, "Get out!" again. I started to move forward. She became very angry. She said, "If the Germans didn't make you into soap like they did with the rest of your family, I will do it with these dogs."[25]

The farmer returned in the nick of time, although his wife still harbored hopes of deceiving the Jews. When Bouena pointed to a cushion in the house that she personally had made, the farmer's wife claimed that it was the work of her mother. The embroiderer also recognized pieces of artwork she and her sister Regina had fashioned, silver candy dishes that she had received as engagement gifts, china from her fiancé's aunt, and a sofa with two seats and four chairs that had been hers. The farmer brought down a large chest containing her trousseau—which included wool for mattresses which she and her family had boiled, washed, and dried; silk for coats and linings; material for dresses; dishes; linen; buttons; thread; and trimmings. Bouena carted off belongings that had been stored there since their first relocation during Passover in 1941, but she was unable to feel any sense of accomplishment. On the contrary, upon seeing her recovered "treasures" all piled in a room, she felt lonely and depressed as she assessed the losses they represented.[26]

A visit with the bank manager who had been in charge of Eliaou's accounts revealed that neither the accounts nor his security boxes had remained intact.[27] Again, the quest to recover articles was extremely traumatic for Bouena.[28] When she tried to reclaim her former home, she was allotted only two rooms, both of which had been stripped of all the family's belongings.[29] As she searched for her lost world, a few old family friends, mostly Greek non-Jews, voluntarily returned some items to her.[30] Apparently, Bouena's experience was not at all unusual, for other returnees bemoaned their fate as well.

Bouena's personal experiences were inextricably tied to those of her community. Her own experiences reflect the developments from the time of the invasion until the deportations and because she was one of the few to escape and to join the partisans, she was able to record subsequent encounters as well. Throughout her life Bouena attempted to save whatever she could: children, songs, belongings, people, and memories.

Years later Bouena sought to memorialize a lost world and culture by expressing herself poetically in her native tongue. Her poetic legacy consists of a rather large collection of Ladino poems, known as coplas, that describe life in Salonika before World War II and a smaller collection of Ladino coplas that describe the Nazi conquest of Salonika in April 1941 and the suffering that followed. The poems in the latter collection are especially poignant. The two oeuvres complement each other and reveal many details of her life. In addition to the poems and her memoirs, Bouena recorded scores of songs, ballads, and proverbs; many of these present previously unknown versions of Ladino songs and sayings. Some of these renditions were recorded by ethnomusicologist Judith Cohen and preserved in the National Music Archives of the National Library in Jerusalem,[31] and many of the traditional songs she recorded have been analyzed in a doctoral dissertation completed at the Center for Judeo-Spanish Studies at Bar-Ilan University.[32] The proverbs have yet to be studied,[33] but the two collections of coplas are what most attract and fascinate the historian. Bouena's verses effectively provide an entrée into the final years of Salonikan Jewry's existence by means of her perceptions of the significant developments during this period. At the same time, a taste of the original language, and of the world of the medieval Spanish spoken by the exiles from Spain,[34] can be acquired by the non-Ladino speaker perusing the verses in Ladino.

One cannot forget that Bouena was writing some three decades after she had lost her home and her family. The writing itself must have served as a catharsis, but the poet also had an historical agenda in mind. In short, her aim was to keep alive a language that was hardly in use by the time she was writing and to commemorate, especially for later generations, a world that had been artificially destroyed. Interestingly enough, because my colleague, Shmuel Refael believes that there is a diary-like feeling about her oeuvre, which is written in the present tense, he attempted to deduce whether or not she had recorded the coplas during the war period. He wondered whether she had notes and whether there was an earlier text or all her poems were based on memory. I highly doubt that she had the time to write while in Salonika; she never mentioned any writing in the postwar period. Her son, Dr. Ely Garfinkle, who has responded to endless queries and graciously supplied me with additional material as well as the photos of his mother's amazing embroidery work taken by him and by his son Michael, confirmed that she wrote the poems from scratch in Montreal.[35]

Two women—both Balkan Sephardim born in the first half of the twentieth century—have proven to be incredibly helpful and generous with their time. My beloved teacher and recently deceased Denah Levy Lida, emeritus professor at Brandeis University, sat with me for many hours during my sabbatical year (2005–2006) and painstakingly helped me through large portions of Bouena's Ladino. By means of e-mail, I have gained endless insights from Mme. Güler Orgun of Istanbul, whom I found after accessing the Ladino website groups.yahoo.com/group/Ladinokomunita with the gracious help of Devin Naar. (My dear friend and colleague Aron Rodrigue also helped me in the early phases of translation and was the angel who sent Devin to me.) Güler is an incredibly gracious woman who has guided me through the perils of understanding a language with so many outside influences and variations. She also insisted upon examining both sets of coplas before the manuscript was submitted. When stymied, Mme. Orgun found two Salonikan colleagues to bail us out: Yehuda Hatsvi of Tel Aviv; and David (Andreas) Kounio of Salonika, whom I finally met on Tisha B'Av, 2011, and who unfortunately passed away a few months later, on December 4, 2011. I cannot describe the amount of time and knowledge from which I benefited thanks to these wonderful people over the years. Each of them responded to my queries enthusiastically and graciously. The hundreds of e-mail messages in my files attest to this; I never could have produced this book without them. David (Andreas) wrote me numerous times that he could not wait to see the book published—which was, unfortunately, literally the case. I am grateful to Erika Perahia Zemour of the Jewish Museum of Thessaloniki for sending me the group photo of the wedding within minutes of my identifying Bouena while visiting the exhibition there. A todos, grasias de todo korason!

Over the years I have given numerous presentations concerning this poetry, the first at a Misgav Yerushalyim conference together with Shmuel Refael, who has been extremely supportive of this enterprise; twice at the World Congress of Jewish Studies; at the Association for Jewish Studies; at City College of New York with the encouragement of Jane Gerber; at Vanderbilt University; to the

Ladino speakers of Ashkelon; in a formal lecture at Yale University during my sabbatical year there; and last, but not least, the plenary talk at the European Association of Biblical Studies in Salonika on the eve of Tisha B'Av, 2011. These talks have helped me gain perspective on the writings and life of Bouena Sarfatty. I am also grateful to Janet Rabinowitch for believing in the value of this project (as did the committee assigned to it, namely Harvey Goldberg and Matthias Lehmann) and for her willingness to brainstorm with me in our search for the appropriate means to make this material accessible to the reader. Janet assigned a highly competent group from Indiana University Press to work with me—Peter C. Froelich; Nancy Lightfoot; and a wonderfully sharp, meticulous, and focused copyeditor, Dawn Ollila—to whom I am truly grateful. Finally, I hope that readers of this book will gain an appreciation of Bouena's insights and uniqueness as well as a new perspective on the history of Jewish Salonika during the first half of the twentieth century.

Corner of Tsimiski and Agias Sofias Streets, where the Sarfatty family lived (exact address unknown).

House on Mitropoleos Street, where the family was moved in 1941 (exact address unknown).

House on Sigrou Street near the Monastir Synagogue, where the family was moved in 1943.

Bouena poses on balcony in her neighborhood, August 8, 1939.
Courtesy of Ely Garfinkle.

AN ODE TO SALONIKA

INTRODUCTION

Twentieth-Century Salonika and Bouena's Ladino Coplas

Salonika provided Jewish exiles from Spain and Portugal with a beloved home for four and a half centuries.[1] The Ottoman rule that began only fourteen years prior to the Expulsion from Spain in 1492 proved conducive to the flowering of a strong, healthy, and productive Jewish community. The reputation of the community was so impressive that by 1553, Samuel Usque coined a biblical term of endearment for the city in his *Consolation for the Tribulations of Israel,* in which he described Salonika as

> a true mother-city in Judaism.[2] For it is established on the very deep foundations of the Law. And it is filled with the choicest plants and most fruitful trees presently known anywhere on the face of our globe. These fruits are divine, because they are watered by an abundant stream of charities. The city's walls are made of holy deeds of the greatest worth.[3]

By 1613, two-thirds of the city's population was Jewish; a Jewish majority was present through the beginning of the twentieth century.[4] The exiles strove to organize themselves religiously, economically, and educationally, and eventually built an impressive Talmud Torah and provided extensive welfare to those in need. The newcomers contributed to the development of weaving and dyeing as well as the manufacture of wool, silk, and tobacco. These Jews—whose professions ranged from bankers and merchants to middlemen and storeowners to porters, fishermen, and tobacco workers—found themselves situated between East and West by virtue of being in Salonika. Although exposed to Westernization and Europeanization, they remained strongly connected to the Ottoman world and to their fellow Sephardi Jews for centuries.

The nineteenth century in particular brought significant changes, including rather sophisticated rail and shipping connections—and, as a result, a boom for the port of Salonika.[5] Europe's presence increased considerably, as firms and individuals made inroads in industry, fashion, education, and finance.[6] Many of these firms employed Jews as maritime, insurance, and tobacco agents.[7] Salonika was considered to be the "most industrially advanced city in the Ottoman Balkans."[8] Visits by luminaries such as Baron de Hirsch resulted in investments of funds as numerous locals and Italians such as the Allatini, Fernandez, and Modiano families followed suit. The Alliance Israélite Universelle (AIU), a Parisian-based society founded in 1860 and devoted to Jewish cultural and professional development, established a school for boys in 1873 and for girls in the following year. Private schools were simultaneously founded by the Pintos, Alshehs, and Gategnos—all active members of the community.[9] Essentially, the principles of modern education were being transmitted by Westernized Jews. The French viewed the developments that transpired in this "Metropolis of Israel" with great satisfaction,[10] for French culture was being advocated and inculcated par excellence.[11] It could be said that

> Salonika at the turn of the century thus lay on the crossroads of two ages as well as of two civilizations. The metropolis of the Southern Balkans acquired a cosmopolitan character and became the main access route for Western capital and ideas to the East . . . as well as major trade center, the most westernized city of the Ottoman Empire. Salonika's uniqueness lay, foremost, in its predominantly Jewish character at a time when the Ottoman Empire was disintegrating and the Balkan nation states rising in its wake. As European economic penetration intensified, Salonika became the coordinator of European hegemony over the Ottoman Empire. Nevertheless, European interests never prevailed over the dynamism of the local entrepreneurs. Economic development laid the basis for modernization, for which European education would provide the means.[12]

Contact with Europe resulted in changes for the city as well as for the Jewish community; some of its members sought to become "local honorary Europeans." Thus, there were Greek and Jewish merchants who obtained the protection of foreign consuls and essentially served as cultural intermediaries.[13] Other developments included the installation of running water in 1898, of electricity by 1899, and—by 1900—the appearance of some fourteen newspapers in print in four different languages. In short, at "the end of the nineteenth century, Jewish Salonika seemed poised for a brilliant future as the capital city of a newly renascent Balkans."[14]

Although the twentieth century held great promise for Salonika, one must realize that certain recurring events always meant disaster for the community. The most devastating of these were conflagrations, particularly during the nineteenth century; the fire of 1890 left twenty thousand Jews homeless. Consequently, public housing complexes for working-class victims of this fire as well as recent Eastern European and Russian immigrants were established in two plots in the Vardar area (Regie Vardar) west of the city as well as in the eastern suburb of Kalamaria.[15] This represents a pioneering initiative on the part of the Jewish community,[16] reflecting its ongoing attempt to aid the impoverished who suffered endlessly from fires, epidemics, and unemployment.[17] The wealthy had insurance policies to cushion these blows, but the less fortunate increasingly suffered losses of homes and property as well as devastating financial complications that followed in each disaster's wake. Among the various charitable activities espoused by the community were fundraisers and the building of hospitals, orphanages, and clinics that offered free medicine and serums. At the same time, the condition of the streets in the poorer areas remained abominable, creating an environment conducive to malaria.

Bouena Sarfatty was witness to the currents of change and turmoil that took place in the first half of the twentieth century, which would alter and eventually destroy this "mother-city in Israel."[18] Her poetry and her memoirs reflect these developments and the turbulence of life in twentieth-century Jewish Salonika, by then composed of seventeen neighborhoods comprising numerous schools, synagogues, stores, and assorted clubs whose members belonged to different social strata. Bouena's birthplace was "a Jewish Salonika which was on the one hand, westernized, modern and cosmopolitan, on the other traditional, religious and parochial; a city full of life."[19]

The twentieth century brought with it tensions and conflicts between absolutism and nationalism, authoritarianism and the workers' movement, Ottomanism and Balkanism, and among the different Balkan groups as well. The ideals of nationalism were spreading and gaining a foothold in the Christian world; its influence grew and affected Muslims in the Ottoman Empire. The Young Turk Revolution of 1908 aimed to replace traditional leaders such as Sultan Abdul Hamid by substituting loyalty to the sultan with loyalty to a government representing the people. The Jews, certain that Ottoman rule had been and would continue to be beneficial to them, remained faithful to the sultan. This stance was logical due to a longstanding sense of mutual trust that had developed between them: "None can have thought that Salonica in particular— the city they dominated—would develop to their benefit if it became part of Greece or Bulgaria."[20] Because the sultan did not succeed in countering this revolution, the imminent changes did not augur well for the pro-Ottoman Jews; nevertheless, the revolt managed to create an illusion of universal freedom and equality for the inhabitants of Salonika,[21] as well as a short-lived optimism among the Sephardim. However, once Jews could be drafted as Greek citizens, young men seeking to avoid the draft represented the majority of emigrants leaving Salonika at that juncture.[22]

By 1910, because the notion of an Ottoman nation had not yet taken hold, numerous movements began to compete for political control of the community.

The workers' movement was led mainly by Bulgarian and Jewish intellectuals who advocated wage increases and strikes. The socialists also sought the support of the workers while Zionist groups, once they were permitted to organize, became more militant in their platforms. Slowly, but surely, the Jews were being politicized. Many Jewish workers, especially those in the tobacco industry,[23] were attracted to workers' organizations and strikes and demonstrations became more commonplace. Meanwhile, antisemitism began to rear its head as numerous Greeks expressed their frustration at not being able to oust the Jewish middlemen with whom they were competing. Although these popular manifestations did not reflect any official policy, their very existence was a serious cause for concern.[24]

Salonikan Jewry made an effort to inculcate a sense of Greek patriotism, but the Balkan Wars were to alter the situation irrevocably. In the latter part of 1912, the Ottoman Empire lost the majority of its European territories to the Balkan States as the result of a joint Balkan offensive. Thus, in October of that year, Greek troops entered the city and began to manifest their antisemitism quite violently.[25] The Jews were perceived as being "interlopers who enjoyed the patronage of a hated foreign conqueror and benefited economically from their ties to it."[26] By November 10, the Jews, few of whom knew Greek, found themselves in a city annexed by the Greek state. The state quickly made declarations promising protection for the community that included permitting the Jews to observe their Sabbath and to keep accounts in their native Spanish-based language, freedom of the press, and providing them with the option of paying a fee in order to avoid the draft.[27] Nevertheless, the message of harmony,[28] which had been advocated by the new regime, was dissipating—especially because Greece and Bulgaria were at odds over the rule of Macedonia. As a result, their armies clashed between March and April 1913, resulting in a readjusted division of territory. In June, because of dissatisfaction with the division of spoils, Bulgaria began a second short-lived and unsuccessful fight. This move essentially solidified the rule of the Greek troops in Salonika.

Proposals were made to establish an international rule in the city; the Jews favored this idea, but the Greeks vehemently objected to it.[29] At this time, some 2,400 Jews preferred to declare their nationalities as Spanish, Portuguese, or Austrian so as not to be counted as Greek citizens;[30] an additional wave of emigration took place as well. Many of those who remained hoped they would receive legal protections similar to those that had been in effect under Ottoman rule.[31] Be that as it may, Hellenization of the city proceeded apace: one could no longer wear a fez to work (European hats were preferable); the language of administration was now Greek, especially because non-Salonikan officials were being recruited to the city; and street names were altered, among other things.[32] Although the city had been conquered quickly, the new government would discover that the lengthy Ottoman rule had left some long-lasting spheres of influence that would not disappear as easily as the fez.

The transition from Ottoman to Greek rule would lead to the creation of a modern Jewish Salonika, but the path was full of pitfalls. This was a fledgling modern nation state that aimed to erase the distinctiveness of individual groups; the Jewish community clearly presented an obstacle to this goal. World War I likewise created serious challenges regarding the future of Greek Salonika.[33] Although Greece remained technically neutral, King Constantine clearly displayed pro-German proclivities; the Jews were traditionally supporters of the king and remained so despite this incongruous political position. Eleutherios Venizelos, formerly a rebel leader in Ottoman Crete, openly rejected the royal stance. In October 1915, Allied troops from France and Britain were stationed in the city and martial law was declared in June 1916. The presence of these troops instilled confidence in Venizelos, who established a breakaway government in Salonika that directly opposed royal rule. This complicated situation eventually was resolved as the result of pressure from the Allies, which led to the abdication of the king and recognition of Venizelos as prime minister.[34] These developments served to exacerbate the growing alienation of the pro-royal Jews from the loyal Greek nationals.

August 18, 1917, was a disastrous day for the Jewish community. A fire, which ostensibly began as the result of uncontrolled cooking sparks at 2:00 PM on August 17, proceeded to flare up and rage for thirty-two hours, precisely when there was a water shortage on that side of town.[35] Some fifty-two thousand Jews lost their homes, and close to ten thousand businesses and homes were destroyed. Of the property that was devastated, three-quarters had belonged to Jews. The progress that had been made in the past two decades in terms of caring for the Jewish poor, such as the construction of working-class housing projects, was effaced overnight.[36] Thirty-two synagogues and five study houses were burned along with libraries, school, offices, banks, shops, cinemas, and theaters.[37] This devastating catastrophe for the Jewish community afforded the new government the opportunity to renovate and replace the ancient Ottoman city with unexpected ease. The fire served as a catalyst for accelerating the process of Hellenization in the city and provided Venizelos with an ideal means of altering the Jewish character of Salonika.[38] The city could be modernized in one fell swoop while the Jews were being relocated and ostensibly removed from the very center in which they had lived and worked for centuries. The concern for Jewish sensitivities during this process was minimal. According to Ottoman

Jewish historian Minna Rozen, "any action by Venizelos's government aimed at placating the Jews of Salonika was solely due to Jewish intervention in the capitals of Europe and was based on his concern for the city's status."[39]

Allied military personnel had set up tents for the dispossessed. Some Jews opted to relocate to Marseilles, Lyon, Belgrade, Milan, Spain, the United States, and elsewhere in Greece,[40] but for many, state housing was the only option. In light of its new policy, the government elected to settle the fire victims in various new suburbs. The western suburbs of Regie Vardar and the Baron de Hirsch neighborhoods had shacks, sheds, and cabins to offer the workers. Additional sites of relocation included the eastern suburb of Campbell and a neighborhood that would be referred to as 151, the number of a former hospital.[41] In this manner, the center of the city was overhauled and reserved for businesses and administration; businessmen could choose and buy desirable locations. Although certificates were distributed to dispossessed Jewish property owners to enable them to bid in land sales, the certificates' value was reduced so that options were sorely limited. The wealthy managed, more or less, to rebuild their lives, but the workers no longer had easy or direct access to the city or to the port where they had been employed for generations. The subsequent decline of the community was inevitable, as these families could not recoup losses that extended far beyond financial. For example, the communal life that had originated in the courtyards and had been based on social contact between members of extended families suffered tremendously now that these displaced tenants were assigned to live in crowded apartments.[42]

The general atmosphere in the community became even tenser as the result of the "Great Catastrophe." Essentially, in 1923, the Turkish defeat of the Greeks resulted in major population disruptions. This defeat led to the flight of some thirty thousand Muslims from Serbia and Bulgaria who passed through Salonika en route to Turkey. Simultaneously, the arrival of one hundred thousand Christian refugees from Thrace and Anatolia placed pressure on Muslims in Macedonia and environs that led to the latter's emigration. All in all, the refugee population in the area included over a million Orthodox Christians; it is estimated that nearly one hundred thousand refugees from Asia Minor, Thrace, the Caucasus, and the Black Sea arrived in Salonika.[43] Almost overnight, the city housed a Greek majority entitled to numerous rights and exemptions by the government. In order to grant them these rights, a tremendous amount of property was earmarked for the refugees and allotted to the state. This major demographic change led to the displacement of yet more members of the Jewish community. In addition, as the city became more and more Hellenized, the native Sephardim found themselves in a city with a significant hostile Christian presence.

As noted by historian K. E. Fleming, "the shift from Ottoman to Greek rule was an excruciatingly complicated and problematic one for Salonika's Jews."[44] These changing tides are reflected in the ousting of Jewish port workers, and then of Jewish fishermen, in 1922 and 1923. In March, two scrap-metal dealers were falsely accused of tampering with the telephone line in the city and received a death sentence,[45] which was unheard of in the entire history of the Jewish presence in the city. These manifestations of oppression by the state accorded with the attitudes held by the newcomers.[46]

Venizelos, whom the Jews did not support, fought to maintain political power throughout this period, and consistently sought to reduce Jewish strength in the city. Thus, in 1924, Sunday was declared the official day of rest in a city whose port had traditionally been closed on Saturdays, owing to the overwhelming presence of Jewish porters and workers there.[47] It is not surprising to learn that one of the city's nicknames was Savatopolis (City of the Sabbath).[48] Exemption payments from army service for young men who had reached the age of twenty-one were canceled. School curricula had to be altered to accommodate Greek-language requirements. Even the Alliance was eventually forced to change its curricula,[49] although French still remained the language of the "cultured elite."[50] As discriminatory laws took effect, the community continually lost property.[51] Anti-Jewish Venizelist newspapers spread falsehoods and incited the Greeks at every opportunity.

The hostility of the refugees toward the Salonikan Jews did not abate, but was inflamed by Venizelos and his nationalist followers, especially during the last ten days of June 1931. The first attack on a Jewish neighborhood was deflected, but nonetheless led to pogroms later that week in the Campbell quarter, one of the new working-class suburbs in the eastern section of the city. Large groups of rioters—composed mostly of refugees—rampaged, burning homes and stores and leaving destruction in their path. Some 250 families were left homeless, and the Campbell neighborhood was essentially abandoned.[52]

One clear repercussion of this pogrom was an increase in immigration to Palestine and a change in the nature of Zionism within the Jewish community. Originally there had been a low-key Zionism that gained momentum after the Balfour Declaration in 1917. This developed into what has been described as a diaspora nationalism or a bourgeois kind of Zionism, placing an emphasis on local concerns rather than upon emigration. As mentioned above, after the revolt of the Young Turks, Zionist groups were permitted to organize. The first of the seven groups that eventually formed were the B'nai Zion Organization and the Maccabee Sports Association, which was first organized with a focus on gymnastics and sports. The blatant antisemitism encountered in the Campbell riots clearly shifted the direction of the Zionist organizations toward emigration—advocated by both left-wing and right-wing groups.[53]

The twentieth century saw numerous waves of emigration. The first émigrés left in 1908 as well as during World War I in order to avoid the draft; some set forth for Palestine. Between 1908 and 1914 and again between 1920 and 1924, younger unmarried male emigrants began to seek their fortunes in the United States. As of 1913, after the Balkan War, many wealthy individuals opted not to become Greek citizens and left. Rena Molho contends that before 1921, three to four thousand Jews of means arrived in Paris.[54] The 1917 fire led to a scattering of Salonikan Jews around Western Europe and the United States.[55] Wealthy families holding Italian citizenship began to leave as early as 1912 and then again after 1917, often selling their factories or, after assessing the damage, claiming fire insurance and bidding adieu to the city.[56] Alliance education had an impact as well; some of its graduates relocated to France. There were merchant families and fishermen who went to Palestine in the 1920s, but the requirement of a certificate hampered the entrance of other potential immigrants. Dockworkers were given priority, although large families were not encouraged to immigrate. The Recanatis, a politically active Zionist family in Salonika, organized a group of emigrants who set forth for Palestine following the riots of 1931. Five years later, political insecurities led to additional emigration. Until 1930, the options available to émigrés were quite varied, ranging as far as South America; in the following decade, emigrants begin to set their sights again on Palestine.[57] All in all, it is estimated that between twenty and twenty-five thousand Salonikan Jews left their birthplace between 1910 and World War II.

Those Jews who remained were, nonetheless, contending with the winds of modernity that penetrated the once-traditional Sephardi society. One notes the ambivalence of the community's leaders in their stance regarding the appointment of a chief rabbi. Traditionally (and in practice until 1923), a Sephardi rabbi served as the religious head of the community. Yet for an entire decade—from 1923 until 1933—no chief rabbi was appointed because no consensus could be reached. Each of the numerous congregations had its own rabbi so that the community was not completely leaderless, but there was no higher rabbinic authority to unite them. In 1933, however, the younger pro-modern leaders decided to alter the image of the old-fashioned Sephardi community. Consequently, they elected to "import" a non-Salonikan and non-Sephardi rabbi who could modernize the community by means of his more up-to-date and worldly outlook.

The position of those lay leaders, who were anxious to modernize the community in any way possible, was consistent with the steps they and others had taken to promote modern education. The Alliance schools, as impressive as they were, reached only a limited student population. An additional effective means to reach the masses in order to modernize them was by composing plays in their native Ladino, the Jewish language based on medieval Spanish which, although originally written in Hebrew letters, could also be adapted to Roman letters; some of these plays would only be read in newspapers rather than performed in public. According to Rena Molho, these plays "constituted the most expedient instrument for the enlightenment and emancipation of the Sephardim, young and old."[58]

Salonika had attained a solid cosmopolitan character by 1920; this new status also added to the general pressure to modernize, creating pressure that could be discerned in various guises. At the government level, one can point to laws and restrictions passed to promote various changes. In addition, each group—such as the assimilationists, the communists, and the socialists—had its own agenda for change; one can include the Alliance as well as the Zionist organizations in this list. In the long run, each body sought to modernize and alter some aspect of traditional Ottoman-oriented Salonikan Jewish society.

As traditional as a society may be or hope to be, it is never immune to change. For example, as it coped with each catastrophe in turn, the community had no alternative but to seek solutions that inherently involved change. Many wealthy Jews, local as well as foreign, contributed to the creation of institutions that sought to alleviate the burden of the poor. Thus, the community benefited in 1908 from the construction of the Hirsch Hospital; boasting impressive Italian architecture, this hospital was a modern institution offering free public clinics. In addition, boys' and girls' orphanages were established by the Allatini and Aboav families. In 1911, Matanot La-Evionim was founded as a soup kitchen for school children; it served up to four hundred meals per day.[59] One must keep in mind the fact that there was a major imbalance in the economic makeup of the community: 40 percent were taxpayers; 60 percent, among them numerous homeless, were recipients of economic aid.[60] A special society provided dowries for as many as 150 needy brides annually, another impressive yet traditional philanthropic activity.

Salonika was home to a number of extremely wealthy families, most of whom were the forces behind various charitable institutions as well as the modernization of the city.[61] The first private bank in Salonika was established by the Allatini brothers;[62] they also built a shopping arcade, as did the Fernandez family. The Modianos constructed office buildings as well as the customs house. Department stores and factories were also built by these and other wealthy families. Many of these philanthropists and industrial entrepreneurs were also educational innovators who imported teachers from outside Greece and attempted to reform the school system by means of apprenticeship programs for boys and girls.[63] Essentially they served as cultural and economic intermediaries as they introduced the community to European ideas in education as well as in industry, banking, and commerce.

Despite the fact that the 1917 fire and years of inflation as well as a crisis in the tobacco industry following World War I all had deleterious effects upon the community, the 1930s actually saw economic improvement in industry—particularly in textiles—and in banking.[64] During this era, the rich cultural life of the community reflected a combination of traditional and modern. Even Ladino publications displayed the trend toward Westernization; newspapers began to avoid and eventually abandon the more traditional rabbinic and religious language. Although Hebrew and Aramaic as well as Turkish-Balkan words had previously been prevalent in print, they appeared increasingly rarely in these popular publications; eventually they were replaced by French expressions and a more international vocabulary.[65]

At the same time, changes were being promoted in the educational system. The range of schools in the city was quite impressive, for they included Jewish as well as non-Jewish institutions, private as well as communal schools, a Talmud Torah, and numerous schools controlled by the AIU. Most, if not all, of these institutions would be influenced by the French educational system.[66] Outside of the traditional classrooms, there were clubs and cultural societies, such as Kadimah and Sfat Emet, that advocated learning the Hebrew language and Jewish history; there was also a club for Alliance graduates in addition to the clubs affiliated with the aforementioned Zionist organizations.[67] The Zionist movement utilized the theater in order to inculcate its values, as did the communists and socialists. Occasionally, joint public events united these various factions. For example, in April 1909, an impressive celebration in honor of Mehmed Reshad V's coronation was organized by the *Club des Intimes de Salonica* in the Beschinar Park.[68] This was actually a fundraiser for educational purposes and for aiding the community; some ten thousand participants, many of them members of different societies and clubs, attended this fiesta.[69]

Other social innovations in the twentieth century included schools for those who desired to learn ballroom dancing, a skill essential to attending fundraising balls as well as debutante parties for the privileged. The city also housed popular dancehalls, despite the fact that they were viewed as dens of iniquity by the older generation. Interestingly enough, many of the orchestras and their leaders that performed in these halls, as well as the singers accompanying them, were Sephardi Jews. Historian Mark Mazower describes the "insatiable appetite for music of all kinds" in a city where Jews and Christians played together at cafes, and demonstrates how modernity transformed previously unacceptable activities into respectable ones:

> Salonica's pleasure gardens, parks, suburban and seaside centres of
> entertainment and distraction were, in times of exile, unemployment,

poverty and political unrest, the places that people would remember, that made the city itself not only bearable but, to an ever-larger proportion of its inhabitants, home.[70]

The growing presence of women in the public domain was also a sign of modern times. Women could now be found both in places of work and recreation. The young girls whose primary incentive for working in the tobacco industry was to earn sufficient money for a dowry were no longer the only females to be found earning an income outside of their homes.[71] Among those in the women's workforce were singers, dressmakers, and teachers—many of whom acquired impressive reputations.[72] The workshops established for girls produced talented lace makers, embroiderers, and seamstresses.[73] As will be seen in Bouena's poems, these women, in particular those dressmakers who could design European fashions, became quite independent and often demanded exorbitant prices for their creations.[74]

The transition from the domestic to the public domain was not smooth for the more independent Jewish girls tempted by the newly acquired freedom enjoyed by wage earners. The fact that, for the first time, they had means of their own as well as access to new forms of recreation created tensions in traditional families. The truth is that neither Jewish nor Greek women of the older generations had presented a challenge of this nature to their respective societies prior to World War II. The German occupation of Salonika would change life so drastically that the limitations of the past would lose their hold on quite a few members of the younger generation. It was during this period that Greek women in general—and particularly teenage girls who were attracted to the resistance—began to participate in the public sphere.[75] These women subsequently engaged in welfare work; served in food kitchens; and functioned as nurses, washerwomen, and fighters.[76]

Ladino

Language played a central role in Bouena's life and in the life of the community. Until the Alliance began to influence its students, Ladino was *the* spoken language; Greek did not enter the world of the *Selaniklis* until the twentieth century. Essentially, the spoken and written language of the Sephardim in the Ottoman Empire developed from Old Castilian, Hebrew, and Aramaic—and, depending upon the community, could contain elements of Arabic, Greek, and Turkish.[77] The term *Judezmo* literally means "Judaism" or a "Jewish language for the Sephardim"; this language is also called Ladino, Spanyol, and Judeo-Español (Espanyol). Until the middle of the nineteenth century, literary compositions in Ladino were religious or traditional and did not reflect popular spoken language. Just as Hebrew was the universal Jewish language that provided men with access to study and prayer, Judezmo, recorded in the early years in Rashi script, also belonged to the male domain. One can find the influence of Hebrew in concepts and words related to prayers, holidays, and blessings; in words that originated in Hebrew but were altered; in biblical terms that became somewhat symbolic; and in the Spanish forms of some Hebrew words.[78]

At the same time, a spoken and more popular language developed, encompassing a rich oral tradition that included romances and *canciones* that reflected the Iberian culture and heritage the exiles brought with them, but somehow still left leeway for post-Expulsion creativity. As it turned out, women were active in the oral transmission of these songs and tales. Thus, that Bouena herself was a repository of a vast number of songs, stories, and sayings comes as no surprise. When studying the Ladino used specifically in Salonika, one perceives the influence of Turkish, and eventually of Greek words and expressions. In the twentieth century there were members of the younger generation, in particular, who were well versed in French or Italian.[79] Be that as it may, the one language understood by all the Jews of Salonika was Ladino, for even a modern Europeanized Salonikan would need to communicate with members of the older generations.[80]

About the Translation

The fact that one of the first major Ladino dictionaries, prepared by Joseph Nehama, provided a translation into French proved quite helpful in dealing with these verses, as did various French dictionaries. A recent addition to the world of Ladino reference books, *Diksionario Amplio Djudeo-espanyol-Ebreo* has been most useful, particularly regarding difficult words that were specific to Salonika.[81] The geographical origin of my two main living resources was not Salonika but rather Istanbul, Ismir, and Janina, so these dictionaries—as well as Bunis's *Voices from Jewish Salonika,* a study of Salonikan Ladino, albeit in newspapers—were most welcome. The Ladino speaker not familiar with Bouena's idiosyncrasies can reconstruct Ladino expressions in reverse after reading the English translations.

About Coplas

The genre of the copla originated in the eighteenth century as a type of written moral rabbinic literature.[82] The copla was a poetic creation with a narrative style containing strophes and rhymes; a verse might consist of three or four lines, or up to eight or nine lines. The early coplas were essentially commentaries on the Bible and other sacred literature. Unlike the orally transmitted romances and *canciones,* the copla was recorded with the intention of preserving religious knowledge and ties to Judaism as well as to strengthen ties to the Holy Land; many a copla would be recited at the appropriate time in the Jewish life cycle.[83] They often had a moral or educational proclivity intended to educate the masses, clearly reflecting Sephardi values to be passed on from generation to generation. Others transmitted historical occurrences as they affected the community and might include changes of custom and social behavior.[84] Spanish researcher and collector of coplas Elena Romero explains that the themes of the coplas were perceived to be part and parcel of the Sephardi heritage, part of the essence of the community.[85]

According to Shmuel Refael, an expert on Sephardi literature, every Sephardi community in the diaspora had copla poets. It is clear that as time passed, this genre took on new poetic forms and themes; one can also perceive the influence of popular oral traditions upon them. In the long run, changes— such as the interaction between written and oral traditions and between continuity and change—can be discerned in the development of the coplas. By the twentieth century, these poems effectively mirrored many aspects of contemporary life.[86] Susana Weich-Shahak, an expert on Sephardi musicology, emphasizes the educational function of coplas, for they informed less knowledgeable members of the community who lacked access to Hebrew sources about various aspects of tradition and history. As a matter of fact, she claims that they were "especially meant for women and children and were performed at home. They were sung by the man in the family," although the women eventually learned the texts and joined in the singing.[87] In addition to coplas that were recorded, there were also spontaneous verses composed in honor of special occasions.[88] The best-known singer in Salonika was a woman, Bona la Tanyedora, whom Bouena admired and memorialized in her verses.

Salonika was the major center for copla publication. Between 1730 and 1941, Salonikan presses were responsible for publishing more than half of all printed coplas.[89] Refael attributes this to three factors: demographics, available printing presses, and the presence of a solid base of writers whose ideology was the perpetuation of Sephardi tradition.[90] Bouena followed an established tradition yet veered from its conventions at the same time. By the twentieth century, copla poets maneuvered between oral and written literature. Bouena also crossed gender boundaries, since coplas were usually created by men and preserved by women.[91] As a matter of fact, Refael believes that hers are probably the first coplas ever written by a woman.[92]

Bouena referred to her own poems as *komplas* (the Salonikan term), although they are not necessarily composed according to traditional rules. In her large corpus on Salonikan life, she was more concerned with describing the lost world than with creating perfect and uniform coplas. The verses in her Holocaust poetic piece seem to conform more consistently to the mold of the classic copla. If viewed as an epic poem, the piece carefully follows the developments in wartime Salonika by providing detailed descriptions mirroring the terror the community experienced during the occupation; because Bouena used the present tense in her coplas, portions of the historical analysis maintain that sense of here and now.

Unlike that of the original coplas, Bouena's language displays influences of East and West—yet does not abandon Hebrew terminology, a traditional characteristic of all Jewish languages. Thus, in the large corpus one encounters words or expressions such as *besiman tov* (1:3),[93] *lachon* (1:9), *chofar* (1:12), *mingnan* (1:46), *avdala* (1:50), *mizouzotte* (1:62), *tanid* (1:77), *tsavaha* (1:111), *taled* (1:119), *maboul* (1:177), *Bet Amigdach* (1:223), *berechit* (1:263), *geuniza* (1:335), *meguila* (1:340); and in the shorter corpus, *brit mila* (2:40), *Bet Ahaim* (2:41), *mazal* (2:46), and *michibira* (2:63), among others. The glossary contains a list of these and other so-called foreign terms incorporated into Bouena's Ladino poetry.

Her orthography is unique, and, even some of the Hebrew words above reflect French spelling. Bouena's Ladino represents a mixture of popular jargon influenced to a lesser extent by Italian, Portuguese, and Greek—and to a much greater extent by French and Turkish.[94] Her French schooling and fluency in that language seem to have affected her Ladino orthography tremendously. I have opted to leave the text in its original form so as to preserve an example of this type of Ladino often flavored with French dressing.[95] For instance, whereas the verb "to die" would be spelled *morir*, in Bouena's verses, conjugated forms of this verb are based on the infinitive *mourir*. Once one adjusts to her style, it is not difficult to adapt one's reading and comprehension of her Ladino.

French words—sometimes spelled Ladino style—such as *magasin* (*magazin*), *croix, lingère,* and *permi(t)* appear frequently. Expressions such as *dernier krie* [*sic*], *en grève,* and *après-midi* are part of her lexicon. In addition, both collections contain numerous French words ranging from toilets to chocolates, slips, paintings, meetings, municipalities, suburbs, workshops, culottes, cards, telegraph, pince-nez, phonographs, and nuns. Likewise one encounters terms in Turkish, often with Ladino-influenced spelling—in particular those that are related to the military, such as *kourchum* (bullet) or *askierlik* (army service); items of clothing such as *koyar* (removable collar) or *kirim* (fur coat); and numerous professions such as *ichbeteredjis* (middleman), *kieristidjis* (lumber merchant), and *mouchamadjis* (linoleum seller). These words appear together with terms such as *ziara,* an Arabic word for pilgrimage commonly used in the Muslim world. Her vocabulary reflects her milieu and her education and was understood by her fellow Salonikans who had been exposed linguistically to far more than Ladino.

Bouena's Poetry as a Historical Source

In her path-breaking study of women's *tkhines* (prayers), Chava Weissler asks this basic question: "How does something come to be regarded as an important historical resource?"[96] In the case of Bouena's coplas, it is clear that their content has a strong historical bent.[97] Although she did not arrange her poems chronologically, by rearranging them, one gains a new perspective that reveals patterns and themes. The poems deal with the major events in the twentieth-century history of the community. Bouena also had a clear sense of change and continuity and of the importance of Salonika in the Jewish world. The second collection deals with a much more limited time span, reflecting the policy of the Nazi takeover and its effects upon various individuals as well as groups. Because Bouena actively cared for those in need until she had to flee, but later survived and returned, her personal experience accurately reflects many developments during the demise of the community. Bouena included stories of hundreds of her brethren, whose home was twentieth-century Salonika. She documented the daily life of her community in poetic form (an achievement unto itself), took on the role of narrator, as well as played a central figure in some of the poems—and, in the telling, presented us with numerous women's stories.[98]

Although she did not write until thirty years after the events,[99] her memory appears to have served her well; the historical analysis that precedes each set of poems will attempt to assess its accuracy. Bouena's poetry reflects a unique perspective concerning the fate of the Sephardi metropolis. She succeeded in conveying a tremendous amount of information in her poems, although the coplas were not organized chronologically or by subject.[100] I have chosen to reorder them by theme in order to present the reader with a more unified impression of the images her verses create—an order that will be reflected in the historical analysis as well. Her memoirs complement and support the material presented in her poems. Her gender also played a central role in her life experience as well as in her perceptions. The women in her family had been enablers, caring for a household made up of a majority of women. They were master embroiderers and seamstresses whose expertise had earned them renown within the community. Volunteering their time and talents both before and during World War II, they were nurturers who cared not only for their own, but also for the less fortunate members of the community. Bouena was also cognizant of the expectations of society and highly critical of less productive or superficial women. Her verses are often satirical and biting, as she observed these women coping with modernity. There is no doubt that Bouena's writings effectively enrich our knowledge of the Sephardi world that had existed in Salonika for nearly five centuries, from the Expulsion from Spain in 1492 until the deportations of 1943.

The onus of chronicling a destruction of this order was overwhelming at times, but, as pointed out by David Roskies, an expert in Holocaust literature, "the chronicling of destruction . . . became for many a means of combating despair."[101] Bouena's works, particularly her memoirs, discuss the despair Bouena faced at various junctures in her life, and how she would sing to overcome certain difficult moments,[102] yet her writing clearly was a more effective means of coping for her. Bouena's coplas represent an attempt to respond to an overwhelming need that arose as the result of the Holocaust and post-Holocaust experiences.

In many ways, Bouena was unique: not only did she become involved politically with the Greek partisans, but she also did not refrain from entering male-dominated domains. A look at her wartime experience reveals that gender categories definitely meet and intersect. The two domains are not necessarily mutually exclusive, although one might occasionally overpower the other. There were periods in her life when she spent a great deal of time in the domain relegated to women. The result is that like the Ashkenazi women's personal *tkhine* prayers, Bouena's poems reveal a great deal regarding the domains and events in women's lives.[103] This is reflected in the historical analysis devoted to Salonikan life precisely because the social reality is analyzed from a woman's perspective. These poems on the whole deal with such topics as marriage and dowries, birth and circumcision, and family and holidays. However, there were other times when she entered the male domain without hesitation, in particular when she joined the Greek partisans. Despite the fact that as a partisan and as an underground agent after the war she tended to be assigned or even to initiate nurturing roles, she was mostly surrounded by and dealing with the men's world and men's values.

As powerful as the writing of poetry may be, the chronicling of events from the Holocaust period did not save lives—and in Bouena's case, her poetry-chronicles were recorded after the war, well after the fact. Nevertheless, the act of chronicling, whether in Yiddish, Hebrew, or Ladino, "dignified the millions of lives that were lost by incorporating them into a distinct and commanding memorial."[104] This is precisely what Bouena was aiming for: dignifying the memory of her beloved city in the first collection and dignifying those lives that were lost in the second collection. Her memorial is distinctly Salonikan, Sephardi, and most certainly commanding. Bouena's memoirs describe in detail the loss incurred both on a personal as well as on a communal level; some of the coplas in the second collection allude to this as well. For example, although the *judería* (Jewish neighborhood) with its wonderful courtyards had already begun to disappear after the fire and pogroms, the wartime ghetto likewise was a temporary replacement imposed from without. Both of these living quarters are frequently referenced in Bouena's collections.

No matter how she might have tried to preserve a flavor of the old country and to foster a new generation of Jews, "there could be no recompense for the loss of a culture and a language."[105] Nevertheless, her poems have survived to serve as a cultural and historical reminder for the reader.[106]

This book is divided into two sections: the first part deals with the larger corpus of poetry, and the second with the war-related poems. Each section begins with an historical analysis of a chapter or two organized by themes—followed by the poems, organized in the same manner. Because the verses that Bouena composed are so unusual and reveal so much about the last years of life in "Jerusalem of the Balkans," they have been transcribed in their entirety from the handwritten version in Ladino. The transcription project itself was a rather lengthy one, especially because Bouena's handwriting is not always easy to decipher.[107] Fortunately, because I had access to more than one copy of these collections, and because some of the papers contained partial additional copies of identical poems, I was eventually able to decipher all of the material.[108] I did not attempt to rhyme the English, but rather sought to find words and expressions in English that best reflect the Ladino usage.

It should be noted that in both collections Bouena concluded the majority of the coplas with the closing line "Bevamos a la saloud"; *a la saloud* means "to the health of," and *bevamos* is the first person–plural subjunctive of the verb *beber,* "to drink." After this phrase she entered the name of a different individual from Salonika whom she admired or wanted to commemorate.[109] Thus, one could argue that she wanted to close the verse with a toast to the health of a given individual. After consulting with native Ladino speakers, I chose to translate this closing phrase as "Let us drink to the health of (whomever)."[110] This phrase appears to be her personal signature rather than a commonly used formula.

Each copla is listed in its original form and appears together with an English translation. Bouena does not seem to have written them in any particular order, but more or less as the spirit moved her. Although the coplas are organized thematically, each is preceded by the original number that Bouena assigned to it in the collections that she gave to me. The first collection contains 413 strophes describing life in Salonika during the first half of the twentieth century and is simply entitled "Coplas Written by Bouena Sarfatty Garfinkle about Life in Salonika."[111] The second, and smaller, collection of ninety-nine coplas, entitled "Coplas about the Miseries That the Germans Inflicted on Salonika, 1941–1943," describes the Nazi destruction of the community.

Since the poet did not record her memories chronologically, one of the aims of the first portion of each section is to highlight recurring themes found in the text and to attempt to place the poems and their creator in a historical context. These are not epic poems, yet there is a plot behind the scenes. A very full picture of the prewar community is presented to the reader in the first collection. For instance, there is repeated emphasis upon the Jewish life cycle and how tradition continued or was interrupted, what the traditions were, and which traditions were unique to Salonika or to Sephardi Jews. Thus the preparations and ceremonies pertaining to weddings and dowries play a central role in these coplas, as do Sabbath and holiday preparations and observances. Another central theme in these verses is the tension between tradition and modernity, and how and when a transition was made between them.

The very title of the second collection reveals the poet's agenda. Life became full of "miseries" once the Germans occupied the city. Bouena's verses present numerous concrete examples of suffering and hardships experienced by individuals as well as groups. Her presentation of these developments is being examined in light of available historical material concerning the period of the Nazi occupation of Salonika. The deportations essentially ended the lengthy history of this "mother-city in Israel," but because Bouena survived, she was able to record her own unique perspective. These poems do not reflect those of a survivor of Auschwitz, but rather of an activist who survived by joining the partisans, a young woman who did not hesitate to take initiative. Thus the historical analysis examines, for example, the way in which the community leaders—including the chief rabbi and the collaborators who served in the Jewish police force—are depicted. Essentially, both this analysis and the coplas examine the process of the liquidation of the ghetto, the life of the partisan, the return of the survivors, and the options available to those who returned to Greece.

Bouena's verses might not represent the height of literary sophistication in the genre of coplas, but they make an enormous contribution to twentieth-century Sephardi literature, history, and ethnography. By using this particular means of expression the poet, in exile in Montreal, succeeded in keeping herself rooted to her Ladino heritage while striving to preserve and transmit a painfully lost material and spiritual culture. In this case, the loss was truly comprehensive: the vast majority (90–95 percent) of Salonikan Jewry was destroyed. These coplas not only preserve traditions and memories of a diverse and thriving modern Sephardi community in the throes of change, but also provide insights into the trauma faced during World War II. It is high time we let the poems speak for themselves.

CHAPTER 1

Bouena's Ode to Salonika

In order to appreciate the vast array of coplas written by Bouena, one needs to consider the themes that recur in each collection and to attempt to view the verses in a historical context. This poet displayed an uncanny awareness of the intricacies of her community and its history and integrated her perceptions into her poetry. She was also extremely cognizant of the changes that society was undergoing at the time, especially because its younger members were being exposed to modern notions that often threatened ancient traditions. The dissonance that resulted did not escape her attention; it was often unsettling.[1] As a result, she is critical or sarcastic at times about, for example, the greediness of young men seeking marital matches or about the way in which the latest fashions dictated the lifestyles of the youth and of the women. In her writing, she displays the utmost respect for the traditional lifestyle as manifested in her detailed descriptions, often containing Ladino proverbs, woven into her coplas. In order to present a clearer picture of the life that Bouena describes, the themes under discussion appear in the same order as the reordered verses (and their translations) in chapter 3. These themes deal with coplas and expressions (nine verses), dowries and marriages (fifty-one), births and children (twelve), family dynamics (forty-six), social commentary (forty-seven), philanthropy and education (twenty-seven), economic status (twenty-six), women's work (ten), Ladino publications (seven), the Sabbath (twelve), holidays (thirty-five), changes in tradition (twenty-eight), the dictates of fashion (twenty-seven), nationalism (thirty-one), historical developments (eighteen), and assorted anecdotes and expressions (twenty-six).

Coplas

It is interesting to note the attitude Bouena and the Salonikans had toward their rhymed couplets and Ladino expressions. The nature of coplas changed over time, since originally they were more or less part of the rabbinic world and only later were they adopted by laypersons. They also became more satirical and less elitist in the twentieth century; one can see that many of Bouena's poems reflect this particular development. Some modern coplas were published, but many of them were extemporaneous and remained unpublished.[2] The more spontaneous copla was part and parcel of everyday life, a common means of expression in the popular culture. Bouena does not hesitate to inform us that coplas were an integral part of life for the Selaniklis. They were tossed out in informal settings such as the home, often accompanied by a toast to whatever or whomever was appropriate. The workingman returned home at the end of the workday and spontaneously tossed out a verse about what had transpired that day.

There is no doubt in Bouena's mind that there are various levels of talent involved here, from the simplest to the most sophisticated; she insists that coplas are innate to Salonikans who are born to create them. Nevertheless she is well aware that there is an art to creating them, in which she herself engages and seeks to revive or at least to preserve to the best of her ability. In her opinion, there was even a divine aspect to the role of the creator of coplas, for his or her talents are considered to be a gift from God. In her opinion, the finest of the copla versifiers were the journalists whose pens flowed freely, and she specifically mentions two of the many journalists in the city whom she greatly admired.[3] The Jewish residents of Salonika appreciated coplas, especially since they provided a great deal of pleasure to one's family and friends. In this culture, wishing one well with a copla was as effective as, if not more so than, a greeting card or presenting a loved one with flowers or chocolates. Presumably, the more successful coplas were recorded for posterity and copied in order to circulate in certain milieux or families, and some made their way to local printing presses.

One is also advised that the Salonikans had their own expressions and this is not surprising, for every society has its own linguistic proclivities, nuances, and sayings. However, Bouena seems anxious to emphasize the strong Judeo-Spanish tradition of quoting ancient sayings and expressions, a prevalent and pervasive custom among her brethren. There may be many ways to express a particular feeling or describe a situation, clearly a tribute to the rich Ladino heritage; numerous proverbs are included at the end of this collection. Proverbs and coplas were passed down from generation to generation, usually from father to son; as far as the poet is concerned, they are part of the genetic makeup. The irony here is that Bouena wrote her ode as a collection of coplas, and it is she who remembered the poetry and the traditions; a woman was blatantly entering the male cultural domain. Her father was long gone: when she was a toddler (about two years old), he left the city limits despite the prohibition to do so; he explicitly ignored the quarantine that was declared due to an outbreak of the plague. He was determined to check on his granary and paid a heavy price for this decision, for he (and possibly Bouena) contracted the disease that led to his demise. Years later, his only son, Eliaou, perished in Auschwitz; consequently there were neither fathers nor sons remaining in her family. Nevertheless, Bouena did not perceive the fact that she was not male to be a problem, for she continued this age-old tradition, recording both coplas and proverbs galore. This Salonikan lady was extremely prolific, presenting anecdotes and information from her own personal experience and from that of the society in which she lived.

Dowries and Marriages

One of the most salient themes in this collection pertains to marriage and dowries and the socioeconomic repercussions of this complex *rite de passage*. In Salonika, all of the girls were privy to the intricacies of the customs and preparations involved. Bouena herself never had the luxury (as a bride) of experiencing the ceremonies surrounding this major life event, although when she was engaged to a fellow Salonikan, her family did begin the traditional and time-consuming preliminary preparations as was customary. Bouena's fiancé, Chaim, had been recruited by the Greek army when the Italians attacked on October 28, 1940, and subsequently fled from these ranks. Once he took this bold step, the couple sensed that their lives were in jeopardy and decided to arrange to be wed quickly at the "Midrash" synagogue.[4] However, when Bouena arrived at the appointed time, she was shocked to discover that Chaim had been murdered by the Germans.

Despite the fact that she had to contend with this traumatic event, her memories of the varied marriage customs, especially concerning the trousseau and the dowry,[5] are extensive and quite vivid; her poetry is replete with references to different stages of the marriage process. For example, in Salonika, fathers opened special savings accounts earmarked for their daughters' dowries. Many parents were careful to save in increments so that financial disaster would not befall them when faced with the actual expenses of the wedding preparations. At the same time, a young workingwoman did not take home all of her salary; a portion was automatically set aside for her dowry.[6]

Every family was anxious to provide an impressive dowry for its daughters, and, as it turns out, young men were often extremely demanding in their negotiations with the prospective bride's parents. Negotiations between the fathers of the two families were always quite stressful. Bouena paints a scene in which the mother restricts her activities to the women's sphere, busying herself in the kitchen with food preparation,[7] hoping to hear her husband utter the words "Be-siman Tov,"[8] an indication that the deal was closed.

As would be expected, problems and complications arose before, during, or after these financial arrangements were completed. Some brides were fortunate enough to inherit essentials such as linens, a trousseau, or jewelry. Others faced a different reality: a poor girl had difficulty finding a match in this society, although special dowry funds or *dotar* societies strove to replace the parental provision.[9] In her memoirs, Bouena mentions the fact that there was a dowry society in New York called La Ermandad that sent funds for the dowries of less-fortunate girls.[10] She informs us that two girls arrived from France whose parents were Salonikan, but whose prospects for marriage were nil. Although attractive and educated, the absence of a dowry doomed them; one can imagine the frustration caused by such demands.[11] Bouena advocates abandoning this stress-inducing and unfair tradition.

She is not exactly gracious when referring to the young men who belong to the Jeune Juif Association,[12] for she considers them to be gold diggers. The poet is extremely critical of these young men who, in her opinion, were only concerned with obtaining large dowries and profiting from the matches they obtained. Likewise, there is a description of rather self-centered and opportunistic young men—wearing Panama hats in the summer and Borsalino hats[13] in the winter combined with elegant shirts and fine silk socks—gallivanting about in order to impress onlookers. This was a façade; their intention was to obtain the maximum possible from the bride's family, whether in terms of the size of the trousseau or the amount of the dowry. Bouena is clearly disgusted by this behavior and is critical as well of the families that played by these rules and imagined that these young men might actually be worthy of their daughters. Obviously it was difficult to make the correct decision, especially when dealing with less-than-trustworthy characters whose main interest was profit. Despite efforts to achieve a good match, complications resulting from poor judgment sometimes occurred. Although most of her examples point to grooms as being less than honorable, occasionally there were brides who took advantage of grooms as well.

At any rate, accumulation of a dowry is a recurring theme in this collection. Her family was invited to a wedding held in the ballroom owned by the Matanot La-Evionim Association.[14] The bride had a substantial dowry, including a full set of lingerie, a thousand pounds in gold, and an inheritance from her grandmother.[15] Many grooms found themselves profiting nicely from matches made by their parents. In addition to the dowry and trousseau, the bride's parents sometimes provided what is known the *meza franka*, literally "French table," but actually referring to a period of time—usually between twelve and eighteen months—during which the groom lived with his in-laws at their expense, obviously an additional and significant perk.

The poet informs us that there were appropriate days for pursuing each of the wedding-related activities. It should come as no surprise to learn that the chosen days for beginning a trousseau were Mondays and Thursdays, the weekdays designated for Torah reading in the synagogue during the morning prayer service. These were also auspicious days to arrange an engagement or make a significant purchase. Presumably, other days were not as conducive to a felicitous union. Apparently, once the agreement was made, the bride's family planned an open-house reception in honor of the engagement and filled their home with flowers.

In her memoirs, Bouena describes celebrations of engagements: the two families agreed on the size of the *ashugar*[16]—which included linens, jewelry, clothes, and the *biankeria* (linen sets). Bouena explains that these items were included in set quantities; some might be provided in half-dozens, or in quantities of a dozen or two.[17] Teenage girls began preparing their trousseaux well in advance, embroidering their initials on items such as sheets, aprons, and cloth napkins. Bouena, who was an incredibly talented embroiderer, enthusiastically began her preparations, as did all young girls, by age fifteen at the latest.

Since not all prospective brides were as talented as Bouena, other options were sometimes pursued in order to ensure the high quality of the contents of the trousseau. The poems reveal the lengthy and elaborate preparations that transpired in the bride's home. Because the trousseau contained so many different items, some of the work might be commissioned (even if the bride prepared the majority of it), although certain items were traditionally prepared at home. Bouena describes the preparations as being all consuming, claiming that on every balcony one could find a girl embroidering her trousseau. She seems to have been ambivalent about the amount of time involved; in one verse she says that the girls are wasting their time, whereas elsewhere she compliments them.[18] The ability to embroider was highly valued; she praises young women like her cousin who made everything by themselves rather than by purchasing the numerous items required. Her attitude should come as no surprise, since the women in her family were known to have "golden hands." They were expert embroiderers and seamstresses whose handiwork was easily identifiable because of its high quality, and were so talented that their work was sought out even by non-Jewish women.[19]

Clearly, not all fathers managed to save—or to save enough—in advance. The competitive and compulsive need to give only the "very best" to one's daughter is portrayed as nothing other than "madness." One family spent beyond its means because it frequented the high-class shops on Venizelos Street, where imported European clothes were sold for trousseaux and bridal lingerie.[20] Many families were crippled by the costs of dowries and weddings. Again, of course, the mother and daughter wanted only the best for the bride; however, if and when arrangements were made without anticipating the cost, there were obvious pitfalls. The foolishness of such peer pressure and attempts to impress either society or the groom was often overwhelming. Bouena is quite critical of those who overindulged and became totally consumed by wedding preparations.

The very first copla in this collection describes "the old days," a phrase that appears frequently in her writing. A special cloth or bundle for the trousseau was used for storing clothes in the past, but later the bedroom contained a cabinet for this purpose. The demands and expenses of married life grew as time passes, for furniture was clearly more expensive than cloth and tablecloths were embroidered with fine silk thread.

Bouena managed to create a proper trousseau for herself but was uncertain about its fate during the war. Bouena eventually learned that her brother Eliaou gave numerous items from it to Greek neighbors for safekeeping before the deportations. Her memoirs note that she located the *forcel* and the *bugget*, or silk-embroidered cover of the basket, and a bundle of wool large enough to fill three mattresses, prepared or purchased in advance. There was material for covering the mattress, for dresses, eiderdown, and ample material for coats and for silk linings; her trousseau also included a set of dishes, buttons, thread, and trimmings.[21]

Bridal preparations also included the time-consuming process of mattress making; Bouena's trousseau included all of the necessary components. There is a detailed description of the festive atmosphere that prevailed while the wool for the bedding was washed in the courtyard in basins and heated cauldrons.[22] A day known as *el dia de la lana* (the day of the wool) was chosen during the summer before the wedding. Once this date was made known, all the women inherently understood that their services would be required. Female friends and relatives lent a hand, singing and making merry while they worked. After all the wool was washed, ropes for hanging it were correctly arranged so that the mother of the bride could dry it properly in the sun.[23] At the end of six months, the mattresses were ready for the bride and groom. Some mothers added to the basic necessities by providing additional items such as canopies, chests, closets, and night tables.[24]

Quilt making incurred further costs: an eiderdown quilt of fine silk cloth was stuffed with feathers imported from Russia. Clearly, this was a serious and onerous task, physically as well as financially. Bouena remarks facetiously that the trousseau had to be made at all costs, even if the family could no longer afford to eat.[25] Prior to the wedding, there was additional work: items prepared years in advance needed to be accessed in order to wash, iron, starch, fold, and tie the contents with ribbons.[26] This was labor-intensive women's work par excellence.

Before the actual ceremony there was another flurry of activity. On the Saturday night before the wedding, the family hosted the *almosama*—an all-night party or feast for the bride, who sat in the midst of the women from her circle of family and friends. According to Bouena, the custom was to provide the dowry fifteen days before the wedding, although Michael Molho refers to the *preciadores,* or inspectors, who arrived two or three days prior to the wedding to inspect the trousseau.[27] The groom contributed a *coffre,* or box of jewelry—the contents of which were put on display. The *shamay,* or assessor, came to the bride's homes on the *dia del ashugar.*[28] A value was set for all the goods and every item was recorded in the *ketubah,* or marriage contract.[29] Everything was on exhibit; Attias explained that the tables, sofas, chairs, and other furniture—as well as ropes and walls—were completely covered with possessions.[30] Anticipating the arrival of the dowry assessor was another stressful time for the father of the bride.[31] Two or three men carefully assessed each item as their colleague recorded the figures, which were not to be contested. Once the assessor finished, refreshments were served; vocal and instrumental music accompanied the placing of the items in the *forcel.* Porters arrived with the groom's family to carry the trunk off to the couple's new abode. The mother of the bride—having prepared food, including a *korban*[32] and pitas, at home—sent candies to friends and relatives; if the family was wealthy, lamb was barbecued for the guests' consumption as well. The tables were then removed to accommodate dancing; in addition, charitable donations were made, usually to associations caring for the sick.

After receiving the dowry, the groom presented the bride with a basket or with a copper bowl containing a package prepared for her visit to the *mikveh,* or ritual bath. This package, covered with the embroidered silk *bugget,* included a robe, towels, scented soap, a comb, a brass tray, bottles of perfume, the *mikveh* fee, and a tray of sweets.[33] Needless to say, Bouena also writes about the *mikveh* experience, which culminated in the bride's first immersion. The mother of the bride invited friends and female relatives to sing, eat sweets, and wish the bride well in this prenuptial women's celebration.[34]

The coplas also criticize straying from tradition. Apparently weddings began to be held in synagogues rather than in halls that had a larger capacity; Bouena perceives this to be a means for grooms to save funds.[35] "In the old days," the couple followed Jewish law and observed the seven days following the wedding, in which a festive meal was prepared each evening. At the conclusion of the meal seven special blessings were made. Apparently, the more modern couples wanted to travel and go on honeymoons where they spent the dowry money, money they themselves had not earned.[36]

Because the locale is Salonika, twentieth-century historical developments took their toll on everyday life. The April 9, 1941, Nazi takeover of the city made any semblance of normality close to impossible. Traditional wedding celebrations became difficult to arrange and as the community became impoverished, life changed drastically. There were waves of group or mass weddings in Salonika both before and after the war. Some were arranged before the groom's enlistment in the army, others after their return from fighting in Albania. Between summer 1942 and spring 1943, there was another wave of marriages; then, after the first transport in March 1943, Chief Rabbi Koretz encouraged the younger generation to marry before going to Krakow.

After the war, the surviving community had to deal with a myriad of problems stemming from the presence of a disjointed group of survivors, some of whom had experienced the camps.[37] In addition, there were other Salonikan Jews who emerged after years of hiding. Among the young people were about fifteen pregnant girls, one of whom had been raped by a Russian soldier. Rabbi Michael Molho offered a solution in spring 1946: he would perform a group wedding in the hall of the Matanot La-Evionim Building on April 7 (and again on April 14).[38] The girls wanted to be dressed in white, so the Joint Distribution Committee rented dresses and veils and provided the necessary ingredients for baking cakes; Bouena was asked to take charge and prepared the collation. The nineteen brides were anxious to have the hall decorated to evoke memories of the aura of the grand ballroom of yore. This plan was extremely difficult to execute logistically and psychologically, but Bouena did not hesitate to help organize, and prepared the refreshments and the hall.

Developments in Bouena's life reflected these changes as well. Although her intended was murdered before their hastily arranged wedding, she did eventually marry a few months after organizing the group wedding. As previously mentioned, she and Max Garfinkle were sent from Palestine in June 1945 to work in a displaced persons camp. After completing their assignments, Bouena and Max wed in Salonika on July 14, 1946, at the Monastir Synagogue.[39] The ceremony was performed by Rabbi Molho; the Union of Deportees organized a choir to sing a few songs in their honor.[40] Despite her knowledge of and ties to tradition, Bouena's own wedding consisted of a very modest ceremony with no family from either side present to celebrate with the couple. This was the last wedding that she attended in Salonika.

Births and Circumcisions

Marriage generally leads to births, and Judaism has many rules and customs for initiating the newborn into the world. In this traditional Sephardi

Matanot La-Evionim Building (now a primary school).

Group wedding on April 7, 1946. Bouena is located in the center of the third row, between the brides, and is wearing a pin or corsage on her dress. *Courtesy of the Jewish Museum of Thessaloniki.*

community, the birth of a son was of utmost importance. Men felt unfulfilled without sons and often did not value their wives until a proper heir was born.[41] If a family had girls first, the stress level rose as the next birth was anticipated. Bouena recounts the pregnancy of Sarina: this woman was extremely anxious because she had already given birth to four girls. She prayed "that another catastrophe [would] not befall her."[42] Her husband threatened to leave her unless there was a circumcision. Although she appears to be critical of this stance, Bouena informs us that "happiness is being invited to a *brit*."[43] This attitude might be due to the festive nature of a circumcision celebration rather than due to sexual prejudice. Interestingly enough, Bouena's poems do not mention celebrations upon the birth of a daughter, although the *hadas* or *fadas* were common in Sephardi communities upon the birth of a male or a female child.[44]

As intimated above, many husbands received the news of the birth of daughters poorly. Pregnant women began to prepare delicacies such as jam for sesame nougats to be served at birth celebrations, most likely anticipating the appropriate refreshments for the circumcision ceremony. The poet explains that although a boy's birth was greeted with joy, when girls were born, the wife wept and the husband sulked.[45] Some women tried to guarantee the birth of a boy by superstitious means. One attempt involved three *kaparot*,[46] entailing the slaughter of two hens and one rooster in order to guarantee the birth of a male.[47] In the case of a pregnant widow, a boy's birth was preferable since the male descendant would perpetuate his father's seed and name.[48]

An unusual account concerns multiple births—in this case, fraternal twins. On the eighth day, the day of the circumcision of the male baby, an unusual array of participants was present: two godmothers, two godfathers, and two circumcisers to perform the ritual act. The godmothers were there most likely in order to take the babies from their mother's arms. The godfathers might have received the honor of returning the newborns to their mother, although the godmothers might have been present to receive and return the female child while the godfathers were assigned to receive and return the male child. In the Middle Ages, women were active in circumcision ceremonies, and terms such as "master" or "mistress" of the circumcision or godfather and godmother appear in rabbinic discussions.[49]

At any rate, after pointing to Elijah's chair (where the godfather usually sits), the poet explains, "The *circumcisers* (my emphasis) start to perform the circumcision." The boy's mohel (ritual circumciser) obviously performed the halakhic deed, but the innovation here is is the presence of a second circumciser. According to Bouena, the "mohel" of the girls said, "Lord of our Fathers, here one has to add and not remove."[50] In Ladino the word *meter*, or "add," also means to present or hand over; thus, the meaning of this expression is that the child was to be presented or returned to her mother rather than taken away. One is relieved to learn that nothing was to be removed from the girl's private parts and simultaneously impressed by the originality of this double ceremony. One assumes that the standard fare of almond balls, wine, and ouzo was served.[51]

Family Dynamics

Bouena is caught between having the utmost respect for families and a high regard for the beauty of traditions they upheld and her criticism of various individuals. She is convinced that tradition keeps families together, and that the members of the younger generation have a great deal to learn from their elders. She is often annoyed with the youth for not respecting tradition and for not understanding its value.

The traditional image of the Sephardi male head of household is subjected to criticism, although praise is lavished upon the men in her own family—including her grandfather, father, and the brother who had taken their deceased father's place at a relatively early age. Her criticism and barbs are aimed at the general male population; many of them are depicted as rather chauvinistic. The older generation is criticized for not keeping up with the times, but the men in particular are singled out for having "a mindset from antediluvian times."[52] Even when the girls worked outside the home, and many did work in tobacco factories, they were still expected to arrive home by sunset. The strictness of fathers was extreme; daughters could not go out at night with friends without the accompaniment of a male family member—and even so, their parents still waited up until they returned.[53]

In three separate verses, part of a blessing that is included in the recitation of the men's daily morning prayers is invoked. In the original blessing, a man thanks the Lord for not being created as a woman;[54] in contrast to the original intention of this blessing, which refers to privileges and commandments solely for men, the poet presents rather mundane reasons for this gratitude. For example, not being a woman means that he does not have to face an irate father when he returns home in the evenings. In the same vein, the poet employs a play on words based on the same daily prayer, this time displaying cynicism concerning the traditional roles of husbands and wives; the man is relieved not to have the responsibility of cooking meals. A traditional interpretation of the blessing might assume that it allows the man to be dissociated from any responsibilities in the women's domain, the kitchen. However, the verse overflows with sarcasm as the poet remarks, tongue in cheek, that those served were so involved in eating their food that no one noticed that "the housewife was burned instead of the pot."[55]

Nonetheless, Bouena is well aware of the important role played by fathers in maintaining tradition, and at times she seems loath to belittle them. In general, she attributes very positive qualities to grandfathers. In one verse, everyone sat around the hearth while the grandfather dispensed advice.[56] One of her grandfathers is described as an ascetic who imposed prolonged fasts on himself.[57] Bouena accepts him uncritically, explaining that because he was considered wise, people consulted him daily.[58] He was the transmitter of tradition, serving as a scribe who prepared ritually needed parchments, and most likely also composed or copied texts for amulets and the like.

An interesting family tradition is described; her grandfather apparently had a beautiful wine cup for the *kiddush* blessing that was to be inherited in each generation by the oldest grandchild in order to avoid fighting among the grandchildren.[59] Presumably, her grandfather had also been the oldest grandchild, and by this means continued the family tradition. Later she describes in detail her grandfather's elegant manner of dressing: he wore a bowler hat and sported a cane with a silver head.[60] She also discusses her grandfather's passing,[61] pointing out that he taught them love, respect for one another, and how to remain united as a family; she was pleased that their widowed grandmother would be residing with them. Grandmothers seem to have been more in touch with the children and less formal than their male counterparts.

Mothers, of course, were the central figures in the household. The truth is that in the prewar period, husbands traditionally expected their wives to occupy themselves in their domestic domain and to serve them; the kitchen also served as a place of refuge when needed. In a typical home, everything was ready in anticipation of the father's return from work: the wife, the dinner table, his slippers, hot water, and a clean dressing gown; the children were waiting to kiss the man of the house.[62] This was a picture of perfect decorum.

Bouena writes that a woman's strength derives from the "love of her husband," whereas "the strength of the man is his wallet."[63] Obviously, this is a rather limited view of the power play, for it ignores the divorcée, the widow, as well as the single woman and leaves poor men in powerless positions as well. At any rate, it is interesting to imagine how love might provide power for women but not suffice for men. Where does this leave the independently wealthy woman or the beloved man who is less than successful financially? Be that as it may, this comment sheds light on the *mentalité* of this society.

With the father as the sole or main breadwinner, it is only logical to find the mother fulfilling the role of homemaker. Even when not preparing a mattress or embroidering linens and the other components of the trousseau, these women were extremely busy. The mother seems to have been a victim of endless work, resting only on the Sabbath.[64] During the rest of the week, she was arranging the house as she returned to post-Sabbath mode, tending to laundry, ironing, sewing, preparing pastries, and engaging in elaborate preparations for the Sabbath and its special cuisine. Because so many of the familiar smells and flavors of the past no longer existed by the time these verses were composed, the sense of nostalgia is quite tangible.[65]

Social Commentary including Philanthropy and Education

Salonikan Jewry was a diverse group economically as well as socially. Its members ranged from the unemployed to fisherman and porters, artisans, bourgeoisie, and the extremely wealthy. Bouena differentiated between these groups, and was well aware that many of her neighbors were putting on airs, whether in order to obtain an advantageous marriage or in imitation of the truly cultured members of society. For example, she points out that the local baths were not considered as desirable as Baden-Baden or Vichy because there was no attractive shopping available in the vicinity. In the verses, descriptions abound of collations, from informal indulgence in melon seeds at home or on one's balcony to delicacies served at parties and social functions. She comments on the joie de vivre of the Selaniklis, whether they socialized at cafes, had afternoon gatherings, strolled by the sea, or danced to one of the numerous bands that performed in the city.

Honor is a theme that appears and reappears in these verses; sometimes one gained honor by means of education, and sometimes due to one's wealth. Bouena describes non-aristocratic and aristocratic individuals and families, and their varying lifestyles, values, and proclivities. The Molho family brought honor to the community,[66] especially because of its beautiful library.[67] In this case, the Molhos were continuing the medieval tradition in which the wealthy, who had tremendous collections, were gracious enough to offer them to the public as libraries.[68]

Importance is attributed to the honor of the wealthy and of the educated, who tended to contract endogamic marriages; at the same time, the fact that the city housed a plethora of congregations is noted. Yet in the long run, exigencies often blurred social and economic barriers, for in times of crisis the Selaniklis united.[69] This essentially optimistic view of *Clal Israel*, of taking responsibility for one's fellow Jew, served to assuage the undercurrent of discrimination and division among the different classes that characterized the prewar community. There were many humanitarians and generous individuals who functioned within the community as well as from outside it. They took care of medical needs and even provided food for the less fortunate and their families in times of crisis. A less prosperous or even a middle-class family would not have the benefit of servants in the home; thus, help with childcare and cooking was most welcome during difficult and stressful times.

Contact between the different economic groups was also fostered by the *mitzvah*—or good deed of *zedakah,* or charity giving—although obviously one class gave and the other was destined to receive. The philanthropists in Salonika engaged in many activities such as taking care of the Hassid Clinic, the Allatini Orphanage, the Aboav Orphanage, the community school, the Bikkur Holim Hospital, and the Gifts for the Needy Association. At the same time, some individuals chose to contribute to the synagogue; donations included money for decorations as well as hand-embroidered covers for the ark, the Torah scroll, and the like.

The Beit Shaul Synagogue, also known as Kahal de la Siniora Fakima, was built by the widow of Samuel Shaul Modiano on family-owned land in about 1898. Although it was not in the center of the city, its establishment eventually led to other institutions being built nearby. Because of its location, it survived the fire of 1917 and became the central synagogue. Unfortunately, the Germans demolished the building in 1943, following the deportations. In the previous decade it had served to shelter refugees.[70]

Baron de Hirsch was a well-known Jewish philanthropist who did not neglect the community of Salonika; as a matter of fact, an entire neighborhood, albeit an impoverished one, was named for him. He gave money for the building of the beautiful Hirsch Hospital.[71] Needless to say, medical care was among the most crucial needs of the poor in the community; philanthropists donated money for hospitals and clinics, for medicine, and for personal operations.

The great fire of 1917 devastated the community and the damage suffered was irreparable.[72] Many of the old neighborhoods were destroyed and disappeared because the government actually discouraged the Jews from rebuilding their homes in the center of the city. The poor were hit the hardest; many never recovered from this blow, despite the fact that the community built houses for the homeless.

Orphanages played a major role in a society that continually lost numerous adults to disasters such as disease and fire. The Allatini and Aboav institutions named above were both important communal establishments that provided options for less fortunate youth, especially since education was a critical means of improving one's circumstances. The former clearly had a fine reputation as its graduates were "well distinguished" at the end of their studies; some were sent to Paris to study at the Sorbonne in a program funded by none other than the Rothschilds. The director of this institution, Isaac Covo, helped to educate students and devoted himself to finding them employment after their military service.[73] The traits that were valued in the men in this traditional society are

Hirsch Hospital, with its Italian architecture; today it is Ippokrátio Hospital.

education, honesty, and maintaining the stance of a good husband, presumably by properly providing for the family.

The latter institution, the Aboav Orphanage, impressed the poet with theatrical productions by its students. These productions were staged in the hope of inspiring members of the audience to make donations and pledge support to the school. This girls' establishment fostered multilingual student performances featuring portions in French, Greek, and Ladino. Bouena praises this program, like the Allatini, for producing honest and learned girls who brought honor to the community.[74] Here one can see how successful these two institutions were and how they received major support from certain influential members of the community.[75]

These orphanages served as schools alongside the other educational institutions in the community, some of which were long lasting and others not as successful. The majority of the schools in the city seem to have been affiliated with the Alliance. The first, known as the Moise Allatini School, was established in 1873 as a French school for boys.[76] One perceives that there was competition among the various schools, some of which were communal and others of which were private—one was even Zionist. For the wealthy, there was always the option of studying abroad.[77] As impressive as the French schools became, one must take note of the fact that the French Jewish community in general was condescending toward its far less cultured brethren in the East who were in dire need of acquiring Western and French culture and education. This was the primary motivation behind the educational system they funded, the Alliance Israélite Universelle. Interestingly enough, Bouena, who received this French education, displays no sense of inferiority whatsoever, but rather reflects a distinct pride in her community; Paris was not viewed as a competitor or as superior in the eyes of the proud Balkan bearers of the Sephardi heritage.

Another school is mentioned a few times, most likely because Bouena's brother, Eliaou, participated in its establishment. This was Sara Primo, a school for navigation; since Salonika is a port city in which the Jews were involved on every imaginable level, one can understand the appeal of such an institution. Its establishment clearly expressed signs of Jewish pride as nurtured by the Zionist movements in the city that emanated naturally from the members of the Jewish port community of Salonika.

Work and Workers

There are numerous verses that contain information concerning professions and workers that provide additional insight into the socioeconomic reality of prewar Salonika. As in any society, each member of the community fared differently; sometimes one's status changed as the result of education, marital alliances, or good fortune and investments. Some succeeded despite the catastrophes and setbacks, and others were not so fortunate. As Western trends and modernization permeated this society, new ideas, whether socialist or capitalist, were adopted and adapted.

It is clear that many of the members of the working class, such as the tobacco workers, struggled in order to survive. As mentioned earlier, in 1908 there were between eight and ten thousand Jewish workers in the tobacco factories, most of whom were girls. Bouena refers to a strike that they organized that made a lasting impression.[78] In times of stress, such as the wake of a disaster, the insurance agent could either save a business that appeared to be doomed or doom that very business. In light of the fact that fires were so prevalent in this city, the insurance companies were frequently quite busy. The fate of the customer was in their hands; he would either be reimbursed and begin anew, or face economic disaster.

As East faced West and sought to modernize, there are areas in which Salonika excelled and displayed pride. However, tradition was not completely forsaken, for there were time-honored professions that proved lucrative. For example, the Almosninos had the largest pastry bakery in town thanks to the high quality of its baked goods. Because the wealthy ordered from them, they could charge higher prices and increase their profit margin; in this way, their reputation was maintained along with their economic status.

The Cohens' shoe store on Venizelos Street was au courant because some members of this family went to Paris, presumably to learn more modern techniques and how to become independent merchants. Upon their return, they set up an artisans' workshop at the port, where shoes were produced by cheap labor; samples were sent to Paris to bypass payment of local taxes.[79] In other words, they adapted to the demands of Parisian fashion, and catered to the Parisians as well as to the Salonikans. By employing inexpensive local labor, they produced shoes at a lower cost than they could elsewhere, and then increased their potential profit by finagling and avoiding local taxes. This lowered the price of their product and also deprived the local government of tax payments. Here was a family that straddled the worlds of fashion and supply and demand, taking advantage of the opportunities afforded by capitalism, which enabled the exploitation of workers.

Factories, the bastion of exploitation of the worker, began to flourish in twentieth-century Salonika. Numerous investments were made in order to build them. The Attias family owned the first spinning factory,[80] importing inexpensive cotton to make thread and fabric; the manufacturer imitated the forerunner of modernity, the United States, by labeling its product as American. Sometimes the government provided incentives for businesses. Just as it did not tax the shoe manufacturers, it encouraged imports by providing stipends for those engaging in these ventures, including a family of lumber merchants.[81] One had to choose wisely as to how to invest one's money. Yet most of the businessmen had to take the initiative. Bouena cites the examples of luggage makers; paint merchants; and builders of factories for soap, candles, and inexpensive clothing. In her verse about Singer sewing machines, Bouena seems to be caught between her admiration of innovation, incentive, and modernization on a grand scale and her personal investment in traditional embroidery and sewing—which she valued and at which she excelled.

One of the most lucrative businesses was, of course, banking—in which some of the most respected members of the community were involved.[82] Nevertheless, one did not have to be wealthy in order to be honored by the community. Alice Aelion, a teacher, was awarded a prize by the Greek government. In addition, she had an uncanny penchant for preservation of tradition; she joined forces with a musician, and the two approached all of the older women in the community in an effort to collect and record all the songs they recalled. Clearly, this project was highly regarded by Bouena as well as by others. Little did she know that her own collections of songs, romances, and verses would also be recorded for posterity.

Other women pursued more traditional professions and were not necessarily as highly educated as Alice. Some of the seamstresses who specialized in sewing items to be included in the trousseau had a high standing, especially among the young women and their mothers. Other seamstresses were valued for their sharp sense of fashion regardless of their formal education or level of literacy. Sarika Florentin and her brother had a workshop, which she ran successfully because of her sense of innovation.[83] Her brother-partner was the salesman who distributed her creations to the women's shops.[84] Because Sarika's reputation preceded her, the brother-sister team made a nice living by working together.

One of the more interesting workingwomen, who was also extremely well known in the community, was Bona la Tanyedora (the tambourinist). The legendary Bona, whose reputation was unequaled, lived in the latter years of the nineteenth century. Bouena remembered hearing her grandmother's stories about this entertainer.[85] Bona is said to have brought a unique liveliness to every family event. Bona even appears in Joseph Nehama's French dictionary of Judéo-Espagnol, which claims that she was without a doubt the most talented musician in her field.[86] This performer adapted herself to every situation, whether joyous or sad, and her flair for tambourine playing was extraordinary. She was present at women's gatherings when the items for the trousseau were to be washed and prepared; this was an occasion for singing in which the tambourinist enhanced the festive atmosphere. The consensus was that no one could compete with Bona, a clever woman with a wonderful temperament: cheerful, humorous, and delightful. She composed spontaneous coplas for her hosts and was a living repository, offering a virtual goldmine of songs.[87]

Another valued professional field was journalism. Bouena mentions that Jews generally read books, but that on the Sabbath, the women read the newspaper *El Gayo* purely to keep abreast of the latest gossip.[88] Although it is clear that these women did not read highbrow literature, Bouena shows respect for the more serious journalists, in particular, Besantsi and Abravanel. Both were polyglots and apparently fearless authors of poems, books, and articles through-out their lives.[89] Abravanel dispensed advice in the last decades of his career, for in 1940 he wrote, "Don't be Jewish." But in 1945 he wrote, "Don't be German."[90] His first declaration was a warning of the dangers facing the Jews; his second declaration was a damnation of the nation that had created the tragedy that ensued.

These journalists dealt with the rapidly changing reality to the best of their abilities. They were devoted to Ladino, to the Sephardi heritage and culture, and discerned that their identities had become problematic in the 1940s. Bouena, on the other hand, did not write until later, and clearly had the advantage of retrospection. Nevertheless, her analysis of Jewish life in Salonika in the first four decades of the twentieth century, although composed from memory, was written from the perspective of someone still living in the Jerusalem of the Balkans. She succeeded in conveying the value of the copla in Salonikan life and commenting upon the role of dowries, weddings, births, circumcisions, and—above all—of the family. Her analysis contrasts the different levels of socioeconomic status in Jewish Salonika and some of the professions that her brethren had chosen for themselves; she displays affection for writers, having eventually become one herself. As will be revealed in the second collection of verses, her two favorite journalists suffered tragic fates.

CHAPTER 2

Tradition versus Modernity and Historical Developments

Bouena had a natural affinity for traditions and for the traditional, partly due to her upbringing as a proud Sephardi, and partly due to her deep roots and vast acquaintance with Ladino folksongs and refrains along with her artistic ties to the world of embroidery. Tradition is an essential element that serves to bind any society—and, consequently, serves to keep families together. Tradition elicits respect and honor and is the antithesis of change. Therefore, if one is to protect traditions, one cannot blindly accept change for its own sake or on the assumption that all change is positive.[1]

Needless to say, knowing the fate of the community under discussion alters the lenses through which one perceives the traditional; this altered perception holds true for the poet-memoirist as well as for the historian. Although modernity and modern ways might have eventually eroded and even overtaken the traditional, the opportunity to do so naturally was thwarted. Tradition is mainly relegated to the memories of the survivors, and in Bouena's case, geographical distance made it nearly impossible for her to continue many of the traditions that she treasured so dearly. But her admiration of the traditional and connection to her tradition served as a catalyst for writing hundreds of verses and for recording numerous proverbs that are devoted to traditions and that recreate the aura of the cherished world that has been lost.

By saying that "tradition passes from father to son," she presumably refers to the more halakhic or legal aspects of Jewish life, since the men are expected to perform most of the commandments.[2] The traditional world evokes nostalgia on her part and stands in sharp contrast to the cynicism and sarcasm she displays toward the younger generation's attraction to change.[3] The ideal image she projects is one of harmony, peace, and love fostered by the family that clings to tradition.

Sabbath and Holiday Observance

Despite the fact that modernity was knocking at the city's door, customs and holidays were not abandoned quite so quickly in many of the homes in

Salonika.[4] At the beginning of the century, the Jewishness of the city was quite apparent and could not be easily dismissed. Consequently, the Sabbath played a central role in the Jewish world of pre–World War II Salonika, especially while there was a Jewish majority in the city. Thus it was not perceived to be problematic or unusual to close the port on the Jewish Sabbath, since the majority of the dockworkers were Sephardi Sabbath observers. Life at the port revolved around the Jewish day of rest until 1923, when the Greek government passed Sabbath decrees to force the Jews to rest on Sunday rather than Saturday,

Bouena describes weekday eating habits such as the special traveling food box or tiered lunch pail that contained hot meals for the workingmen. On Fridays, simple meals were eaten in anticipation of the delicacies to be served on the Sabbath. She refers to the elaborate Sabbath preparations such as cooking and shopping along with the joy in the family after Friday night services; in the poet's nostalgic eyes, this was how a Sephardi household should look and sound on the eve of the Sabbath.

Once they cooked and served the food, the women did not play a major role on this day of rest. The poet claims that the women sat around eating melon seeds.[5] This custom is still common in Mizrahi homes: different seeds taken from pumpkins, watermelon, or sunflowers are washed, dried, salted, and cracked open one by one as a pastime. Other pastimes included strolls to the White Tower or watching boats and socializing.[6] These walks were part of an intergenerational activity that also served as a family outing and did not conflict with the halakhic limitations of the Sabbath. The end of the day of rest was traditionally marked by the *havdalah* ceremony, at which time brides and grooms were often toasted.

Bouena loved the annual cycle of the Jewish holidays, beginning with the New Year and Yom Kippur and the proximity of these three High Holidays to the festivals of Sukkot (Festival of the Booths) and Simhat Torah. She enjoyed watching the erection of temporary booths for Sukkot, which often occurred directly after breaking the Yom Kippur fast. (This is a tradition maintained by Jewish families throughout the world and symbolizes the connection between one holiday and the next, linking one outstanding deed to another.) The excitement of the children is described as they are allowed to help in the construction of this important temporary structure.

The custom in Salonika was to auction the four species, the *lulav* (palm, willow, and myrtle branches) and *etrog* (citron), needed for Sukkot on Yom Kippur; many other honors were also sold to the highest bidder, but this was an important annual sale. During the seven days of the holiday, except for the Sabbath, the lulav and etrog are traditionally used at morning prayers.[7]

One of the verses reveals a highly unusual practice: "(On) Sukkot, the women recite the prayer over the lulav every day!" Although, according to

The White Tower, symbol of the port of Salonika.

Jewish law, women are not forbidden to take the four species or to recite the appropriate prayer, one would not have expected to discover this practice in a premodern Sephardi community.[8] Not only did the women make the blessing, but their sincerity was lauded. Finally, the continuity of this tradition was cherished and advocated, for mothers extracted promises from their daughters to continue this tradition.[9] This tradition seems to have been unique to the women of Salonika and predated developments in modern Western communities by at least half a century. It seems that this custom was indeed continued by the Selaniklis who immigrated to Israel, for after Sukkot services in the neighborhoods of south Tel Aviv, husbands offered their wives the opportunity to bless the lulav and etrog. In addition, volunteers visited the homes of the members of the synagogue and offered those women who had not attended services the option of taking the four species and saying the blessing. Those who needed coaching repeated the blessing after the volunteer, who often received a small payment for his "services."[10]

The end of Sukkot, Simhat Torah, always includes a celebration of the completion of the reading of the Five Books of Moses as well as beginning the reading anew. The *Hattan Torah* (Torah groom) is a member of the community who is traditionally given the honor of completing the cycle of that year's reading of the Torah; Bouena was moved by this annual celebration.

The next holiday on the Jewish calendar is Hanukah—which, unlike most of the others, has no religious restrictions concerning carrying or using money. Consequently the community, particularly the Zionist organizations, took advantage of the opportunity to organize dances and card games for the purpose of fundraising. The following holiday is Tu Bi-Shevat—the fifteenth day of the month of Shevat, or Jewish Arbor Day; Bouena remembers that dried fruits are traditionally eaten on this day.

In Salonika, the month of Adar was a time for making marital arrangements as well as weddings. The Sabbath before Purim, Shabbat Zachor (the Sabbath of Remembrance), was known in Salonika as the Brides' Sabbath. Sugar, lemon, and food coloring flooded the market in anticipation of the creation of sugar dolls. As of the Thursday prior to this Sabbath, there were outdoor displays on tables adjacent to stores that included figures of brides, grooms, the evil Haman, bracelets, scissors, the Eiffel Tower, cars, and the like; the sugar artists were famous for their gallows made of sugar, symbolizing the hanging of Haman and his sons.[11] The traditional portions prepared were called Purim plates, which, according to Bouena, were well received.[12] Brides sent their mothers and mothers-in-law a plate of *kopita,* or sesame halva. The brides in turn received generous gifts from the older women and other relatives as a gesture intended to help the newlyweds establish themselves; hence the aforementioned nickname for the day as the Brides' Sabbath. Children delivered the trays, laden with cookies and sweets and sugar figures of grooms or brides. Bouena details these customs while emphasizing how the bride and groom received special treatment from both sides of the family.

Young couples and families with children of marriageable age received gifts sent on trays made of sugar or copper. The children received gifts as well. In addition, the Sephardim in Salonika seem to have adopted the Ashkenazi custom of baking fruit-filled triangular pastries called *hamantaschen,* or "ears of Haman." Many customs are mentioned in these verses—beginning with the fast of Esther on the day before Purim; the aforementioned baking of pastries; the Purim meal; the sending of *platicos,* or portions, to at least three (but usually more) individuals; and the giving of charity to the needy and small sums of money to children.

Bouena explains that it was an honor for a family to own its own Scroll of Esther and to read it either publicly or privately or just follow along with the chosen public reader. Elsewhere, she describes a classic Purim: first the *megilla* scroll, or Book of Esther, was read while the children grasped wooden hammers with which "to finish off Haman"; in actuality they were following the custom whereby the children make noise each time the name of the evil archenemy of the Jewish people in Persia is read aloud, in order to blot out his memory.[13] Noisemakers take different shapes and forms—such as groggers, hammers, and the like.

There was extensive celebration on this holiday, although it seems that the congregation of descendants from Sicily or Syracosa observed its own Purim on the eighteenth day of the month of Shevat.[14] They organized balls and prepared sweets, bride dolls, and baked goods for one another as part of the aforementioned portions. Apparently Bouena was not aware that this celebration could be traced to a fifteenth-century miracle story. According to this source, during the king's annual procession in this Italian locale, the Jews were expected to join a march in public with their Torah scrolls, which are traditionally stored in special protective cases. One year, the Jews decided to march with empty cases rather than to defile the Torah because the king was considered to be a nonbeliever; unfortunately, before the procession, their scheme was revealed to the court. Needless to say, punishment for such treachery would have led to the demise of the community. However, the community was miraculously saved: the night before the procession a member of the community foresaw the disaster in a dream, which convinced the Jews to place their scrolls in the cases. The end of the story is remarkably similar to that of Shushan Purim—as was their celebration of this miracle, which was marked by a day-long fast, reading from a scroll, partaking of meals, and sending portions to others.[15] Their celebration was similar, but not identical, to that of the other congregations in Salonika. There were colorful treats, a carnival and ball, costumes, songs, operettas, and merrymaking galore.

Passover has always been a highly significant holiday, which might account for the fact that many verses are devoted to it. *Shabbat Ha-Gadol*—the "Great Sabbath," or the Saturday prior to the Passover holiday—played a significant role in communal life both in and outside the synagogue. Many families in Salonika were rather large and as a result, the children were accustomed to wearing hand-me-downs. As would be expected, the older and larger children received new clothing and passed on whatever they had outgrown; each successive child wore his or her sibling's clothes in order to get the most use from them. But once a year, regardless of one's station in life, everyone anticipated receiving new clothes; Bouena enlightens us about various customs unique to this community. Collections were taken, contributions made, and benefits organized precisely for this purpose. On Friday nights, the community attended Sabbath services at the Great Talmud Torah Synagogue, where ropes were strung up temporarily in order to hang the new clothes. After the prayers, there were special sermons in honor of this important Sabbath; then songs were performed by a choir of *paytanim,* or poets, which were followed by speeches. At long last, the ceremony ended as the students and the less fortunate received their new clothes.[16]

There are discussions of matsah production and distribution, for the community had total control of its production and sale; in Salonika, the price was set according to one's ability to pay. The community also took charge of the sugar preparation for the holiday—presumably making sure that it was pure, well refined, and kosher for Passover; needless to say, it was also expensive. In order to ascertain that distribution was fair and honest, special means were taken to properly weigh the sugar. Food preparation is mentioned; despite the severe dietary restrictions of this holiday, there were delicacies in each household. The Seder ceremony was led by the father, who was compared to royalty.[17] During the day, the mothers seem once again to have been sitting on the balcony, observing the children, and—at the same time—eyeing one another. In this community, the balcony was a central place for the women, especially for those of the older generation. The balcony enabled some to see outside without having to leave the safety and modesty of their home, and provided others with protection from the outside world. Many of the older women preferred to remain in the private sphere, either by choice or by conditioning and habit; being adjacent to the outside, the balcony appears to have provided access, however limited, to the public sphere.

The third of the annual pilgrimage festivals, namely Shavuot, merits less attention than the other two, but is not ignored completely. Special food was prepared and outings were planned—such as to Bes Tsinar, a large garden in which one could walk for miles on end. The garden was located on the shore of the gulf, where a dip in the ocean was possible. The locally acclaimed Nahmias family's ouzo was brought to these picnics.[18] This was a classic mixture of tradition and modernity: after attending synagogue services, the family remained together but engaged in less-than-holy or scholarly activities. Nevertheless, no rules were abrogated and a festive atmosphere was maintained, although it is highly doubtful that rabbis or highly observant families participated in these particular festivities.

The last event in the Jewish calendar year is the only other fast day that, like Yom Kippur, lasts from sundown to sundown, for it is a day of mourning in memory of the destruction of the Temple. The Ninth of Av is briefly described as the day one sits on the floor and fasts; some Jews wore black as a sign of mourning.[19] Although Bouena did not mention the other mourning customs that are observed on this day, such as refraining from wearing leather or reading the Book of Lamentations, she nevertheless presents a traditional image of this fast day.

Whether observing the Sabbath and holidays or just enjoying themselves, families spent a great deal of time together. Bouena informs the reader that the younger generation was changing the age-old traditions and, as a result, quality family time was diminishing. Modernity affected almost every aspect of one's life.

Changes in Tradition

In a traditional world, many customs are related to rites of passage, such as those following a death in the family. Even among the least observant Jews, the loss of a loved one tends to elicit an inner urge to display respect for the dead and to cope with the loss; such responses help to preserve mourning customs. Sephardi and Mizrahi funerals are traditionally more vocal than those of Ashkenazim, and female keeners are often present to accompany the deceased with the proper fanfare.[20] Bouena differentiates between the emotional experience one undergoes at the funeral of a young person who has been taken before his or her time and that of dealing with the passing of an older person. Bouena herself experienced numerous losses, including the death of her father when she was young, of her brother and sisters at Auschwitz, and—the most painful loss of all—the death of a child. The members of her family who remained in Salonika could never be honored with a proper burial and her own daughter died at a very early age. Nevertheless, she is cognizant of the fact that the passing of an elder, natural as it may be, still merits the utmost respect.

Simultaneously, signs that the times are changing appear in these verses, such as a diminishing of the degree of respect paid to fathers and the shaving of beards by some of the men who were hastening their own transformation. Weddings were being streamlined and no longer seemed to be as grand as before. Even the Jewish court was not immune to the wheels of change; it attempted not to appear outdated by ordering the rabbis to exchange their cassocks for turbans. Note that in this case, the state was not commanding the rabbis to abandon their traditional dress; it was the rabbinic court that initiated this transformation.

Nevertheless, one cannot deny that some advances improved the quality of life. Instead of carriages, taxis appeared on the scene.[21] Once running water became available in the 1890s, a water company installed meters, which changed life considerably.[22] This innovation led to a quick lesson in industrialization and privatization, for a billing system is impersonal and effective and must be taken seriously. A contract, rather than a verbal agreement, became the legally binding means of conducting business, whether between supplier and consumer or between two private individuals. Modernity canceled out many familiar personal and interpersonal relationships; formality and the impersonal were integral characteristics of modernization that imposed themselves on the recipient, neutralizing much of the traditional informality that was once the norm.

Household life in Salonika was also transformed in various ways. Not only were transportation motorized, water companies formed, and new heating systems developed, but the advent of electricity also resulted in far-reaching changes both inside and outside the home. By the 1890s, gas and electricity lit up the city for the first time. Bouena refers to a newer heating system by means of a stove with continuous fire in the middle of the house; it was lit at Hanukah and extinguished at Passover.[23] Note that even though heating methods were gradually modernizing, the Jewish calendar year still was the basis for mapping time in the Salonikan mindset.

While Bouena sees the value in those advances that improved the heating and lighting of houses, she seems to have doubts about whether any advances were being made by installing telephones in homes. She was certain that the women were using it for idle chatter.[24] The poet is far more critical of women than of men and belittles the simple women who were so enthralled with their new toy that they used it at every opportunity, conversing about the most mundane and inane topics. One assumes that she did not object to the installation of a telephone as long as it was being used for appropriate purposes. The women who, in her eyes, abused this privilege were most likely the less educated of the housewives, who sought to impress others by obtaining a tangible symbol of modernity in their homes.

Bouena frequently criticizes the materialism that is often associated with progress and is concerned about the price of modernity. Instead of having the "inviter" announce upcoming events and name the guests aloud, invitations were being sent to homes.[25] This method was more efficient but was a sign of the depersonalization brought about by modernity. It was a process that dispensed with tradition and was destined to make the old methods obsolete.

In the long run, there is no doubt that these modern developments improved the quality of life of many a Salonikan. Reading the description of the pre–washing machine era in a typical household serves as a reminder of the labor-intensive nature of laundry.[26] Bouena admires the hard work and industriousness of the women, but also reveals the nature of their toil. Nonetheless, her wariness of modernity was well founded, for she saw so many less-than-impressive advances that one begins to wonder who was marching in which direction.

The Dictates of Fashion

On the whole, the women appear to have been attracted to modern styles and fashions. Their lives were often dictated by the latest styles, and Bouena remarks upon this extensively. Her criticism usually pertains to women, but not all allusions are gender specific. There were those who aimed to display their new clothes while riding in open carriages.[27] When she comments about fez wearers, she is most probably casting aspersions on men. Interestingly enough, the fez became a symbol of affinity with the old Turkish regime, and wearing it was interpreted as a reversion to the days of old. Apparently it was sometimes a fashion statement and at other times a sign of days long gone.

The geographical location of Salonika was crucial to its development as a cosmopolitan center that tended to be influenced by the West—particularly by trendsetting Paris. As Michael Molho points out, this city served as a bridge between the conservative East and the enlightened West, a place where European culture found a comfortable home.[28] The Jews were among the most ardent proponents of Europeanism; some moved back and forth between the two worlds, while others' moves were more permanent. Those who dabbled between the two worlds served as bearers of change on all levels—from fashion and style to politics and economy. However, change in this city emanated from the West as well as from the East.

The end of the first decade of the twentieth century heralded an unending series of changes with which the community had to cope.[29] Many of the Jews were influenced by the modern nationalistic ideas of the Young Turks and their revolt in 1908. It was at that time that Zionist groups slowly but surely developed, although they did not necessarily reflect any desire to relocate to Palestine.[30] At the same time, the draft law of 1908 propelled numerous young men who lacked the funds to pay for an exemption to flee to Alexandria and to the United States, especially during World War I (1914–18) and immediately afterward.

The Balkan Wars created numerous problems for the community, as Hellenization proceeded apace.[31] At the same time, political frictions developed between the royalist supporters of the king and the nationalist prime minister, the antisemitic Elepheterios Venizelos, as the polarization of the Jews and the Greeks widened. It was no accident that wealthy members of the community who had Italian citizenship began to emigrate, especially since the transition for them was a relatively easy one.[32]

The next and incredibly damaging blow to the community was the aforementioned fire of 1917 and its aftermath. Salonikans experienced more than their share of fires in the nineteenth century and their communal leaders had a great deal of experience in coping with disasters, but never had they suffered a conflagration as devastating as that in 1917. Neither Salonika nor its Jewish community, which was originally composed of seventeen neighborhoods, would ever be the same.

Ultimately the fire proved to be a blessing for Venizelos, who took advantage of the opportunity to rid the city center of its Jewish majority and changed the entire face of Salonika. His message came through loud and clear as he forbade the rebuilding of edifices on their original locations and seriously limited options for growth, investment, or relocation. Many of the factory owners who had Italian citizenship made insurance claims and left for Italy. Although the wealthy could abandon their homeland, the options open to the homeless poor were limited; no one could return to the old neighborhoods as access to the city center and to work became more difficult. The suburbs and new, courtyard-less neighborhoods, lacking the flavor of days of yore, were the only option.[33] In addition, by passing various laws—such as making Greek the primary language of instruction in all schools—the government was able to manipulate the entire community and speed up the process of Hellenization.[34] All of the progress that had taken place between 1900 and 1920 was effectively canceled out by a two-day disaster.[35]

In the meantime, the Greeks and the Turks continued fighting, resulting in massacres and relocations. The 1923 Treaty of Lausanne essentially arranged for population exchanges; Greeks in Turkey could relocate to Greece, and vice versa. Bouena mentions one group of Muslims that relocated to Turkey, namely, the descendants of the infamous Donmëh, the followers of Sabbatai Zevi who remained loyal to him even after he converted to Islam in 1666 (Salonika had been the home of numerous Sabbateans in the seventeenth century).[36] Bouena calls them "Jews at home and Muslims in the market"; she learned that they went to Turkey. She writes that she supposedly bought the house of a believer—claiming, tongue in cheek, that she "found a synagogue in the attic."[37]

Needless to say, these relocations seriously affected the Jews of Salonika. The arrival of more than one hundred thousand Greeks in Salonika, most of whom were penniless, was disastrous for many Jews because of the competition and tension that resulted. The factories and rights that Jews once had were being given to Greeks, whose presence became almost overwhelming. New laws were passed that crippled the Jewish community economically. Bouena provides an example concerning Jewish pharmacists. Originally, in order to practice legally, the pharmacist needed and obtained a Turkish diploma, but "with the Greek laws, / They were obliged to have a Greek partner [pharmacist] who has Greek papers." Consequently, the Greeks were in a superior position and could overtake Jewish professional businesses in certain fields. Bouena notes that the Greeks became homeowners overnight without investing anything, whereas the Jews were apt to lose their homes or their investments.[38] The Sabbath decree of 1923, which obligated Jews to work on Saturday, also proved to be yet another catalyst for immigration. Between 1922 and 1926, thousands of Jews moved to Paris as well as to Italy, for Savatopolis had been relegated to nostalgia.

Tensions flared at the start of the next decade and erupted more than once—as in the Campbell quarter, a poor Jewish neighborhood, in June 1931; the result was a pogrom. According to Dublon-Knebel, the instigators were members of the EEE (National Union of Greece), an antisemitic group that became fascist as of the late 1920s. Their initiative was bolstered by many unemployed Anatolian refugees who seized the opportunity to enter the fray.[39] Bouena offers interesting information concerning this disaster, which included a fire in this southern suburb. In an unusually long copla, one discovers that the lives of the Jews of this neighborhood were spared because of a chance occurrence. A Jewish pharmacist named Isaac Tivoli was awakened during the night by a patient in need of medicine. Tivoli responded; when he opened the door to his pharmacy, he encountered raging flames and immediately awakened his family of six, sent them to safety, and then proceeded to save the residents of the Jewish Quarter.[40] Fortunately this was not a repeat of the 1917 fire. Nevertheless, the pogrom and fire took their toll, both physically and psychologically.

The combination of the draft, the fire of 1917, serious government restrictions, Hellenization, relocations, and antisemitism convinced many a Jewish Salonikan that the time had come to abandon this beloved city. Consequently, the Jewish population dropped to about 52,350 by 1935; as the result of an incoming flow of immigrants, a Greek majority populated the center of the once Jewish "Jerusalem of the Balkans." Although many Turks moved to Turkish soil, a similar move was not made by the Jews. They were not as mobile; in their eyes, their new Balkan home replaced Spain at the end of the fifteenth century. Despite the fact that the Jews flourished under Turkish rule, the Salonikans were not anxious to move to mainland Turkey. Bouena's verses describe the fate of different members of the community, including lawyers who needed to retool time and again, and who eventually emigrated because of the ever-changing laws.[41] This example aptly reflects the frustrations and continuous attempts by the Jewish community to adapt and rebuild after each disaster—until such point that the situation simply became unbearable.

Bouena's poetry incorporates these events along with information about new waves of immigration—whether to Paris, the United States, or to Palestine. She refers to an uncle from America who bore gifts, found a bride, and returned to his new home.[42] Elsewhere, she notes, "The shipping agencies are working well." Every week the ships were filled with the belongings of Salonikans who were leaving for either Palestine or Paris. She saw the loads of furniture being sent abroad—most likely to Paris, since the poorer emigrants did not have large amounts of furniture to take along. Her awareness of the deteriorating situation owing to government decrees and Greek immigrant hostility is also reflected here; she writes, "We hope that there will not be antisemitism wherever they are going."[43] This seems to be a reference to the westbound travelers.

The motives behind immigration were, on the whole, economic—which comes as no surprise in light of the extreme poverty faced by a large percentage of the Jewish population.[44] Despite valiant attempts by the communal committee to alleviate the situation, the fire of 1917 only added to the bleakness of life for the very poor. Some Selaniklis opted to leave, for they feared that the Venizelos government, with its incendiary publications, would continue to discriminate against them; others, having lived through the Campbell pogrom, were also convinced that it was time to leave. Bouena's verses reflect the fear and frustration that pervaded the community.

Some of Bouena's coplas reflect a growing sense of helplessness in the community under Greek rule—whether in dealing with the municipality, in reaction to new laws, or as the result of antisemitism. The scrap-metal workers who were falsely accused of cutting the telephone or telegraph wires and sentenced to death made a deep impression upon the community.[45] In the long run, they were declared not guilty, but he who was to relay the verdict intended to save them was an antisemite and withheld this information. This resulted in the original sentence's being carried out on the Sabbath, something previously unimaginable; the community was understandably traumatized.

A look at the Jewish community in the 1930s reveals a religiously, politically, and culturally diverse group; Bouena is well aware of this diversity. This reality reflected "deep divisions" that concerned "thorny issues" such as assimilation or separatism; Zionism or Hellenization; private versus public education; linguistic affinities, and others.[46] Zionism, in particular, raised suspicion in the eyes of the Greek nationalists. In the long run, there was no single or correct option for the community.

Nationalism in Greek Communities

When General Metaxas became dictator of Greece in 1936, albeit with the king's support, the Selaniklis again experienced fear and trepidation; many began to wonder if they had the thousand liras needed to purchase a permit to go to Palestine. Bouena was especially sensitive to the temptations of Zionism and emigration to the Holy Land because two of her sisters ultimately immigrated to Palestine. The Balfour Declaration came three months after the fateful fire of 1917. Although historically speaking the majority of Salonikan Jews did not belong to Zionist associations, Bouena has a distinctly different impression, probably due to her own family's deep commitment to Zionist values. She believes that Zionism should be part and parcel of every child's education and mentions various Zionist societies, often pointing out their socioeconomic characteristics. She informs us that the wealthy belonged to the Keren Hayisod Association,[47] but that there were numerous other organizations—including Bnai Zion, Maccabee, the Young Hebrews, Theodor Herzl, Betar, Mizrahi, and Tel Aviv. In one verse, there are details about a successful plan for a Sephardi moshav. This plan was conceived in 1917 by Dr. Moshe Coffinas, a Jew in the Greek parliament, but did not materialize until 1937—when the necessary funds were raised with the help of the Zionist Federation.[48] Eventually, an agricultural moshav in the Sharon area was founded and named Tsur Moshe in memory of Coffinas. The original plan was for fifty Greek families, mainly from Salonika, to live and work in the moshav, but when it was allocated more land after 1948, families from Bulgaria and Turkey joined them.[49]

Some of the Salonikans only visited the Holy Land—Bouena refers to this journey as a *ziyara,* the Arabic word for pilgrimage; others only invested from afar. There were fundraising activities galore, with an eye to building Tel Aviv. Bouena explains that the Young Hebrew Association organized an annual bazaar in order to collect money for the Jewish National Fund (JNF). Some of the communal efforts at fundraising utilized the talents of the local women, who contributed highly professional artwork to the cause.[50]

Bouena alludes to the fact that immigration to Palestine was not an option for everyone because of government limitations pertaining to financial demands, marital status, occupational needs, or family size. Some arranged unconsummated marriages and adopted children in order to deceive the authorities.[51]

The realities of the developing country and relations between the Jews of Salonika and Palestine, especially following the establishment of Tsur Moshe, are reflected in these verses. Bouena presents the view of a Salonikan mother whose daughter and grandchildren immigrated. Her daughter was having considerable difficulty learning the language, in sharp contrast to her grandchildren.[52] This is a realistic reflection of the learning curve as well as the uneven adaptation to a new environment among members of different generations. Children up to a certain age adapt quickly to new cultures and new languages, whereas adults experience a slower and more difficult process, especially when there is a language barrier. Elsewhere, Bouena hints at the obliviousness of an emissary from Palestine to the realities of the diaspora world. The delegate from the JNF addressed the Zionist leaders in the community, but was insensitive to the fact that he was visiting a traditional community—or at least a community that, despite its attraction to modernity, still respected tradition. The secular Zionist arrived and, without a moment's hesitation, dined in a non-kosher establishment. Needless to say, his behavior caused "a scandal for our city."[53] Such brash behavior would later be affiliated with the secular *sabra,* or native-born Israeli, for whom religion and tradition would often take a backseat to political idealism.

Some Historical Developments

Although some Salonikans eventually moved to Israel and served in the army there, many young men served in the Greek army. In the discussion of dowries, mention was made of the Turkish draft exemption tax, but once Salonika became a Greek city, the rules changed. No one wanted to serve in the Greek military, and those who could not avoid the draft counted the days until they completed their tour of duty.[54]

Bouena's brother, Eliaou, was drafted; one verse presents a humorous account of how he coped during a local assignment at the Yedi Kule citadel.[55] Eliaou was also sent with the army to northwest Morocco, where he was wounded and hospitalized. As a result, many members of the community assumed that he died, despite the fact that the members of his own family insisted that he would return. She describes the hardships he faced upon his return—much to the surprise of his business partners—and how he managed to recoup his losses.[56]

Yedi Koule, a fortress guarding the northern entrance to the city.

The Greco-Italian War appears in the verses as well. Hitler's ally, Italy, initiated a unilateral invasion of Greece in 1940. Most of the fighting that followed took place in Greece and Albania, and the Italians did not fare very well. As the Greeks neared victory, Hitler realized that he could not permit his ally to be humiliated and invaded Greece. Bouena declares that the Italians went to war on the assumption that they would be victorious, but their attitude altered when they heard the shots of 1942, presumably those of the Greek troops overtaking them.[57] In the opinion of the Greeks, the success of their army was guaranteed.

Although this collection is devoted to prewar Salonika, there is some overlap with the wartime coplas. Thus, one already finds comments on the Italian invasion of Albania and the recruitment of Jewish boys into the Greek army.[58] Yet the majority of Bouena's verses are devoted to her beloved holidays and traditions related to weddings and dowries, births and deaths, family life, holidays, and Zionism. She appreciates the beauty of the ancient customs as well as the advantages of many modern technological advances. She is witness to the joys and devastations of Jewish life in twentieth-century Salonika—to the fires, political changes, and immigration patterns. She is cynical about those who leaped into modernity without looking, but is also a realist who adopts Zionist values and expresses support for a Jewish homeland. Unfortunately, once the Axis armies appeared in the Balkans, a snowball effect was set in motion; the Nazis not only overtook the city of Salonika, but also obliterated five hundred years of Jewish life and creativity. Bouena chooses to devote the majority of her verses to the pre-Nazi period, but the experience of the invasion left an indelible mark on the life that is described in her coplas. The era of joyously living a traditional Sephardi life, even as it confronted modernity, came to an abrupt end.

Bouena Sarfatty Garfinkle   Komplas de la vida a Salonique

1) Antes para la biankeria azian bokthas
Para vouadrar la ropa. Agora aye chifoniera
a la ouda de ethar, azen maseros bien
brodados kon birihim de seda fina
buvamos a la saloud de la madre de la novia
        ke se yama   Sarah Medina

2) Los lavoradores de toutoun estan en greve
se averaron al magazin, gritan en las ventanes
ke kieren pan para sous femias
buvamos a la saloud de Daniel Atias

3) El Padre de Maurice vino a demandar la mano
de Marie, duho ke ese kazamiento de amor
ma! estouvo aziendo bazar por la dota
Por la biankeria i la achougar i la djoya de la tia
ke a Marie le dicho
La madre a la kouzina aparejando raki i mezet
asperando de sinter el Besiman tove
buvamos a la saloud de este par ke va atener
bouen   mazal

4) El marido de Sarika es oun tembel despoues
de seich mezes non avia de la dota ni oun
Penez, el esfouegro foue ouvligado de le pagar
el beidel buvamos a la saloud de Haim Abravanel

First page of the first collection of coplas, in Bouena's original handwriting.

CHAPTER 3

Komplas eskrito de Bouena Sarfatty Garfinkle de la vida a Salonique

Coplas about Coplas

20. Las komplas a Salonique es parte de la vida.
    Ningounos alevantan el vazo sin dezir eviva,
    Souetan a los amigos de boueno korason: parnasa, saloud i amor.
    Bevamos a la saloud de los Sassons.

108. Saver ether komplas eze oun dono del dio.
    Los selaniklis las saven dezir kon savor.
    Las mejores son de loz djornalistas,
    Besantsi o Abravanel,[1] ke tienen la penina fatsile kada dia.
    Bevamos a la saloud de Albert Attias.

374. Saver ethar komplas eze art.
    Mouthos las saven kopiar.
    Se kiere hen para laz dezir,
    Eze oun plazer de souhaitar boueno a loz haverim.
    Bevamos a la saloud de Avraam Eshkenazi.

142. Los livros de estoria non moutha djente loz meldan.
    Ma! Los selaniklis ethan komplas, para ke todos sepan eze plazer
    De las sentir i souhatamos boueno a amigos i a los ermanos de Salonique.
    Bevamos a la saloud de Salomon Shaki.

13. A Salonique las komplas es la vida de kada dia.
    El hombre kouando viene del lavoro,

---

1. These two journalists (the first is sometimes spelled Bessanthi or Besanthi) are mentioned numerous times as talented and prolific authors; see Ladino Publications 9, 307, 88, 278, and 279, below. Besantsi founded *El Impartial* (1909–11), then edited *El Liberal* (1912), a journal of general interest, and the daily *El Pueblo* (1917–33), a Zionist publication he cofounded. See Rena Molho, *Salonica and Istanbul,* 251.

CHAPTER 3

Coplas Written by Bouena Sarfatty Garfinkle about Life in Salonika

Coplas about Coplas

20. Coplas in Salonika are part of life.
    No one raises his glass without saying a toast,
    Toasting friends heartily: to a livelihood, good health, and love.
    Let us drink to the health of the Sassons.

108. Knowing how to create[2] coplas is a gift from God.
    The Salonikans know how to recite them with relish.
    The best are those of the journalists,
    Besantsi or Abravanel, who have a flowing pen every day.
    Let us drink to the health of Albert Attias.

374. Knowing how to toss out complas is an art.
    Many know how to copy them.
    It is necessary to have grace [in order] to recite them,
    It is a pleasure to wish one's friends well.
    Let us drink to the health of Avraham Eshkenazi.

142. The history books are not read by many people.
    But! The Salonikans toss out coplas, so that everyone knows this pleasure
    Of hearing them and we wish friends and siblings in Salonika well.
    Let us drink to the health of Salomon Shaki.

13. In Salonika, the coplas are [part of] everyday life.
    When the man comes home from work,

---

2. Literally, "toss out."

La moujer le apareja el raki[3] i el mezet,[4] i las pantouflas.
El marido para la (r)engrasiar, la etha ouna kompla,
De lo ke se paso (d)el dia.
Bevamos a la saloud de Bienvenida.

102. Los Selaniklis tienen sous expretiones.
    Ounos dizen me flato; otros dizen me dio enchavonada.
    Ounos dizen se arezvalo; otros dizen se mourio.
    Ounos dizen kayadez, otros dizen amoudesian.
    Bevamos a la saloud de Avraam Sion.

159. Las expresiones nounka mankaron a Salonique.
    Ma todas reviene a lo mezmo.
    Ounos dizen eze deskalso [*sic*]; otros dizen eze pimienta.
    Ounos dizen machka ougnas;
    Otros dizen mira atrase kouando sourte.
    Bevamos a la saloud de Daniel Sotto.

190. Los selaniklis tienen en la sangre los refranes
    Ke los pasan de padre a ijo.
    Las komplas sin se oulvidar,
    En kada reunion de famia se siente, mas i mas.
    Bevamos a la saloud de Eliaou Amar.

Dowries and Marriages

110. Louenes i djoueves eze dia de Thora, achougar, fatos.
    Biankeria se empesan estos dias.
    Tambien despozorios o merkar artikolos de valor,
    Ese lounes o djoueves sin exeption.
    Bevamos a la saloud de Rafael Sion.

208. Despozorio ese alegria.
    Kazamiento ese frouvoir famia.
    Bevamos a la saloud de Salomon Negria.

300. El padre ke tiene ijas aze ekonomias, i merka liras apoko, apoko.
    Las mete en ouna oya para la dota de las nignas.

---

3. Raki is an anise-based aperitif like ouzo consumed by both men and women of all classes of society, which served as "medicine, payment and celebration" (Rodrigue and Stein, introduction to Halevi, *A Jewish Voice*, xxxvii).

4. *Mezet* is hors d'oeuvre—usually a selection of fried pastry, liver, stuffed vegetables, and the like.

The wife prepares ouzo and tidbits to eat and his slippers.
The husband, in order to thank her, tosses out a verse
About what happened on that day.
Let us drink to the health of Bienvenida.

102. The Salonikans have their expressions.
Some say he flattered me; others say he pulled the wool over my eyes.
Some say he slipped away; others say he died.
Some say be quiet; others say shut up.
Let us drink to the health of Avraham Sion.

159. Expressions were never lacking in Salonika.
But they all come down to the same thing.
Some say: he is barefoot; others say he is pepper.
Some say he bites fingernails;
Others say he looks back [at his rear end] when he defecates.
Let us drink to the health of Daniel Sotto.

190. Salonikans have proverbs in their blood
Which they pass from father to son.
The couplets, without forgetting them,
At each family meeting they are heard more and more.
Let us drink to the health of Eliaou Amar.

Dowries and Marriages

110. Mondays and Thursdays are the day of Torah, trousseau, layettes.
Linen sets are begun on these days.
Also engagements or purchasing items of value.
It is [on] Mondays and Thursdays without exception.
Let us drink to the health of Rafael Sion.

208. Engagement is happiness.
Marriage is building a family.
Let us drink to the health of Salomon Negria.

300. The father who has daughters saves, and buys gold coins, little by little.
He puts them in a pot for the dowry of the girls.

Las konta kinze dias antes de la boda, kon alegria.
Bevamos a la saloud del novio i la novia i toda la famia.

124. Eliaou dize ke si tou padre dechava oun milion de liras,
Ese tou ke ivas a heredar.
Ma! Le decho kouatro nignas.
Eze yo ke las devo de mirar i las kazar.
Bevamos a la saloud de Samuel Lazar.

156. A Salonique aye mouthos monastirlis.
Son honorados i muy rikos.
Gentelle se kazo.
El vestido de novia se brodo kon perlas finas i oun vello de grande valor.
A Marie mi ermana se lo empresto kouando se kazo.
Bevamos a la saloud de Reyna Serror.

301. Josepo Menache se kazo kon la gneta de Daoût,
El director de la komunitad.
Korbeyes de flores resevieron
Ke al otro dia las tomo el estierkero.
Bevamos a la saloud de Daniel Serrera.

380. A los ballos venden kartas.
Los nignos merkan para kitar la reyna de ballo.
Las ke tienen mas mouthas eze la popular.
Le meten korona i bayla kon el prezidente de los sosieta.
Bevamos a la saloud de Daniel Amar.

381. A loz ballos los nignos se van al bar.
Beven i rompen kopas para amostrar.
Azen doubara para se distinguar.
Bevamos a la saloud de Rafael Yakar.

382. A loz ballos aye karnet de bal.
Los nignos eskriven ke bayle van a baylar.
Si la nigna tiene mouthas parás, todos apera la sira.
Bevamos a la saloud de Salomon Amar.

383. Al ballo de Pourim me visti de blanko,
Kon Maguin David de flores bleus parsemados.
El Leon del Juda amario,

He counts them with joy fifteen days before the wedding.
Let us drink to the health of the groom and the bride and the whole family.

124. Eliaou says if your father had left a million pounds,
You would have been the one to inherit.
But! He left behind four girls.
It is I who has to take care of them and to marry them off.
Let us drink to the health of Samuel Lazar.

156. In Salonika, there are many from Monastir.
They are honored and very wealthy.
Gentelle married.
The bridal dress was embroidered with fine pearls and a veil of great value.
She loaned it to my sister Marie when she got married.
Let us drink to the health of Reyna Serror.

301. Joseph Menach married the granddaughter of Daout,
The head of the community.
They received bouquets of flowers
That the garbagemen took [away] the next day.
Let us drink to the health of Daniel Serrera.

380. At balls, they sell cards.
The boys buy them to choose the queen of the ball.
Those who have more are popular.
They crown her and she dances with the president of the society.
Let us drink to the health of Daniel Amar.

381. At the balls, the boys go to the bar.
They drink and break glasses to show off.
They make a racket in order to stand out.
Let us drink to the health of Rafael Yakar.

382. At the balls, there is a dance card.
The boys write which dance they are going to dance.
If the girl has a lot of money, everyone waits his turn.
Let us drink to the health of Salomon Amar.

383. I wore white to the Purim ball,
With a Star of David strewn with blue flowers.[5]
The Lion of Judah was yellow,

---

5. From the French *persemer un chemin de fleurs,* "to strew a path with flowers."

Oun koutiko del Keren Hakayemeth
Metido al bel de la tsintoura.
Gani el primo premio;
Foue oun grande evenimiento para toda la famia.
Bevamos a la saloud de Yechoua Nahmias.

384. El ballo del Matanoth eze el mijor.
Las nignas vistidas de Tamarika, dande Katina Paximada
O de Eujenie o ke trayen de Paris.
Los padres kieren amostrar ke tienen dota, biankeria i achougar.
Bevamos a la saloud de Isaac Lazar.

429. A Salonique a loz ballos, ke sea del Matanoth,
      o del Keren Hakayemet,
Las nignas kon sous toilettas i la djoya,
Ke ese para amostrar lo ke tienen.
Los nignos kon smoking i papion blanko,
Baylando kon la ke tiene papa kon dota.
Bevamos a la saloud de Samuel Saporta.

430. A Salonique la djouventud dia al Alhad se va a baylar,
A las organisationes sionistas ke lo yaman aprè midí.
La semana entera las nignas estan pensando koualo se van ameter
O trokando la lithoura[6] del vestido.
Bevamos a la saloud de Avraam Tsimino.

378. A Salonique kouando salimos de loz ballos,
Moz vamos a komer k(o)ul(o)urias kaentes kon kezo.
Koumiendo i baylando, fina ke arivamos en kaza.
Al otro dia tenemos dolor de pathas.
Non dizimos nada a mama porke moz va agritar.
Vivamos a la saloud de Rachel Amar.[7]

171. Doz ijikas vengneron de Paris, de parientes Selaniklis.
Moz ambezaron la karioka.
Edukadas i ermozas, ningounos laz demandan
Porke non tienen dota para dar.
Esperamos ke oun dia esta dota se va abandonar.
Bevamos a la saloud de Leon Amar.

---

6. Lishura.
7. In one draft of the verses, the name is Behar.

A little box from the Jewish National Fund
Placed at the back of the belt.
I won first prize;
It was a great event for the whole family.
Let us drink to the health of Yeshua Nahmias.

384. The ball at the Gifts for the Needy Association is the best.
The girls dressed by Tamarika, chez Katina Paximada,
Or by Eugenie or [with clothes] that they bring from Paris.
The parents want to show that they have a dowry, linens and a trousseau.
Let us drink to the health of Isaac Lazar.

429. At the balls in Salonika, whether they be at the Gifts [for the Needy],
    or at the Jewish National Fund,
[One finds] the girls with their gowns and their jewelry
That is for showing off what they have.
The boys with smoking jackets and white bow ties,
Dancing with those who have a father with a dowry.
Let us drink to the health of Samuel Saporta.

430. In Salonika the youth goes dancing on Sundays
To the Zionist organizations which they call an afternoon get-together.
The entire week the girls are thinking about what to wear
Or adjusting the smoothness of their dress.
Let us drink to the health of Avraham Tsimino.

378. In Salonika when we leave the balls,
We go to eat hot sesame bagels with cheese.
Eating and dancing until we arrive home.
The following day we have pains in our legs.
We don't say anything to Mother because she is going to scold us.
Let us drink to the health of Rachel Amar.

171. Two girls whose parents are from Salonika came from Paris.
They taught us the karioka dance.
Educated and pretty, [but] no one asks for them
Because they do not have a dowry to offer.
We hope that one day this dowry [custom] will be abandoned.
Let us drink to the health of Leon Amar.

256. Antes teniamos otho dias de houpa.
Agora se van aviajar;
Gastan la dota porke vino sin soudar.
Bevamos a la saloud de Salomon Behar.

257. Antes se kazavan kon koredor.
Agora se kieren kazar por amor.
Ma! Kouando se apersive ke non tiene el milion,
Decha la nigna kon dolor de korason.
Bevamos a la saloud de Maurice Sasson.

119b. Mi madre vendio el bono para dar a Rachel dota,
Komo kieria amostrar.
Biankeria de Karadimo le merko
Sin pensar ke aye kouatro de detras.
Para Marie vindio la djoya;
Para Daisy kon Hadji, se mando la dota de samara presioza.
Ma! Eliaou mos prometio ke a mozotros mos va a dar amor i todo lo mijor.
Bevamos a la saloud de Eliaou ke mos da lo ke moz aprometio.

3. El padre de Maurice vino a demandar la mano de Marie.
Dicho ke ese kazamiento de amor,
Ma! Estouvo aziendo bazar por la dota,
Por la biankeria i la ashugar i la djoya de la tia ke a Marie le decho.
La madre a la kouzina aparejando raki i mezet,
Asperando de sintir el Besiman Tov.[8]
Bevamos a la saloud de este par ke va a tener bouen mazal.

164. El padre de la novia, antes ke diga Besiman Tov,
Toma enformationes, se aseventa kouanto pouede
I lo eskrive koualo le dicheron.
Viene en kaza, lo melda kon atention
Ke persona ez el yerno ke deskojo.
Bevamos a la saloud de Eliaou Guerchon.

243. Le dieron al novio ashugar, biankeria,
I mille liras de oro, de dota i meza franka.
Bevamos a la saloud de Malka.

---

8. Literally, "may it be a sign of good fortune"; with good wishes.

256. In the old days, there were eight days of wedding celebration.
    Now they want to go traveling;
    They spend the dowry because it came effortlessly.[9]
    Let us drink to the health of Salomon Behar.

257. In the old days, they married using a marriage broker.
    Now they want to marry for love.
    But! When he [the groom] realizes that she does not have the million,
    He leaves the girl with a broken heart.
    Let us drink to the health of Maurice Sasson.

119b. My mother sold the bond in order to give Rachel a dowry,
    As she wanted to show off.
    She bought linens from Karadimo[10] for her
    Without thinking that there are four after her.
    For Marie, she sold the jewelry;
    For Daisy with Hadji, she sent the dowry of precious fur.
    But! Eliaou promised to give us love and all the best.
    Let us drink to the health of Eliaou, who gives us what he promises.

3. The father of Maurice came to ask for the hand of Marie.
    He said it was a marriage of love,
    But! He kept bargaining for the dowry,
    For linens and the trousseau and the jewelry of the aunt who left it for Marie.
    The mother was in the kitchen preparing ouzo and hors d'oeuvres,
    Waiting to hear the toast "with good wishes."
    Let us drink to the health of this pair that is going to have good luck.

164. Before the father of the bride says "with good wishes,"
    He gets information, clarifies as much as he can
    And writes down what they told him.
    He comes home, carefully reads
    What [kind of] person the son-in-law whom he chose is.
    Let us drink to the health of Eliaou Gershon.

243. They gave the groom a trousseau, linens,
    And a thousand gold liras as dowry, and free room and board at
        his in-laws'.[11]
    Let us drink to the health of Malka.

---

9. Without perspiring.
10. A firm.
11. Usually for a period of twelve to eighteen months.

276b. Salomon se kazo; a la boda non mos invito.
Tomo moutha dota, meza franka
I kamas altas kon kourtinas.
Bevamos a la saloud de Regina.

19. Dr. Beja vino a Salonique, kon moujer Françaisa.
Se kazo a Paris; el padre se avia mouerido.
La madre non le kijo dar ni oun vestido.
Bevamos a la saloud de los keridos.

241. Marido viejo dan los parientes a sous ijas.
Solo miran ke sea riko; lo resto non lez emporta.
Bevamos a la saloud de Haim Saporta.

288. Antes vestia bragas.
Agora mos tomo baston
Porke tomo ashugar, biankeria, meza franka, grande dota,
I la boutika del esfouegro ke heredo.
Bevamos a la saloud de los Mordos.

235. A la J. J.[12] aye mansevos
Ke vouelen i mouthos f(i)eden.
Toman grandes dotas; se azen mas rikos de lo ke son.
Bevamos a la saloud de Mika Hasson.

49. Los mansevos visten el enverano tsapeos de panama,
El envierno de Borsalino, bien elegantes kamizas i kalsas de seda fina.
Todo esto azen para amostrar i tomar moutha achougar i dota sin kontar.
Bevamos a la saloud de akeyos ke se dechan engagnar.

202. Rabi Chimon Barioha fiestan los Sarfattys.
Eze ouna grande boda kon tsalguin.
Bevamos a la saloud de los ke mos aze bevir.

308. A Salonique azemos korban.
La madre del novio desparte pitas.
Ese alegria de ver el kodredo,

---

12. Jeune Juif Association.

276b. Salomon got married; we were not invited to the wedding.
He took a large dowry, free room and board at his in-laws'
And high beds with curtains.
Let us drink to the health of Regina.

19. Dr. Beja came to Salonika with his French wife.
They wed in Paris; the father had died.
The mother did not even want to give her a dress.
Let us drink to the health of the lovers.

241. The parents give their daughters an old husband.
They only see that he may be rich; the rest is not important to them.
Let us drink to the health of Haim Saporta.

288. He used to wear breeches.[13]
Now he took up a walking stick
Because he got a trousseau, linens, free room and board at his in-laws',
A large dowry, and his father-in-law's shop that he inherited.
Let us drink to the health of the Mordos.

235. In the Young Jews Association, there are young men
Who smell and many who stink.
They take large dowries; they get richer than they already are.
Let us drink to the health of Mika Hasson.

49. The young men wear Panama hats in the summer,
Italian fedora hats in winter, quite elegant shirts and socks of fine silk.
All this is done to show themselves off and to get a large trousseau and
huge dowry.
Let us drink to the health of those who allow themselves to be deceived.

202. R. Shimon Barioha marries the Sarfattys.
It is a large wedding with a Turkish music band.
Let us drink to the health of what makes us live.[14]

308. In Salonika we offer a [pseudo-] sacrifice.[15]
The mother of the groom serves pitas.
This is happiness, to see the lamb,

---

13. Figuratively, he was very poor.
14. Literally, "those who make us live."
15. See Michael Molho, *Traditions and Customs,* 12, where he refers to sesame-covered loaves replacing a sacrifice; this is supposed to protect the groom from the evil eye.

Alcheh raki i mezet para loz envitados.
Bevamos a la saloud de Avraam Toledano.

4. El marido de Sarika es oun tembel.
Despoues de sech mezes non avia de la dota ni oun penez.
El esfouegro foue ouvligado de le pagar el be(i)del.
Bevamos a la saloud de Haim Abravanel.

92. Merki kaza, se afondo.
Merki liras, abacho.
Kazi a ija; el novio ez ladron,
Se fouyo; la decho kon dolor de korason.
Bevamos a la saloud de mi ija i ke le pase esta dolor de korason.

324. Marika la lingère mos izo la biankeria.
Toma ouna lire de oro el dia.
El padre de la novia grita.
La madre non sale de la kouzina preparando la koumida.
Bevamos a la saloud de Salomon Atias.

412. Estamos invitados a la boda de Marie
Ke se va azer al salon del Matanotte Laevionim.
Dio achougar, i biankeria de kouatro saizon,
Mille liras de oro, i la djoya de la nona ke le decho.
Bevamos a la saloud de Haim Guerchon.

162. El photographe viene en kaza a photographiar a la novia.
Despoues al salon ande va aser la boda.
Kon esta louz ke sale de la makina,
Todos aseran los ojos, ke paresen siego.
Bevamos a la saloud de Rachel Gaegos.

1. Antes para la biankeria azian bokthas,[16]
Biankeria para vouadrar la ropa.
Agora aya chifoniera a la ouda de ether.
Azen maseros bien brodados kon birihim de seda fina.
Bevamos a la saloud de la madre de la novia ke se yama Sarah Medina.

---

16. Also spelled *bohcha* or *bogcha*.

The Alcheh ouzo and hors d'oeuvre for the guests.
Let us drink to the health of Avraham Toledano.

4. Sarika's husband is a good-for-nothing.
After six months there was nothing left of the dowry, not even a penny.
The father-in-law was forced to pay the military exemption tax.
Let us drink to the health of Haim Abravanel.

92. I bought a house; it collapsed.
I bought gold coins; they devaluated.
I married my daughter off; the groom is a thief.
He fled; he left her with heartache.
Let us drink to the health of my daughter and that this heartache
   should pass.

324. Marika the linen seamstress made us the bridal linens.
She takes a lira of gold a day.[17]
The father of the bride yells.
The mother preparing the food doesn't come out of the kitchen.
Let us drink to the health of Salomon Attias.

412. We are invited to Marie's wedding
That is going to be in the ballroom of the Gifts for the Needy
   [Association].
She gave a dowry, lingerie for four seasons,
A thousand gold coins and jewelry that her grandmother left her.
To the heath of Haim Guerchon.

162. The photographer comes to the house to photograph the bride.
Then he goes into the ballroom where the wedding will be.
With this light that is emitted from the camera,
All close their eyes, so they appear [to be] blind.
Let us drink to the health of Rachel Gaegos.

1. In the old days, they made bundles[18]
For the linens to store the clothes.
Now there is a cabinet in the bedroom.
They make tablecloths embroidered with thread of fine silk.
Let us drink to the health of the bride's mother, whose name is Sarah
   Medina.

---

17. As payment.
18. They were wrapped in a silk shawl.

422. A la kaye Venizelos aye groutas de valor.
    Venden ropa emportada de la Europa,
    Para achougar i biankerias, ke ya se izo ouna lokeria.
    Todos kieren lo mejor darle a sous ijas.
    Despoues de la boda, el padre non tiene ouna drakme
    Para el resto de la famia.
    Bevamos a la saloud de Daniel Nahmias.

165. La lana de la novia se lava al kourtijo.
    Emprestan basinas de todas las vezinas, kaldera para la bouyir.
    Vienen amigos i parientes para lavar.
    Por sech mezes la madre la mete al sol, para ke se seke bien,
    I fazer los mendeles[19] para el novio i la novia
    Ke van a tener mazal tov.
    Bevamos a la saloud de Rafael Simantov.

316. Sarika se kazo.
    Sou madre le dio kamas de bronzo, kon baldakino,
    Boron, i biezavi[20] i tambien doz komodinos.
    Bevamos a la saloud de todos los souvrinos.

325. Agora mos aze el edredon kon plouma fina ke se yama duve,
    Emportada de rusia, la (e)stofa eze de seda fina.
    Bevamos a la saloud del padre de la novia
    Ke eskapo de kazar ijas.

64. Komo loz kodredoz, todoz keren aver a la novia.
    Asperan va avenir ande kore el avoua, kon el kantaro a la kavesa,
    El moumi i la antari[21] i el koyar de dentela.
    Bevamos a la saloud de Daniel Ferrera.

45. Antes ivamos en las grandes bodas; koumiamos i beviamos.
    Tagnavamos el pandero, el oût, sin mos oulvidar el kanon.
    Agora se aze kidouchim a la kiyila,
    Ke eze ouna grande ekonomia para el novio ke se va a kazar.
    Bevamos a la saloud de Dino Lazar.

---

19. *Minder* in Turkish.
20. This is *vizaví* in Ladino.
21. Also spelled *entari*. According to Michael Molho, this was a "sleeveless dress of smooth fabric, in striped or floral material which crossed and buttoned on the left side" (*Traditions and Customs*, 35–36).

422. On Venizelos Street there are high-class stores.
     They sell merchandise imported from Europe
     For trousseaux and linens, that already became a folly.
     They all want to give the best to their daughters.
     After the wedding, the father does not have a Greek cent [left]
     For the rest of the family.
     Let us drink to the health of Daniel Nahmias.

165. The bride's wool is washed in the courtyard.
     They borrow basins from all the neighbors, a cauldron for boiling it.
     Friends and relatives come to wash.
     For six months, the mother puts it out in the sun, so that it will dry well,
     And to make the mattresses for the bride and groom
     Who will have good luck.
     Let us drink to the health of Rafael Simantov.

316. Sarika married.
     Her mother gave her bronze beds, with canopies,
     A chest of drawers, and a cupboard with mirrors and also two night tables.
     Let us drink to the health of all the nieces and nephews.

325. Now they make the eiderdown quilt with fine feathers that is called down,
     Imported from Russia, the cloth is of fine silk.
     Let us drink to the health of the father of the bride
     Who survived marrying off his daughters.

64. Like the sheep in a flock, everyone wants to see the bride.
     Waiting [until] she will come where the water runs, with a pitcher
         on her head,
     The chevesse and the robe and the detachable collar of lace.
     Let us drink to the health of Daniel Ferrera.

45. We used to attend large weddings; we ate and we drank.
     We played the tambourine, the oud, and we cannot forget the dulcimer.
     Now they have weddings at the synagogue,
     Which is a serious saving for the groom who is about to be wed.
     Let us drink to the health of Dino Lazar.

323. Kazar ija eze komo meter oun vapor en medio de la mar.
    Si aye grande fortouna, se pouede baterear.[22]
    Esperamos i arogamos ke va a tener bouen mazal.
    Bevamos a la saloud de Avraam Amar.

267. A Salonique en kada balkon, aye ouna nigna brodando sou biankeria.
    Kitando de sous manos; todas las kozas finas.
    Bevamos a la saloud de todas las mosas ke azen sous biankeria.

276. Signores i signorinas, portoukales i mandarinas,
    Komo la gneve, kaye a vilya a vilya,[23]
    Ansi se der(r)ite la ija a azer sou biankeria.
    Bevamos a la saloud de Esther Negria.

5. A Sarika la demando oun ijiko.
    Lo refouzo porke era bachiko.
    El padre i la madre kierian este kazamieno porke era riko.
    Bevamos a la saloud de Leon Tsiko.

14. Mochon se kazo kon la servidera.
    La komunitad lez dio kidouchim a la eskalera.
    El padre se mourio, non le decho ni ouna lira.
    Yevo a la madre al Beth Din, ke le dieron manias,
    Kordon del padre, oun kouchak yeno de liras.
    Bevamos a la saloud de los talmide hakamim i toda sou kompagnia.

194. Mochon imbivdo; a la fin del mes, se kazo.
    Le paresio ke va a tomar novia djovena.
    Le va a mirar las kriatouras, ma se yero.
    Los ijos estan souzios, i komen a la mizoura.
    Las etha a la kama sin senar i mezmo sin las bezar.
    Bevamos a la saloud de Eliaou Lazar.

250b. Tomamos lingères para ke aga la biankeria.
    Todos las toman mezmo ke non tienen koumida.
    Bevamos a la saloud de las souvrinas.

246. El padre souda fina kouando viene el presiador.
    La madre i la ija, kieren lo mijor.

---

22. This is a double entendre. *Fortuna* also means "property" or "good fortune"; *baterear* also means "to cause bankruptcy."
    23. Presumably *nyeve*, or "snow," and *velija*, or "flakes."

323. Marrying off a daughter is like launching a ship in the middle of the sea.
     If there is a major storm, it can sink.
     We wait and pray that there will be good luck.
     Let us drink to the health of Avraham Amar.

267. In Salonika on every balcony, there is a girl embroidering her linens.
     [All] her own handicraft; everything is excellent.
     Let us drink to the health of all the maidens who make their own linens.

276. Ladies and gentlemen, oranges and tangerines,
     Like the snow falls flake by flake.
     Thus the girl wastes herself by making her linens.
     Let us drink to the health of Esther Negria.

5. A young man asked for the hand of Sarika.
   She refused because he was short.
   Her father and mother wanted this marriage because he was rich.
   Let us drink to the health of Leon Tsiko.

14. Moshe married the maidservant.
    The community made his wedding at the staircase.
    His father died and did not leave him a gold coin.
    He took his mother to the rabbinical court, where they gave her bracelets,
    His father's chain, a belt full of gold coins.
    Let us drink to the health of the scholars and all of their entourage.

194. Moshe was widowed; at the end of the month, he married.
     It seemed to him that he was going to take a young bride.
     She was going to take care of his children, but he was wrong.
     The children are dirty, and their food is rationed.
     She puts them to bed without dinner and without even kissing them.
     Let us drink to the health of Eliaou Lazar.

250b. We hire linen seamstresses so that [they] will make the linens.
      Everyone hires them, even if they have nothing to eat.
      Let us drink to the health of the nieces.

246. The father perspires until the dowry assessor comes.
     The mother and the daughter want the best.

Todo rekamado sin saver kouanto kosto.
Bevamos a la saloud de ke se amojo.

166. La novia la yevaron al bagno del Kapan.
Va azer la prima tevila.
Kantan kantigas de novia de tradition,
    i parmathetes ascenden para esta ocazion.
Se desparte doulsoura, la mejor, i todos dizen mazal tov.
Bevamos a la saloud de la madre de la novia ke moz koumbido.

411. La novia mos kounbido al bagno.
Todas mos estamos aparejando,
Kombinezones de seda i dantella fina,
Porke mos vamos a deznoudar delantre las vezinas.
Bevamos a la saloud de todas estas vazias.

Births and Children

114. Sarina tiene trenta agnos de kazada.
Solo esta semana e apersevio ke esta pregnada.
Dr. Louis Modiano le dicho ke se este a la kama todo el pregnado.
Ez ouna grande alegria para el marido e toda la famia.
Bevamos a la saloud de Sarina Nahmias.

222. Ouna nigna eze ouna gravina.[24]
Bevamos a la saloud de Regina.

85. Sarina esta pregnada.
Tiene kouatro nignas i esta bien espantada ke non le venga otra gravina.
El marido prometio ke se va afouyir,
Si non aye beraha de Brith a la venida.
Bevamos a la saloud de Ichoua Negria.

220. Alegre de estar invitado a brith.
Bevamos a la saloud de Eliaou Eshkenazi.

---

24. This word appears as *graveína, graviyina, klavina,* and in other forms.

Everything is embroidered without knowing what it cost.
Let us drink to the health of he who got soaked.[25]

166. They took the bride to the bath in the covered market.
She is going to make her first immersion.
They sing traditional bridal songs,
and candles are lit for this occasion.
Sweets are passed around, the best [there are], and they all say good luck.
Let us drink to the health of the mother of the bride who invited us.

411. The bride invited us to the ritual bath.
We are all getting ready,
With silk slips and fine lace,
Because we are going to undress in front of the [female] neighbors.
Let us drink to the health of all these empty-headed women.

Births and Children

114. Sarina is married for thirty years.
Only this week she noticed that she is pregnant.
Dr. Louis Modiano told her that she is to remain in bed for the entire
pregnancy.
This is a great [and] happy occasion for the husband and the entire family.
Let us drink to the health of Sarina Nahmias.

222. A girl is a carnation.[26]
Let us drink to the health of Regina.

85. Sarina is pregnant.
She has four girls and is extremely anxious lest another carnation comes.[27]
Her husband promised that he is going to flee,
If there is not a blessing for a circumcision upon the arrival [of the baby].
Let us drink to the health of Yehoshua Negria.

220. Happy to be invited to a circumcision ceremony.
Let us drink to the health of Eliaou Eshkenazi.

---

25. She means soaked from perspiration, or "taken."
26. Here Bouena means that she is lovely like a rose or carnation.
27. Güler Orgun explained that this is Sephardi sarcastic humor; a girl is lovely—
but try to convince this terrified mother of that, should she give birth to another
(personal communication, February 20, 2011).

89. Merkimos konfites i marotsinos para el Brith,
    Mas oulvidimos el raki.
    La vezena foue abacho, troucho ouna damedjana.
    Ouvo bastante ke el parido se emboracho de alegria,
    Porke la moujer eze nigno ke pario.
    Leon Botton, kon el pandero, alegro loz envitados i a los kousfouegros.
    Bevamos a la saloud de Daniel Gaegos.

46. Avia oun Hakam ke se iva kada viernes al kazal
    Ke Shabat avia mingnan.
    Loz bandidos lo kijeron matar, a la atornada, dia de Alka,
    Para lo arovar las paras.
    En medio del kamino, lo yamaron para ouna beraha de Brith Mila.
    Se kedo la nothe ande el parido,
    Ke avia fiesta kon parientes i amigos.
    Este modo se salvo de la mouerte,
    Porke non refouzo la beraha del Brith Mila.
    Bevamos a la saloud de los ke non se oulvidan de dezir beraha.

318. Las pregnadas aparejan bronda,
     Para azer tajos de susan para el parimiento.
     Si ese nigno ese kon alegria; si ese nigna ese kon yoros,
     Porke el marido se esta anojado.
     Bevamos a la saloud de todos los anojados.

326. Karolina esta pregnada.
     Le izieron tres kaparas: doz gäinas i oun gayo,[28]
     Porke non saven koualo aye a la tripa, si ese nigna o nigno.
     Bevamos a la saloud de Avraam Medina.

371. Fouemos a vijitar a Karolina, ke esta pregnada i eze bivda.
     El marido se mourio i eya va aparir al kanton.
     La esfouegra eze mouy bouena.
     La enkoraja i le ayouda al etho.
     No la decha oun pounto sola.
     Arogamos ke para nigno
     I ke meta el nombre del marido.

---

28. *Kapparot* (sacrifices) usually involved a chicken or rooster being swung over the head of an ill person. Michael Molho describes a practice intended to predict the baby's sex; if the gall bladder of a chicken held over a fire burst, the baby would be male, and if it quietly collapsed, female (*Traditions and Customs,* 41–42).

89. We bought candied almonds and almond balls for the circumcision,
    But we forgot the ouzo.
    Our neighbor went downstairs, brought demijohn.[29]
    There was enough so that the father became drunk with joy,
    Because his wife had given birth to a boy.
    Leon Botton, with his tambourine, made the guests and the in-laws merry.
    Let us drink to the health of Daniel Gaegos.

46. There was a scholar who went to the village every Friday
    As there was a quorum there on the Sabbath.
    Bandits wanted to kill him on his return [trip], on Sunday,
    In order to rob him of his money.
    Midway home, he was called to make a blessing at a circumcision.
    He spent the night at the father's house [of the newborn]
    Where there was a celebration attended by relatives and friends.
    In this way, he was spared death,
    Because he did not refuse to make a blessing at the circumcision.
    Let us drink to the health of those who do not forget to say blessings.

318. The pregnant women prepare jam
     To make sesame nougats for the birth.
     If it's a boy, it is with joy; if it is a girl, it is with tears,
     Because the husband is sulking.
     Let us drink to the health of all the sulkers.

326. Caroline is pregnant.
     They made three *kapparot:* two hens and one rooster,
     Because they don't know what is in her belly, if it's a girl or a boy.
     Let us drink to the health of Avraham Medina.

371. We went to visit Caroline, who is pregnant and is a widow.
     Her husband died and she is going to give birth in a corner.[30]
     Her mother-in-law is a very good woman.
     She encourages her and helps her with the work.
     She doesn't leave her alone for a minute.
     We pray that she bears a boy
     And that she gives him the name of her husband.

---

29. This is a large, wicker-covered bottle (Güler Orgun, personal communication, February 18, 2011).

30. Perhaps she means she will give birth all alone.

357. Kouando el marido se mouere i non tiene ijos,
    Los ermanos del marido tienen priorita.
    Si [non] refouzan de le dar halisa,[31]
    Mouthos la dechan bivda la vida entera.
    Bevamos a la saloud de Estrea.

143. La moujer de Isaac Sarfatty esta pregnada.
    Kiere ninio ke le venga, ma! Foue nigna; se anojo.
    Despoues soupo ke eze doz; otro vino.
    Le dicho ke eze trese.
    La koumadre le dicho ke eze kouatro.
    Al pounto se foue kouriendo aver a la moujer, antes ke venga la de sinko.
    Bevamos a la saloud de Abraam Pinto.

273. El ke tiene medios, ouna nigna i oun nigno:
    El dia del Brith Mila aye doz kitaderas,
    Doz kitadores i doz moelim.
    Despoues de dezir: "ze a kise chel Eliaou Anavi,"
    Los mohalim empesan azer el brith.
    El moel de la nigna dize:
    Signor de Rabotay, aki aye ke meter i non ke kitar.
    Bevamos a la saloud de los Amars.

342. Al Brith se desparte marothinos,
    Vino, raki para parientes i amigos.
    Bevamos a la saloud de Albert Tsimini.

Family Dynamics

81. La tradition viene de padre a ijo.
    Ese alegria para la famia.
    Los detiene todos endjountos, sin pelear ni djousgar.
    Bevamos a la saloud de los ke se adjountan.

215. Los Benrubis son grande famia
    De esprito de alegria, i kon amor a sou famia.
    Bevamos a la saloud de los Nahmias.

330. Los Sarfattys tienen bouenas bozes.
    Kouando kantan, paresen Rosignol operas,

---

31. According to Jewish law, a childless widow needs to continue her husband's
line. She must turn to her brother-in-law, who may elect to marry her or to release her
by means of the *halitsa* ceremony in the Jewish court.

357. When the husband dies and there are no children,
    The brothers of the husband have priority.
    If they [don't] refuse to grant a release,
    Many are left as widows for their entire life.
    Let us drink to the health of Estrea.

143. Isaac Sarfatty's wife is pregnant.
    He wants a boy to come forth, but! It was a girl; he was annoyed.
    Then he found out that there are two; another came.
    They told him that there are three.
    The midwife told him there are four.
    At that point, he went running to see his wife before the fifth one arrived.
    Let us drink to the health of Abraham Pinto.

273. He who has twins, a girl and a boy:
    On the day of the circumcision, there are two godmothers,[32]
    Two godfathers, and two ritual circumcisers.
    After saying: "this is the chair of the prophet Elijah,"
    The circumcisers start to perform the circumcision.
    The circumciser of the girl says:
    "Lord of our Fathers, here one has to add and not remove."
    Let us drink to the health of the Amars.

342. At the circumcision they serve almond balls,
    Wine, ouzo for family and friends.
    Let us drink to the health of Albert Tsimini.

Family Dynamics

81. The tradition comes[33] from father to son.
    This is happiness for the family.
    It keeps them all together, without fighting or judging.
    Let us drink to the health of those who get united.

215. The Benrubys are a great family
    With a spirit of joy and with love for their family.
    Let us drink to the health of the Nahmiases.

330. The Sarfattys have good voices.
    When they sing, it resembles Rossignol operas

---

32. The godmother takes the baby from the mother and gives it to the mohel; David Bunis describes the birth of a twin boy and girl in *Voices from Jewish Salonika*, 142.
33. Passes.

O romansas ke alegran korasones.
Bevamos a la saloud de los Sassones.

61. En mouestro pouertal,[34] tenemos oun arvole de tilio.
Ese mi tio ke lo asembro kouando kazo al ijo.
El kousfouegro se lo regalo ke tiene vouerta[35] al depo.[36]
Bevamos a la saloud de Leon Kapon.

401. Mi padre tenia kaveyos pretos i mostachos royos.
Ningounos se fiavan ke eran souyos.
Oun dia en medio de la kaye, le travaron el mostatho.
Este modo se fiaron ke eran souyos, i era sou natoura.
Bevamos a la saloud de Avraam Segoura.

228. Mi padre i mi madre se mourio kouano eramos tsikos.
Mi tia mos engrandesio i mos ambezo koualo ese la vida.
Bevamos a la saloud de Bienvenida.

83. Kouando loz Nahmias alevantan el vazo para dizer lehaim,
Eze de korason.
Souhaitan saloud i gana de komer, i bouen mazal a las ijas.
Bevamos a la saloud de toda la famia.

47. Antes metian a la kriatouras a la kouna.
La madre o la tia las dava para las ijas.
Era tradition de se ethar a la kouna del tio o de la souvrina.
Agora azen berseau de seda i dentela fina.
La lingère lo aze ke toma ouna lira de oro el dia.
Bevamos a la saloud de estas vazias.

176. A Salonique las nignas non salen la nothe kon amigos.
Deve de ser akompagnada del ermano o el tio.
La madre asentada al balkon fina kouando atornan.
El padre gritando ke eze moutho tadre i enda[37] non vegneron.
Bevamos a la saloud de Samuel Serrero.

---

34. *Pwertal* in Ladino.
35. *Gwerta* in Ladino.
36. This was the train station "on the waterfront" at the southwestern end of Salonika, and later an area of Jewish residence (Michael Molho, *Traditions and Customs*, 135). David (Andreas) Kounio commented that there were individual houses there and ample room for gardens (personal communication, February 19, 2009).
37. *Ainda,* meaning "yet."

Or romances that make hearts merry.
Let us drink to the health of the Sassons.

61. In our doorway, we have a linden tree.
My uncle planted it when he married off his son.
His [son's] father-in-law who has a garden in the Depot neighborhood
gave it to him as a gift.
Let us drink to the health of Leon Kapon.

401. My father had black hair and a red mustache.
No one believed that they were his.
One day in the middle of the street, they pulled his mustache.
In this way, they believed that they were his, and his naturally.
Let us drink to the health of Avraham Segoura.

228. My mother and father died when we were small.
My aunt brought us up and taught us what life is.
Let us drink to the health of Bienvenida.

83. When the Nahmiases raise the glass to make a toast,
It is from the heart.
They wish for health and a good appetite and good luck for the girls.
Let us drink to the health of all the family.

47. In the old days, they put the children in the cradle.
The mother or the aunt gave it for the daughters [to use].
It was a tradition to lay them down in the cradle of the uncle or of
the niece.
Nowadays they make cradles of silk and fine lace.
The lingerie maker who makes it charges a gold coin per day.
Let us drink to the health of these empty-headed women.

176. In Salonika, the girls don't go out at night with friends.
They have to be accompanied by a brother or an uncle.
The mother sits in the balcony until they come back.
The father shouting that it is very late and they haven't come home yet!
Let us drink to the health of Samuel Serrero.

177. A Salonique los hombres tienen kavesa del tiempo de maboul.
     Non dechan respirar a las nignas, mezmo ke lavoran al toutoun.
     Deven de estar en kaza apenas el sol se ensero.
     Bevamos a la saloud de Salomon Sasson.

277. Kouando el padre alevanta el vazo de vino,
     I dize "lehaim," a sou famia, todos responden kon grande alegria.
     Bevamos a la saloud de toda la famia.

121. Saloud i senter boueno de los alondjados
     Eze lo mejor ke se pouede souhaitar.
     Mazal boueno a los ijos, la madre dezia sin kedar.
     La korona de la kaza ke non manke; esto tambien ez de arogar.
     Bevamos a la saloud de Samy Yakar.

369. Regina kouando nasio, mi padre oun anio a la mama le merko.
     Kouando se estava mouriendo, mi souvrina se lo tomo del dedo.
     Se lo demandi al marido, nounka me lo dio.
     A la ermana, se lo aregalo despoues ke la moujer se arrevento.
     Vivamos a la saloud de Stella Anjer i todo sou soy.

181. Las kriatouras djougan a bachilaki.
     Dezegnan el djougo en la kaye, ke eze asfalt,
     Kon ouna piedra ke traye el padre.
     Vienen en kaza i es senar, lavar i yir a ethar.
     Bevamos a la saloud de Leon Behar.

247. El vendedor apregona: naradja boyida i bouena.
     La moujer aze doulse para kouando va avenir la kriatoura.
     Bevamos a la saloud de Eliaou Segoura.

184. La nina viene a vijitar kada dia el enverano.
     Mos aze taharinas[38] judeos; este modo tenemos para el envierno,
     Sin mos oulvidar ke tora el kaffe en arodeando la toradera.
     Mama mouele a poko a poko; kouando se eskapa, mouele otro.
     Bevamos a la saloud de Gabriel Sotto.

362. En kaza tenemoz sia de mecher.
     Todos moz kieremos asentar.
     Mos peleamos mezmo ke non ese mouestra sira.
     Mama metio fin a esto:

---

38. *Tayarinas* in Ladino.

177. In Salonika the men have a mindset from antediluvian times.
     They don't let the girls breathe, even if they work in tobacco.
     They have to be home as soon as the sun sets.
     Let us drink to the health of Salomon Sasson.

277. When the father raises his glass of wine,
     And toasts his family "to life," everyone responds with great joy.
     Let us drink to the health of the whole family.

121. Health and feeling well for those away from home
     Is the best that one can wish for.
     Good luck for the children, the mother repeatedly said.
     May the head of the house never be missing; this too is to be prayed for.
     Let us drink to the health of Sammy Yakar.

369. When Regina was born, my father bought a ring for my mother.
     When she was dying, my niece took it off her finger.
     I asked her husband to give it to me, but he never did.
     He gave it as a present to his sister after his wife died.
     Let us drink to the health of Stella Anjer and all of hers.

181. The children play hopscotch.
     They design the game in the street, which is of asphalt,
     With a stone that father brings.
     They come home and it is time for dinner, to take a bath and to go to bed.
     Let us drink to the health of Leon Behar.

247. The seller calls out: oranges, boiled and good.
     The woman makes jam for when the child gets home.
     Let us drink to the health of Eliaou Segoura.

184. The girl comes to visit every day in the summer.
     We make Jewish spaghetti; in this way we have for the winter,
     Without forgetting to roast the coffee by turning the roaster.
     Mother grinds little by little; when it is finished, she grinds more.
     Let us drink to the health of Gabriel Sotto.

362. At home we have an oak chair.
     We all want to sit in it.
     We fight even though it is not our turn.
     Mother put an end to it:

Mos dio tiketas kouando la pouedemos ouzar.
Este modo no aye mas pelear.
Bevamos a la saloud de Julia Amar.

363. Al kourtijo papa mos metio mechidera.
Mos pouedemos asentar todos los sinko, algouna vez sech.
Mechemos i tomamoz plazer.
Yo tengo vente u sech; inda me asento a mesher.
Bevamos a la saloud de Acher Abravanel.

60. Las gardenias eze la flor la mejor.
Me la meto a la boutoniera.
Tiene bouena golor, korsage para mi moujer,
Para ke me se alegre el korason.
Bevamos a la saloud de Daniel Sasson.

30. Haimaki Cohen eze oun hombre de valor.
Kito ijos, komo el i sou soye.
Fredy eze el major, ke aze honor a los djidios.
Bevamos a la saloud de esta famia ke eze ouna de la mejor.

390. Daniel koumplo mignan ke en Hebreo lo yaman bar mitzvah.
Izieron ouna bouena fiesta.
El padre i la madre estavan kontentes.
A la nothe touvieron Leon Botton.
Bayles a la tourka se baylo.
Todos dieron donation para las ovras djoudias.
Bevamos a la saloud de Sarina.

334. Benditho [el] ke me izo hombre i non moujer,
Mi padre non grita kouando vengo en kaza a las diez.
Bevamos a la saloud de Oly Abravanel.

84. Benditho el ke me izo hombre i non moujer.
Este modo non tengo responsabilitad del tendjere.
Todos komen sin se apersevir,
Ke la balabaya se kemo alougar del tasin.
Bevamos a la saloud de Rafel Nisim.

She gave us tickets [for] when we can use it.
This way there is no more fighting.
Let us drink to the health of Julia Amar.

363. Father placed a rocking chair on the patio for us.
All five [of us] can sit [in it], sometimes six.
We rock and we enjoy ourselves.
I am twenty-six years old; I still sit to rock.
Let us drink to the health of Asher Abravanel.

60. The gardenias are the best flowers.
I put them in my buttonhole.
They have a good fragrance, a corsage for my wife,
So that my heart rejoices.
Let us drink to the health of Daniel Sasson.

30. Haim Cohen is a fine man.
He produced sons, like him and his own people.
Freddy is the oldest, who does honor to the Jews.
Let us drink to the health of this family that is one of the best.

390. Daniel completed a minyan, which in Hebrew they call bar mitzvah.[39]
They made a nice celebration.
His father and mother were satisfied.
At night they had Leon Botton.[40]
They danced Turkish-style dances.
All gave donations for Jewish organizations.
Let us drink to the health of Sarina.

334. Blessed [is he] who made me a man and not a woman.
My father doesn't shout when I come home at ten p.m.
Let us drink to the health of Oly Abravanel.

84. Blessed be he who made me a man and not a woman.
This way I have no responsibility for the pot.
Everyone eats without noticing
That the housewife was burned instead of the pot.
Let us drink to the health of Rafael Nissim.

---

39. To be of age.
40. She meant Botton and his orchestra. Botton began composing classical oriental music at the age of ten, and played the oud in his ten-man orchestra (Bouena Garfinkle, undated [1989] letter to the author).

180. Benditho el ke me izo hombre i non moujer.
Tengo privileges en kaza, komo si era el rey.
Todos me sienten lo ke digo.
Me akavido i non exajerar porke el ijo grande se va a revoltar.
Bevamos a la saloud de Eliaou Moktar.

100. Daniel eze siego.
Le dio a kontar las liras al yerno.
Tenia sien pedasos; le metio a la bolsa kouartos.
Kouando la moujer las konto a la otra vez,
Vido ke el yerno lez arovo la feze.
Bevamos a la saloud de los Rozales ke kedaron sin feze.

101. Kouando los hombres vienen del lavoro, tienen todo pronto.
La mujer apareja las pantouflas, avoua kaente, i la djoube limpia.
La meza meteda para senar, i las kriatouras prontas para lo bezar.
Bevamos a la saloud de Eliaou Lazar.

80. La fouersa de la moujer ese el amor del marido.
La fouersa del hombre eze la bolsa.
La fouersa de loz ijos eze la amistad de la famia.
Bevamos a la saloud de Boulisa.

185. Boulisa non tiene gana la nothe para komer kon el marido.
Ouna magnana el balabay le metio yave al kanier.[41]
A la nothe Boulisa estava mouerta por komer.
Bevamos a la saloud de Daniel Kounee.

90. Se ouza kalsas blankas ke paresen ounos doundourmadjes[42]
Karosikas para las kriatouras el padre la arempoucha
Ke paresen ounos yagourthis.
Bevamos a la saloud de Mochon Nadjari.

93. El saleptsi[43] pasa la mangnana
Apregonando el salep.
La madre sale a la pouerta a enthir el tendjere.
Las kriatouras alegre de lo bever.
Bevamos a la saloud de Daniel Abravanel.

---

41. *Kaniye* in Ladino.
42. The traditional spelling is *dondurma*.
43. The traditional spelling is *salepchi*.

180. Blessed be he who made me a man and not a woman.
   I have privileges at home, as if I were a king.
   Everyone listens to what I say.
   I am careful and don't exaggerate because the oldest son will rebel.
   Let us drink to the health of Eliaou Moktar.

100. Daniel is blind.
   He let his son-in-law count the gold coins.
   He had a hundred pieces; he placed quarters in his purse.[44]
   When his [Daniel's] wife counted them once again,
   She saw that the son-in-law had stolen his fez.[45]
   Let us drink to the health of the Rozaleses who were left without a fez.

101. When the men come from work, everything is ready.
   The wife prepares the slippers, hot water, and the clean dressing gown.
   The table is set for dinner and the children are ready to kiss him.
   Let us drink to the health of Eliaou Lazar.

80. The strength of the woman is the love of her husband.
   The strength of the man is his wallet.
   The strength of the children is the love of the family.
   Let us drink to the health of Boulisa.

185. Boulisa doesn't feel like eating with her husband at night.
   One morning the head of the house locked the pantry.
   That night Boulisa was dying to eat.
   Let us drink to the health of Daniel Kounee.

90. They use white socks that make them look like ice-cream sellers,
   Little carriages for the children [which] the father pushes
   That make them look like yogurt sellers.
   Let us drink to the health of Moshe Nadjari.

93. The salep vendor passes the morning
   Calling out to sell the drink of salep root.
   The mother comes out of the door to fill the pot [with salep].
   The children are happy to drink it.
   Let us drink to the health of Daniel Abravanel.

---

44. Gold coins, to this day, come in quarters, half-liras, one lira, and "five liras in one" (Güler Orgun, personal communication, February 19, 2011).

45. This expression means "to abuse one's trust."

353. El enverano mama mos apareja para la eskola:
Frankas pretas de satin, kon blanko brodado,
Thapeo de Panama, i polo para el invierno.
Bevamos a la saloud de mama ke lavora en verano para el envierno.

94. Despoues de medio dia, tenemos la bouza.
Todos la kriatouras, kon el penez i la michtraba[46] alegres i kontentes.
Beven kon savor; el bozadji kanta kantigas de amor.
Bevamos a la saloud de Abraam Serror.

178. Salonique se troko de kouando se tsamouchko.
Respectar el padre i la madre kedo.
El nono i la nona tienen la oultima palabra,
I el ermano grande se entremete a la desizion.
Bevamos a la saloud de Julia Sion.

218. El nono i la nona se respecta a la famia.
Bevamos a la saloud de Albert Fany i kompagnia.

372. Dizen ke el mez de Tevet la barva bate frio i louvia;
I loz dias kourtos, arodeados todos al deredor del fogadero
I el nono kontando konsejas a los nietos.
Bevamos a la saloud de Eliaou Beja.

129. Mi nono era Afsakadji.
Asara be-Tevet azia tanid othos dias.
Kon sou barva blanka
Ke azia plazer i honor a la famia.
Venian djente a tomar konsejo, kada dia.
Bevamos a la saloud de Abraam Atias.

104. El nono tiene intojos para meldar la thora o los pasoukes de Shabat.
Kanta mouy ermozo i mos ambeza a alegrar korasones.
Bevamos a la saloud del nono i la nona i toda la famia.

105. El nono eskrive kon lettras de merouba.[47]
Aze parchemenes para la kiyila, mizouzotte

---

46. *Maşrapa* in Turkish.
47. "These are square letters," referring to the cursive Hebrew script used by scribes.

353. In the summer, mother prepares us for school:
     Black aprons[48] of satin with white embroidery,
     A Panama hat, and a knitted cap for the winter.
     Let us drink to the health of mother who works in the summer for
        the winter.

94. After midday we have the *boza.*[49]
    All the kids with their pennies and their mugs are happy and content.
    They drink with gusto; the boza vendor sings love songs.
    Let us drink to the health of Abraham Serror.

178. Salonika changed since it burned.[50]
     Respect for one's father and mother ceased.
     The grandfather and grandmother have the last word,
     And the oldest brother gets involved in the decision.
     Let us drink to the health of Julia Sion.

218. Grandfather and grandmother are respected by the family.
     Let us drink to the health of Albert Fany and company.

372. They say that in the month of Tevet, the beard fights the cold and rain;
     And on short days, everyone is around the brazier
     And the grandfather is telling stories to his grandchildren.
     Let us drink to the health of Eliaou Beja.

129. My grandfather was someone who imposed prolonged fasts on himself.[51]
     On the tenth of Tevet he fasted for eight days.
     [He,] with his white beard
     That gave pleasure and honor to the family.
     People came to consult him every day.
     Let us drink to the health of Abraham Attias.

104. Grandfather has eyeglasses for reading the Torah or the Sabbath verses.
     He sings beautifully and he teaches us to rejoice.
     Let us drink to the health of grandfather and grandmother and all
        the family.

105. Grandfather writes with square [Hebrew] letters.
     He makes parchments for the congregation, parchments for the doorpost

---

48. This was part of the outfit worn to school.

49. This was a drink of fermented millet. In reality, it is non-alcoholic, according to Güler Orgun (personal communication, February 19, 2011).

50. Literally, "scorched."

51. See chapter 1, note 56; for more details, see Michael Molho, *Traditions and Customs,* 149.

I kameotte para loz vezinos.
Bevamos a la saloud de Abraam Tsimino.

399. Mi nono veste ora kon luvientena [*sic*],[52]
Chapeau melon i kol bien enkolado i vestido eskouro;
Por kravata, oun fiongo ke ese ermozoura,
Getres beige kon botones eskouros, gilé de mouthas kolores,
Baston kon kavesa de plata.
Bevamos a la saloud de Salomon Atias.

42. El kopo de kidouch el maz ermozo eze del nono.
Eze tradition de lo dechar al maz grande gneto de la famia.
Esta modo non aya pelear.
Apenas el viejo se mouere, el vazo va alougar.
Bevamos a la saloud de Abraam Parnas.

106. El nono se mourio; moz decho heredation.
Moz ambezo el amor i la honor del djidio,
Ke seamos haounados en la famia,
I tener respecto del denfrente i de toda la djouderia.
Bevamos a la saloud de la nona
Ke la vamos a tener en mi kaza kon alegria.

123. La nona moz vino a vijitar.
Komo kada semana, roskas[53] mos ezo,
I metio raki a la masa.
Las reoucho tanto bouenas ke mos tresalimos kouando laz goustimos.
Bevamos a la saloud de Alegra Almoznino.

158. La nona viste antari i tiene grandes aldikeras.[54]
Kouando mos viene a vijitar, estan yenas.
Moz da amozotros, ke semos loz gnetos.
Tambien a vezinos i amigos, sin se oulvidar de ningounos.

---

52. This word does not appear in any dictionary, nor do any of the Ladino speakers I consulted recognize it. The best educated guess was that of Yehuda Hatsvi, who described it as "an integral cover of the watch so as to protect it from the rain (*luvia*)" (e-mail message to author, February 22, 2009).

53. *Roskas* was also a game that involved betting, using these cookies. "A small segment was cut off the periphery, one edge of the roska was placed in the mouth, and the better, with head uplifted, attempted to eat it all without touching it with his hands. Amid the general hilarity the cookie would often break or crumble before it could be rolled into the mouth" (Sciaky, *Farewell to Salonica*, 71).

54. *Faldukwera* in Ladino.

And amulets for the neighbors.
Let us drink to the health of Avraham Tsimino.

399. My grandfather wears a watch with a rain cover,
A bowler hat and well starched collar and a dark suit;
As a tie, a bow tie that is beautiful,
Beige spats with dark buttons, a waistcoat of many colors,
A cane with a silver head.
Let us drink to the health of Salomon Atias.

42. The most beautiful kiddish cup is that of our grandfather.
It is a tradition to leave it to the oldest grandchild in the family.
In this way there is no fighting.
As soon as the old man dies, the cup goes to its [rightful] place.
Let us drink to the health of Abraham Parnas.

106. Grandfather died; he left us an inheritance.
He taught us love and honor of the Jew,
That we should be united in the family,
And have respect for others and for the whole community.
Let us drink to the health of grandmother
Whom, to our delight, we are going to have in my house.

123. Grandmother came to visit us.
[As she does] every week, she made wheel-shaped cookies
Sprinkled with sesame for us, and put ouzo in the dough.
They [the cookies] turned out so well that we were thrilled when
we tasted them.
Let us drink to the health of Allegra Almosnino.

158. Grandmother wears a traditional dress[55] and has large pockets.
When she comes to visit us, they are full.
She gives to us, since we are the grandchildren.
Also to neighbors and friends, without forgetting anyone.

---

55. This was part of the traditional costume described above.

Bevamos a la saloud de la nona,
Ke le souhaitamos nothe i dia.

254. Mi nona viste antari; ese plazer de verla
Kon koyar, el devantal, i el mumi.
Bevamos a la saloud de Neomi.

Burials

48. Se yora al viejo por honor; al mansevo por dolor.
En kada enteramiento, aye yoras i gritos de korason.
Bevamos a la saloud de Yeouda Sadok.

86. Djamila se mourio a los sien i diez agnos.
La akompagnaron kon tsalguin[56]
Fina la meara del Bet Hahaim.
La foue a vijitar doz dias antes ke mouriera.
Oun ermozo charki me kanto.
Bevamos a la saloud de la famia de Djamila ke izieron koualo demando.

Social Commentary

131. El mas grande ensulto para el selanikli
Ez dezirle sose soye de Amalikim.
El mas ermozo komplimento ez sos soye de Juda.
Bevamos a la saloud de los ke non saven insultar.

355. A Salonique kouando ouno kiere insultar al otro,
Le dizé: sos vazio komo ouna kampania,
Oh sos oun kavayo de la askerier.
Bevamos a la saloud de Alberto Abravanel.

118. Merki ouna kaza a la kampagna ke oun bey morava.
Topi mobles, sin kontar, ke solo al palasio del rey se topa esta ermozoura.
Bevamos a la saloud de Levy Segoura.

216. Los Koanim son de vanda de tomar.
Algouna vez se dethiden de dar.
Bevamos a la saloud de Eliaou Amar.

---

56. *Çalgi* in Turkish.

Let us drink to the health of grandmother,
Whom we wish well night and day.

254. My grandmother wears a traditional dress; it is a pleasure to see her
With a detachable collar, the [full-body length] apron and the chevesse.[57]
Let us drink to the health of Naomi.

Burials

48. One cries for the old out of honor; one cries for the young out of pain.
In each burial, there are cries and heartfelt shouts.
Let us drink to the health of Yehuda Sadok.

86. Jamila died at the age of 110 years.
She was accompanied by musical instruments[58]
Until the cave of the cemetery.
I went to visit her two days before she died.
She sang a lovely song for me.
Let us drink to the health of Jamila's family that did what she asked.

Social Commentary

131. The greatest insult to a Salonikan is to tell him
He is a descendant of Amalek.
The greatest compliment is to say he is [descended] from Judah.
Let us drink to the health of those who do not know how to insult.

355. In Salonika when a person wants to insult the other,
He says: you are empty like a bell.
Or—you are a military horse.
Let us drink to the health of Alberto Abravanel.

118. I bought a house in the countryside in which a bey had lived.
I found tons of furniture, which only in a king's palace can one find
such beauty.
Let us drink to the health of Levy Segoura.

216. The priests are on the side of taking.
Sometimes they decide to give.
Let us drink to the health of Eliaou Amar.

---

57. Nehama describes this as a gauze cloth with beads that women wear on their
hair (*Dictionnaire du Judéo-espagnol,* 373).

58. This Turkish "orchestra" included a lute, violin, and tambourine.

217. La moujer del Haham las yaman roubisa.
Bevamos a la saloud de Miriam i Boubesa.

221. Haim kiere dezir vidas.
Bevamos a la saloud de los Albertos i las Bienvenidas.

268. La trambouka eze mouzika si la saves tagner.
Si non, eze ouna doubara ke aze estremeser.
Bevamos a la saloud de los Amiels.

289. Sarika tiene gramophone kon todas las plakas de Leon Botton.
Kouando lo tagne, todos aver las pouertas del balkon
Para sentir el tsalguin mijor.
Bevamos a la saloud de el ke moz alegra korason.

269. Kamas de bronzo se merko para amostrar
Ke non tiene dolor de korason.
Bevamos a la saloud de Daniel Sasson.

354. Mi vezina se merko kamas de bronzo
Kon mendeles inthidos i bilidi de flores.
Parese ouna kamareta de novia a la houpa.[59]
Mos alegremos ke se lo pouede pagar.
Bevamos a la saloud de Samuel Behar.

270. Bienvenida se kazo kon ouno de la aristokrasia.
Non savia asentarse ni a la sia.
La esfouegra le ambezo todos los ouzos de los Atias.
Bevamos a la saloud de Bienvenida,
La esfouegra i toda la famia.

328. Las nignas a Salonique todas son koketas.[60]
A vale la pena, meszmo ke en kaza non aye pan ni mezmo sena.
Bevamos a la saloud de Estrea.

175. Tenemos kantaro; el avoua eze mas freska de la glasiera.
Lo merkemos a Langada,[61]

---

59. The Jews of Salonika used to put a decorated cover over the bed. As Yehuda Hatsvi explained, it was called a *baldakino* and looked like a huppah (e-mail message to author, February 24, 2009).

60. Smart in appearance or dress, dapper.

61. These thermal springs were a popular spa located 25 to 30 km from the city (David [Andreas] Kounio, forwarded communication from Guler Orgun, February 18, 2007).

217. The wife of the rabbi is called the *roubisa*.
    Let us drink to the health of Miriam and Boubesa.

221. Haim means life.
    Let us drink to the health of the Albertos and the Bienvenidas.

268. The drum is musical if you know how to play it.
    If not, it is noise that makes one shudder.
    Let us drink to the health of the Amiels.

289. Sarika has a phonograph with all the records of Leon Botton.
    When she plays it, everyone opens the balcony doors
    So that they can hear the music better.
    Let us drink to the health of he who lightens our hearts.

269. He bought himself beds of bronze
    To show that he doesn't have heartache.[62]
    Let us drink to the health of Daniel Sasson.

354. My neighbor bought herself bronze beds
    With stuffed mattresses and floral fabric.
    It looked like a bedroom for the bride at the [bridal] canopy.
    We are happy that she can afford it.
    Let us drink to the health of Samuel Behar.

270. Bienvenida married a member of the aristocracy.
    She didn't even know how to sit on a chair.
    Her mother-in-law taught her all the customs of the Attias's.
    Let us drink to the health of Bienvenida,
    Her mother-in-law and the entire family.

328. All the girls in Salonika are coquettes.
    It is worth it! Although in the house there is no bread, not even dinner.
    Let us drink to the health of Estrea.

175. We have a pitcher; the water is fresher than that of the refrigerator.
    We bought it at Langada,

---

62. Regrets.

Ke fouemoz a tomar bagnos kaentes de avoua natural.
Kon la kalor de Salonique, te afreska moutho kouando beves oun kopo.
Bevamos a la saloud de Salomon Sotto.

282. Los Selaniklis se van azer bagno a Baden Baden or a Vichi;
Ke tenemos a ouna ora de Salonique, avoua de Langada,
Ma non aye bouen charchi.
Bevamos a la saloud de la avoua saloridoza al lado de Salonique.

423. Komo Adler, kortate el mostatho.
Komo Elio Haim, bayla valse.
Komo Peppo [*sic*] Basso, bezar.
Esto ese tener mazal.
Bevamos a la saloud de la parea ke se adjountan a la paralia kada alkad.

424. Antes las moujeres ivan avijitar.
Agora se van adjougar poker.
Se les ijo hazinoura komo los komardjes.
Bevamos a la saloud de Avraam Nadjari.

407. A laz nothadas, se desparte revanadikas.[63]
Al kazamiento, pastas o tortas finas,
Pagadas por el novio sin ekonomia.
Al despozorio, kounfites rose o blanko, se mete a la table de la famia;
Al Brith Mila, marothinos.
Bevamos a la saloud de los Tsiminos.

196. Pepitas de melon se kome moutho al balkon,
En djousgando a la vezina, si ese alta o bacha, o oun ballon.
Bevamos a la saloud de Rofel Aelion.

197. Si foumas, kome karpous.
Ez el ijo del Rey ke lo kito esta melezina.
Koumio moutho, fina ke se arevento.
Ma! A mozotros mos ambezo.
Bevamos a la saloud de Daniel Azouz.

225. La mas grande bendition del dio
Ez de tener amigos kon senseridad i honestedad.
Bevamos a la saloud de Rachel Amar.

---

63. According to Yehuda Hatsvi, these were made of simple cake, but baked a second time like biscotti. They were usually served not at parties but at *nochadas,* or memorial evenings for the dead (e-mail message to author, February 24, 2009).

Where we went to take the hot baths in natural water.
With the heat of Salonika, it refreshes you greatly when you drink a cup.
Let us drink to the health of Salomon Sotto.

282. The Salonikans go to the baths in Baden Baden or in Vichy;
While we have water from Langada one hour from Salonika,
But there is not a good shopping area [there].
Let us drink to the health of the healthful waters next to Salonika.

423. Like Adler, cut [off] your moustache.
Like Elio Haim, dance a waltz.
Like Peppo [*sic*] Basso, kiss.
This is to have [good] luck.
Let us drink to the health of the group that joins the wealthy every
    Monday.

424. In the old days, the women went to visit [each other].
Now they go to play poker.
It has become a disease to them like the gamblers.
Let us drink to the health of Avraham Najari.

407. In the evening parties, they serve biscotti.
At a wedding, pastries or fine tortes,
Paid for by the groom without scrimping.
At the engagement, they put red or white comfits[64] on the family's table;
At a circumcision, almond balls.
Let us drink to the health of the Tsiminos.

196. One often eats melon seeds on the balcony,
While judging the neighbor, whether she is tall or short, or rotund.
Let us drink to the health of Rafael Aelion.

197. If you smoke, eat watermelon.
It is the king's son who figured out this remedy.
He ate so much that he burst.
But! He taught us something.
Let us drink to the health of Daniel Azouz.

225. The greatest blessing of God
Is to have friends who are sincere and honest.
Let us drink to the health of Rachel Amar.

---

64. Sugar-coated nuts.

226. Si avlan de mi, de bien, or de mal,
Ese ke se interesante.
Bevamos a la saloud de Miriam Parente.

137. Los djidios de Salonique son maestros de ethar ballon.
Todos dizen ke el souyo esta mas alto, alado de el dio.
Bevamos a la saloud de los ke se asentan al balkon.

209b. Baylar a la pista del Phaler, eze vida.
Bevamos a la saloud de Bienvenida.

147. Loz Selaniklis saven bevir.
Non dechan okazion para se devertir:
Bodas o beraha de Brith.
Los djovenos azen Après-Midi i baylan al faler
O a la pista de kaffe.
Kada nothe salen a kaminar al bodre de la mar.
Bevamos a la saloud de Leon Amar.

283. Loz ke moran a la Rejie se asentan al kaffe Ramona,
Beven bira, raki i limonada savroza.
Bevamos a la saloud de Jako Roza.

210. La phamphara de la makaby eze la mejor a Salonique.
Bevamos a la saloud de Jacque Sarfatty.

211. El 25 mars se ve mouthas phampharas a Salonique.
Ningounos asemeja komo la de la makaby.
Bevamos a la saloud de Jacque Sheby.

236. Al Kloub de Zentin, djougan poker,
I mouthas vezez piedren los pantalones.
Bevamos a la saloud de los Pitilones.

245. El bayle a la tourka se alegra el korason.
Meten papeles a la frente del baylador.
Bevamos a la saloud de Haim Sasson.

226. If people talk about me, for better or for worse,
    It means that they are interested.
    Let us drink to the health of Miriam Parente.

137. The Jews of Salonika are masters of kite flying.
    All say that theirs is the highest, next to God.
    Let us drink to the health of those who sit on the balcony.

209b. To dance at the dance floor of the Phaler,[65] that's the life.
    Let us drink to the health of Bienvenida.

147. The Salonikans know how to live.
    They do not miss an occasion to enjoy themselves:
    Weddings or circumcisions.
    The young people have afternoon gatherings and dance at the Phaler
    Or at the dance floor by the coffee house.
    Every night they go out to stroll along the seaside.
    Let us drink to the health of Leon Amar.

283. Those who live in the Regie quarter sit at the Ramon café,
    Drinking beer, ouzo and tasty lemonade.
    Let us drink to the health of Jako Roza.

210. The band of the Maccabees is the best in Salonika.
    Let us drink to the health of Jacques Sarfatty.

211. On the twenty-fifth of March, one sees many bands in Salonika.
    Nothing equals that of the Maccabees.
    Let us drink to the health of Jacques Sheby.

236. At the Zentin Club,[66] they play poker
    And often they lose their trousers.[67]
    Let us drink to the health of the Pitilons.

245. The Turkish dance makes the heart merry.
    They put paper money on the forehead of the dancer.
    Let us drink to the health of Haim Sasson.

---

65. This was a coffeehouse; she spells it both with "ph" and "f."
66. This was an anti-Zionist, but not anti-religious, group of Salonikans who were pro-Ottomanization. Most of the members were educated in AIU or foreign schools, but they were not assimilationists. See Michael Molho, "Spaniolit Newspapers in Salonika," 105.
67. Equivalent to the English expression "to lose one's shirt."

337. Salonique esta devizado en mouthas keyelottes.
Kouando te kazas, la komunitad manda haham de tou kiyila.
Pagas tou petha komo tu situation.
Bevamos a la saloud de esta bouena organization.

338. A Salonique aye mouthas keyelotte.
Tou chamach te yama la magnana a la prima tefila
Kon ouna boz de tenor: "ha tefila, tefila ah ah."
Eze mouy ermozo de te despertar
I empesar de dia kon mouzika i religion.
Bevamos a la saloud de akeyos ke alegran korason.

348. Los Saportas son grande famia.
Kierian arkilar kaza ke ningounos los kierian.
Tomo kaza; dicho ke eran kouatro.
A poko a poko, troucho loz vente i kouatro.
Bevamos a la saloud de los Saportas kon toda sou famia.

314. La djente non aristokratika las yaman koulibera.
Non tienen servidera ni mezmo vouadradera[68] para la esfouegra.
Bevamos a la saloud de Alegra.

63. Los Selaniklis saven viajar.
Viajan kon vagon-lit;
Se akavidan ke la kama non sea al karo.
Valijas de kouero, a vestidos sport.
La moujeres koundourias de tako bacho i jaquetas kon botones de palo.
Bevamos a la saloud de los Pintos ke viajan kon araba de kouatro kar(r)os.

68. A las moujeres non se pouede aserar la boka; al hombre la bolsa.
Al novio la dota,
A las kriatouras baylar i saltar i yirse a la eskola.
Bevamos a la saloud de Isaac Sola.

87. Las bouenas mansanas vienen de eskopia.
Komemoz ouna, kieremos otra.

---

68. Or *guadradera,* "a nurse."

337. Salonika is divided into many congregations.
When you marry, the community sends a rabbi from your synagogue.
You pay the [community] tax according to your [financial] situation.[69]
Let us drink to the health of this fine organization.

338. In Salonika there are many congregations.
Your beadle wakes you in the morning for the first set of prayers
With a tenor's voice: "[time for] prayers—aha, prayers."
It is lovely for you to be awakened
And to begin the day with music and religion.
Let us drink to the health of those who make the heart rejoice.

348. The Saportas are a large family.
They wanted to rent a house[70] but no one accepted them.
He rented a flat; he said they were four.
Slowly[71] he brought the twenty-four.
Let us drink to the health of the Saportas with their whole family.

314. The non-aristocratic people are called lower class.[72]
They don't have servants, not even a caretaker for the mother-in-law.
Let us drink to the health of Alegra.

63. The Salonikans know how to travel.
They travel on the sleeper;
They make sure that the bed will not be [located] on the wheel.
Leather suitcases, sports clothes.
The women are wearing low-heeled shoes and jackets with wooden
      buttons.
Let us drink to the health of the Pintos, who travel in a four-wheel-
      drive car.

68. [As] for women, one cannot close their mouths; [as] for men, [their]
      purses.
[One cannot avoid] giving the groom a dowry.
[Or keep] the children from dancing and jumping and going to school.
Let us drink to the health of Isaac Sola.

87. The good apples come from Skopje.
We eat one, we want another.

---

69. This was an internal community tax, not one paid to the government.
70. Most likely this was a flat rather than a house.
71. Step by step.
72. Literally, "hut dwellers"—from the Turkish (actually, Persian) *kulube,* "hut"
(Güler Orgun, personal communication, January 14, 2009).

Eze boueno para la saloud.
Tambien el vino kouando tagnes el oût.
Bevamos a la saloud de Isaac Efendi
Ke moz alegra el korason kouando tagne el oût.

99. Los Kavalalis djougan poker para se devertir
Porke non tienen ande yir.
Viajan ouna vez el agno a Paris o en Suisse;
Kouando atornan, djougan bridge.
Bevamos a la saloud de Daniel Benruby.

24. A Salonique aya kloub de los Joseph.
Ouna vez la semana se ven.
Dizen ke todos son bovos.
Bevamos a la saloud de Chana Kovo.

73. Los Molhos tienen ouna ermoza libreria.
Pouedemos topar livros para toda la famia,
Djornales en todas las linguas.
Mos aze honor, a toda la djouderia.
Bevamos a la saloud de los Molhos i toda la famia.

119. Levy, Cohen i Hassid vienen de la mezma famia.
Si la moujer ese de estos nombres,
La deve de merkar kon un pedaso de djoya.
Los hombres a la kiyila se meten un taled a la kavesa,
Para dezir la tifila de los koenes.
Bevamos a la saloud de los Levys,
Cohen i Hassid i toda la djouderia.

40. Tenemoz ouna vezina ke se yama Palomba.
Eze brouta ke da goumito de verla.
Todos los souvrinos la respectan
Porke tiene el portofolio a la mano kouando vienen averla.
Bevamos a la saloud de Adella.

151. A Salonique entre loz djidios aye tres classas:
Los rikos, los medianeros i los proves.
Kada ouno, se kazan kon los souyos.
Ma! Kouando la djouderia esta en perekolo,

It is good for one's health.
Also wine when one plays the oud.
Let us drink to the health of Isaac Efendi
Who gives us joy when he plays the oud.

99. The Kavalalis[73] play poker to amuse themselves
Because they have nowhere to go.
They travel once a year to Paris or to Switzerland;
When they return, they play bridge.
Let us drink to the health of Daniel Benruby.

24. In Salonika there was a club of the Josephs.
They meet once a week.
People say that they are all stupid.
Let us drink to the health of Chana Kovo.

73. The Molhos have a beautiful library.
We can find books there for the entire family,
Newspapers in every language.
They honor us, the entire community.
Let us drink to the health of the Molhos and their whole family.

119. Levy, Cohen, and Hassid come from the same family.
If the woman is from these families,
One must buy her with a piece of jewelry.
The men in the synagogue put a prayer shawl on their heads,
In order to recite the prayer of the priestly descendants.
Let us drink to the health of the Levys,
Cohens, and Hassids, and the entire community.

40. We have a neighbor whose name is Palomba.
She is so ugly that it makes one retch to see her.
All the nieces and nephews respect her
Because she has her wallet in her hand when they come to see her.
Let us drink to the health of Adella.

151. In Salonika there are three classes of Jews:
The rich, the middle class, and the poor.
Each one marries its own.
But! When the Jewish community is in danger,

---

73. Kavala is a port in central Macedonia.

Todo se aounan i ayoudan.
Bevamos a la saloud de Alberto Segoura.

138. Los djidios de Salonique son umanetarios.
Si el vizino esta hazino, le miran las kriatouras
I le dan el kinino, ouna soupa de gaïna kon minestra kaente,
Fina kouando lo meten empies en los dos piezes.
Bevamos a la saloud de Eliaou Parente.

23. Mochon Sadok se emprovisio; oun amigo non le kedo.
Malhorozamente tenia solo amigos del vazo.
La moujer le dicho mouthas vezez ke esta hevra non es parati.
Bevamos a la saloud de Gabriel Alfandary.

12. Marika Kotopouli es artista non djoudia.
A la chena, djougo Dibouk.
La foue aver toda la djouderia.
Todos se enkantaron komo tangneron el chofar.
Bevamos a la saloud de Marika Kotopouli i toda su kompagnia.

15. Los Fernandez son grande famia, de honor de instruction
I tambien de mouthas liras.
Azen honor a los djidios de verlos, komo pratikan moustra religion.
Bevamos a la saloud de los Fernandez kon todo el soye.

16. Los Fernandez se van ayir de Salonique.
Es ouna grande piedrita para los Selaniklis:
Dirijentes de la komunitad, philantrope, ke dan sin kedar.
Bevamos a la saloud de los Fernandez ande van apozar.

Philanthropy and Education

234. El philantrope tiene kavod.
A Salonique se okupan del despanser[74] Hassid,
O pinkas orphelinato Allatini, o Aboav,
Las eskolas komunales i el Bikour Holim.
Bevamos a la saloud de los Revah
Que nounka mankaron de se okoupar del Matanoth Laevionim.

111. Shemtov Saporta ese miembro del Bikour Holim.[75]
Da paras sin kontar para melezinas,

---

74. This is *dispensaire,* French for "dispensary" or "clinic."
75. This institution dated back to the sixteenth century and was reorganized at the end of the nineteenth.

Everyone unites and helps.
Let us drink to the health of Alberto Segoura.

138. The Jews of Salonika are humanitarians.
If a neighbor is ill, they look after the children
And give him quinine, chicken soup with hot tiny-cut pasta,
Until they get him back on his [own] two feet.
Let us drink to the health of Eliaou Parente.

23. Moshe Sadok became impoverished; he has no friends left.
Unfortunately he only had drinking friends.
His wife told him frequently that this crowd is not for you.
Let us drink to the health of Gabriel Alfandary.

12. Marika Kotopouli is a non-Jewish artist.
She appeared in *The Dybbuk* onstage.[76]
The entire community went to see her.
All were surprised at how they blew the shofar.
Let us drink to the health of Marika Kotopouli and her entire company.

15. The Fernandezes are a great family, educated and honorable,
Also very wealthy.
It does honor to the Jews to see them, how they practice our religion.
Let us drink to the health of the Fernandezes, with all that is theirs.

16. The Fernandezes are going to leave Salonika.
It is a great loss for the Salonikans:
Leaders of the community, philanthropists, who give unceasingly.
Let us drink to the health of the Fernandezes wherever they will settle.

Philanthropy and Education

234. The philanthropist deserves credit.
In Salonika they take care of the Hassid Clinic,
Or registry in the Allatini Orphanage or the Aboav,
The community schools and the Bikur Holim [Hospital].
Let us drink to the health of the Revahs
Who never failed to attend to the Gifts for the Needy Association.

111. Shemtov Saporta is a member of the Bikur Holim.
He gives money endlessly for medicines,

---

76. This was a translation of the famous Yiddish play written by S. Ansky in 1914.

Abedouwoua desmazalados de Salonique.
Nounka se kanso de ayoudar
Fina el dia de sou mouerte ke decho tsavaha.
Bevamos a la saloud de Rafel Beraka.

28. Los proves a Salonique tiene livro de Bikour Holim.
Toman melezinas de baldes
I tambien es fathile de tener kama al hopital Hirsch.
El Dr. Alalouf lez aze la operation sin pagar
Kaza de la komunitad sin kiera.
Isaac Tivoli lez etha la injection, ke eze oun hombre de korason.
Bevamos a la saloud de Rafael Sasson.

271. El ethador de injection se yama Isaac.
Las kriatouras solo de lo ver, se meten agorar.
Tivoli ese el nombre ke los azen trembler.
Bevamos a la saloud de Avraam Amar.

409. Los Haleguas saven brodar sirma,
Parohet i mapa para la thora.
Nounka se kansaron de dar lo ke rekaman
Para la kiyila.
Bevamos a la saloud de Parnas.

183. El marido de Sarina etha mekanes.[77]
Kouando kanta, todos abren pouertas i ventanas.
Tiene boz para kantar al konak del rey.
Eze hazan de la kiyila[78] de Signora Fakima
Ke la yaman agora Bet Saoul.[79]
Bevamos a la saloud de Sarina i el marido i toda la kompagnia.

387. La Barone de Hirsch dio paras al Dr. Misrahi hopital
Ke frouvouare a Salonique.
Todos los djidios se enteresaron.
Oun ermozo hospital frouvaron.
El governo para lo rengrasiar, la kaleja foue yamada Misrahi.
Bevamos a la saloud de Alberto Kamhi.

---

77. This is classical Turkish music; see the glossary.
78. *Kiyila* can mean "a congregation" or "a synagogue."
79. This synagogue was discussed in chapter 1.

Aids the unfortunate of Salonika.
He never tired of helping
Until the day of his death when he left a will.
Let us drink to the health of Rafael Beraka.

28. The poor of Salonika have a Bikkur Holim membership book.
They get free medicine
And it is also easy to get a bed in the Hirsch Hospital.[80]
Dr. Alalouf will operate on them gratis
In the building of the community that doesn't pay rent.
Isaac Tivoli gives them an injection, for he is a sincere man.
Let us drink to the health of Rafael Sasson.

271. The person who gives injections is called Isaac.
The kids only have to see him, they begin to cry.
Tivoli is the name that makes them tremble.
Let us drink to the health of Avraham Amar.

409. The Haleguas know how to embroider gold thread,
A curtain for the ark and a cover for the Torah.
They never tired of giving that which they embroider [with raised work]
For the synagogue.
Let us drink to the health of Parnas.

183. Sarina's husband tosses out Turkish melodies.
When he sings, everyone opens doors and windows.
He has a voice suited for singing in the royal mansion.
He is the cantor of the synagogue of Sra. Fakima
Which is now called Beit Shaul.
Let us drink to the health of Sarina and her husband and all those present.

387. Baroness de Hirsch gave money to the Dr. Mizrahi Hospital[81]
That was built in Salonika.
All of the Jews were interested.
They built a beautiful hospital.
The government, in order to thank him:[82] the street was named Mizrahi.
Let us drink to the health of Albert Kamhi.

---

80. The hospital was built in 1907.
81. Since Dr. Mizrahi was the driving force behind the fundraising campaign for the hospital, Bouena and others most likely referred to the hospital by his name rather than the major donor's name, or used the names interchangeably.
82. That is, the government took action.

260. Antes se mouerian de ouna dolor de tripa.
     Agora se van a la clinique para se operar de Apandasite.
     Asperan ke le salga el pedo, ke agora lo yaman aire o pouf.
     Bevamos a la saloud del Dr. Alalouf.

261. Al hospital de Hirsch, aplikan el radion
     Grasias a Madame Curie ke lo invento.
     El Bikour Holim paga por los proves.
     Bevamos a la saloud de todos los doctores.

373. El Dr. Matalon rekomenda
     Ke merkemos las melezinas a la pharmasia Franseza.
     El pharmasien estoudio a Paris i eze honesto.
     Non te vende avoua a lougar de bevida.
     Bevamos a la saloud de Daniel Medina.

 18. Moutho se avlo del orphelinato Allatini,
     Ke salen mansevos, bien destinguidos.
     Los bouenos elevos, los mandan a Paris,
     A la Serbone stoudian, grasias a Rotchild.
     Bevamos a la saloud de estos ke estoudian para bien bevir.

287. El orphelinato Allatini kita mansevos de honor, edukados,
     Honestos, i bouenos maridos.
     Isaac Covo se occupa de lez topar lavoro despoues del servisio militar.
     Bevamos a la saloud de este grande hombre ke nounka se kanso.

239. Komo todos saven ke los derijente del orphelinato Allatini dizen:
     Lo karo eze barato i lo barato eze karo.
     Bevamos a la saloud de este grande hombre, Isaac Covo.

145. El orphelinato Aboav izo theatro: las kouatro ijikas ermanikas baylaron.
     En Frances, foue la hetsizera Audette;
     En Grego, mes[a] [s]to Perivolaki;[83]
     En Ladino la bandiera,
     Ke foue kompozada del director ke ese Mr. Botton.
     Bevamos a la saloud de Daniel Matalon.

146. Este theatro izo konoser el orphelinato.
     Todos dieron paras para ameliorar el Aboav.

---

83. This is a song with a small theatrical sketch (David Kounios, personal communication, February 20, 2009).

260. In the old days, they died of a bellyache.
Today they go to the clinic to be operated on for appendicitis.
They wait until one lets out the fart, which they now call air or puff.
Let us drink to the health of Dr. Alalouf.

261. In the Hirsch Hospital, they use radium
Thanks to Mme. Curie who invented it.
The Bikur Holim Society pays for the poor.
Let us drink to the health of all the doctors.

373. Dr. Matalon recommends
That we buy our medicines at the French pharmacy.
The pharmacist studied in Paris and is honest.
He doesn't sell you water instead of an elixir.
Let us drink to the health of Daniel Medina.

18. Much was said about the Allatini Orphanage,
That they emerge as young men, well distinguished.
The good students are sent to Paris.
They study at the Sorbonne, thanks to Rothschild.
Let us drink to the health of those who study in order to live better.

287. The Allatini Orphanage produces young men of honor, educated,
Honest and good husbands.
Isaac Covo deals with finding them work after their military service.
Let us drink to the health of this great man who never tired.

239. As everyone knows that the administrators of the orphanage say:
The costly is cheap and the cheap is costly.
Let us drink to the health of this great man, Isaac Covo.

145. The Aboav Orphanage put on shows: the four little sisters danced.
In French, there was "The Witch Audette";
In Greek, "Inside the Small Garden";
In Ladino, "The Banner,"
That was composed by the director who is Mr. Botton.[84]
Let us drink to the health of Daniel Matalon.

146. This theatre made the orphanage known.
Everyone gave money in order to improve the Aboav.

---

84. This was Solomon Botton, a member of the committee that translated and adapted plays in Ladino (Rena Molho, *Salonica and Istanbul,* 255).

Salieron nignas honestas i balabayas i estoudiadas.
Mouthas de eyas estan bien kazadas en Palestina
Ke azen honor a la djouderia.
Bevamos a la saloud de Jacques Nahmias.

386. El orphelinato se formo Mr. Aboav; paras decho.
Avia kouatro vouerfanikas ke el padre i la madre mourio;
Ni parientes ni amigos.
Solas en el moundo kedaron.
El komitato devouado, setenta i sinko nignas tomaron,
Resivieron instruction i amor i bien vistidos en kada okazion.
Bevamos a la saloud de komitato de esta institution.

329. El terreno de Aya Sofia le dio Alchek
Ke aga eskolas amozotros, ouna hevra por noventa i moueve agnos.
Le devemos de lo dar atras.
Bevamos a la saloud de Haim Atas.

144. La eskola Alchek sero.
La Gategno tomo a loz elevos.
Malhorozamente, despoues de doze agnos non existio
Porke loz gastes son grandes; la ruino.
Bevamos a la saloud de los elevos ke estoudiaron a esta eskola de djidios.

309. Las nignas a Salonique azen gymnastic.
El maestro Mauro Skoufas.
Si son godras, dizen ke ese para se aflakar.
Si son flakas, dizen ke ese para se aflakar [*sic*].[85]
Bevamos a la saloud de las ke kieren amostrar.

125. Tenemos oun souvrino ke nounka lo vimos.
Estoudio a Paris; le parese ke non tenemos edukation.
Ayer lo vimos por prima vez a la boda de Sarina.
Mos demando pardon i demando si pouedia venir avermos.

---

85. This was probably an error and was meant to be a different verb, such as *enforteser,* "to become stronger."

They produced honest girls [and] housewives and learned.
Many of them married well in Palestine
Which brings honor to the community.
Let us drink to the health of Jacques Nahmias.

386. Mr. Aboav formed the orphanage; he left money.
     There were four orphaned little girls whose mother and father had died,
     [Leaving] neither relatives nor friends.
     They were left alone in the world.
     The devoted committee took seventy-five girls,
     [Who] received instruction and love and were well dressed on every
         occasion.
     Let us drink to the health of the committee of this institution.

329. The building plot of Saint Sophia[86] was given by Alchek
     So that he built schools for us; a house of learning [created][87] for
         ninety-nine years.
     We have to give it[88] back.
     Let us drink to the health of Haim Atas.

144. The Alchek school closed.[89]
     The Gategno[90] took the students.
     Unfortunately, after twelve years it could not survive
     Because the expenses were great; it was bankrupt.
     Let us drink to the health of the students who studied at this Jewish
         school.

309. The girls of Salonika exercise.
     The teacher is Mauro Skoufas.
     If they are heavy, he says it is in order to get thinner.
     If they are thin, he says it is so that they will be thin [*sic*].
     Let us drink to the health of those who want to show [off].

125. We have a cousin whom we have never seen.
     He studied in Paris; it seems to him that we do not have an education.
     Yesterday we saw him for the first time at Sarina's wedding.
     He asked our forgiveness and asked if he could come to visit us.

---

86. This street, Agias Sofias (and the cathedral by the same name), is located in the
southeast part of the city.
87. *Hevra* can mean *heder,* "Talmud Torah," or even "synagogue."
88. It refers to the land.
89. It was established in 1898.
90. It was also known as the Franco-Allemande.

Le dichimos ke mozotros estoudymos a la eskola de l'Alliansa,
Ke non ambezemos solo a meldar i eskrevir,
Ambezemos koualo ez la vida de la djouderia de Salonique.
Bevamos a la saloud de Alberto Hassid.

126. Perogravoura i Peroskultoura las nignas estan ambezando.
Eliaou vido ke estamos moutho enteresadas.
Al otra dia se asavento ande pouedemoz ambezar este Art.
A la eskola italiana moz mando i nounka regretimos de lo ke ambezimos.
Bevamos a la saloud de este ermano ke mos dio todo lo ke deseyemos.

280. Mr. Nehama eze oun bouen pedagogue.
Moz dio instruction a todos los djidios.
Mademoiselle Saporta se izo director.
Bevamos a la saloud de esta djente de valor.

163. Al Dr. Louis Modiano lo honoraron.
En Italia viajo; diplome de profesor tomo.
Eze honor para la djouderia i alegria para los djidios.
Bevamos a la saloud de Nico Sasson.

288b. Mademoiselle Saporta se kazo kon Charle Beraha.
Mr. Saltiel se izo el director.
Troucho a la ermana de Paris ke estoudio a la Serbone.
Eze la maestra mejor ke konosko.
Bevamos a la saloud de todos los elevos.

427. Alice Aelion ese maestra de la eskola komunala.
Kada agno la komunitad la honora porke ese moutho devouada.
Ogagno gano el primo premio.
Se lo dio el governo grego.
Bevamos a la saloud de Alice, el padre, la madre i sous ermanos.

188. Sarah Primo ese ouna eskola de navigation.
Grasias a Besanthi i Eliaou Sarfatty ke vino a Salonique,
Son los primos marineros djudios.
Bevamos a la saloud de Haim Amario.

We told him that we studied at the Alliance school,
That not only did we learn to read and write,
But we learned about the life of the community of Salonika.
Let us drink to the health of Alberto Hassid.

126. The girls are studying pyrogravure[91] and sculpture.
Eliaou saw that we were very interested.
The other day he found out where we can learn this art.
He sent us to the Italian school and we never regretted what we had
learned.
Let us drink to the health of this brother who gave us everything we
desired.

280. Mr. Nehama is a good teacher.
He taught all of us Jews.
Mademoiselle Saporta became principal.
Let us drink to the health of these virtuous people.

163. Dr. Louis Modiano was honored.
He traveled to Italy; he got a professor's degree.
It is an honor for the Jewish community and happiness for the Jews.
Let us drink to the health of Nico Sasson.

288b. Mlle. Saporta married Charles Beraha.
Mr. Saltiel became principal.
He brought his sister from Paris who studied at the Sorbonne.
She is the best teacher that I know.
Let us drink to the health of all the students.

427. Alice Aelion is a teacher in the communal school.
Every year the community honors her because she is extremely devoted.
This year she won first prize.
The Greek government gave it to her.
Let us drink to the health of Alice, her father, her mother, and her siblings.

188. Sarah Primo is a navigation school.[92]
Thanks to Besantsi and Eliaou Sarfatty who came to Salonika,
They are the first Jewish sailors.
Let us drink to the health of Haim Amario.

---

91. This is a technique for etching wood with a metallic pencil.
92. This school was run by the Jewish Agency, and sat in the port on the gulf on
Nikis Street (or Boulevard) (Garfinkle, "The Memoirs of Bouena Garfinkle," 91).

189. Fouemos al bodre de la mar aver a Sarah Primo.
     Parese perlas en medio de la mar, asendido.
     Estamos fieros de ver esto.
     Esperamos ke oun dia biylikas djoudias van a venir.
     Bevamos a la saloud de Mochon Amir.

360. Merkimos marothinos para parientes i amigos.
     Samuel salio doctor; a la Serbone estoudio.
     Fizo oun stage al Institu Pasteur.
     Passo los examenes kon kolores, i oun premio tomo.
     Souetamos a Samuel mazal tov.

Economic Status

96. Las Iforia mos vino a vijitar, examinaron loz livros sin kedar.
    Komo non toparon anomalia, dijeron:
          regalo para sous famias.
    Bevamos a la saloud de Salomon Atias.

97. Salomon Segoura se rouvino; merko liras i abacho.
    Pago a todos los kreditores, ma! El kedo sin pantalones.[93]
    Bevamos a la saloud de Joseph Kapones.

79. A Salonique mouthos se emprovisieron.
    Dieron las liras emprenda, i les pagaron a venti doz i noventa.
    Bevamos a la saloud de estos ke kedaron sin fouersa.

172. Tramouz viene kada mez kon el violino.
     Tagne oun poko i la mama lo da ounas kountas drakmes.
     Este modo gana sou vida, para el i Bienvenida.
     Bevamos a la saloud de los ke reseven a Tramouz kon alegria.

74. Loz Leones tienen fabrika de chavon.
    Eze blanko i vedre, bouena koualitad.
    Mitieron oun hourtoum a la kaye
    Ke sale avoua enchavonada para loz proves del vizendado.
    Bevamos a la saloud de Daniel Modiano.

---

93. The same expression appears in copla 236.

189. We went to the seaside to see Sarah Primo.
     It looked like pearls in the middle of the sea, lit up.
     We were proud to see this.
     We hope that one day Jewish warships will come.
     Let us drink to the health of Mochon Amir.

360. We bought almond balls for relatives and friends.
     Samuel became a doctor; he studied at the Sorbonne.
     He did his residency at the Pasteur Institute.
     He passed his exams with flying colors, and received a prize.
     We toast Samuel, [wishing him] good luck.

Economic Status

96. The tax collectors came to visit us, examining the books endlessly.
    Since they did not find anything wrong, they said:
       a gift for their families.[94]
    Let us drink to the health of Salomon Atias.

97. Salomon Segoura is bankrupt; he bought gold coins and they devalued.
    He paid all the creditors, but! He lost his "shirt."
    Let us drink to the health of Joseph Kapones.

79. In Salonika, many have become impoverished.
    They gave their gold coins as collateral, and they paid them
       back at 22.90.[95]
    Let us drink to the health of those who are left helpless.

172. Tramouz comes every month with his violin.
     He plays a little bit and Mama gives him a few drachmas.
     In this way he earns his living, for himself and Bienvenida.
     Let us drink to the health of those who receive Tramouz gladly.

74. The Leons have a soap factory.
    It is white and green, of good quality.
    They put a hose in the street
    That spouts soapy water for the poor of the neighborhood.[96]
    Let us drink to the health of Daniel Modiano.

---

94. They asked for a "tip," known as *baksheesh* (*bakşiş*).

95. The original value of each coin was probably 25 or 30 (Güler Orgun, personal communication, February 25, 2011).

96. Presumably this water can be used in the summer for outdoor showers, especially for the young, or for washing clothes or utensils, on the assumption that there is water available for rinsing off the soap.

2. Los lavoradores de toutoun estan en greve.
   Se aseraron al magazin, gritan en las ventanas
   Ke kieren pan para sous famias.
   Bevamos a la saloud de Daniel Atias.

237. A Salonique a los Sarfattys loz yaman tsitsikeros.[97]
   Nounka vendieron ouna flor o asembraron oun pipino.
   Bevamos a la saloud de Albert Tsimino.

141. A Salonique los hombres komen la medio dia al tsarchi.
   El empyegado viene a tomar la komida kon el sefertasin.[98]
   Todo esta pronto kouando viene,
   I se va presto para ke se lo koma kaente.
   Bevamos a la saloud de Salomon Parente.

391. Los hamales de Lachtira tienen albadra.
   Se meten sien okas de trigo
   A la aspalda komo nada.
   Komen la magnana oun pan i kezo;
   A la medio dia, oun pan ke kitan la miga.
   Lo inthen de fijon[99] o garvansos o lenteja.
   A kindi se komen la miga kon oun raki.
   Dizen minha a Lachtira; siempre tienen mignan.
   Si algouna vez algouno manka, yaman al patron ke siempre esta pronto.
   Se moueren viejos i yenos de saloud.
   Bevamos a la saloud de Salomon Alalouf.

392. Eliaou tiene oun emprigado; se yama Avramiko.
   Tiene othenta i moueves agnos.
   Empeso a lavorar para el nono kouando tenia vente.
   La magnana avre el magazin fina kouando viene Eliaou i el de Cohen.
   Despoues viene en kaza, a demandar koualo tiene de menester la mama.
   Mos merka toda la zarzava o le ke mos manka de bakal.
   Traye la legna ariva, asiende la sova, kome de medio dia.
   Mama apareja el sefer tasin para Eliaou.

---

97. This word reflects the development of Ladino beautifully: Because the sound "ch" is prounounced like "ts" in Greek, the spelling in Ladino of *chichekchi* (actually çiçekçi), Turkish for florist, begins with "ts," but ends with a Spanish suffix. The glossary contains the term for flower rather than seller of flowers, upon which this term is based (Güler Orgun, personal communication, April 8, 2012).

98. *Sefer-tasi* is an alternate spelling in Ladino.

99. *Fijónes* are white or navy beans eaten at midday on Tuesdays and Fridays. See copla 128.

2. The tobacco workers are on strike.
They shut themselves up in the store, yelling in the windows
That they want bread for their families.
Let us drink to the health of Daniel Attias.

237. In Salonika, the Sarfattys are called florists.
They never sold a flower or planted a cucumber.
Let us drink to the health of Albert Tsimino.

141. In Salonika, the men eat the midday [meal] at the market.
The employee comes to fetch the meal with the "lunch pail."[100]
Everything is ready when he comes,
And he leaves quickly so that the boss can eat it while it is still warm.
Let us drink to the health of Salomon Parente.

391. The porters of Lachtira[101] have saddles.[102]
They put one hundred measures[103] of wheat
On their shoulders as if it were nothing.
They eat bread and cheese in the morning;
At midday, a bread from which they remove the soft center.
They fill it with beans or chickpeas or lentils.
In the afternoon, they eat the soft part with an ouzo.
They recite minha in Lachtira; they always have a minyan.
If sometimes, someone is missing, they call the boss who is always ready.
They die of old age and full of health.
Let us drink to the health of Salomon Alalouf.

392. Eliaou has an employee; his name is Avramiko.
He is eighty-nine years old.
He began to work for grandfather when he was twenty.
In the morning he opens the store until Eliaou and Cohen have come.
Afterwards he comes [to our] home to ask what Mother needs.
He buys us all the vegetables or whatever we are lacking from the grocer.
He brings the wood up, lights the stove, eats lunch.
Mother prepares the "lunch pail" for Eliaou.

---

100. It was akin to a traveling food box, actually made up of a number of pots of exactly the same dimension, superposed and held by a handle.

101. Lachtira is from the Greek *istira* or *sitira,* "wheat"; this was the center of the wholesale grain trade, where the wheat silos were located by the port of the city (David Kounio, personal communication, August 26, 2006).

102. With ropes to carry things.

103. This equals 1282 grams.

Yeva el komer al mouelino i se va ande sou moujer Bienvenida.
Bevamos a la saloud de los hamales de Lachtira i todas sous famias.

115. Tsiko i Bitran tienen fabrika de vestidos prontos
Para los kazalinos o los ke kieren pagar poko.
Tienen makinas de electrisita
I todo se aze presto i sin penar.
Bevamos a la saloud de Shimon Amar.

116. Shimon Amar tiene banka.
Es konsiderada despoues de la banka automana.
Azen tranzaktiones en todo el moundo.
Son modestos i umanitarios.
Se pasean kon Rubin i Shimon por todas las kayes.
Bevamos a la saloud de esta grande famia honorada.

117. Los Rodrigues son reprezentantes de Singer a Cairo.
Vingneron a Salonique a amostrar mouevas makinas.
Kouando vieron ke mozotros estamos mas avansados de eyos,
Se foueron komo los kodredos sin dezir adios a los ke lo troucheron.
Bevamos a la saloud de Michelle Serrero.

168. A los deskarsos a Salonique loz yaman: "Eze economiozo."
Mi vizino se mourio. Decho konakes de valor.
Nounka merko antari a la moujer ni mezmo para el.
Bevamos a la saloud de los [h]eredadores ke van a baylar.

213. Panoutho merko el mouelino Allatini[104] kon condition
Non van a trokar el nombre del mouelino.
Bevamos a la saloud de los Allatinis.

302. Es difithile de me[r]kar mouchama[105] para el pasaje
O para la ouda o la kouzina.
Los mouchamadjis tienen trost: fouetes ande Basso, o ande Elio Haim,
Kon el telephone se komunikan ke aye mouchteri.
Bevamos a la saloud de los komeres.[106]

---

104. This mill was founded in 1854, and in 1882 became the "first steam-driven flour mill" (Michael Molho, *Traditions and Customs*, 331).

105. Also spelled *muŝamá*, which is from the Turkish *müsamba* (linoleum).

106. This is a lovely Ladino expression taken from *komer*, "to eat"; *dar a komer* or *komer* is "a bribe," and this is the plural (Güler Orgun personal communication, February 25, 2011).

He brings the food to the mill and goes to his wife Bienvenida.
Let us drink to the health of the porters of Lachtira and all their families.

115. Chico and Bitran have a factory of ready made clothes
For the villagers or for those who want to pay little.
They have electrical machines
And everything is done quickly and effortlessly.
Let us drink to the health of Shimon Amar.

116. Shimon Amar has a bank.
It is considered second [only] to the Ottoman bank.
They make transactions throughout the world.
They are modest and humanitarian.
They stroll with Rubin and Shimon throughout all the streets.
Let us drink to the health of this great honorable family.

117. The Rodrigues are representatives of Singer in Cairo.
They came to Salonika to display new machines.
When they saw that we were more advanced than they,
They left like sheep without saying goodbye to those who invited them.
Let us drink to the health of Michelle Serrero.

168. In Salonika the barefoot are called "thrifty."
My neighbor died. He left valuable estates.
He never bought a gown for his wife, nor even for himself.
Let us drink to the health of the heirs who are going to celebrate.[107]

213. Panoucho bought the Allatini mill on the condition
That they wouldn't change the name of the mill.
Let us drink to the health of the Allatinis.

302. It is difficult to buy linoleum for the corridor,
For the room, or the kitchen.
The linoleum sellers have a "trust":[108] if you went to Basso or to Elio Haim,
They communicate to each other by telephone when there is a customer.
To the health of the illegal benefits.

---

107. Literally, dance.

108. This was a group of commercial enterprises combined to control the market for commodities; the aim was to keep the price high (Güler Orgun, personal communication, February 19, 2007).

238. Non te pouedes imajinar kountas difikultad aye al palasio del Rey.
     Akontentate de tou baraka i non bevir komo el.
     Bevamos a la saloud de Oly Abravanel.

127. Los Amozninos tienen la mas grande pastetheria.
     Las pastas ke azen se sierve a las salones de los rikos.
     La savor keda al palada
     I la rekomendas ande vas.
     Bevamos a la saloud de Leon Amar.

71. Loz Cohenes tienen las mas moderna grouta de koundourias
    A la kay Venizelos.
    Se foueron a Paris, atornaron despouez de doz mezes.
    A Salonique avrieron athelier al porto.
    Azen kalsados kon lavaro barato.
    Mandan las mestas a Paris sin pagar petha a los selaniklis.
    Bevamos a la saloud de Eliaou Kabeli.

130. Atias la prima fabrika de filado a Salonique.
     Trayen el kotton en ballas del Egypto, azen la filatoura,
     I ropa, ke se yama merikana.
     Bevamos a la saloud de Rofel Arama.

231. El governo dio kilos para emportar del estragneron.
     Los Saltielim se izieron rikos porke eran kieristidjis.
     Bevamos a la saloud de los Amalikim.

182. Los ermanos de Alegra Sarfatty son valijeros.
     Eran kacheros.
     Oun dia troucheron ouna kachika en kaza.
     Komo la madre non la pouedia arempouchar,
     Le metieron ouna mano de kouero.
     La enfodraron la misma kolor de las vellas
     Para ke sea ermoza a la kamareta.
     Ez ansi ke empesaron los primos a Salonique a azer valijas.
     Izieron honor a los Selaniklis.
     Bevamos a la saloud de Alegra la madre i suz ermanos.

135. Los Karassos son boyadjis.
     Empesaron kon ouna kaldera al tsametsi.
     Agora tienen fabrika ke azen honor a la djouderia de Salonique.

238. You cannot imagine how many problems there are in the king's palace.
Just be satisfied with your own hut and not [wanting] to live like him.
Let us drink to the health of Oly Abravanel.

127. The Almosninos have the largest pastry bakery.
The cakes they make are served in the homes of the wealthy.
The flavor remains on the palate
And they are recommended wherever one goes.
Let us drink to the health of Leon Amar.

71. The Cohens have the most modern shoe store
On Venizelos Street.
They went to Paris, returned after two months.
In Salonika, they opened a workshop at the port.
They made shoes with cheap labor.
They send the samples to Paris without paying taxes to the Salonikans.
Let us drink to the health of Eliaou Kabeli.

130. Attias [had] the first spinning factory in Salonika.
They bring cotton in bales from Egypt, make the thread
And fabric that they called American.
Let us drink to the health of Raphael Arama.

231. The government gave lots of money for importing from abroad.
The Saltiels became rich because they were lumber merchants.
Let us drink to the health of the Amaleks.[109]

182. Alegra Sarfatty's brothers are luggage makers.
They were chest makers before.
One day they brought a little chest home.
Since their mother couldn't move it,
They put a leather handle on it.
They lined it with the same color of the curtains
So that it would look nice in the room.
That is how they became the first in Salonika to make suitcases.
They brought honor to the Salonikans.
Let us drink to the health of Alegra, the mother, and her brothers.

135. The Karassos are paint merchants.
They began with a cauldron at the market.
Now they have a factory; they do honor to the Jews of Salonika.

_____

109. This is extremely odd, as it is highly doubtful that there was a family named Amalek; one suspects that this was an error or misspelling of another name.

Foueron los primoz de developar esta industri.
Bevamos a la saloud de los Karassos aounados
Lavoraron fouerte para parvenir.

136. Mi nono Salomon Ichoua empeso
A azer parmethetes al anko de la kouzina.
Los thiketikos mos enteresemos ke amelioremos.
Kouando moz izimos grandes, fabrika avrimos.
Fouemos los primos a Salonique de esta industri.
Bevamos a la saloud de Rachel Kabeli.

91. Los Nadjaris tienen magazen a Lachtira.
Azen konkerensia a los Sarfattys sin kedar.
El benadan decha a otros ke koman pan.
Bevamos a la saloud de los Nadjaris
Ke lez parese ke aki van akedar.

65. Las moujeres a Salonique non tienen derito de voto,
Ni para el mayor o la komunitad o el governo.
Si se mouere el marido, non pouede jerar[110] los bienes.
Deven de meter oun hombre mezmo si el non tiene meoyo.
Bevamos a la saloud de Clara Mayo.

Women's Work

21. Bienvenida tiene basina i kaldera enterado a la kouzina.
El dia de la kolada ez reyna de las vezinas.
Bevamos a la saloud de Daniel, Alberto i Sarina.

397. A Salonique en kada kouzina aye oun palo para manear
La kolada ke bouye a la kaldera enter[r]ada.
Eze ouna grande limpieza.
Las savanas salen blankas komo ouna velija de gneve.
Bevamos a la saloud de Karolina i Genevieva.

394. A Salonique tenemos la Boulgarika
Ke vende envouente[111] para panarizes.
No kreen en doktor.

---

110. This is *djirar,* "to operate" or "to handle business." It is similar to the French expression, *gerer ton argent,* "to manage your money" (Yehuda Hatsvi, personal communication, February 19, 2009).
111. This is traditionally spelled *enguente.*

They were the first to develop this industry.
Let us drink to the health of the united Karassos
Who worked hard in order to succeed.

136. My grandfather Solomon Yehoshua began
     To make candles on the kitchen bench.
     We, the little ones, were interested in improving.
     When we got older, we opened a factory.
     We were the first in Salonika in this industry.
     Let us drink to the health of Rachel Kabeli.

91. The Nadjaris have a store in Lachtira.
    They compete with the Sarfattys endlessly.
    The [good] person lets others earn their bread.
    Let us drink to the health of the Nadjaris
    As it appears that they are going to be staying here.

65. The women of Salonika do not have the right to vote,
    Not for the mayor nor [in] the community nor [for] the government.
    If the husband dies, she cannot manage his belongings.
    She has to give them to a man even if he has no brains.
    Let us drink to the health of Clara Mayo.

Women's Work

21. Bienvenida has a basin and a cauldron "buried"[112] in her kitchen.
    On laundry day she is queen of the neighboring ladies.[113]
    Let us drink to the health of Daniel, Alberto, and Sarina.

397. In Salonika, in every kitchen there is a wooden stick for stirring
     The laundry that boils in the cauldron set in the ground.
     It is a large wash.
     The sheets emerge white as a snowflake.
     Let us drink to the health of Caroline and Genevieve.

394. In Salonika we have the Bulgarian lady
     Who sells ointment for boils.[114]
     They do not believe in doctors.

---

112. It was probably sunken.
113. One is struck by the sarcasm here—that is, the image of royalty in such quotidian surroundings.
114. Or furuncles.

Van kada dia a trokar el pansement.
Bevamos a la saloud de Eliaou Amar.

408. Dizen ke los Sarfattys tienen mano de oro.
Yo vide que kitan de loz bastidores.
Rachelika, la de la tia Palomba, eze la mejor.
Todo lo ke kita de la mano ese para exposision.
Bevamos a la saloud de Madame Ichoua ke le ambezo.

160. Se ouza vellas de fillet; non todos las reuchen bien.
A la ventana de Liaou, aye ouna ermoza rêucheda.
Bouena la izo de el livro ke merko Regina.
Bevamos a la saloud de Avraam Medina.

120. Marika la lingère
Tomo renome kon las ijas del Dr. Matalon.
Lez dieron clientes de savor.
Toma oua lira de oro el dia.
Se izo rika kon la djouderia.
Bevamos a la saloud de Isaac Azaria.

39. Tamarika eze ouna grande chastra.
Lavora para todas las ke moran a las kampangnas.
Non save ni meldar ni eskrevir,
Ma! Loz vestidos ke azen son dernier krie.
Bevamos a la saloud de Abraam Shaki.

200. Alice Aelion akompagno oun mouzekante,
Yendo en kada vieja de Salonique, arekojer kantes.
Ouna kantega al katalogue le dedikaron.
Alice se allegro en meldando.
Bevamos a la saloud de Albert Toledano.

169. Sarika Florentin aze ermozas tsintouras.
Aze el bel bouena figoura.
El ermano se okupa de vender en loz grandes magazenes de moujer.
Bevamos a la saloud de David i Moche Amiel.

170. Sarika Florentin eze el brasso deretho del ermano
E okupa de la Atelier i azer lo ke eze menester.
Tiene cada dia mouevas ideas komo va azer oye las tsintouras.
Bevamos a la saloud de Michelle Segoura.

They go every day to change the bandage.
Let us drink to the health of Eliaou Amar.

408. They say that the Sarfattys have golden hands.
I saw when they removed [their work] from the embroidering frames.
Rachelika, Aunt Palomba's daughter, is the best.
Everything that emerges from her hand[iwork] is for display.
Let us drink to the health of Madame Yehoshua who taught her.

160. One uses curtains of mesh; not all work well.
On Liaou's window, there is a beautiful successful one.
Bouena made it from the book that Regina bought.
Let us drink to the health of Avraham Medina.

120. Marika the lingerie maker
Became famous by means of Dr. Matalon's daughters.
They gave her clients with taste.
She charges a gold coin a day.
She made herself wealthy via the community.
Let us drink to the health of Isaac Azaria.

39. Tamar is a great seamstress.
She works for all those who live in the countryside.
She doesn't know to read or write,
But! The clothes that she makes are the latest fashion.
Let us drink to the health of Abraham Shaki.

200. Alice Aelion accompanied a musician,
Going to every old woman in Salonika, collecting songs.
They dedicated one song in the catalogue to her.
Alice was pleased upon reading it.
Let us drink to the health of Albert Toledano.

169. Sarika Florentin makes handsome belts.
She gives the waist a nice shape.
Her brother attends to selling [them] in the fancy women's stores.
Let us drink to the health of David and Moshe Amiel.

170. Sarika Florentin is the right hand of her brother
And takes care of the workshop and does whatever is necessary.
Every day she has new ideas as to how she is going to make the belts today.
Let us drink to the health of Michelle Segoura.

Ladino Publications

195. Para los djidios de Salonique,
Eze grande plazer de meldar livros de ley, no romansas.
Ma! Shabat las moujeres meldan djornal, El Gayo,
Para saver lo ke se pasa:
Si Sarika se kazo o Rekoulika pario.
Bevamos a la saloud de Mochon Sasson.

27. Bona la Tagnedera se mourio.
Para los selaniklis esta biva i sana.
Los djornales umoristike avlan de eya i mouthos livros se ekrivieron
Ke van aser meldados de generationes a generationes.
Bevamos a la saloud de los ke eskrivio.

9. El maz seriozo djornal djidio es El Aktion,
Dan novedades de França, Amerika, mezmo de Estambol.
Besantsi eskrive ladino i algouna vez en lachon.
Moz mete al kouriente
Kouantos kiboutzim a Palestina ya se fravouo.
Bevamos a la saloud de Samuel Guerchon.

307. Bessanthi eze djornalista.
Nounka se espanto de eskrevir la djoustisia.
Avla otho lenguas, bien perfectionadas.
Bevamos a la saloud de Bessanthi i sou famia amada.

88. Tener la penina fathile ese bendition del dio.
Besanthi i Acher Abravanel eskriven libros, artikolos, poemas kon savor.
Son eskrivanos de natoura, eskrevian kouando eran kriatouras.
Bevamos a la saloud de Abraam Segoura.

278. Ounos de loz bouenos eskrivanos eze Acher Abravanel.
Eskriven djounto kon Acher Amiel livros, artikolos de valor.
Bevamos a la saloud de los ke mos da information.

279. Acher Abravanel eskrivio al '40: non seas djidio.
Al kouarenta i sinko: non seas alman.
Bevamos a la saloud de eskrividor.

Ladino Publications

195. For the Jews of Salonika,
     It is a great pleasure to read books of law, not novels.
     But! On Shabbat the women read the newspaper *El Gayo*
     In order to know what is going on:
     If Sarika got married or Rekulika gave birth.
     Let us drink to the health of Moshe Sasson.

27. Bona the tambourinist died.[115]
    For the Salonikans she is alive and well.
    The humoristic papers speak of her and many books were written
         [about her]
    That will be read for generations and generations.
    Let us drink to the health of those who wrote.

9. The most serious Jewish newspaper is "El Aktion,"
   Providing news from France, America, even from Istanbul.
   Besantsi writes in Ladino and sometimes in Hebrew.
   He keeps us up to date [about]
   How many kibbutzim have already been built in Palestine.
   Let us drink to the health of Samuel Gershon.

307. Besansti[116] is a journalist.
     He never was afraid to write the truth.
     He speaks eight languages, quite perfectly.
     Let us drink to the health of Besantsi and his beloved family.

88. To have the talent for writing is a blessing from God.
    Besantsi and Asher Abravanel write books, articles, tasteful poems.
    They are natural writers; they wrote when they were children.
    Let us drink to the health of Abraham Segoura.

278. One of the good writers is Asher Abravanel.
     He writes books [and] worthy articles together with Asher Amiel.
     Let us drink to the health of those who give us information.

279. Asher Abravanel wrote in 1940: "Don't be Jewish."
     In 1945: "Don't be German."
     Let us drink to the health of the writer.

---

115. See the discussion of Bona in chapter 1.
116. In Hebrew his name is pronounced like Ben Sangi.

Shabbat

134. Foue ande el Dr. Gauthier kon mi marido.
A la kamareta de asperar avia oun Hassid.
Este modo me akodri la kompla del Shabat de Salonique.
Bevamos a la saloud de los Hasidim.

36. El zembil[117] yeno moz trayen djoueves la nothe zarzava
I frouta i salata freska, pipinos de savor.
Eze alegria para la madre ke el marido vino kon laz manos yenas.
La madre empesa a moundar la pinzela
Para viernes lo guizar i eskapar temprano, antes del Shabat.
Bevamos a la saloud de Daniel Rabat.

109. Djoueves kouando venemos de la eskola,
La kaza esta parfoumada del vouezmo
Del pastel de hojas de espinaka o de merendjenas.
Mama mos da agostar; moz dize esto eze para Shabat.
Bevamos a la saloud de mama ke nounka se kanso de moz akontentar.

128. A Salonique kada viernes fezan fijones.
Ese tradition kon savoya moradeada i voueos
Ke tiene bouena savor.
Ounos se lo komen regolar al plato;
Otros toman la bodra del pan,
Kitan la miga i la enthen de fijon.
Otros kon boukados[118] al plato.
Bevamos a la saloud de Esther Romano.

112. Mi madre se repoza solo el Chabat.
Alhad arekoje la kaza, i alegre ke todos mos fouemos a la eskola.
Lounes la kolada; Martes dar fiero sin kedar.
Mierkoles kouzir moueva o vieja ropa.
Djoueves aparejar para los pastels.
Viernes azer el chabat, alegre despues ke moz dio el bagno.
Se viste komo ouna reyna para el Kidouch ke va azer el papa.
Bevamos a la saloud de mama ke lavora sin kedar.

187. Chabat de mangnana, kouando venimos de la kiyila,
Azemos kidouch kon raki Nahmias,

---

117. This is a flat basket woven of straw or wool and carried on the shoulder.
118. *Bokado* appears in copla 418 and is translated as "morsel" or "bite-size piece."

Shabbat

134. I went to Dr. Gauthier with my husband.
      In the waiting room there was a Hassid.
      This way I remembered the coplas about the Sabbath in Salonika.
      Let us drink to the health of the Hassidim.

 36. On Thursday nights they bring us a basket full of vegetables
      And fruit and fresh salad, tasty cucumbers.
      It is a joy for the mother that the husband came with loaded arms.
      The mother begins to shell the peas
      So that she can cook them on Friday and finish early before the Sabbath.
      Let us drink to the health of Daniel Rabat.

109. On Thursdays, when we come home from school,
      The house is perfumed with the smell
      Of the filo pastry with spinach or with eggplant.
      Mother gives us a taste; she tells us it is for Shabbat.
      Let us drink to the health of mother who never tired of pleasing us.

128. In Salonika, on every Friday, beans are cooked.
      This [is a]tradition with browned onion and bones
      That have a wonderful taste.
      Some eat them normally from the plate;
      Others take the crust of the bread,
      Removing the soft dough in the center and fill it up with beans.
      Others take bite-size pieces [to soak up the juice or gravy] on the plate.
      Let us drink to the health of Esther Romano.

112. My mother only rests on the Sabbath.
      [On] Sunday she arranges the house, and is happy that we all went to
         school.
      Monday, the laundry; Tuesday, to iron nonstop.
      Wednesday, to sew old or new clothes.
      Thursday, to prepare the pastries.
      Friday, to prepare [make] the Sabbath, happy after she gave us a bath.
      She dresses like a queen for the kiddush that father is going to make.
      Let us drink to the health of mother who works endlessly.

187. On the Sabbath morning, when we come from synagogue,
      We make kiddush with Nahmias ouzo,

Borekas de merendjena, i boyos de kezo.
Ez oun plazer de ver la famia koumiendo estas kozas finas.
Bevamos a la saloud de Daniel Atias.

242. Chabat kouando los selaniklis vienen a la kiyila,
Azen kidouch kon raki i pastel de foja i vouevos enhaminados.
Bevamos a la saloud de los mouevos kazados.

199. A Salonique, el kidouch se aze kon vino, kasher i vazo de plata.
Esperamos ke esta tradition nounka moz manke.
Todos arodeados en la meza, Papa kantando kon alegria.
Bevamos a la saloud de toda la famia.

346. Las moujeres se asentan Chabat al pouertal a komer pipitas de melon,
A la nothe beven avoua d'azar
Porke el estomaguo se kiere ar[r]embouchar.
Bevamos a la saloud de Samuel Behar.

252. Dia de Shabat mos vamos apasear a la tore blanka.
Vemos vapores, yendo i vingnendo, a Bakthe-Thiflik,
O Aritzou.
Bevamos a la saloud de Jacque Azouz.

275. El golf de Salonique eze el mejor del moundo.
Se pasean kada Shabat:
Los nonos, las nonas i toda la famia.
Bevamos a la saloud de los Nahmias.

50. La avdela se aze kon limon o klavos de kanela ke tiene golor.
Souhaitamos al novio i a la novia: larga vida kon saloud i amor.
Bevamos a la saloud de Samuel Hasson.

Holiday Observance: The Old and the New

403. Pourim, los djidios de Salonique dizen, non bevas vino.
Pessah, dizen: ijos de mis ijos son doz vezes mios.

Eggplant borekas, and cheese pastries.
It is a pleasure to see the family eating these fine things.
Let us drink to the health of Daniel Attias.

242. On Shabbat when the Salonikans come to the synagogue,
They make kiddush with ouzo and filo dough pastries and hardboiled
eggs.
Let us drink to the health of the newlyweds.

199. In Salonika, they make kiddush with kosher wine and a silver cup.
We hope never to be deprived of this tradition.
Everyone around the table, father singing joyously.
Let us drink to the health of all the family.

346. The women sit on Shabbat at the doorway to eat melon seeds.
At night they drink orange-blossom water
Because the stomach needs to be pushed.[119]
Let us drink to the health of Samuel Behar.

252. On the Sabbath day, we go on an outing to the White Tower.[120]
We see boats, coming and going, to Bakthe-Thiflik Beach[121]
Or the Aritzou Beach area.
Let us drink to the health of Jacques Azouz.

275. The gulf of Salonika is the best in the world.
[All] stroll there every Sabbath:
The grandfathers, the grandmothers and the entire family.
Let us drink to the health of the Nahmiases.

50. Havdalah is made with lemon or cinnamon bark, which have an aroma.
We toast the bride and groom: to a long life with health and love.
Let us drink to the health of Samuel Hasson.

Holiday Observance: The Old and the New

403. At Purim, the Jews of Salonika say: Don't drink wine.
At Passover, they say: Children of my children are twice mine.

---

119. Stimulated for digestion.
120. This was the only remaining tower of a number that were constructed in 1430. They were built along the walls of the city, but all were eventually destroyed except the Beyaz Kule, the White Tower (see Michael Molho, *Traditions and Customs,* 135, and photo in chapter 2).
121. Today it is called Neoi Epivates and is opposite the city's seafront (David Kounio, personal communication, February 18, 2009).

Le chana aba be-Jeruchalaim.
Chevoutte: si non viene Chevoutte, non te kites el samar[r]on.
Roch Achana: tiskou lechanim rabotte.
Hanouka: Hanoukia, bayla tou tia hanouka;
Bayla tou vava!
I enviernada bouena.
Bevamos a la saloud de Salomon Morena.

11. El kalendario mos da las datas: Pourim, Pessah i Chevouotte.
Ke son fiestas de kolor, sin mos oulvidar Soukot,
Simha Tora i Hanouka, ke tenemos mouthos balles.
Baylamos sin kedar.
Bevamos a la saloud de Avraam Behar.

263. Primeros de Pessah i oultimos de Soukot:
Pessah la ermozoura del seder, kon toda la famia.
Soukot en kada balkon se ve ouna souka.
Ma la ermozoura del Hatan Torah i Berechit non se pouede deskrevir.[122]
Bevamos a la saloud de los Hatanim ke vamos a tener al avenir.

69. La primavera tenemos flores.
Pessach a la meza las bendezimos.
Chevouotte tenemoz karpouz i melon
I sotlathi travado;
Soukotte mangrana ke eze la frouta de la saizon.
Bevamos a la saloud de Abraam Guerchon.

249. Yom Kipour venden *mitsvot* a la kiyila.
El ke da mas moutho la merka.
Eze grande honor para el merkador.
Bevamos a la saloud de Theodore.

426. Yom Kipour Eliaou ayouda al Hazan Reyna
El dia entero a la Znoak.
Regina i Bouena, kada ouna a sou kama,

---

122. See Michael Molho, *Traditions and Customs*, 213, for a description of the Salonikan customs.

Next year in Jerusalem.

At Shavuot: If Shavuot does not come, don't take off the short fur coat.

At Rosh Hashana: You should merit a long life.

At Hanuka: Hanukah lamp, your aunt dances, Hanuka;

So does your grandmother![123]

And [have] a good winter season.

Let us drink to the health of Salomon Morena.

11. The calendar gives us the dates: Purim, Passover and Shavuot.

These are colorful festivals, without forgetting Sukkot,

Simhat Torah and Hanukkah, when we have many balls.

We dance continuously.

Let us drink to the health of Avraham Behar.

263. The first days of Passover and the last days of Sukkot:[124]

Passover [is] the beauty of the Seder, with the whole family [together].

Sukkot, in every balcony one sees a booth.

But the beauty of those honored to read the Torah cannot be described.[125]

Let us drink to the health of those honored Torah readers who we will
   be having in the future.

69. In spring we have flowers.

[During] Passover we bless them at the table.

[At] Shavuot we have watermelon and melon

And slightly burnt rice pudding;

[At] Sukkot, pomegranate, which is the fruit in season.

Let us drink to the health of Abraham Guerchon.

249. On Yom Kippur they buy the four species at the synagogue.

The one who offers the most buys it.

It is a great honor for the buyer.

Let us drink to the health of Theodore.

426. On Yom Kippur, Eliaou helps Cantor Reyna

The entire day at the Znoak [club].[126]

Regina and Bouena, each one in her bed,

---

123. Regarding this Hanukah expression, see Bunis, *Voices from Jewish Salonika*, 130, 404.

124. Festival of Sukkot, which lasts eight days in the diaspora.

125. She is referring to the reading of the end of Deuteronomy and the beginning of Genesis on the last day of Sukkot called Simhat Torah. See Bunis, *Voices from Jewish Salonika*, 219–22, for descriptions of variations of this custom in different congregations in Salonika.

126. Presumably prayer services were held in the club auditorium on the high holidays.

Meldando el livro ke aparejaron.
Vivamos a la saloud de los Kalderon.

77. Kipour despoues del Tanid, komemos, mos repozamos oun poko.
I toda la famia empesamos azer la souka.
Eze oun plazer de ver los tsiketikos lavoran, trayen los clavos.
Papa loz enclava sin kedar.
Bevamos a la saloud de Salomon Adar.

72. Soukotte las moujeres dizen kada dia la beraha de la loula!
Eze de verlas kon tanto senseritad.
Kouando la ija se kaza, la madre la hize prometer
Ke i eya lo va azer.
Bevamos a la saloud de Ichoua Azriel.

264. Hanouka asendemos hanoukias.
Djougan kartas al profito de la Palestina.
Las organizationes sionistas organizan ballos,
Venden los parmachetes para el Keren Hakayemet.
Bevamos a la saloud de todos los dirijentes.

266. Toubichvat ese la fiesta de las froutas.
Vamos a vijitar a las tias, mezmo si aye louvia.
Bevamos a la saloud de Daniel Rachel i Louna.

312. Pourim eze grande fiesta.
Las moujeres se van a la kama medias mouertas.
El dia azen orejas de Aman[127] i charope de almendra.
Bevamos a la saloud de Moche Amenda.

402. Pourim ese fiesta de alegria.
Las novias, las aresevimos kon plazer,
I las atornamos kon savor de toda las kolores.
Vestimiento de karnavalia, ballos, baylar i reir;
Kantes de Pourim, opereta de Esther.
Aye en todas las kazas i las eskolas.
Bevamos a la saloud de Avraam Sola.

286. Los platos de Pourim son bouenos aresevidos.
Ese alegria kouando se mando a loz parientes o a los amigos.
Bevamos a la saloud de los ke non tienen enemigos.

---

127. "Ears of Haman"; triangular pastries with different fillings.

Reading the book that they prepared.
Let us drink to the health of the Calderons.

77. After the fast on Yom Kippur, we eat, we rest a bit.
Then the whole family begins to erect the booth.
It is a pleasure to see the little ones working away, bringing the nails.
Father nails them in endlessly.
Let us drink to the health of Salomon Adar.

72. [On] Sukkot, the women recite the prayer over the lulav every day!
It is [something] seeing them with such sincerity.
When the daughter marries, her mother makes her promise
That she will continue doing this.
Let us drink to the health of Yehoshua Azriel.

264. On Hanukah we light the candelabrum.
They play card games for the good of Palestine.
The Zionist organizations organize balls,
Sell candles for the Jewish National Fund.
Let us drink to the health of all the administrators.

266. Tu Bi-Shevat is the festival of the fruits.
We are going to visit the aunts, even if it rains.
Let us drink to the health of Daniel, Rachel, and Luna.

312. Purim is a great festival.
The women go to bed half dead.
All day they make Purim pastries and almond syrup.
Let us drink to the health of Moshe Amenda.

402. Purim is a festival of joy.
We receive the sugar dolls with pleasure,
And we send them off with flavors of all of [the] colors.
Outfits for the carnival, balls, to dance and laugh;
Purim songs, the Esther operetta.
There are in all the houses and the schools.
Let us drink to the health of Avraham Sola.

286. The Purim plates are well received.
This is happiness when they are sent to relatives or to friends.
Let us drink to the health of those who do not have enemies.

43. A Salonique, la esfouegra dan regalo de Pourim.
   A laz novias, yadran de perla, o anio de valor o algouna alfinetika
   Ke la merko al basheste viejo.
   La madre de la novia da al yerno ora kon kordon,
   O meguila de oro, o plata, o de tavla
   Segoun la situation.
   Bevamos a la saloud de akeos ke dan kon korason.

248. Pourim se desparte novias[128]
   I a las nignas lez dan bastidor; a loz nignos penina.
   Bevamos a la saloud de Salomon Nahmias.

41. A Salonique en todas las kazas aye livros:
   Arbaa ve estrim i parchemenes de famia
   Sin se oulvidar la meguila ke la meldan Pourim a la kiyila.
   Bevamos a la saloud Yakiel Bar Illal.

340. Pourim meldamos la meguila.
   Las kriatouras kon martios de tabla para akavar aman.
   Atornamoz en kaza a komer doulsoura.
   Kantamos kantiguas de pourim kon alegria.
   Bevamos a la saloud de Eliaou Kattan i toda sou famia.

310. Los Saragosis fiestan Pourim aparte de todos los djidios.
   Azen ballos i desparten doulsoura entre eyos.
   Bevamos a la saloud de Avraam Gaegos.

393. A Salonique, por las mas parte, son grande famias.
   La vestimienta se pasa de ouno a otro.
   Los grandes siempre mouevo.
   Los tsikos asperan Shabat agadol para dezir:
   Oun kon saloud mille doukados.
   Bevamos a la saloud de Alberto Sadok.

313. Shabat agadol todos visten mouevo.
   Viernes el koundouriero traye los kalsados en oun sesto para toda la famia
   I a la servidera tambien.
   Bevamos a la saloud de Daniel Amiel.

---

128. *Las novias* or *novikas* were sugar figures (with lemon and food coloring) shaped like brides as well as like different objects such as clocks, towers, gallows, etc. The Sabbath before Purim was called the Brides' Sabbath, and future brides were given the bride figures. See chapter 2 for details.

43. In Salonika, the mother-in-law gives Purim gifts:
    To the brides, a pearl necklace, or a ring of value or a little pin
    That she bought her in the old section of the market.[129]
    The bride's mother gives the son-in-law a watch with a chain,
    Or a scroll [cover or case] of gold, or silver, or of wood
    According to her financial situation.
    Let us drink to the health of those who give from the heart.

248. On Purim, they distribute bride dolls
    And they give the girls an embroidery ring; the boys [receive] a pen.
    Let us drink to the health of Salomon Nahmias.

41. In Salonika in every house there are books:
    Twenty-four family parchments without counting the Scroll of Esther
    That is read at the synagogue on Purim.
    Let us drink to the health of Yehiel Bar Hillel.

340. On Purim we read the megilla.
    The children have hammers of wood to "finish off" Haman.
    We return home to eat sweets.
    We sing Purim songs happily.
    Let us drink to the health of Eliaou Kattan and his entire family.

310. The Saragossans celebrate Purim separately from all the other Jews.
    They make balls and distribute sweets among themselves.
    Let us drink to the health of Avraham Gaegos.

393. In Salonika, for the most part, families are large.
    Clothing passes from one to another.
    The older ones always get new [clothes].
    The younger ones wait until the Sabbath before Passover in order to say:
    One "kon salud"[130] is worth a thousand ducats.
    Let us drink to the health of Albert Sadok.

313. Everyone wears new clothes on the Sabbath before Passover.
    On Friday the shoemaker brings shoes in a basket for the whole family
    And for the servant as well.
    Let us drink to the health of Daniel Amiel.

---

129. This was where the notion stores were located.

130. This is a special phrase used to wish someone wearing new clothing for the first time good health (Güler Orgun, personal communication, February 26, 2011).

333. Antes de Pessah para Shabat agadol,
Mos treyian los kalsados en oun sesto.
Para toda la famia esa ouna grande alegria.
El padre asentado a la poltrona, mirando las fathas de las kriatouras.
Bevamos a la saloud de Joseph Segoura.

414. Los boyos de afekoumin mos troucheron.
Ese segouro ke en doz dias, ya ese Pessah.
Matza de vino i roskas de raki.
Esto ese ouna grande alegria a Salonique.
Bevamos a la saloud de Alberto Eshkenazi.

415. La matza los proves la toman debaldes.
Los rikos la pagan moutho karo.
Aye matza de makina o de mano
Ke solo la komounitad la vende kon sous manos.
Bevamos a la saloud de Yakiel Mano.

416. La komunitad tiene machguia para azer la matza.
Si la matza non esta etha a nouestra tradition,
Todo so etha aporey sin dolor de korason.
Bevamos a la saloud del machguia Sasson.

417. La ashouka de Pessah viene komo ouna kavesa.
La komunitad la importa, i la desparte a la djouderia.
Eze mouy kara i bien rafinada.
Las moujeres la pezan a la almirez ke parese oro.
Bevamos a la saloud de Sarika Oro.

418. Pessah semos venti i kouatro a la meza.
La Agada se melda en kantando.
Los bokados ese kon alegria.
La koumida ese pinzela freska kon kodredo, ese al sason,
Ke se alegra el korason.
Sin oulvidar Eloenou che ba chamaim i el kavretiko.[131]
Bevamos a la saloud de Daniel Tsiko.

---

131. For a detailed discussion of this song, see Michael Molho, *Traditions and Customs*, 323–28.

333. For the Shabbat before Passover,
   They brought us the shoes in a basket.
   This is great joy for the whole family.
   The father sitting in the armchair, looking at the faces of the children.
   Let us drink to the health of Joseph Segoura.

414. They brought us the pieces of the afikoman.
   It is certain that in two days, it is already Passover.
   Wine matsah[132] and ouzo cookies.
   This is a great celebration for Salonika.
   Let us drink to the health of Albert Eshkenazi.

415. The poor receive matsah gratis.
   The rich pay very dearly.
   There is machine made matsah or hand made
   That only the community sells by itself.
   Let us drink to the health of Yakiel Mano.

416. The community has a supervisor in order to make the matsah.
   If the matsah is not made according to our tradition,
   It is all thrown in to the garbage without heartache.
   Let us drink to the health of the rabbinic supervisor Sasson.

417. The Passover sugar comes [shaped] like a head.
   The community imports it and distributes it to the community.
   It is very expensive and well refined.
   The women mash it with the brass mortar that looks like gold.
   Let us drink to the health of Sarika Oro.

418. At Passover we are twenty-four at the table.
   The Haggadah is read by singing.
   The morsels [of matsah] are [eaten] happily.
   The meal is fresh peas with lamb, being in season,
   Which brings joy to the heart.
   Without forgetting [to sing] "Who Knows One?" and "One Kid."
   Let us drink to the health of Daniel Tsiko.

---

132. There was a tradition to celebrate "Second Passover" on the fourteenth of the month of Iyyar, when wine matsah would be eaten. This was for those who were ill or unable to celebrate the holiday on time.

78. Eze tradition, el vinagre de loz dinim.[133]
Mama los etha al bily; la ija grande la akompagna,
Ke paresen doz prensesas en kampagnas.
Bevamos a la saloud de las ke se akompagnan.

419. Pessah demangnana todas las kriatouras salen a la kaye,
Bien vestidas de blanko, kourdelas a la kavesa.
Las madres al balkon ke paresen prensesas.
Bevamos a la saloud de la famia parente.

76. Pessah tenemoz oun ermizo kavesal
Ke el papa se va asentar a dezir la agada.
Arodeado de sou famia, parese el rey de la djouderia.
Bevamos a la saloud de el papa, mama i toda la famia.

22. Pessah de mangnana el padre i la madre se alevantan temprano
Para moueler la matza ke se mitio en mojo la nothe.
El padre partiendo vouevos; la madre aziendo boumouelos.[134]
Las kriatouras se alevantan kon alegria
A komerlos kon miel o asouka bien fina.
Bevamos a la saloud de Rachel, Julie i Josephina.

157. Pesah los hombres de la famia moz vienen a vijitar.
Vouevos enhamidados[135] aparejamos
Ke estan ethos kon kachkas de sevoya i oun poko de azeyte
I boyidos kon loumbre amakada.
Bevamos a la saloud de Rofel Benaroya.

405. Las moujeres avren [f]oja para Chevouotte para pastel o
Rodanthas de kalavasa rosa.
Mouthos se van en exkurtion para trayer la ley le Moche en sou korason.
Bevamos a la saloud de Mochon Sasson.

209. Chevoutte moz vamos en excurtion a la pounta tsika[136] o al b[o]urako.
Bevamos a la saloud de Pepo Basso.

---

133. Here the "laws" refer to a custom at the Seder related to the Ten Plagues. After the head of the household recites the plagues, he surreptitiously washes his hands in a basin of water, which will miraculously turn into vinegar. Then two women (in this verse, the wife and daughter) dispose of the vinegar (without looking) in the toilet or outhouse (David Kounio, personal communication, February 19, 2009).

134. In Spanish they are called *buñuelos*.

135. *Haminados* are the hardboiled eggs that cook overnight on the Sabbath and holidays, often as part of a stew for the meal after morning services.

136. The Gulf of Thessaloniki forms two semi-peninsulas, the big one and the small one (*la grande i la chika punta*—or, in Turkish, *Karaburnu i Karaburnaki*); (David Kounio, personal communication, February 23, 2009).

78. There is a tradition, the vinegar of the laws.
    Mother throws them in the outhouse; the oldest girl accompanies her.
    They look like two princesses in the countryside.
    Let us drink to the health of those who accompany each other.

419. [On] Passover morning all the children go out into the street,
    Nicely dressed in white, ribbons on their heads,
    The mothers on the balcony who look like princesses.
    Let us drink to the health of the extended family.

76. [On] Passover we have a handsome cushion
    On which father is going to sit to recite the Haggadah.
    Surrounded by his family, he looks like the king of the Jews.
    Let us drink to the health of father, mother and all of the family.

22. On Passover morning the mother and father get up early
    In order to grind the matsah that was soaking all night.
    The father cracking the eggs; the mother making pastries.
    The children wake up cheerfully
    In order to eat them with honey or powdered sugar.
    Let us drink to the health of Rachel, Julie, and Josephina.

157. On Passover the men of the family come to visit us.
    We prepared hardboiled eggs
    Which are made with onion skin and a little bit of olive oil
    And boiled over a low flame.
    Let us drink to the health of Raphael Benaroya.

405. The women knead the filo dough for Shavuot for pastries or
    Rolled cheese pastry (filled) with red pumpkin.
    Many go on an excursion to bring the Law of Moses into their hearts.
    Let us drink to the health of Moshe Sasson.

209. On Shavuot we go on an outing to the small point or the hole.
    Let us drink to the health of Pepo Basso.

51. Beytsinar eze ouna vouerta grande.
Se kamina kilometros i nounka se ve entera.
Chevouotte debacho el arvole mos asentamos kon la mujer i las kriatouras.
Yivamos sestos yenos de koumida,
Sin moz oulvidar el sotlatsi e raki Nahmias.
El golf komo kristal; azemos bagno de mar.
Bevamos a la saloud de Daniel Amar.

150. Ticha be'ave mos asentamos en bacho atomar tanid.
La mama se veste de preto por honor de loz djidios
Ke foueron masakrados a esta dato.
Bevamos a la saloud de David Dassa.

Changes in Tradition, Confrontations with Modernity

339. Antes despoues del Avdela avia fiesta de famia.
Agora se van al cinema o al saler kon amigas.
Los parientes non estan kontente de esta moueva vida
Ke se esta aziendo ipedemia.
Bevamos a la saloud de Rachel i Bienvenida.

167. Antes laz moujeres se ivan al bagno.
El empregado de la grouta lo yevava el obogo.[137]
Agora ese mas fathile.
Tienen valejas ke parese ke se van ayir en viaje.
Bevamos a la saloud de Daniel i Djamila.

396. A Salonique al tiempo del tourko,
Las moujeres non dizian a ningounos kouando estavan hazinas.
Eze yousourin non ese menester ke lo sepa la vezina.
Se mouerian sin tomar melezina.
Bevamos a la saloud de Yakiel Medina.

400. En mi kaza tenemos cabinet de asentar ke non me pouedo ouzar.
El medio bagno me ize cabinet a la tourka.
Sarina mos vino a vijitar.
Me dicho ke yo vine de Bakdad.
Bevamos a la saloud de Eliaou Bakar.

---

137. *Bogo* is from the Turkish *boğmak.*

51. Bes Tsinar[138] is a large garden.
    One can walk for miles and never see its entirety.
    On Shavuot we sit under the tree with the wife and children.
    We bring baskets filled with food
    Without forgetting the rice pudding dessert and the Nahmias ouzo.
    The Gulf [of Salonika] is (clear) like crystal; we take a dip in the sea.
    Let us drink to the health of Daniel Amar.

150. On Tisha B'Av, we sit on the floor and fast.
    Mother wears black in honor of the Jews
    Who were massacred on this date.
    Let us drink to the health of David Dassa.

Changes in Tradition, Confrontations with Modernity

339. In the old days there was a family party after Havdalah.
    Now they go to the movies or out with friends.
    The parents are not happy with this new lifestyle
    That has become an epidemic.
    Let us drink to the health of Rachel and Bienvenida.

167. In the old days the women went to the bath.
    The employee of the office carried a bundle.
    Now it is easier.
    They have suitcases, which makes it seem like they are going on a trip.
    Let us drink to the health of Daniel and Jamila.

396. In Salonika at the time of the Turks,
    The women did not tell anyone when they were sick.
    It is not necessary for the neighbor to know of these sufferings.
    They died without taking medicine.
    Let us drink to the health of Yehiel Medina.

400. In my house we have a toilet for sitting that I cannot get used to.
    I made the half bathroom into a Turkish-style bathroom.[139]
    Sarina came to visit us.
    She told me that I came from Baghdad.
    Let us drink to the health of Eliaou Bakar.

---

138. *Beşçınar* literally means "five sycamore trees."
139. This means "without a basin."

179. Sarika se va ayir a viajar.
    Dizen ke se va ayir kon aeroplane.
    Yo si me souvo en este pachariko, me vo a sourtir al pantaloniko.
    Bevamos a la saloud de Alberto Tsiko.

349. Antes eskrevian kon lettras de merouba.
    Agora eskriven kon makinas de eskrevir.
    Las eskolas estan yenas para ambezar este chechit.
    Bevamos a la saloud de Liza Charki.

224. A Salonique en kada balkon aye oun tiesto de amber.
    La kolor amario, el vouezmo ke aranka el korason.
    Bevamos a la saloud de Daniel Sasson.

364. Antes bezavan la mano al padre.
    Tenian barva i las kriatouras se pountsavan.[140]
    Agora bien arapados se ethan al garon
    I los abrasan de korason.
    Bevamos a la saloud de Alice Bensasson.

365. Agora le bezan la mano al padre solo Pessah.
    El padre lez mete sou mano a la kavesa.
    Loz bendize de korason.
    Les souhouta ke non tengan nounka dolor.
    Bevamos a la saloud de Michelle Sasson.

410. Las moujeres se vestieron a la franka.
    Solo las nonas visten antari i kofia kon yadran de perla.
    Los hombre se araparon la barva i el mostacho
    I visten koundourias de loustrin ke aze kri kri.
    Bevamos a la saloud de Ovadia Coumeri.

366. Al tiempo todos los djidios Shabat se ivan a pasear a la tore blanka
    Kon faldoukeras yenas de pepitas de mellon.
    Agora ese djouventud ke se va
    A enkontrar konesidos o amigos.
    Bevamos a la saloud de Rachel i Sarina.

367. El tiempo del Tourko la tore blanka era prisión.
    Agora eze para loz skouts ke azen exposition.

---

140. *Punchaban* in Ladino.

179. Sarika is going to travel.
They say that she will be going by airplane.
If I get on this little bird, I am going to soil my pants.
Let us drink to the health of Alberto Chico.

349. In the old days they wrote with square letters.
Now they write with typewriters.
The schools are filled in order to study this type of thing.
Let us drink to the health of Liza Charki.

224. In Salonika in each balcony there is a clay planter with amber.
Yellow in color, the smell tears at the heart.
Let us drink to the health of Daniel Sasson.

364. In the old days they kissed the father's hand.
They had beards and the children got pricked by it.
Now they [the fathers] are well shaved
And they [the children] embrace them heartily.[141]
Let us drink to the health of Alice Bensasson.

365. Now they kiss the father's hand only on Passover.
The father places his hand on the head.
He blesses them from his heart.
He wishes [for] them never to suffer.
Let us drink to the health of Michelle Sasson.

410. The women dressed European-style.
Only the grandmothers wear the robe and headdress with a pearl necklace.
The men shaved their beard[s] and mustache[s]
And wear patent leather shoes that creak.
Let us drink to the health of Ovadia Coumeri.

366. Once all the Jews went strolling on the Sabbath to the White Tower
With pockets filled with melon seeds.
Now it is the youth that goes
To meet acquaintances or friends.
Let us drink to the health of Rachel and Sarina.

367. During Turkish rule, the White Tower was a prison.
Now it is for the Scouts who put together exhibitions.

---

141. As Güler Orgun suggested, they now can throw their arms around their father's necks and embrace them with all their hearts (personal communication, February 23, 2009).

Venden kozas de art ke loz azen eyos mezmos
Para abedouwar[142] tsiketikos.
Bevamos a la saloud de Moche Tsiko.

253. Antes azian bodas kon tsalguin,
    I talamo de flores.
    Agora eze solo kiduchim.
    Bevamos a la saloud de Daniel Hakim.

311. Todos suiven la moda.
    El bet din ordeno a los Hakamim
    Ke se troken la djo[u]ben a las tokas.
    Bevamos a la saloud de Eliaou Saporta.

331. El hût esta pasando de moda; los Sarfattys inda lo sonan.
    Avrimos pouertas i ventanas
    Kouando Eliaou sona las romansas o sharkis.
    Bevamos a la saloud de Albert Shaki.

332. Antes kouziamos solo a la mano.
    Agora Singer mos troucho makinas kon kar(r)o.
    Las chastres estan bendiziendo al dio,
    Ke eskapan sou lavoro a la ouna doz.
    Bevamos a la saloud de Avraam Sadok.

230. A Salonique avia karosas; agora aye taxis.
    Bevamos a la saloud de los Kabelis.

413. Antes las kriatouras venian de la eskola,
    Koumian de kindi i se asentavan a eskrevir.
    Agora kon este kouti, se asentan a sentir ke lo yaman radio a Salonique.
    Bevamos a la saloud de laz madres
    Ke non poueden mas engloutir.

388. A Salonique tenemos agora avoua de la compagnia.
    Aye kontor para ver kouanto konsumimos.
    Viene el kouento i al pounto pagamos.
    Si non, la avoua mos van akortar.
    Bevamos a la saloud de Acher Behar.

303. Antes non se azia kontrato; era solo dar la mano.
    Agora van el notario i signan kon el lape.
    Bevamos a la saloud de Daniel Amar.

---

142. *Abediguar* in Ladino.

They sell artistic things that they make themselves
To help the little ones.
Let us drink to the health of Moshe Tsiko.

253. In the old days they made weddings with a Turkish band
And a wedding canopy of flowers.
Now there is just the ceremony.
Let us drink to the health of Daniel Hakim.

311. Everyone follows the latest style.
The Jewish court ordered the rabbis
To change their cassocks to the turbans.[143]
Let us drink to the health of Eliaou Saporta.

331. The oud is going out of style; the Sarfattys still play it.
We open doors and windows
When Eliaou plays the ballads or slow oriental tunes.
Let us drink to the health of Albert Shaki.

332. In the old days we used to sew only by hand.
Now Singer brought us machines with wheels.
The dressmakers are blessing God,
For they can finish their work at one [or] two.
Let us drink to the health of Avraham Sadok.

230. In Salonika there were carriages; now there are taxis.
Let us drink to the health of the Kabelis.

413. In the old days the children came home from school,
Ate the afternoon meal and sat themselves down to write.
Now with this box, they sit down to listen to what is called Radio Salonika.
Let us drink to the health of the mothers
Who are not able to swallow any more.

388. In Salonika we now have water from the [water] company.
There is a meter in order to see how much we consume.
The bill comes and we pay it promptly.
If not, they are going to cut off our water.
Let us drink to the health of Asher Behar.

303. In the old days there was no contract; it was only a handshake.
Now the notary comes and one signs with a pen.
Let us drink to the health of Daniel Amar.

---

143. These were worn by the Muslim religious leaders, the imams.

304. Ez tradition ke la madre de la novia vouadre la ketouba.
Agora kon la Eforia, la ketouba non vale ni ouna lira.
Bevamos a la saloud de Shimon i toda la kompagnia.

113. Antes mos kaentavamos
Kon fogarero brazero de kovre kolor de oro
I todos mos asentavamos al deredor.
Despoues foue la soba kon legna i la kamareta entera esta kaente.
Agora tenemos salamandre en medio de la kaza.
Se asiende Hanouka; la amatamos Pessah.
Kaenta la kaza ma!
La ermozoura del fogarero non se pouede remplasar.
Bevamos a la saloud de Samuel Behar.

406. Antes mos areloumbravamos kon gaz.
Agora tenemos electricita; el fiero era kon karvon.
Agora metez la prize i ya se kaento.
Bevamos a la saloud de Leon Botton.

345. Antes teniamos kombidador;[144] agora se manda invitation.
Moutha djente tienen theleophone; avlan kon loz maridos.
Kouantas vezes picho oye.
Bevamos a la saloud de Aaron.

379. Antes las nignas se ivan a las après-midis
De las sosietas sionistas a baylar.
Agora se van i al dansing.
Isaac Pitilon eze el djazbonista.
Aze ouna doubara para romper los ouyidos.
Bevamos a la saloud de Leon Almoznino.

385. Mos fouemos al cinema kon Djamila i Tamar.
Se amatava i asendia i todo no se via.
Bevamos a la saloud de Rachel i Bienvenida.

319. Mi nouera non kiere kriatouras.
Kiere salon i komedor i glasiera a la kouzina.
Bevamos a la saloud de estas vazias.

---

144. The list of invitees was given to the *combibador,* who went from house to house, or courtyard to courtyard, calling out the name of those invited and all the details of the wedding. In the nineteenth century, women were the official announcers.

304. It is a tradition that the mother of the bride keeps the ketubah.
    Now with the tax collectors, the ketubah isn't worth a nickel.
    Let us drink to the health of Shimon and the whole company.

113. In the old days we used to warm ourselves
    With a coal-burning copper brazier, the color of gold,
    And all of us sat around it.
    Afterwards there was a wood-burning stove and the whole room is warm.
    Now we have a stove with continuous fire in the middle of the house.
    It is lit on Hanukah; we extinguish it on Passover.
    It warms the whole house, but!
        The beauty of the brazier cannot be replaced.
    Let us drink to the health of Samuel Behar.

406. In the old days we would illuminate the house with gas.
    Now we have electricity; the iron was heated with coal.
    Now you plug it in and it is already hot.
    Let us drink to the health of Leon Botton.

345. In the old days we had an invitation announcer; now one sends invitations.
    Many people have telephones; they talk with their husbands.
    How many times did he piss today?
    Let us drink to the health of Aron.

379. In the old days the girls went to the afternoon gatherings
    Of the Zionist society in order to dance.
    Now they go to dance halls.[145]
    Isaac Pitilon is the jazz band musician.
    He makes a racket that destroys the ears.
    Let us drink to the health of Leon Almosnino.

385. We went to the cinema with Djamila and Tamar.
    The lights went on and off and everything was not seen.[146]
    Let us drink to the health of Rachel and Bienvenida.

319. My daughter-in-law doesn't want children.
    She wants a living room and a dining room and a refrigerator in the
        kitchen.
    Let us drink to the health of these [female] fools.

---

145. "*Le Dancing*" were dance halls (Güler Orgun, personal communication, February 8, 2009).
146. She is implying that it was an opportunity for misbehavior.

262. En esta generation todos kieren salir hazan.
    Non se kieren yir al servisio militar.
    Bevamos a la saloud de los ke van a la prima tefila.

The Dictates of Fashion

38. Oye todo eze a la moda.
    Antes madres azian kouklas de handrajo.
    Las kriatouras djougavan mejor.
    Agora si se lez roumpio el braso o la patha, yoran sin apozar.
    Bevamos a la saloud de Haim Lazar.

251. Las nignas se bo[y]adean las ougnas komo las maminas.
    La diferensia ese ke lo yaman manicure.
    Bevamos a la saloud de Signor Manzour.

356. Se ouze tsantas de plata para las moujeres
    Ke visten a la franka, manias a los doz brasos, orejales elouengosos,
    Kon anio en kada dedo.
    Bevamos a la saloud de Avraam Toledo.

290. Laz rikas merkan biankeria de ande karadimo seda fina
    I rekamo excluzivo i tambien fino.
    Bevamos a la saloud de los padres ke tiene ijas.

359. Mi moujer se merko tsapeo mouevo d'ande Eujenie,
    Ke se va doz vezes el agno a Paris.
    Traye modeles de valor kon vello ke lo yaman voil.
    Parese komo ouna tourka kon feredje[147] i non vale ni oun penez.
    Bevamos a la saloud de Samuel Perez.

82. Los ke kieren amostrar
    Se asentan al size[148] de la karosa
    Para ke todos los veyan ke tiene noueva Fez, antari de estofa.
    Bevamos a la saloud de David Saporta.

---

147. The Turkish women wore the *feradje,* which included a head cover of the same material and also covered their faces with a veil when appearing in the street. This term, the *ferace,* is a kind of overall formerly worn by Turkish women when they went out. Bouena refers both to veils and to the outer clothing (Güler Orgun, personal communication, March 1 and 3, 2011). See also copla 66.

148. This should be *sis* (Yehuda Tsvi, personal communication, February 19, 2009). This is from the expression *asentarse al sis,* "to sit on the side of the coach."

262. In this generation everyone wants to be a cantor.
     No one wants to go to military service.
     Let us drink to the health of those who go to morning prayers.

The Dictates of Fashion

38. Today everything is according to the latest style.
    In the old days mothers used to make rag dolls.
    The little girls played better.
    Now if they break an arm or leg, they cry endlessly.
    Let us drink to the health of Haim Lazar.

251. The girls paint their fingernails like their mommies [do].
     The difference is that they [the latter] call it a manicure.
     Let us drink to the health of Mr. Mansour.

356. It is the fashion to have silver handbags for women
     Who dress European style, bracelets on both arms, long earrings,
     With a ring on every finger.
     Let us drink to the health of Avraham Toledo.

290. The rich women buy linens from Karadimo's fine silk
     And exclusive embroidery and [which is] also fine.
     Let us drink to the health of the fathers who have daughters.

359. My wife bought a new hat at Eugenie's,
     Who goes twice a year to Paris.
     She brings quality samples with a veil that they call a "voile."
     She looks like a Turkish woman with her *ferace* and it isn't worth a penny.
     Let us drink to the health of Samuel Perez.

82. Those who like to show themselves off
    Sit on the coachman's seat of the carriage
    So that everyone can see that they have a new Fez or a robe of silk.
    Let us drink to the health of David Saporta.

431. A Salonique se ouza pliser.
Kon el ayre del vardar[149] se les alevanta el faldar.
Ese kepazelik, tambien maskaralik.
Ese vrouensa de verlas, ma! Eyas se alegran.
Bevamos a la saloud de los ke tienen pasensia.

132. Antes las godras eran ermozas.
Agora se meten korse para se estrethar el bel.
Los Sarfattys lo enventaron; modeles trayen de Paris.
Todas estan en kadenas kouando se meten esta koza estretha.
Bevamos a la saloud de Estreia.

258. Madame Koretz aze tsai para las damas.
Estan pensando koualo se van a meter.
Bevamos a la saloud de Acher Abravanel.

361. A Salonique se ouza jupe-kulotte
Para excurtion o asentar al balkon.
Ese konfortable, i non se ve el pantalon.
Bevamos a la saloud de Eleonora Matalon ke lo envento.

44. Antes las moujeres a Salonique vestian bragas de makatli.
Agora visten pantalones kon dentela o kulotes de seda, ethas de birchim.
Los hombres lavoran komo aznos para poueder dar a sou moujer i sous ijas
Todo lo ke sale de nouevo i visten las vezinas.
Bevamos a la saloud de Alegra kon toda sou famia.

244. Imprimero se yamava Estherina, despoues se troko Esthela.
Agora se yama Esther.
Bevamos a la saloud de la esfouegra.

272. Mi moujer antes se yamava Sarah; agora se yama Sarina.
Kiere servidera para se repozar todo el dia,
Moujer para la kolada de la famia.
Bevamos a la saloud de todas las djoudias.

250. Las nignas se kortaron los kaveyos.
Paresen oun hombre sin pantalon.
Bevamos a la saloud del Dr. Matalon.

---

149. Vardar is the Serbian name for the river that runs from Yugoslavia to the Gulf of Thessaloniki.

431. In Salonika they use pleats.
    With the breeze of Vardar it lifts the petticoat.
    This is a degradation, also a disgrace.
    It is an embarrassment to see them, but! They [females] are happy.
    Let us drink to the health of those who have patience.

132. In the old days, the heavy women were [considered] beautiful.
    Now they wear a corset to pull in their waists.
    The Sarfattys invented it; they bring samples from Paris.
    Everyone is in chains when they put on this tight thing.
    Let us drink to the health of Estrella.

258. Mrs. Koretz makes tea for the ladies.
    They are thinking about what they are going to wear.
    Let us drink to the health of Asher Abravanel.

361. In Salonika one uses the divided skirt
    For picnics or to sit on the balcony.
    It is comfortable and no one sees the underpants.
    Let us drink to the health of Eleonora Matalon who created it.

44. The women of Salonika used to wear wide pants of rough cotton.
    Now they wear pants with lace or culottes of silk, made of silk thread.
    The men work like dogs in order to give their wives and their daughters
    Everything that is of the latest style and is worn by the [female] neighbors.
    Let us drink to the health of Alegra with her entire family.

244. At first, she was called Estherina, then she switched to Esthela.
    Now she is called Esther.
    Let us drink to the health of the mother-in-law.

272. My wife used to be called Sarah; now she's called Sarina.
    She wants a maidservant so that she can rest all day,
    A woman for [doing] the family's laundry.
    Let us drink to the health of all the Jewish women.

250. The girls cut their hair.
    They look like men without pants.
    Bevamos a la saloud de Dr. Matalon.

347. Antes las moujeres tenian kaveyos elouengos ke esto era ermozoura.
Agora se ar[r]apan a la garçon ke paresen krevadoura.[150]
Visten pantalon i soultouka de hombre i pedrieron la ermozoura.
Bevamos a la saloud de Michel Segoura.

58. Laz moujeres se kortaron los kaveyos.
Mouthas de eyas dan goumito de verlas;
I manzia de las ke tenian grande koda
Ke paresia sirma para rekamar la koltha.
Bevamos a la saloud de Loutha ke non salio loka.

59. Las moujeres salieron lokas.
Todas se estan vistiendo a la franka, venden el yadran
I la podya para se merkar kandrajos sin kedar.
Ese las chastras laz ganadas,
Non kedan ni oun dia sin djornal.
Bevamos a la saloud de estas djokas.

148. Las nignas son elegantes, trokan la garnetoura del vestido,
Koles i dentella i rekamos finos ke salen aver todos los vezinos.
Bevamos a la saloud de Daniel Tsimino.

174. Las moujeres de las kampagnas visten lourginon.
Se lo meten kon kadena de oro komo kordon.
Ven mejor kon sous ojos, ma se lo meten para amostrar
I se destingar, ma! Ningounos lez dizen ke non tiene savor.
Bevamos a la saloud de Rachel Amon.

149. Se ouza orejales pretos.
Las moujeres vesten ke paresen en louyto.
Mi fija los viste a la kaye.
Se los kita a la pouerta antes de entrar en kaza.
Bevamos a la saloud de las
Ke sienten al marido kouando se kazan.

186. Todas kieren estar a la moda.
Ma! Charpas a la kavesa non se meten,
Mas tsapeos grandes ke parese oun table
I oun paradi[s] para lo engrasiar.
Parese el vendedor de la mala.
Bevamos a la saloud de Nehama Mallak.

---

150. *Krevadura* is literally a "hernia" or "bulge."

347. In the old days, the women had long hair that was beautiful to see.
     Today they have it cut like a boy and it looks awful.
     They wear pants and men's short jackets and have lost their beauty.
     Let us drink to the health of Michel Segoura.

 58. The women cut their hair [off].
     Seeing many of them makes one want to retch;
     And even worse for those that had long ponytails
     That looked like gold threads for embroidering quilts.
     Let us drink to the health of Lutha, who did not go crazy.

 59. The women went crazy.
     All of them are dressing European style, selling necklaces
     And fancy embroidered aprons in order to buy rags nonstop.
     It is the seamstresses [who are] the profiteers,
     [Who] never remain even one day without a day's wages.
     Let us drink to the health of these fools.

148. The girls are elegant, changing the accessories of their clothes,
     Collars and lace and fine brocades which all the neighbors come out
          to see.
     Let us drink to the health of Daniel Tsimino.

174. The women in the countryside don pince-nez.
     They wear it with a gold chain like a cord.
     They see better with their eyes, but! They put it on to show off
     And to stand out, but no one tells them that it is not nice.
     Let us drink to the health of Rachel Amon.

149. Black earrings are fashionable.
     The women wear[ing them] look like they are in mourning.
     My daughter wears them in the street.
     She takes them off at the door before entering the house.
     Let us drink to the health of those
     Who listen to their husbands when they get married.

186. Everyone wants to be fashionable.
     They don't wear scarves on their heads,
     But! Big hats that look like a tray
     And [the feather of] a bird of paradise to make it graceful.
     It looks like the street seller.
     Let us drink to the health of Nehama Mallak.

152. El bachiste viejo era de loz Tourkos.
 Aye magazenes de louso, kozas ethas de mano,
 Fina pechtemal para el bagno.
 Bevamos a la saloud de Daniel Massarano.

155. En Komotini aye mouthos djudios rikos.
 Vienen a Salonique a se vestir ande Eujeni.
 Merkan todos los modeles.
 Pagan el do[u]pio para ke non loz vendan a ningounos.
 Bevamos a la saloud de las ke saven azer louso.

219. Vestiamos fez; mos vino tsapeo.
 Bevamos a la saloud de Eleonora Serrero.

66. Las tourkas visten feredje.
 Toman i ougnas[151] koreladas.
 Las kazas son adientro de oun kourtijo i sin ventanas.
 Laz moujeres mouestras tienen balkones para la kaye,
 Moumi[152] i antari i kirim[153] de Silvi.
 Bevamos a la saloud de Abraam Levy.

343. Kouando los Shakis viajan, ese solo kon wagon lit.
 Van a Paris o a Londra para desmersar a vestir.
 La djente los miran para saver koualo eze la moda.
 Bevamos a la saloud de Haim Sotta.

122. Se ouza vestidos trikotados.
 Todos kouriendo a merkar lana ande Saltiel, Tsimino o Halegua.
 Todos tienen magazin yenos.
 Mos ambezan mouevos pountos.
 Mos asentamos a trikotar de dia i de noche
 Para [e]skapar la prima antes ke la otra lo vista.
 Bevamos a la saloud de Daniel Ventoura.

Nationalism

133. Los magazenes de los djidios empesaron a avrir el chabat.
 Ma! Non viene el balabay.
 Toman impiegados gregos para los remplasar.

---

151. *Unyas* in Ladino.

152. This is a gauze square with embroidery or beads at the edges; it is worn on the hair at home.

153. Or *kilim;* see the glossary.

152. The old bazaar belonged to the Turks.
     There are elegant stores, things made by hand,
     Even towels for the bath.[154]
     Let us drink to the health of Daniel Massarano.

155. In Comotini there are many wealthy Jews.
     They come to Salonika to buy clothes at Eugenie's.
     They buy all the models.
     They pay double so that they do not sell them to anyone else.
     Let us drink to the health of those who know how to dress elegantly.

219. We used to wear the fez; now we have the hat.
     Let us drink to the health of Eleonora Serrero.

66. The Turkish women wear an outer layer of clothing.[155]
    They take red fingernails.
    The houses are inside a courtyard and without windows.
    Our women have balconies facing the street,
    The chevesse and robe and a fur coat by Silvi.
    Let us drink to the health of Avraham Levy.

343. When the Shakis travel, it is only by sleeper.
     They go to Paris or to London to go shopping for clothes.
     Everyone watches them in order to know what the fashion is.
     Let us drink to the health of Haim Sotta.

122. One uses knit clothes.
     Everyone runs to buy yarn at Saltiel, Tsimino, or Halegua.
     All of them have well-stocked stores.
     They teach us new stitches.
     We sit knitting day and night
     In order to finish first before the other one wears it.
     Let us drink to the health of Daniel Ventura.

Nationalism

133. The Jewish stores began to open on the Sabbath.
     But! The owner does not come.
     They use Greek employees to replace them.

---

154. These special towels were wrapped around the body, like those used in saunas.

155. See copla 359, above, for details concerning this outer layer of women's clothing.

Komo aye moutha konkerensia,
son ouvligados de dechar la pouerta avierta.
Bevamos a la saloud de Samuel Parente.

6. A la askierlik azemos poria.
No tengo tiempo de pensar a mi kerida.
Te djouro ke me se mitio meoyo
En kontando los dias ke va a tomar el apouliterio.[156]
Bevamos a la saloud de los askieres ke estamos poudridos.

103. Salomon Alalouf eze officier de reserva de la armada grega.
Non save ke sentir; non se pouede djousgar al amigo.
Siente, Salomon, mi madre dizia,
Non agas al malo ni mersed ni grado.[157]
Esto foue ouna bouena lision para mi,
Ke kreyites al malo i non a los faktos.
Por segouro ke tou moujer la va a entender ke ize sakrifisio
Para ke non vos peleyech i ke vos kazech.
Bevamos a la saloud de los Saltiels.

306. Las moujeres estamoz trikotando kalsas
Para kaentar mouestros mansevos ke estan gareando.
Bevamos a la saloud de Avraam Toledano.

398. Eliaou Sarfatty se foue al askierlik.
Joseph Nahmouly le izo uniforma kaki.
En primero estouvo i peresia para oun officier.
Al segoundo dia le dicho: Non pouedes lavorar para mi.
Estas vestido mejor de mi.
Le dio regalo oun vestido al oficier.
Nahmouly lo izo otras ves.
Bevamos a la saloud de Avraam Abravanel.

425. Eliaou ese soldado.
A Yedi Koule esta beileando.
Vido pasar ouna hombra de la grande tore.

---

156. This term comes from the Greek *apolitirio.*

157. *Mersed* is a term to address an honored person—e.g., *Su Mersed;* likewise, *grado* can be a title of honor (Yehuda Hatsvi, personal communication, February 22, 2009).

Since there is a lot of competition,
    they are obliged to leave the door open.
Let us drink to the health of Samuel Parente.

6. In our military service we have to march.
    I don't have time to think of my beloved.
    I swear to you that I am losing my mind
    By counting the days until I am going to get the certificate of discharge.
    Let us drink to the health of us soldiers, for we are fed up.[158]

103. Salomon Alalouf is a reserve officer in the Greek army.
    He does not know what to feel, [but] one cannot judge one's friend.
    Listen, Salomon, my mother used to say,
    Have neither mercy nor sympathy for an evil person.[159]
    This was a good lesson for me,
    That you believed the evil person and not the facts.
    Surely your wife will understand that I made a sacrifice
    So that you would not quarrel and that you got married.
    Let us drink to the health of the Saltiels.

306. We, the women are knitting socks
    To warm up our young men who are fighting.
    Let us drink to the health of Avraham Toledano.

398. Eliaou Sarfatty went to military service.
    Joseph Nahmouly made him a khaki uniform.
    On the first day[160] it looked as though it was for an officer.
    On the second day he[161] told him: "You can't work for me.
    You are dressed better than I am."
    He gifted the clothes to an officer.
    Nahmouly made it again.[162]
    Let us drink to the health of Avraham Abravanel.

425. Eliaou is a soldier.
    He is fighting in Yedi Kule.[163]
    He saw a shadow pass by the great tower.

---

158. Literally, "rotten."

159. This proverb instructs one to ignore bad people, not to give them what they do not deserve (Yehuda Hatsvi, personal communication, February 22, 2009).

160. When he went there.

161. His officer.

162. A less elegant uniform was made that was more appropriate for a soldier.

163. This was a prison from Ottoman times located just outside the city walls.

Dicho mouthas vezes: Alt!

La hombra siempre kaminando.

Tiro; la hombra kayo.

Tomaron feneles para ver ke prizoniero se esta fouyendo.

Pasaron la nothada en mirando.

Ese solo a la magnana ke toparon oun gato mouerto.

Bevamos a la saloud de Eliaou ke se espanto en matando oun gato.

173. Eliaou se foue soldado; a boukia lo mandaron.

Estouvo ferido en gareando; al hospital lo mandaron.

Estouvo mouy hazino; non teniamos novedades.

Todos loz vezinos dezian ke se mourio.

Mozotros deziamos ke esta biva i sano i va atornar a Salonique.

Al mouelino foue aver los haverim kouando atorno.

Non topo ni oun grano de trigo.

Todo se arovaron porke lez paresio ke non va atornar.

Eliaou loz arojo; kon ardor lavoro.

Despoues de ounos kouantos agnos Eliaou tenia mas de lo ke decho.

Moz tomo bouena kaza kon salon i komedor,

Vestimienta la mejor para mi i Regina.

Bevamos a la saloud de Eliaou ke reucho.

358. Los varsanos tienen pharmasia a todos los karties de Salonique.

Tenian diplome tourkia.

Agora kon laz leyes gregas,

Foueron ovligados de tomar haver grego ke tiene papel grego.

Tienen milizinas i parfumes sin kontar.

El otro sin meter oun penes se izo balabay.

Bevamos a la saloud de Hadji Zakay.

139. Recanati i Benruby son ichbeteredjis.[164]

Estoudiaron a la idadier; avokato salieron.

El grego vino; el diplome no lez valio.

La tourkia los demando ke a Estambol se foueron.

Non kijeron kitar Salonique.

Fina ke oun dia entraron en politika.

Touvieron moy reouchida; foueron respectados de la djouderia.

Kouando kemaron el fobourgo Kambel se izieron bezer.

---

164. In the Turkish world, these are facilitators (*bitirici*) who maneuver via bribes.

He called out many times: Halt!
The shadow kept walking.
He shot; the shadow fell.
They took lanterns to see which prisoner is fleeing,
They passed the night watching.
It was only in the morning when they discovered a dead cat.
Let us drink to the health of Eliaou who was scared by killing a cat.

173. Eliaou became a soldier; they sent him to Bouquia.[165]
    He was wounded while fighting; they sent him to the hospital.
    He was very ill; we had no news.
    All the neighbors said that he died;
    We said that he's alive and well and that he's going to return to Salonika.
    He went to the mill to see his associates when he returned.
    He didn't find even a grain of wheat [there].
    They robbed everything because they thought that he wouldn't return.
    Eliaou threw them out; he worked hard.
    After a few years Eliaou had more than what he had left behind.
    He got us a good house with a living room and a dining room,
    The best clothes for me and Regina.
    Let us drink to the health of Eliaou who succeeded.

358. The Varsanos have pharmacies in all the neighborhoods of Salonika.
    They had a Turkish diploma.
    Now with the Greek laws,
    They were obliged to have a Greek partner who has Greek papers.
    They have countless amounts of medicines and perfumes.
    The other, without putting in a penny, became a proprietor.
    Let us drink to the health of Hadji Zakay.

139. Recanati and Benruby are middlemen.
    They studied at the idadier;[166] they graduated as lawyers.
    The Greeks came; their diploma was not valid.
    The Turks asked them to go to Istanbul.
    They did not want to leave Salonika.
    Until one day they entered politics.
    They were very successful; they were respected by the community.
    When they burned the Campbell suburb they became exasperated.

---

165. Bouquia is in northwestern Morocco.
166. *Idadi* is a Turkish lycée, or state-supported high school.

A Paris se foueron i estan mouy bien.
Bevamos a la saloud de Rachel Regina i Bienvenida.

107. Kon la bilidier, non tengan alechek.[167]
Dale lo ke demandan porke non eze chelit.[168]
Eyos van a ganar mezmo si tienes razon.
Te va kostar el doupio de lo ke te demando.
Bevamos a la saloud de Leon Botton.

344. Dos djidios foueron matados i enterados en chabat,
Akuzados de kortar el filo del thelegraphe.
Touvieron la grasia,
Ma! Oun antisemithe vouadro el telegrapho a la posta.
Solo al otro dia se soupo ke eran inosentes.
Foue oun loyto para loz djidios de Salonique
Ke la prima vez
Ke se vido djoudiria kondanada.
Arogamos ke esto ke non se repete en nouestra sivdad.

321. Los djidios estan imigrando a Palestina o en Françia.
De kouando Metaxas formo la neolea,
Ke todos se estan espantando.
Si tienes mil liras, al pounto tomas permi
Para te yir a mouestra tierra santa.
Bevamos a la saloud de la famias ke arivaron oye a Haifa.

322. A Salonique eze moutho la moda de azer mariage blanc
I aporfijar ijos.
Ese la sola manera de se yir a Palestina.
Bevamos a la saloud de Alberto Medina.

320. Metaxas organizo la djouventoud en todas las eskolas.
Ordeno ke los djidios non poueden vestir uniforma.
Las kriatouras mouestras vienen yorando
Ke non visten kravata i kamisa komo toda la clasa.
Bevamos a la saloud de Rahel Sarina i Adassa.

317. Al porto de Salonique lavoravan moutha djouderia.
Oun dia se foueron todos a Palestina a Haifa.
Dezbarkan los vapores ki vienen.

---

167. *Ilişki* in Turkish.
168. Yehuda Hatsvi explained that *shilit* is "a comical situation," but I have not yet found the etymology of this word (personal communication, March 6, 2011).

They went to Paris and are very well.
Let us drink to the health of Rachel, Regina, and Bienvenida.

107. With the Municipality, do not have any relations.[169]
   Give them what they want because this is no joke.
   They are going to win even if you are right.
   It will cost you twice as much as was asked of you.
   Let us drink to the health of Leon Botton.

344. Two Jews were killed and buried on Shabbat,
   Accused of cutting the telegraph wire.
   They received a pardon,
   But! An antisemite hid the telegram in the post office.
   Only the other day was it known that they were innocent.
   It was a day of mourning for the Jews of Salonika
   Because it was the first time
   That they saw the Jewish community condemned.
   We pray that this will not repeat itself in our city.

321. The Jews are immigrating to Palestine or to France.
   Since Metaxas formed the new law,
   [So] that everyone is afraid.
   If you have a thousand liras, immediately you have a permit
   To go to our Holy Land.
   Let us drink to the health of the families that arrived today in Haifa.

322. In Salonika it is very fashionable to make a marriage of convenience
   And adopt children.[170]
   It is the only way to go to Palestine.
   Let us drink to the health of Alberto Medina.

320. Metaxas organized the youth in all the schools.
   He decreed that the Jews[171] cannot wear [school] uniforms.
   Our children come crying
   That they can't wear a tie and shirt like everyone else in the class.
   Let us drink to the health of Rachel, Sarina, and Hadassah.

317. Many Jews worked in the port of Salonika.
   One day they all went to Palestine, to Haifa.
   They unload the ships that come.

---

169. That is, do not have anything to do with them.
170. The marriage is fictitious, allowing them to claim to have children.
171. Jewish students.

El porto de Tel Aviv se avrio, grasias a esta djouderia.
Bevamos a la saloud de esta djouderia.

227. Ay dos mil agnos ke estamos asperando el estado de Israel.
Agora kon la declaration Balfour,
Ese por segouro ke no vamos a asperar mas.
Bevamos a la saloud de mama i papa.

229. Mi madre enbivdo kouando eramos tsikos.
Mos mando a la eskola i mos ambezo koualo ese el sionizmo.
Bevamos a la saloud de todas las bivdas djoudias.

285. Loz djidios de Salonique merkan chekalim
Para poueder votar para loz sionistas general o loz revizionistas.
Bevamos a la saloud de los derijentes de estas grandes famias.

420. A Salonique tenemos mouthas organisationes sionistas:
La J. J., Theodore Hertzel, el Betar, Misrachi.
Agora tenemos la Tel Aviv.
Vital Avayou se okoupo de la formar.
Bevamos a la saloud de estos komitatos
Ke arekojen para Naalal.

421. Kada djidio a Salonique eze miembro de ouna sosieta sionista
En sou milieu o en sou kartier.
Solo el Keren Hayisod eze para los rikos.
Arekojen grandes soumas para Palestina.
Bevamos a la saloud de Rafael Medina.

17. Richon le Sion las primas vignas en Palestina.
Los Rocheld izieron esto possible.
Nounka se oulvidaron ke son djudios.
Lo amostran en kada okazion.
Bevamos a la saloud de Samuel Sion.

10. A Palestina se fraguouo oun mochav para los Sepharadim.
Tsour Moche se yama.
La mayorita son de Salonique.
El Keren Hakayemet les arkilo la tierra.
El kontrato es por noventa i noueve agnos.
Bevamos a la saloud de Samuel Toledano.

The port of Tel Aviv opened up, thanks to this Jewish community.
Let us drink to the health of this Jewish community.

227. It is two thousand years that we are waiting for the State of Israel.
Now with the Balfour Declaration,
It is certain that we are not going to wait any longer.
Let us drink to the health of mother and father.

229. My mother became a widow when we were young.
She sent us to school and she taught us what Zionism is.
Let us drink to the health of all the Jewish widows.

285. The Jews of Salonika buy shekels
To enable them to vote for the General Zionists or for the Revisionists.
Let us drink to the health of the leaders of these great families.

420. In Salonika we have many Zionist organizations:
The Young Jews Association, Theodor Hertzl, Beitar, Mizrahi.
Now we have the Tel Aviv.
Vital Avayu dealt with forming it.
Let us drink to the health of these committee members
Who collect money for Nahalal.[172]

421. Every Jew in Salonika is a member of a Zionist society
In his social group or in his neighborhood.
Only the Keren Hayisod is for the wealthy.
They collect large sums of money for Palestine.
Let us drink to the health of Rafael Medina.

17. Rishon le Tsion[173] had the first vineyards in Palestine.
The Rothschilds made this possible.
They never forgot that they are Jews.
They manifest this on every occasion.
Let us drink to the health of Samuel Sion.

10. In Palestine they founded a moshav for the Sephardim.
It is called Tsur Moshe.
The majority is from Salonika.
The Jewish National Fund leased them the land.
The contract is for ninety-nine years.
Let us drink to the health of Samuel Toledano.

---

172. Nahalal, the first worker's moshav in Israel, was established in 1921.

173. Rishon Le Tsion was a settlement outside Tel Aviv; today it is a densely popu-
lated city.

62. David se foue a Ziara [ziyara][174] en nouestra tierra santa.
   Etho kadich al kote maravi, troucho mizouzotte, livros de ley,
   I moz dio regalo a todos, los souvrinos, tambien a loz vezinos.
   Bevamos a la saloud de este bouen amigo.

255. Las organizationes sionistas azen Après-Midis
   Para azer paras por frouvoir Tel Aviv.
   Bevamos a la saloud de los Azouvis.

98. Los Sionistas general dizen
   Ke vamos a tomar la palestina kon las bouenas.
   Los Misrakistas dizen:
   Machia va avenir i la Palestina moz van adar.
   Loz revizionistas dizen ke la vamos a tomar kon pelear.
   Devemos de aparejar kanones, tankes, i kourchounes.
   Sin mos oulvidar loz kiboutzin ke mos van adar komidas.
   Bevamos a la saloud de los Komeris i toda sous famias.

7. Moraotte aya en Palestina.
   El Moufti kiere destrouyir los kiboutzim.
   Non eze mijor ke se arangen
   I non matarse de parte i otra?
   Todo eze politika porke el moufti kiere ser Rey de la Palestina.
   Bevamos a la saloud de loz Haverim
   Ke lavoran la tiera para azer estado de Israel en Palestina.

8. Chernovitz, delegado del Keren HaKayemet, vino a Salonique.
   Avlo kon los dirigentes.
   Despoues de la reugnon a la lokanda non kacher koumio.
   Es oun skandal para moustra sivdad.
   Bevamos a la saloud de Tamar.

404. Los Abravanel tienen otho ijos i dos ijas.
   Tomaron permi para la Palestina.
   Se aporfijaron sech i kazaron kouatro en mariage blanc.
   Ya voz imajenach ke se intho oun vapor de esta famia.
   Bevamos a la saloud de Sarah Nahmias.

327. Tomi lettra de mi ija ke esta a Palestina.
   Tiene moutha difikultad kon la lengua,

---

174. *Ziaras* were usually visits to graves, either of family members (especially during the week of mourning) or of saintly rabbis, but here the term refers to a pilgrimage.

62. David went on a pilgrimage to our Holy Land.
    He recited kaddish at the Western Wall, brought parchments,[175] law books
    And gave gifts to all of us, the nephews, also to the neighbors.
    Let us drink to the health of this good friend.

255. The Zionist organizations make afternoon gatherings
    To make money to build Tel Aviv.
    Let us drink to the health of the Azouvis.

98. The Zionists in general say
    That we are going to take Palestine with good will.
    The Mizrahis say:
    The messiah is going to come and they are going to give us Palestine.
    The Revisionists say that we are going to take it by fighting.
    We have to get cannons, tanks and bullets ready.
    Without us forgetting the kibbutzim that are going to provide us
        with food.
    Let us drink to the health of the Komeris and all their families.

7. Incidents occurred in Palestine.
    The Mufti wants to destroy the kibbutzim.
    Wouldn't it be better for them to come to an agreement
    And not kill each other?
    It's all politics because the Mufti wants to be king of Palestine.
    Let us drink to the health of the kibbutz members
    Who work the land to make the State of Israel in Palestine.

8. Chernovitz, the delegate of the Jewish National Fund, came to Salonika.
    He spoke with the leaders.
    After the meeting he ate in a non-kosher restaurant.
    It is a scandal for our city.
    Let us drink to the health of Tamar.

404. The Abravanels have eight sons and two daughters.
    They received a permit for Palestine.
    They adopted six and married off four in a marriage of convenience.
    You can already imagine that they filled a boat with this family.
    Let us drink to the health of Sarah Nahmias.

327. I got a letter from my daughter who is in Palestine.
    She is having a lot of difficulty with the language,

---

175. This small parchment (*mezuzah*) is placed in a container and hung as a sign on the doorpost.

Ma! Las kriatouras, solo de yir a la kaye adjougar,
Paresen ke son ayi nasidas.
Bevamos a la saloud de Rachel Nahmias.

265. El bazar de la J. J. eze Hanukalik para el Keren Hakayemet.
Todas laz moujeres azen oun lavoro de art para merkar mouestra tierra.
Los magazenes dan oun regalo de lo ke tienen
Para rezhatar Israel mouestra tierra.
Bevamos a la saloud del nouestro presidente Salomon Parente.

428. La makabi se foue a viajar a Paris.
Rochild los resevio i los mitio en ouna pansion.
Les amostro l'ark de triomph, Champ Elise,
I la Serbone,
Sin mankar las mas grande kiyila mouy ermoza.
Bevamos a la saloud de Rochild
Ke alegro a los macabeos de Salonique kon honor.

Historical Developments

191. Madame Levy vino a vijitar a la nona,
Yorando ke en sou kaza ez peguima.
La ija se izo sabatista.
Las soeurs la mandarin en ouna clisa[176]
Para ke los parientes non la veyan ni ke troke de idea.
Bevamos a la saloud de akeyos
Ke non mandan a sous ijos a la eskola de las soeures.

67. Loz maminim son djidios en kaza i muzulmanes a la plasa.
Lo ambeze agora ke se foueron en Turkia; merki la kaza de la mamina.
Topi kiyila al mosandara.[177]
Bevamos a la saloud de Rofel Medina.

153. Levy Masarano ese kachero.
Kazo a las ija kon loz Haleguas.

---

176. *Kilise* in Turkish.
177. *Musandara* in Ladino.

But! The children, just by going out to play in the street,
They seem as though they had been born there.
Let us drink to the health of Rachel Nahmias.

265. The bazaar of the Young Hebrews is the Hanukah present for the JNF.
All the women make artwork in order to buy our land.
The stores give a gift from what they have
In order to rescue our land of Israel.
Let us drink to the health of our president Salomon Parente.

428. The Maccabees[178] went on a trip to Paris.
Rothschild received them and put them up in a pension.
He showed them the Arc de Triomphe, the Champs-Élysées,
And the Sorbonne,
Without overlooking the very beautiful largest synagogue.
Let us drink to the health of Rothschild
Who made the Maccabees of Salonika happy by honoring them.

Historical Developments

191. Mme. Levy came to visit grandmother,
Crying that in her house there is a defect.
Her daughter became a Sabbatean.[179]
The nuns sent her to a church
So the relatives won't see her and won't change her mind.
Let us drink to the health of those
Who don't send their children to the nuns' school.

67. The Sabbateans are Jews at home and Muslims in the market.[180]
I learned now that they went to Turkey; I bought the house of a believer.
I found a synagogue in the attic.
Let us drink to the health of Rafael Medina.

153. Levy Masarano is a crate maker.
He married his daughters [off] to the Haleguas.

---

178. This was a Zionist boy scout troop. See Molho, *Traditions and Customs*, 126, for a photo of a group on a field trip in 1937.

179. This refers to the descendants of followers of Sabbatai Zevi, the seventeenth-century false messiah, who ultimately converted to Islam in 1666. They lived in the city until they were forcibly relocated to Turkey in 1922; at that time, they numbered an estimated ten thousand.

180. "In the market" means in public; these were the *Dönme,* or Muslim Sabbateans, who converted as did their leader.

Vida, Alegra i la gneta Fifi se foueron a Paris.
Despoues de ounos kouantos mezes partio sou moujer kon el tio Levy.
Bevamos a la saloud de Mochon Nadjari.

154. El tio Jecob vino a viajar de la Amerika.
Mos troucho kalsas i pyjamas de seda.
Kon Dora mi souvrina se kazo i la Amerika se foueron.
Touvieron mazal; partieron antes de la guerra.
Bevamos a la saloud de loz ke touvieron mazal.

281. Loz Haleguas se foueron a Paris; regretaron de dechar Salonique.
Toda la famia lavorando i soudando;
　　　los viejos se mourieron proves i anis.
Bevamos a la saloud de los A(g)malikim.

140. Las adjensias de vapores estan bien lavorando.
Kada semana se va vapores yenos de mobles de los Selaniklis
Para Paris o Palestina.
Esperamos ke non va aver antisemitezmo ande van ayir.
Bevamos a la saloud de Yakiel Amir.

259. Despoues del fouego la komounitad frouvouo kazas a la rejie
Para akeyos ke kedaron sin oun bakir.[181]
Bevamos a la saloud de los Selaniklis.

274. El fouego a Salonique ounos se emprovesieron.
Otros se enrikesieron.
El ke keria frouvoir,
El governo dezia ke el plano de la sivdad non esta pronto.
Mos dieron papeles por el tereno; los yamavan bonos.
El ke lo vouadro se enrekisio.
El ke lo vindio se enprovisio.
Bevamos a la saloud de akel ke non penso.

37. Los Segouras son sougritadjas de generationes,
Asegourean kazas i groutas al tsarchi.[182]
Kouando aye fouego son los primeros ke van aver.
Miran en ke dezgrasia esta el mouchteri.
Bevamos a la saloud de Alberto Shaki.

---

181. A worthless copper coin.
182. Also spelled *tsatchi.*

Vida, Alegra and the granddaughter Fifi went to Paris.
After a few months his wife left with Uncle Levy.
Let us drink to the health of Moshe Nadjari.

154. Uncle Jacob came to visit from America.
He brought us socks and silk pajamas.
He married my niece Dora and they went to America.
They were fortunate; they left before the war.
Let us drink to the health of those who had good fortune.

281. The Haleguas went to Paris; they were sorry to leave Salonika.
The whole family worked and sweated;
    the older ones died poor and destitute.
Let us drink to the health of the Amaleks.

140. The shipping agencies are working well.
Every week ships filled with furniture of the Salonikans set forth
For Paris or Palestine.
We hope that there will not be antisemitism wherever they are going.
Let us drink to the health of Yakiel Amir.

259. After the fire the community built houses in the Regie
For those who were left without a cent.
Let us drink to the health of the Salonikans.

274. The fire in Salonika caused some to become impoverished;
Others became rich.
To he who wanted to build,
The government said that the plan for the city was not ready yet.
They gave us papers for the land; they called them bonds.
Whoever kept them became rich.
Whoever sold them was impoverished.
Let us drink to the health of he who did not think.

37. The Segouras are insurance agents for generations,
Insuring houses and businesses in the marketplace.
When there is a fire they are the first to go to see.
They see the degree of disaster the client is in.
Let us drink to the health of Alberto Shaki.

70. Yangoula eze oun ladron, mata por savor, terorizo la grecia entera.
    La djente se espantan de salir despoues de las siete.
    Bevamos a la saloud de la polisia ke lo afero kon pena.

29. Venizelos eze oun grande antisemith.
    Eze del partido de los resfouyidos ke vigneron de Zmirn.
    Kouando ven djidios
    Lez da mal de korason ke eyos biven a la toumba
    I la djouderia a los konakes moderno ke se fragouo despoues del fouego.
    Bevamos a la saloud de los Gregos.

315. El governo explouzo a los djidios Italianos.
     En Livorno foueron mandados.
     Atornaron a Salonique, ounos kon moutho oro.
     Otros kon moutho lodo.
     Bevamos a la saloud de Isaac Covo.

350. Isaac Tivoli eze pharmasien del fobourg kambel.
     Ouna nothe ouna moujer le esperto ke kieria melezina
        para sou ija ke se dezmayo.
     Avrio la pouerta de la pharmasia ke estava en flamas,
     Desperto sou moujer i las sinko kriatouras.
     Laz mando al kampo i el foue a salvar la djouderia.
     Al otro dia se soupo ke los simpatezadores de Hitler
     Ke loz yamavan senkieme kolome
     Tenian torthas en las manos, asendiendo las kolon(i)as.
     Bevamos a la saloud de este hombre ke salvo seines de mouestros ermanos.

351. El Bikour Holim lo honoro ke foue machia para loz djidios.
     Ningounos mourieron a este fouego,
     Grasias a Isaac Tivoli ke loz abidourvo.[183]
     Bevamos a la saloud de Isaac Tivoli kon todo sou soy[e].

---

183. From the Ladino *abediguar.*

70. Yangoula is a thief, killing for the fun of it, terrorizing all of Greece.[184]
    People fear going out after seven.
    Let us drink to the health of the police who caught him with difficulty.

29. Venizelos is a great antisemite.
    He belongs to the party of the refugees that came from Izmir.
    When they see Jews
    It gives them heartache because they live in the Toumba[185]
    And the Jews [live] in the modern mansions that were built after the fire.
    Let us drink to the health of the Greeks.

315. The government expelled the Italian Jews.
     They were sent to Livorno.
     They returned to Salonika, some with a great deal of gold.
     Others with a great deal of mud.[186]
     Let us drink to the health of Isaac Covo.

350. Isaac Tivoli is a pharmacist of the Campbell suburb.
     One night a woman woke him up who wanted medicine
         for her daughter who had fainted.
     He opened the door of the pharmacy that was in flames.
     He woke up his wife and their five children,
     Sent them out to the countryside and he went to save the Jewish quarter.
     The other day it became known that the Hitler sympathizers
     That are called the Fifth Column
     Had torches in their hands, setting fire to the neighborhoods.
     Let us drink to the health of this man who save hundreds of our brethren.

351. Bikkur Holim honored him because he had been a savior for the Jews.
     No one died in this fire
     Thanks to Isaac Tivoli who aided them.
     Let us drink to the health of Isaac Tivoli and all his lineage.

---

184. Yang[o]ula (also spelled Yangoulas/Yangulas/Yankoulas) was a well-known bandit active in the mountainous areas of Greece in the 1920s; he was killed by the authorities in 1925. His exploits became legendary and stories that had appeared in Greek were even translated into Ladino (in Rashi script—namely, Hebrew letters) by Y. S. Kazis. They were published in Salonika in 1927 in two small volumes entitled *Los amores de Yangulas* (Devin Naar, personal communication, January 25, 2011). Regarding this figure, see Koliopulos, "Brigandage and Irredentism," 226n18; and Mazower, "Policing the Anti-Communist State," 134.

185. La Toumba is an area outside the city that at the time was deserted and poor; consequently Venizelos placed the refugees there. Obviously they were jealous of some of the Jews who resided in better neighborhoods (David Kounio, personal communication, February 19, 2009).

186. Humiliation.

352. Los djidios empesaron a se espantar.
     Ounos imigraron a Palestina, otros a Paris,
     Ma! Ese difithele de tener permi.
     Mouestra sierte eze aki.
     Bevamos a la saloud de los Shakis.

186b. Los Italianos salen en guerra.
      Les parese ke van aganar, ma!
      Koundo sienten el tiro de kourenta i doz, se sourten al pantalon.
      Bevamos a la saloud de Albert Matalon.

368. El tiempo de la guerra kon los italianos, bogadearon la torre
     Kaki i beige para la kamouflar i ke el enemigo ke non la veya.
     Despoues ke ethavan las bombas, todos tenian los ojos a la torre,
     Ke fouera djidio o ermeni.
     Todos se espantavan ke no la van a estrouyir.[187]
     Vivamos a la saloud de Edgar Hassid.

305. Estamos ganando la guera en Albania.
     Mouthas madres estan yorando; los Italianos vingneron a garear
     Kon mandolinos, guitaras i ploumas al koyar.
     Mozotros tenemos el Tsolia[188] ke mos aze avansar.
     Bevamos a la saloud de mouestros mansevos a Koritza.

Assorted Anecdotes or Expressions

95. Ovadia Serror tiene bouena boze.
    El rey lo demando a kantar para el i sou deredor en dia de Kipour.
    Lo tomaron de la kiyila
    Para lo yevar al palasio del rey a kantar.
    El rey regalo le dio.
    Al otro dia atorno i moz konto koualo se paso.
    Bevamos a la saloud de Eliaou Sasson.

75. Paro se sogno ke las sietes vakas flakas
    Se koumio a las siete vakas godras.
    Joseph lo expliko komo avia ambrera.
    Los ermanos vingneron a merkar grano.

---

187. *Estruir* in Ladino.

188. *O Tsolia* is the Greek national costume for men with a white skirt (David Kounio, personal communication, February 18, 2009).

352. The Jews began to be frightened.
Some immigrated to Palestine, others to Paris.
But! It is difficult to get a permit.
Our fate is here.
Let us drink to the health of the Shakis.

186b. The Italians go to war.
They think that they are going to win, But!
When they hear the shots of 1942, they defecate in their pants.
Let us drink to the health of Albert Matalon.

368. At the time of war with the Italians, they painted the tower[189]
Khaki and beige to camouflage it and so that the enemy would not see it.
After they threw the bombs, everyone turned their eyes to the tower,
Whether Jewish or Armenian.
Everyone was afraid that it would be destroyed.
Let us drink to the health of Edgar Hassid.

305. We are winning the war in Albania.
Many mothers are weeping; the Italians came to fight
With mandolins, guitars, and feathers in their detachable collars.
We have the elite Greek unit so we are going to forge ahead.
Let us drink to the health of our young men in Koritza.

Assorted Anecdotes or Expressions

95. Ovadia Serror has a good voice.
The king asked him to sing for him and his court on Yom Kippur day.
They took him out of the synagogue
To bring him to the king's palace to sing.
The king gave him a gift.
The next day he came home and told us what happened.
Let us drink to the health of Eliaou Sasson.

75. Pharoah dreamed that the seven lean cows
Ate the seven fat cows.
Joseph explained to him it was because there would be a famine.
His brothers came to buy grain.

---

189. This was the fifteenth-century Crusader landmark located in the center of the entrance to the bay of Salonika that was used as a prison—which was probably why they were hoping it would be destroyed.

Joseph tomo a Benjamin prisoniero para ke Yacob vignera averlo.
Bevamos a la saloud de Esther Serrero.

375. Enfrente de mi kaza aye oun kampiko.
En medio oun marmoliko.
Las kriatouras en djougando vimos oun bourako.
La mama yamo a papa ke vino al pounto
I eze ansina ke toparon la klisa.
Ikonas i mezaïkas de valor i oun basin de avoua se topo.
Mi padre entro el primo kon el vizino.
Bevamos a la saloud de Salomon Almoznino.

212. La alma djoudia existe i va existir
Komo existio Avraam, Isaac i Jacob.
Bevamos a la saloud de Salomon Jacob.

335. Los Taletim non se poueden arojar.
La kiyila los etha en Gueniza.
El chamach se okoupa de los vouadrar.
Bevamos a la saloud de Salomon Amar.

336. Los djidios de Salonique non van al korte.
Van a la komunitad ke tiene Beth Din.
La oultima palavra tienen los Hakamim.
Bevamos a la saloud de los Talmide Hahamim.

341. Los hahamim son de vanda de tomar.
Nounka dieron ni van adar.
Les parese ke todo krese al arvoliko.
Bevamos a la saloud de Daniel Tsiko.

161. Kouando doz personas estan siempre en ouna
Dizen: non se kitan de la manga.
Otro dizen: son piojo entre kostoura.
Otro dizen: ande va Hana, va plata.[190]
Bevamos a la saloud de Ichoua Beraha.

192. Dizen ke se manean loz de abacho.
Se manean los de ariva.

---

190. Yehuda Hatsvi explained that there are a number of expressions that relate to Hannah; in one she appeared with the *plato,* or "tray," for serving guests. He suggested that Bouena chose *plata,* "money," rather than *plato* simply for the sake of the rhyme (personal communication, February 20, 2009). Hannah was not a common Sephardi name so few women would have been offended by this mockery.

Joseph took Benjamin hostage so that Jacob would come to see him.
Let us drink to the health of Esther Serrero.

375. Opposite my house there is a little field.
In the middle [there is] a little piece of marble.[191]
While we children played in it we saw a hole.
Mother called Father who came at once
And in this way they found the church.
Icons and mosaics of value and a basin of water were found.
My father entered first with the neighbor.
Let us drink to the health of Salomon Almosnino.

212. The Jewish soul exists and is going to exist
Just like Abraham, Isaac and Jacob.
Let us drink to the health of Salomon Jacob.

335. Prayer shawls cannot be discarded.
The community puts them away in special storage for holy items.
The beadle takes care of storing them.
Let us drink to the health of Salomon Amar.

336. The Jews of Salonika don't go to court.
They go to the community that has a rabbinical court.
The rabbis have the final word.
Let us drink to the health of the learned rabbis.

341. The rabbis like to take.
They never give or are going to give.
It seems to them that everything grows on trees.
Let us drink to the health of Daniel Tsiko.

161. When two people are always together,
They say that they don't get out of one sleeve.
Others say: they are fleas in a seam.
Others say: wherever Hannah goes, the silver goes.
Let us drink to the health of Yehoshua Beraha.

192. They say that those below move about.
The ones above move about.

---

191. This was probably a tombstone.

Ya me kansi de me manear, ma todo ese sin mazal.
Bevamos a la saloud de las ke tienen mazal.

193. De fazer paras non ese kokma.
De saverlas vouadrar ese art.
Kien ese desfazedor[192] non tiene azlaka.[193]
Bevamos a la saloud de los ke tienen beraha.

198. Las kozas ke te plaze, komes ouna i kieres otra.
Las tsoupas kon savor komo si fouera oun bombon.
Bevamos a la saloud de Michel Aaron.

201. El major vouezmo[194] eze el ambrer [sic].[195]
Bevamos a la saloud de Joseph Menache.

203. Primavera ese tiempo de amor.
Primavera ese tiempo de la flor.
Bevamos a la saloud de Leon Botton.

204. La amistad non se merka, la salud tambien.
Bevamos a la saloud de Albert Amiel.

205. La mouzika adoulse el alma.
La kantiga alegra al alma.
Bevamos a la saloud de Isaac Amar.

206. La yerva krese al kampo.
La honestedad krese en la famia.
Bevamos a la saloud de Avraam Nahmias.

240. La karosa del kazalino esta yena de lodo.
La karosa del rey esta yena de oro.
Bevamos a la saloud de Isaac Covo.

232. Nigna kon ojos pretos i karas koreladas,
Las yaman eze ouna mansana de Yugoslavia.
Bevamos a la saloud de la famia Azaria.

---

192. "The *desfazedor* does not necessarily spend money, but throws away a slice of bread or throws away yesterday's food, or gets rid of an item of clothing just because it was stained (while it was possible to clean it!)" (Yehuda Hatsvi, e-mail message to author, March 27, 2011).

193. This is the Hebrew term for "success," but also means "having plenty," or "in abundance."

194. *Guesmo* in Ladino.

195. Literally "famine," as in copla 75 about Joseph and Pharoah; food smells best when one is hungry.

I am tired of moving about, but everything is without luck.[196]
Let us drink to the health of those who are lucky.

193. Making money takes no brains.
To know [how] to save it is an art.
He who is prodigal does not have prosperity.
Let us drink to the health of those who have a blessing.

198. The things that please you, you eat one and want another.
You chew them with gusto as if it were candy.
Let us drink to the health of Michel Aaron.

201. The best smell is hunger.
Let us drink to the health of Joseph Menache.

203. Spring is the time of love.
Spring is the time of the flower.
Let us drink to the health of Leon Botton.

204. Friendship is not bought; neither is health.
Let us drink to the health of Albert Amiel.

205. Music sweetens the soul.
The song pleases the soul.
Let us drink to the health of Isaac Amar.

206. Grass grows in the fields.
Honesty grows in the family.
Let us drink to the health of Avraham Nahmias.

240. The carriage of the villager is full of mud.
The carriage of the king is full of gold.
Let us drink to the health of Isaac Covo.

232. A girl with black eyes and red cheeks,
They call her an apple from Yugoslavia.
Let us drink to the health of the Azaria family.

---

196. That is, things go wrong.

284. Laz blondas son bovas.
Laz morenas son savrozas.
Bevamos a la saloud de Eleonora.

370. Todos tenemos diziluziones en la vida,
Ke sea Rachel, Julie or Bienvenida.
Mos oulvidamos koualo se passo
Porke mos vamos amouerir kon dol[l]or de korason.
Vivamos a la saloud de Moche Kapon.

233. La ermozoura de la persona empesa de la honestedad
I de l'amistad i del korason.
Bevamos a la saloud de Haim Sasson.

207. Rogar por saloud.
Rogar por parnasa.
Bevamos a la saloud de Avraam Amar.

214. El avoua aze mal; el vino aze kantar.
Bevamos a la saloud de Salamon Amar.

389. Avlemos tanto de Salonique, ma non avlemos del garbi.
Ese oun ayre kon arena.
Todos seran ventanas i pouertas
Kouando se alevanta sin moz avertir.
Bevamos a la saloud de Daniel Shaki.

395. A Salonique a los deskarsos lez dizen: Si, tienes frios.
No das o se las meté debacho del kavesal
O lo van a enterer kon las paras
O el ke va akedar va a baylar.
Bevamos a la saloud de Regina Behar.

223. El Bet Amigdach kayo; la pare kedo.
Oun dia los vamos a frouvoir.
Bevamos a la saloud de Rachel Amar.

284. The blondes are stupid.
    The brunettes are pleasant.
    Let us drink to the health of Eleonora.

370. We all have disappointments in life,
    Whether it be Rachel, Julie, or Bienvenida.
    We forget what happened
    Because [otherwise] we are going to die of heartache.
    Let us drink to the health of Moshe Kapon.

233. The beauty of a person begins with honesty
    And friendship and from the heart.
    Let us drink to the health of Haim Sasson.

207. Pray for health.
    Pray for a livelihood.
    Let us drink to the health of Avraham Amar.

214. Water does harm; wine makes one sing.
    Let us drink to the health of Salomon Amar.

389. We speak so much of Salonika, but we don't speak of the strong wind.
    It is a wind with sand.
    Everyone closes windows and doors
    When it blows without warning us.
    Let us drink to the health of Daniel Shaki.

395. In Salonika to the barefoot[197] they say: Yes, you are cold.
    One doesn't give; one either puts it under one's pillow
    Or they will bury one with the money
    Or he who is going to remain is going to dance.[198]
    Let us drink to the health of Regina Behar.

223. The Temple fell; the wall remained.
    One day we are going to [re]build it.
    Let us drink to the health of Rachel Amar.

---

197. That is, the destitute.
198. The survivor, or heir, is going to have a ball.

CHAPTER 4

"The Miseries That the Germans Inflicted on Salonika"

The Nazi invasion of Salonika on April 9, 1941, would determine the fate of the twenty-five-year-old Bouena and her family as well as all of Salonikan Jewry. Bouena survived by fleeing and joining the partisans, at first the EDES Royalists[1] and later the ELAS Communists.[2] She eventually reached Palestine, accompanying a group of children she had smuggled out of Greece. She later returned to work as a dietitian in the displaced persons' camp in Siderokastro, Greece, and encouraged Jews to immigrate to Palestine.

This particular collection of verses, entitled *Komplas de las mizerias ke izo lo[s] almanes a Salonique del 1941–1943* (in English, "Coplas about the Miseries That the Germans Inflicted on Salonika, 1941–1943"), contains ninety-nine strophes. The traumas that Bouena as well as the community had experienced remained with her until her dying day. Interestingly enough, one perceives that events are often represented in the verses as belonging to the present rather than to the past, for she relived them time and again. The use of this tense seems to add a sense of authenticity and realism, as if the verses were part of a diary.[3] The lost world here is not one whose heyday passed as the result of modernization or secularism, but rather the result of war and manmade devastation. In his collection of Sephardi Holocaust poetry, Isaac Jack Lévy writes, "[T]he primary duty of Sephardic writers is not the verbalization of the message but rather the message as a means of retaining their own identity through remembrance of fallen brothers and sisters."[4] Bouena is clearly engaged in remembrance but her verses are unusual in that their message does more than help the survivors retain their identity, for the verses simultaneously send an informative message of historic significance.

On October 28, 1940, Mussolini, without consulting with Hitler, decided to invade Albania with the intention of pushing onward into Greece.[5] On November 14 the Greek army mounted a counteroffensive in order to deter the Italians; its troops crossed over into Albania and were successful in their campaign against the Italians. In Bouena's opinion, Mussolini was unsuccessfully imitating Hitler and he inadvertently created an embarrassing military situation. Hitler realized that he had no choice but to bail out his ally, and quickly sent troops via Bulgaria in order to quash the Greek army. Bowman notes that after the Greek surrender the defeated soldiers (one of whom most likely was Bouena's fiancé) were not interned as prisoners, but rather were released; it seems that most of them simply walked home.[6]

In the very first verse in the collection, Bouena notes that at Passover rumors of a pending German invasion began to circulate. The reaction of the community was to close down its shops and for each family to wait at home; soon after, the sounds of the destruction of stores reverberated in their ears as their food supplies were plundered.[7] No one knew precisely what to anticipate, but it was clear that this first action augured ill for the Jews of Salonika.

The Nazis wasted no time upon entering the city. The tentacles of the Rosenberg Commission reached into Greece because there were valuables worth confiscating. Between May and November 1941, Alfred Rosenberg and a unit of German officers and academics raided synagogues, schools, banks, presses, hospitals, private homes, and other institutions, and carried off invaluable books, religious items, manuscripts, and the like.[8] Their workers quickly located and pillaged the homes of the cultured and the wealthy, sending truckloads of treasures to Germany. Bouena describes the day they plundered the Sarfatty home,[9] noting that they had done their homework, for they knew exactly what in each home was of value; for instance, they were aware that her family possessed valuable paintings. The reactions of her family members and her neighbors varied from hysteria to an acceptance of the inevitable.

The Nazi pillaging was focused and steady. Germany was in dire need of iron for the war effort; one Jewish family possessed a formidable supply of iron and the Germans were overjoyed to discover such a valuable cache in Salonika.[10] In essence, the Germans looted, requisitioned, and attempted to claim as much as possible as quickly as possible. As it turns out, even the most basic commodities were of value to the Nazis. Bouena recalls that they took everything from everyone—including essentials such as meat, fish, and bread.[11] They succeeded in undermining the community by simultaneously causing serious unemployment as well as starvation.[12]

Bouena deduced that if it were not for Matanot La-Evionim,[13] starvation would have been even more widespread. A special committee was set up to compile lists of taxpayers and collect funds for soup kitchens: "The project started with 200 children and by mid-April it had reached 2,000 children who each received a warm midday meal and a portion of bread gratis. This foundation was supported exclusively by the contributions of Jews, without any municipal or governmental assistance whatsoever."[14]

Bouena was concerned about not only her own family, but also the welfare of the community as a whole. Thus, Bouena and her friend Sarah served as volunteers and busily prepared milk from powder provided by the

International Red Cross.[15] The shipments of milk arrived in boxes; her friend's father instructed them to save the nails and boxes from the containers so that he could trade them for food for the workers.[16] They distributed it at the Matanot La-Evionim refectory.[17] The entire operation was supervised carefully, for the Red Cross representatives wanted to ascertain that the milk was prepared properly.[18] While working under the tutelage of the Red Cross representative, the two young women gained a sense of usefulness and satisfaction.

Nevertheless, Bouena was well aware of the fact that a community with more than its share of impoverished members cannot properly care for the needy. Everyone was suffering from shortages of basic staples, and yearning for that which is lacking. Unfortunately the situation worsened and many could no longer manage at all; shortages were no longer temporary and death from starvation became commonplace. The picture was gloomy indeed, and without hope of improvement.

The world of old rapidly faded once the Nazis imposed themselves upon the Selaniklis. With the removal of paintings and other objects of value, appreciation of art and culture eventually disappeared as well; when books were not available, an additional channel to culture was blocked. As radios and newspapers were confiscated, one could no longer remain in touch with the outside world. Slowly but surely, the Germans deprived the Jews of their possessions as well as of their ability to function. Their goal was to strip the Jews of their dignity along with the more tangible objects that filled the coffers of the Third Reich, which was always desperate for funds.[19] In her verses, Bouena seeks a way in which to find a ray of light and advises all to be patient; this might seem odd to the reader who knows that she wrote this after the fact, but it is the tone she wanted to convey and reflects the manner in which she encouraged her fellow Jews at the time.

The Nazi invasion created many unexpected traumas for every Jewish family. Bouena recalls the foreign soldiers taken as prisoners of war who were marched to and from the city daily. Because the local population displayed sympathy for these young men, the Germans declared that anyone who made contact with them would be punished.[20] As it turned out, each day some of them passed by the Sarfatty home en route to their work assignments. In blatant defiance of the German decree, Bouena's sister Regina offered the soldiers water and bread as they marched by. The two sisters noticed that one of the wounded British soldiers wore a chain with a mezuzah and decided to help him. The women of the family joined forces and managed to smuggle this Jewish soldier into their home.[21] Despite the fact that this placed them in a very precarious position, they elected to care for him as best as they could. Together with their cook and their aunt, they bathed the soldier who, it turned out, was burning up with fever. Unfortunately, the saga of their English patient did not end well, for he perished while under their care. The Sarfatty women deliberated as to the appropriate next step, and decided to sneak the body out of their home in the middle of the night, but they held onto his necklace as a keepsake.

During the course of the occupation, there were specific incidents and dates that became part of the group memory. Every Salonikan survivor recalls the Sabbath in which the men were humiliated; Bouena includes her own description of this event. These verses refer to July 11, 1942, an unbearably hot Sabbath, when all the men of the community (except those of Italian[22] and Spanish citizenship) between the ages of nineteen and forty-five were ordered to appear in Liberty Square in order to register for the workforce. She describes the humiliation suffered by those made to stand for six hours in the hot sun, during which time most of them dehydrated; anyone who collapsed was beaten, and bulldogs attacked some of them.[23] Eventually, all were sent home because the turnout was too small; the actual conscription took place the following week. This humiliating experience is referred to as the Black Sabbath.[24]

In an attempt to express the sense of humiliation and helplessness that permeated the community, the poet uses the image of the Jews behaving like sheep when "facing the Germans," an image that appears in post-Holocaust descriptions criticizing the passivity of the Jews as they met their fate.[25] She contends that the youth wanted to revolt but were not able to initiate resistance in face of such a powerful foe.[26] Some had already been drafted into the Greek army when it first mobilized to repel the Italian invasion of Albania; a few verses in the collection relate to them.

Ultimately, the Nazis recruited young men between the age of eighteen and twenty-eight for forced labor.[27] Because of Bouena's position as a volunteer worker for the Red Cross, she had an entrance pass to the labor camps and recorded eyewitness accounts. She noted the sorry state of nutrition there, and was impressed that these boys suffered without complaint.[28] Their diet consisted of a hundred grams of bread and some cabbage soup; many suffered from dysentery, malaria, sunstroke, and beatings.[29] Bouena often provided the only means of communication between these young men and their families. Her descriptions of the encounters with the young men as well as her contact with their mothers are painful and poignant.[30] Bouena was very strongly affected by this experience.[31]

Bouena was well aware that not all of these young men would survive the work camps.[32] She continued to visit them, helping them to the best of her ability, and regretting her inability to help more of them. She helped her neighbor smuggle her son out of the camp, but unfortunately he did not survive the ordeal.[33] His mother, a widow, was left at the mercy of her neighbors—who were well aware of the biblical injunction to provide for widows and orphans.[34] Many young men perished at the labor camps, particularly during the summer months. The Italian consul reported that of 7,500 sent to work, nearly 300 died and that most of the returnees had contracted malaria.[35] The parents of young men had real cause for concern.

The community eventually negotiated the release of those in the labor camps, but at a high price. In winter 1942, it had no choice but to comply with the demand to relinquish its ancient cemetery. As early as 1937, the Greek municipality had coveted this expansive tract of land; it intended to build a university there and to discontinue burials as of 1940. It is not clear if Bouena was aware of the politicking that preceded the German negotiations, but the community knew that there were Greeks who were extremely active in the destruction of tens (and even hundreds) of thousands of tombs, some of which dated to the fifteenth century. Marble slates and fragments from the ancient cemetery still can be found in unexpected and unsettling locales such as roads, pools, urinals, dance floors, and churchyards.[36]

The general ambience of fear and apprehension in the Jewish community permeates the coplas; Bouena tries to offer encouragement and a show of strength.[37] The fear created by the Nazi presence was at first experienced by the Jews, but eventually it spread to the general Greek population. Although some Greeks managed to help their Jewish friends, the Jews did not reveal that they desperately needed supplies, escape routes, food, money, and more. Nevertheless, the encouragement communicated to them by their Greek friends was clearly appreciated.[38]

Bouena alludes to the wise counsel taken by individuals who were not present at the time of the invasion and did not return to Salonika; such a decision was not easy to make, but in retrospect it was the clear path to choose. Relative to the other (all smaller) Jewish communities in Greece, the proportion of Selaniklis who fled, hid, or joined the partisans was minimal. A serious consideration for anyone pondering whether to leave was the language barrier; many of the Salonikan Jews did not speak Greek. Inability to communicate with the non-Jewish Greeks paralyzed those who spoke only Ladino or French (or Italian). The Selaniklis were not entirely isolated from the rest of the country, but the majority of these Jews lacked the connections—whether geographical, linguistic, or political—to join the partisan circles and thus, in 1941, few did. Apparently, as starvation became more severe, some changed their minds.[39]

Many members of the younger generation chose to remain at home not because of the language factor, but due to a strong sense of family loyalty.[40] At the same time, the fact that Salonika is located in the mountains and was at a considerable distance from the centers of resistance must be taken into account. Mazower also attributes this "passivity" to the fact that Salonika was the first

Greek-Jewish community to experience the occupation, and at a time when the resistance was not yet well organized.[41] According to historian Daniel Carpi, the Germans exploited the power of family ties in the Jewish community and of the Jews' alienation from the local Greeks.[42] Yosef Ben points out that the men in the work camps were warned by the Greeks and Italians not to return home but to join the partisans; most did not heed this warning. Some returned, only to discover that their families were gone and that they, too, were being deported.[43]

Bouena mentions two groups that were permitted to leave by virtue of their foreign citizenship, the Spaniards and the Italians. Although it was rumored that they were being sent to the same destinations as the rest of the Jews, the 367 Spanish nationals were indeed told that they have special rights. Nevertheless, there is a great deal of truth in the verse claiming that "no one knows what is going to happen."[44] Bouena's supposition regarding their fate was not erroneous. The promise of going to Spain was slow to materialize. When this group of Jews was sent to Bergen-Belsen, American Sephardim pressured Franco to take action. As a result, in the first week of February 1944, after six months in the camp, these privileged Jews were sent to Barcelona for five months and then moved to Casablanca for four additional months. Ultimately, 150 of them arrived in Tel Aviv; the rest, a group of 217, returned to Salonika.

The Italian nationals began to panic, especially since it was unclear precisely who qualified for inclusion in this category. One possibility was that only the 281 Jews who had registered immediately following the Germans' arrival would be permitted to leave; an alternative was to allow the emigration of spouses of Italian citizens as well as anyone with familial ties to Italian Jews. There were also those who did not fit neatly into any of these categories but had made a serious economic or cultural contribution to Italy; in the long run, the consul decided on the basis of his own judgment.[45] It should come as no surprise to learn that there were many disagreements between the German and Italian officials on this issue. Needless to say, the number of Jews saved—which included Bouena, who was issued an Italian passport—exceeded the official number of registered Italians.[46]

Carpi located documentation revealing the negotiations between the Germans and the Italians. The Italian government was anxious to guard all of its assets in the area, whether industrial, commercial, cultural, or social. Since Jews were in control of an unusually large amount of Italian assets, Italian priorities were clearly at odds with those of the Germans.[47] Because Italians were anxious to protect their own interests, the "Italian" Jews were sent to Italian-ruled Athens—although once there, no one's fate was certain.[48]

Bouena pays attention to those who left the city, whether intentionally or by chance, and how they fared. Asher Abravanel, the eminent journalist mentioned in chapter 1, wrote an article advising all to flee while it was still an option. Asher's suspicions about Nazi plans might have been based on instinct or on his own sources of information; he attempted to motivate Jews not to wait and suffer at the hands of the enemy. Bouena adds that ultimately, this journalist was imprisoned in Pavlos Melas, the same prison where she would be incarcerated; she is uncertain of his fate.[49] Abravanel's fellow journalist, Besantsi, published a series of articles condemning the Nazis and he was classified as an enemy of Germany. He escaped the city and managed to hide for two years; Bouena toasts those who helped him survive during that time.[50] Unfortunately, the Germans later apprehended him.[51]

Restrictions on movement, such as being forbidden to leave one's house prior to 10:00 AM, prevented Jews from attending morning services at the synagogue, especially during the month of repentance before the New Year, when *selihot* prayers were held very early in the morning. Jewish police patrolled the neighborhood, ascertaining that this restriction was enforced.[52] Bouena cannot fathom the complicity of her fellow Jews, but the head of the police supposedly cooperated because he was promised that he would be allowed to remain in the city.[53]

Despite the incredibly strict limitations imposed upon the community, attempts were made to maintain a sense of normality. If a son was born, there was to be a circumcision; couples married despite the aura of gloom. If songs were traditionally sung on these occasions, the Nazi terror tactics were not going to silence them as long as there were Jews alive to sing. But there is little joy in the coplas describing weddings; either there was no appropriate venue for the occasion or the rabbi was missing. In one case, she credits the Italian consul, Guelfo Zamboni—who ultimately saved Jewish lives as well—with facilitating a wedding ceremony.

During the German occupation, three Italian consuls served in Salonika. Pietro Nobili Vitelleschi, despite his presence during the conquest of the city, is rarely mentioned in the historical records. Guelfo Zamboni, the second consul general, served from April 11, 1942, until June 18, 1943. Carpi emphasizes that it was Zamboni who negotiated with the Germans over the fate of the Jews, whom he considered to be "entitled to Italian citizenship." Zamboni sent hundreds of telegrams to Athens and Rome in order to procure Italian backing, and managed to release some Jews who had already been confined in the Baron de Hirsch ghetto.[54] The third consul, Giuseppe Castruccio, served until Italy's surrender on September 8, 1943; at this point, the Germans closed the consulate, dismissing Castruccio four days later because he refused to pledge allegiance to the new fascist ruling party.[55]

The poet devotes many verses to the process of the destruction of the community and the creation of the ghettos. Bouena compares the ghetto to a mousetrap that offers no means of escape.[56] The cramped quarters of the ghetto were unbearable despite the poet's attempt to describe it as an opportunity to achieve togetherness.[57] Needless to say, the community was shocked and dismayed by the imposition of such severe physical limitations.[58]

There was only one synagogue, the Monastir congregation, to which the community had access in the final stages of its isolation.[59] The fear of the unknown provided incentive for prayer and repentance for those hoping to avert punishment for their sins or to at least end their lives with a clean slate.

Bouena is under the impression that the Germans organized the deportations in order to distance the Jews from their surroundings. It is unclear whether she believes that if they had remained in their original neighborhoods, the non-Jews would have offered help or resistance or if the Germans' intention was simply to remove the Jews from Salonika so that no one would witness their fate. She devotes a few verses to the actual removal of individuals from their homes on the day of their deportation. Two coplas refer to the physically infirm, who were most likely included in the first group of deportees. One verse concerns the deportation of war veterans, namely, young men who, while serving in the Greek army, took part in the fighting in Albania between November 1940 and April 1941. Some of them returned as disabled veterans and would normally have been considered heroes, having successfully fought in locales such as Koritza. However, the Germans showed them no respect and treated them like useless invalids.[60] Although Bouena did not remain in Salonika to witness the rest of the deportations, she saw enough to have been deeply affected by the experience and to know that remaining in the city was not a viable option for her.

The poet devotes many verses to those leaders who were considered to be collaborators with the Nazis. The survivors named 53 or 54 Jews who aided the Nazis in the deportations, who had abused Jews who had been caught attempting to flee, and who had turned in Greeks who had hidden or otherwise helped Jews. At the top of this list were Vital Hasson, Rabbi Zvi Koretz, and Jacques Albala; all three appear in numerous coplas in this collection.[61] When the SS ordered the community to organize its own *politofilakas* (police force), the Jews were far from pleased. Jacques Albala, a travel agent who knew German because he had lived several years in Vienna, was chosen to form a unit of civil guards under the tutelage of Laskaris Papanaoum, the Greek collaborator assigned to supervise this unit from its inception.[62] References to the *politofilakas,* which numbered between 200 and 250 unarmed young men from wealthy families, appear repeatedly in these verses.[63]

In Bouena's eyes, Albala was a thief[64] who was more ardently antisemitic than the Germans.[65] It turned out that many of those chosen to serve in the *politofilakas* were almost as cruel to their fellow Jews as were the Nazis and instilled terror among their brethren. Bouena always found herself looking over her shoulder wherever she went, for she was convinced that no one could really be trusted; one never knew who worked for the Nazis officially or who might be a collaborator. In particular there was a feeling within the community that these policemen were ubiquitous, or at least they seemed to be; thus the utmost care should be taken on all fronts. Ladino had been a means of communication to which the Nazis had no access, but these Jewish "police" unnerved the Selaniklis, who realized that it was no longer safe to speak their mother tongue in public. Distrust of this group proved to be completely justified. Bouena specifically states that the Jewish police inspected the passengers of outgoing trains in order to catch any Jew attempting to flee.[66] In her eyes, these men were as evil as the Germans.[67] Toward the end, on April 12, 1943, the Nazis appointed Jacques Albala president of the community as a replacement for the chief rabbi; Albala in turn chose Vital Hasson to serve in his stead as head of the Jewish police.

Vital Hasson is the second collaborator about whom Bouena writes at length. This Salonikan made certain that he would not perish with the rest of the community. Yosef Ben reports that many survivors characterize Hasson as a cruel man who cheated, robbed, beat, terrorized, and abused his fellow Jews incessantly.[68] Hasson had major dealings in the black market that enabled him to supply the German soldiers with difficult-to-obtain goods. Bouena was well acquainted with him and his family; it is clear that she always expected the worst from this immoral individual. She was well aware of his dishonest and irredeemable behavior toward all except his inner circle; he did not hesitate to locate fellow Jews in flight or in hiding and to turn them over to the authorities. She remarks that he allowed himself to behave so despicably because he was so certain that he had the unqualified support of the Germans.[69] In addition to being power hungry, he was ostentatious; for example, he was said to have paraded about on a horse while brandishing a whip.[70] Bowman calls him a "sadistic criminal" who tortured, raped, extorted and was "an ugly parody of the SS," dressing like them and marking his enemies for death.[71]

The poet witnesses the manipulation of her dear friend Sarah Trabout, coerced by Hasson to marry his brother in the wake of a conversation with Sarah's father, who was told, "either this wedding is going to take place / Or your children are going to disappear"; the prospective bride had no choice but to acquiesce. While the community was being terrorized, Hasson organized a bombastic wedding that included floral decorations for the bridal canopy and a limousine (and driver) instructed to show off the newlyweds touring the streets of the ghetto. Sarah was terribly upset, "crying that she didn't want to hear mention of the groom's name." Hasson planned for the couple ultimately to be sent to a camp for the privileged, but when the transports were organized, Sarah refused to be separated from her beloved family.[72]

Sarah was only one of many female victims who suffered at Hasson's hands; apparently he enjoyed mistreating girls in the presence of their parents.[73] René Molho, a survivor, speaks derogatorily of the Hasson brothers, singling out the older brother as being a German-speaking Gestapo informer who turned in Jews who attempt to flee; it seems that he sought out wealthy Jews in particular. In addition, he forced girls "to submit to him sexually."[74]

Hasson's path crossed Bouena's all too often, especially because of her position as a volunteer for the Red Cross; Hasson attempted to humiliate her and derail her plans at almost every opportunity. She relates numerous harrowing accounts in her memoirs, including a confrontation on March 15, 1943, the day of the first transport.[75] One copla alludes to this incident, which occurred because none of the women relocated to the Baron de Hirsch ghetto was permitted to come with her children to the Regie Vardar neighborhood at the usual time for the milk distribution. The Red Cross had no idea that no one was allowed to leave Baron de Hirsch on this day and the Nazis clearly did not want to jeopardize their plans.

As a result, the Salonikan delegate of the International Committee of the Red Cross, René Burkhardt, arranged for the driver of the Red Cross car to take Bouena to distribute the milk to the starving children.[76] Upon entering the ghetto, she was unnerved at the sight of the barbed wire and the tight security, a clear sign of danger. The neighborhood adjacent to the railroad station was a closed and secured port for deportation; Bouena rightly feared for her life as she entered this ghetto.[77] She wrote in her memoirs, "I thought to myself, I came in, but they will never let me leave again. I had the flag of the International Red Cross on my car, and this gave me some consolation. They took me to the Soupe Populaire in the school. We brought in all the containers of milk."

At that moment, she encountered her nemesis, Hasson, who was determined to punish her for crossing the line.[78] She describes the traumatic incident at the distribution station thus:

> With much anger in his voice, Hasson said to me, "Drink!" He gave me a mug full of milk, and I drank. As soon as I finished, he poured some more. I couldn't drink any more. I was vomiting and drinking, and my dress was soaked with milk. I was thinking of all the babies who would be without milk on account of this brute. I couldn't drink anymore and was desperate. When Hasson saw this, he took the mug from me and forced me to drink until my gums were bleeding. He kept pushing the mug into my mouth. He pushed some more, and my teeth began to shake. My white uniform was covered with milk and

blood. Hasson began to beat me on the face. When I was exhausted, he decided that I should distribute the leftover milk.[79]

Bouena also refers to his ties to Papanaoum, the aforementioned Greek collaborator with the SS who supervised the recruitment of young men for Hasson's (and earlier for Albala's) police force. Bouena refers to their amicable relationship and to the irony resulting from this arrangement: "What is this antisemite doing with a Jew? / They are making plans together for the deportation of the Jews / And to take all the belongings of these unfortunates." All they could do is hope these two would fail; events seemed to be completely out of their control. At any rate, Bouena seeks to append an optimistic note to this verse by pointing out that if they should fail, it would be "[b]ecause Salonika is a city of miracles."[80]

Hasson was crafty and eager to exploit almost anyone at every opportunity. The fact that his sister worked for the Jewish community and was privy to inside information provided him with an advantage that proved devastating for his victims. Hasson's sibling passed on all the information at her fingertips, serving as the enabler who guaranteed the success of Hasson's "snakelike business," for he readily used anything he knew in order to blackmail his fellow Jews. Bouena condemns the Hassons: at the time of the deportations, his sister took a share of gold from the stash that had been accumulated through theft. Needless to say, her brother arranged for her to be sent to a camp for the privileged.[81]

The ultimate fate of Vital Hasson belongs to this story as well. Because of his involvement with the roundups, this collaborator was entitled to freedom of movement. Hasson made sure to negotiate his own escape from the furnaces of Poland by procuring Italian passports from the Italian consul in exchange for the release of a number of Jews from the Baron de Hirsch ghetto. The consul wished to save thirty-four former Italian citizens, including women married to Greeks; this was the basis of their exchange, but Hasson was charged for the car and food provided.[82] Entry into Albania was ultimately negotiated for his group. Consequently, on August 19, 1943, the day of the nineteenth and final deportation, Hasson escaped to Albania with an entourage of fourteen including his wife, daughter, and mistress and scores of suitcases filled with jewelry and gold coins;[83] at first he drove a German car but then switched to a Greek model. Because Consul Castruccio was aware of the crimes Hasson committed, he submitted a description of him to the authorities in Albania in order to enable the Italians to arrest him. In a telegram sent by the consul that very month, he was termed "a Jew with a murky past, a tailor by trade" who used his power with "unusual ferocity" and perpetrated infamies.[84] Apparently the accusations were not taken too seriously, since Hasson was placed in a minimum-security concentration camp in Kavaje. After this site was liberated in September 1943, Hasson bought a boat and landed in Bari, Italy, where a dentist from Salonika recognized him.

Although he was arrested again, he was released shortly thereafter and fled to Alexandria, Egypt; a Salonikan refugee there recognized him, so he was apprehended a third time.[85] At this point, Hasson was sent to Athens by the British police but freed when Greece was liberated. In November 1945, upon returning to reclaim various items of value that he had hidden with friends, he was recognized by a survivor; this final arrest led to the courtroom.[86] Bouena was in Greece when the proceedings began on July 2, 1946; they lasted three days, with the sentencing pronounced at 3:00 AM. The poet expresses her dismay combined with a sense of helplessness during the trial because the voices of the most convincing witnesses could no longer be heard; they had already been condemned to death in the crematorium.[87] Despite this fact, Hasson was sentenced to death by firing squad and transferred to a prison in Corfu in 1948.[88]

The third controversial figure to whom Bouena devotes many verses is the spiritual head of the community for its final decade—none other than the chief rabbi, Zvi Koretz. There are conflicting views concerning his intentions and the rationale behind his actions. The poet's attitude reflects that of the majority of the Salonikan survivors of the war who lived through this period. Koretz was a rabbi from Rzeszow, Galicia, who attended the Theologischen Seminar in Vienna and was awarded a Ph.D. at the university there; he was first hired by the community in 1933.[89] Bowman describes him as "a dedicated scholar and competent religious and diplomatic leader" who could not handle the Salonikan Sephardim; although he was sincerely concerned for his community's fate, in the community's eyes, he was formal and rigid.[90] At the same time, his nonaggressive stance and his naïve dealings with the Nazis simply facilitated the execution of their plans. Despite the fact that he learned Ladino, many resented him for being an outsider, an attitude that is somewhat understandable;[91] the press describes him as arrogant and ostentatious. Bouena has the impression that those members of the community who opposed hiring Koretz suffered after he obtained the position. She intimates that when those who did not welcome him were in need of some communal service, such as circumcision, they suddenly encountered difficulties.[92]

One might think that the fact that he could communicate directly with the Germans would have proven advantageous to the community, but as far as the survivors are concerned, the rabbi did not manage to manipulate the Nazis one iota.[93] In the collective Salonikan memory, he did his utmost to cooperate with them, which led to the deception and betrayal of his fellow Jews. Koretz was seen as a foreign traitor who benefited from VIP treatment and made sure to protect his family but was oblivious to the disaster that awaited the community.[94] A survivor wrote, "Dr. Koretz assures us that if we obey orders, we have nothing to fear," for "Dr. Koretz maintains that there is no danger."[95] The resentment that Bouena and so many of her compatriots felt toward him is strongly reflected in her writing as well.

Bouena was aware that Koretz was arrested in Athens on May 17, 1941, and sent to Vienna for eight months. Upon his return to Salonika at the end of January 1942, the rabbi reassured the Jews that their fears were in vain: "Koretz sold us out, the whole Jewish community, / In order to save himself, his family, and his entourage. / He told us that he just came from Europe / And all the Jews are eating well and not just cornbread."[96]

With each progressive development following the Nazi conquest, Bouena points out how Koretz either took advantage of his position or neglected to help the community or to alleviate the situation in any way. Apparently, members of the EAM offered to help Jews flee and even approached Rabbi Koretz to offer their aid, which was refused.[97] When the young men of Salonika were sent out to forced labor camps, the members of the community felt that Koretz exploited his status by procuring exemptions for his own. Most of the young men were suffering from malaria, but "only the sons of the friends of Koretz did not go. / He gave them papers [stating] that they are working for him." The resentment toward the Ashkenazi rabbi grew because he obtained preferential treatment for those around him.[98]

The poet presents her impression of Koretz's negotiations with the Nazis. She claims that he sought Greek citizenship, something the government was not anxious to grant. There was pressure on the Jewish community to relinquish the coveted grounds that contained the five-hundred-year-old Jewish cemetery, part of an attempt to extort tremendous sums of money from the Jews. This cemetery held the remains of Spanish exiles and numerous rabbis and luminaries from eminent Sephardi families.[99] Koretz agreed to give up this sacred ground; it was confiscated in November 1942 and destroyed by the Greeks on December 6. Bouena writes, "They opened the tombs in his presence. / With the skeletons, they found jewels and precious objects. / He took them to his home where he made a room into a museum."[100] According to the poet, any objections to these arrangements were violently stifled. It is shocking to think that the members of a community believed their rabbinic leader to be capable of such complicity—but then again, these were stressful times. Fleming writes, "Koretz, who had already handed over the community's registers to the Germans, continued to comply with German demands; whether he did so out of collusion or the naïve belief that compliance would bring leniency is unclear."[101]

In order to smoothly execute the transports, a great deal of administrative planning must first have taken place, beginning with the relocations to the ghettos. As the Germans proceeded with their plans for Aryanization, they summoned the chief rabbi to inform him of his duties. Bouena could not contain her anger, for she and her fellow Salonikans were convinced that the chief rabbi facilitated the Nazis' systematic disbandment of the community. His orders were to move the large community into smaller living spaces with less humane conditions. The poet refers to the orders to abandon their homes in order to move to the ghettos and how the "first foreign chief rabbi" sold them out so easily.[102]

In a rapid and compressed form, the community experienced the various stages of exclusion leading to ghettoization. In February 1943, Koretz became responsible for all the Jews in German-occupied zones around the city. He promptly announced any orders he received and "urged his listeners to follow German commands"; by March, he was instrumental in helping to perpetuate the myth regarding relocation in Krakow.[103] The community was taxed in order to fund the relocation, which began February 6, 1943, the day of the arrival of Eichmann's Sonderkommando; it was to be completed by the twenty-fifth of the month.

Survivors such as Yaakov Handeli recall how the rabbi recruited high school students such as himself to volunteer, sending them door to door with forms in order to provide the Germans with accurate lists of residences, their inhabitants, their professions, and the like. He emphasized the importance and urgency of their assignments, which included preparing identity cards and ninety thousand yellow badges based on information from the completed forms.[104] Immanuel contends that hundreds of students were involved in these frantic registration activities.[105] When one compares the fate of the Salonikans to that of the other Greek Jewish communities, one understands their rancor. Although the circumstances here were not identical to any other locale vis-à-vis size, geographical location, accessibility, knowledge of Greek, and ties to their neighbors, almost every other Jewish community had a larger percentage of survivors. In many cases, survival was due to being warned by their community leaders and rabbis and advised to flee the roundups.[106]

As of December 1942, the main ghetto was established in the aforementioned Baron de Hirsch neighborhood, conveniently located for the transports since it is adjacent to the railroad station. Koretz negotiated for two quarters rather than one; by February 25, 1943, all were reassigned to even more cramped living quarters. The impression given was that the rabbi was adamant that every order be fully obeyed; carrying "out all these instructions led to a frenzy of activity."[107] Because Bouena herself had premonitions about the fate awaiting the community, she joined a committee that anticipated the deportation and decided to attempt to rescue Jewish children. Together with two other young women, she approached the rabbi with a proposal to hide and shelter newborn babies in monasteries and convents: "The rabbi disagreed with our plan and forthwith denounced us to the Jewish police of the ghetto by whom we were followed." The members of the committee held a secret meeting and decided to defy the rabbi and continue with their plan; each member worked separately in order not to attract attention.[108] Ironically these young women's perceptions were more astute and realistic than those of the German-speaking rabbi.

Thus, it should come as no surprise that the poet continues to condemn the chief rabbi as he tried to allay the fears of his adopted community.[109] On March 14, 1943, a public meeting was held in the ghetto synagogue to announce the relocations; the first transport was scheduled for the following day. Bouena points to the furor that erupted, although the rabbi again tried to defuse the anger, hoping to convince the Selaniklis to comply with the German ordinances. In her eyes, the chief rabbi had "sold [them] out to the Germans," treating his constituents as little more than children. When informed of the deportations, he all too belatedly tried to suggest alternatives. She also refers to his next appearance three days later: "He came to the congregation of Monastir to speak. They began to beat him; they wanted to tear him apart, but the Jewish police saved him."[110] This appears to have been a near lynching; the Jewish police alerted the Germans, who proceeded to imprison those involved.[111] It was an example of cooperation between the Jewish police and the Germans, all anxious to protect the leader chosen to manipulate the Jews, some of whom were interfering with their plans.

That very spring, as Passover approached, the matsah factory was closed; the rabbi informed the community that there was no choice but to eat bread. Because it was impossible to manufacture what was needed for the eight-day holiday, this decision was made in the interest of saving lives so that none would starve. Nevertheless, it was not easy for anyone to accept this decision; in a pun on the very name of this holiday, Bouena toasts "those who are going to 'pass over' the bread."[112]

Anger and resentment are repeatedly expressed toward this leader. When he met with the prime minister, Ioannis Rhallis, his request for help was denied and he was put under house arrest.[113] Sent with his family to Bergen-Belsen rather than to Auschwitz, the rabbi died on June 2, 1945, of typhoid—although his wife and children survived.[114] Rozen refers to the accumulation of anger expressed after the war toward the unpopular Ashkenazi outsider.[115] Gita, his widow, testified at Yad Vashem that he did everything physically possible to save

Remnant of the Baron de Hirsch neighborhood.

Train station opposite Baron de Hirsch ghetto today.

the Jews, who judged him unfairly. Some see the anger as representing a need for a scapegoat or a "postwar passion for vengeance."[116] While his defenders claim that this type of damnation is typical of post-Holocaust sentiments regarding most members of the Judenrat in almost any given community, Bouena feels justified in criticizing him and his actions and in holding him responsible for helping the Germans maintain an aura of secrecy in order to more smoothly execute their plans.

This condemnation of Koretz has been criticized by some scholars; it is interesting to note that not all of the survivors have the same impression of this man. For example, the family of Andreas Kounio that was likewise interned in Bergen-Belsen felt that the rabbi's approach was completely logical for someone with German training;[117] although he was a Polish Jew, he was proud of the orderliness of the German world. Thus he was perceived to have been a naïve Jew who did not realize how the Germans exploited his sense of responsibility and admiration of German order; his compliance was due to his education and his personal inclinations rather than to ill intent.[118] Bouena's memoirs tell of a survivor who refused to join the Jewish police and subsequently lost his entire family; he resented the special treatment that the Koretz family received, even following the return from the camps.[119] From his perspective, the Koretz survivors of Bergen-Belsen had accommodations far superior to those, like himself, who survived Auschwitz and who were sleeping on the floor of the Allatini Orphanage. He and his cohorts were hoping to sneak into Palestine while Koretz's widow was patiently waiting for permits.[120] The atmosphere was extremely hostile at the time of the return of the Bergen-Belsen group: "Survivors, who were drowning in the intricate process of establishing their claims to family property inhabited by squatters or owned by wartime collaborators, at first tried to lynch them." The widow was ostracized and her son (and daughter) were rejected by the community.[121]

Benbassa and Rodrigue contend that Koretz "was certainly predisposed to do the Germans' bidding in order not to alienate them and not to bring further misfortune upon the community, and became, like some of the *Judenrat* leaders in Eastern Europe, a cog in the machinery of destruction, facilitating rather than hindering the Nazis' tasks."[122] According to what Bea Lewkowicz writes of her interviews with survivors, "One person who is commonly perceived as a traitor and held responsible for the fact that so many Jews were deported to Poland is Rabbi Koretz."[123]

Rozen suggests that the portrayal of Koretz "was a function of the community's need to understand its unexpected and colossal tragedy," and since most of the survivors did not write until later, it also was commensurate with the Israeli mindset after the war.[124] As a result, in the writings soon after the liberation, "historians" were creating collective memory, but, in her opinion, additional testimony, particularly if provided at later dates, is less condemning. Rozen points to a change that transpired between 1967 and 1984, at which time Koretz was viewed as having been a fallible leader—perhaps incompetent as well—who was to be condemned because he still had betrayed the community, but was no longer portrayed quite so acrimoniously.[125] Rozen concludes that the "portrayal of Koretz as a collaborator and a traitor should thus be treated with caution and evaluated in the context of the needs of the various actors in this tragic story."[126]

In Hebrew volumes devoted to the memory of Salonika, there is an attempt to determine whether the harsh judgments rendered were justified. Immanuel cites an article defending the rabbi, but is rather successful in refuting its contentions. Surprisingly enough, his interviews of survivors in the United States reveal impressions identical to those of survivors living in Israel. In addition, Immanuel spoke to leaders of other Greek Jewish communities who phoned Koretz for guidance after the first transports had departed. The rabbi continued to encourage them to comply, insisting that the first three trainloads of Jews had been treated well at Krakow; after observing the ninth transport, however, he seems to have arrived at a different conclusion. The harsh words of survivors, based on actual experiences rather than the impressions of outsiders, intrinsically merit a certain degree of legitimacy.[127]

If, as some contend, Zionist ideology or the need to cut ties with the diaspora mentality was responsible for the attitudes of the survivors who relocated to Israel, how can one explain Bouena's stance? Because she lived in Palestine for a very brief period and did not speak Hebrew, she clearly was not influenced by Zionist ideology or bias. After the war, while living in Montreal, Bouena was neither part of a larger community of survivors nor of a Greek Jewish diaspora; she occasionally visited her family in Israel but was not influenced by the Israeli mindset in the least. She drew her own conclusions, having personally witnessed the policy advocated by the chief rabbi. She herself harbored serious doubts in 1943 about the fate of the community; her pragmatic suggestion to save infants was rejected out of hand by the leader. As a result, her criticism of Koretz is extremely harsh.

By the same token, Bea Lewkowicz recorded her assessment of the rabbi's role after conducting postwar interviews with Jews returning to Salonika. In no uncertain terms, they felt bitter and "betrayed by the Jewish leadership, especially by Rabbi Koretz, who convinced the Jews to follow the deportation orders to Poland."[128] The Selaniklis who had remained in Greece were attempting to analyze the "colossal tragedy"; they had been influenced neither by those recording the events nor by those who had moved to Palestine.[129] This was simply their personal assessment, which needs to be understood as such. The behavior of the Salonikan rabbi stands out in distinct contrast to that of rabbis from other, albeit smaller, Greek communities, who had warned their constituents; Koretz never encouraged the younger generation to flee or to join the partisans. One may contend that he has been made into a scapegoat by means of historical memory, but there is general agreement that he acquiesced to German directives at times when he might have been able to delay events, warn people, or save lives. Rozen prefers to view him as having been a fallible leader, but those who survived the camps or returned from hiding have not been able to forgive him for fulfilling German orders quickly and obediently or for ignoring the warning signs that disaster was looming.

As it turns out, the Selaniklis were creative in their attempts to maintain their sanity while under Nazi rule. In this collection, there are only two verses that express ill wishes for Hitler. However, in a separate collection, Bouena lists *maldiciones* galore—some two hundred sayings expressing the equivalent of curses aimed at Hitler, all composed between April 1941 and March 1943. In the collection under discussion, one verse expresses the hope that the Jews will outlast this dictator: "Hitler is going to drop dead and still the Jews are going to remain in Salonika." She adds, "We are going to laugh at him when / He is going to have a black and cruel shuddering [experience]."[130] Here is a clear wish for survival, but since it is written after the fact, it is, unfortunately, nothing more than wishful thinking. Similarly, in one of the first coplas in the collection, she points out that "there were rumors in Salonika that Hitler is going to die, / But I say: Let him suffer and not die. / May a great misfortune befall him and those around him / And may they not be spared great heartache. / I hope that God will hear these curses that I cast upon him."[131] Perhaps Bouena hoped that by hearing her curses, God would take action.

Bouena's fate was to be quite different from that of the majority of her community. Following her run-in with Hasson, the Red Cross volunteer feared for her life. While contemplating her prospects, she discovered that her fiancé, Chaim, had escaped the forced labor camp and returned to Salonika. Knowing that he could not remain in the city, the two planned to marry on the following day and flee together. An impromptu ceremony was to take place at the synagogue. However, when the bride arrived at the appointed hour, she was shocked to discover that her groom had been murdered at the bridal canopy in advance of his fiancée's arrival. Bouena was arrested on the spot and incarcerated in Pavlos Melas. This was (and still is) a Greek army camp located in the northern outskirts of the city expropriated by the SS; it was converted into a prison that mainly contained political prisoners who were condemned to be shot.[132] While Bouena was still in this prison, Greek partisans managed to smuggle her out of

View of Pavlos Melas Greek army camp, where Bouena was imprisoned.

her cell via an ingenious escape plan.[133] Once freed, she was keenly aware that under no circumstances could she remain in Salonika.

Although Bouena needed to leave Salonika immediately, she had to plan carefully and consult with trustworthy friends. With their help, she was hidden in various homes en route to the mountains. She traveled southwest to Veria (Veroia), at the foot of the Vermion Mountains in Macedonia, and from there by bus to a safe home owned by an Albanian from Salonika who was in Egypt at the time. However, the Albanian's wife did not let Bouena stay for long and again, she was on the move. She returned to Veria by bus and en route, witnessed a transport of Jews from Ghetto 151; she noted that the railroad cars were without windows. Once back in Veria, she was followed by a man she recognized, a journalist she knew had served with the Jewish police. Bouena had written verses about the lack of trust in the Jewish police and the eerie sense the Salonikans have that they were being shadowed; she was now experiencing this insecurity firsthand. Somehow she managed to lose him and reached the home of her friend Georgette Modiano, who promised to help her.[134] She spent two nights there and was sent to another home, that of a Dr. Scouros.[135]

While in Veria, she helped her contact, Mme. Soula, in a Christian soup kitchen established for children. Apparently, the workers there were expected to make the sign of the cross either when praying or upon entering the building. Bouena, needless to say, had no idea how to properly perform this; she made the sign backwards. She was fortunate, for a woman who noticed her confusion took her to an office to instruct her, explaining that she was fond of Jews. In other words, not only did this woman notice Bouena's error, but she also realized the reason for the young woman's ignorance. Fortunately, she not only verbalized affection for the Jews, but acted upon her beliefs by helping Bouena learn to dissimulate and by not revealing her secret to anyone. After the war, the poet unsuccessfully attempted to locate this woman in order to thank her.[136]

After about two weeks, her hosts began to lose their mettle, fearing the consequences if caught harboring a fugitive. They notified their contact, Daniel Modiano, that her presence was making them anxious. Consequently, Modiano rented a rather costly room for her until he could hatch a feasible plan. Bouena spent a number of months in limbo, but returned home when she was in need of medical attention;[137] Modiano once again took care of her. This Italian Jew, a friend of the Sarfatty family, proved to be her savior, for he managed to take advantage of his excellent relationship with the Italian consul, Guelfo Zamboni. Zamboni actively helped groups of Italian Jewish women married to Greeks; Jewish men whose wives were Italian citizens; and even those whose names simply sounded Italian.[138] Thus, Bouena was not surprised when Daniel informed her that he had obtained an Italian passport for her. The instructions that she received are these: "Your name is Flora Tivoli, born in Livorno, Italy / And you are going to go to Athens on the Italian train." This unusually long verse ends with an appropriate toast to the health of Modiano.[139]

Because of Bouena's precarious situation as a fugitive from prison who was in cahoots with the partisans, she was extremely nervous about executing a smooth escape. The plan was for her to board a southward-bound military train filled with Italian soldiers; when it stopped midway, she could transfer and board another Italian train bound for Athens.[140] Upon her arrival at the station in Salonika, Bouena realized that the infamous Hasson was standing alongside the consul, examining the passengers and their documents. Despite the fact that her face was covered with a veil, there was no doubt in her mind that he could easily identify her and turn her over to the authorities. According to her memoirs, the only reason he refrained from revealing her identity was because members of the underground were present who would have shot him at a moment's notice. Despite the fact that Daniel accompanied her to the train station, this proved to be a nerve-wracking experience. The poet describes it vividly: "I took Daniel's arm, trembling and farting. / Only once I entered the train did I relieve myself."[141] One is not surprised to discover that Bouena was under tremendous stress, especially upon realizing that Hasson was present at the station. This incident is corroborated by Michael Molho, who attests to the fact that her archenemy was indeed there.[142] Daniel, whom she calls her angel, provided a successful escape route, which entailed two days of waiting in a field for a second train that would be traveling within the Italian zone and then arriving in Athens by truck.

Modiano, as Bouena writes, "took care of smuggling Jews out of the Baron de Hirsch. / The Italian consul gave them false passports to enable them to flee."[143] He himself fled to Italy in spring 1943, but the Germans were anxious to punish him for his treachery. Thus, her savior was their nemesis. In September, the SS located, murdered, and mutilated him and his family along with the Mosseri, Fernandez Dias, and Torres families—three extremely influential Italian Jewish families from Salonika who had helped Modiano and the consul. All were staying in a hotel on Lake Superior (Maggiore) in northern Italy. As Bouena writes, "The Germans came, killed him and his coterie. / The cadavers were thrown into the lake."[144] This strophe does not end with the usual refrain toasting a member of the community, for the pain upon learning of these murders weighs far too heavily upon the poet and her pen. Thus she chooses a less conventional but nevertheless powerful means of closing the verse: "This was done [by] the German more evil than Pharoah and Haman."[145] There is no doubt in her mind that Hitler had outdone the biblical and post-biblical figures who preceded him and similarly sought to annihilate the Jews.

Although the life of Bouena's savior was brutally ended, his charge managed, somewhat miraculously, to preserve her own life. The partisans gave Bouena her undercover name, Maritsa Serafamidou. Once in Athens the Greek-speaking partisan with her new identity made contact with two young Jewish men from the underground named Maurice and Nico; the three of them functioned as a unit.[146] Despite the fact that she escaped Nazi-controlled territory, the Salonikan was still extremely wary of her surroundings, realizing that it was dangerous to tarry in Athens. She explains that while eating in a restaurant in the capital city, the trio experienced a strong sense of discomfort. One never knew who was on which side; seeing a familiar face was not necessarily cause to rejoice, for one never knew who was a loyal Jew and who was a German collaborator. One could never be too cautious.

The threesome left Athens, riding by bus to a small town by the sea. Madame Tsakousti, their contact there, gave them tickets for passage by boat to Evvia (Evvoia), a hilly and thickly wooded region where they rented a barn. Her cohorts were away on an errand when a German boat transporting Jewish prisoners approached the shore. Bouena and some others relocated to a second barn, where a large group amassed to listen to a speech by Hitler on the radio. Bouena herself was neither arrested nor harmed that day purely by luck; because she was suffering from a stomachache, she went outside to a ditch in order to relieve herself. While outside, the Germans arrived and torched the barn; she and a boy who had accompanied her outside survived by hiding in a pit.[147] This is another case of serendipity in a matter of life and death.

The group was then composed of the original threesome as well as a three- or four-month-old infant Bouena rescued from its dying mother's arms and numerous abandoned Jewish children they discovered on the way. They followed the well-known partisan route by sea from the peninsula of Evvia. Locals as well as a Turkish fisherman played a significant role here; Turkish fishing boats were often available for hire in Greece to take passengers to Çesme, on the Turkish coast.[148] Bouena and her cohorts did precisely this, as she relates: "We rented a fishing (steam) boat to Turkey. / We set forth; we debarked at Çesme. / We felt as if we had come to heaven."[149] At long last, they were not surrounded by German or Italian soldiers, Jewish police and collaborators, or any other hostile persons.

The role of the Greek Christians and their attitudes to the Jews varied from place to place and from individual to individual. In Salonika, economic competition fueled antisemitic feelings; in addition, there was a linguistic barrier between Greek speakers and the Ladino speakers. Nevertheless, Mazower contends that antisemitism had a small role in the deportation process.[150] While monasteries and nunneries assumed care for babies, individual Orthodox Christian families took children into their homes and helped young men link up with the resistance.[151] It is estimated that about two thousand Jews were hiding in Athens, in villages or on islands, or fighting with the resistance. Upon leaving Salonika, many Jews entrusted their Greek neighbors and friends with their belongings, which included apartments and shops.

In her memoirs, Bouena details many of her adventures with the partisans. She relates how the fishermen changed the boat's flag from Greek to Turkish halfway so that when they landed on Turkish shores, the soldiers would not ask anyone for papers.[152] In August 1943, the British consulate in Ankara received instructions from London to give entrance permits to every Jew who reached Turkey. The British themselves were concerned about saving members of their air force who were stranded in the area; consequently, they set up headquarters in Çesme while the Americans chose Ismir. The Greek partisans, namely the ELAS and the EAM, cooperated with the Allies. Thus, the aim of the partisans was to move prisoners of war and underground leaders to Turkey, to return with funds and supplies, and to respond to requests made by the Allies. As in Bouena's case, fishing boats and other small vessels served as the means of transport between Ismir and Çesme. The Yishuv representatives learned about this arrangement and sought to save Jews in this manner, eventually preferring to deal directly with the partisans rather than with the Allies. Once news of the March deportations reached the outside world, there was pressure to attempt to save any remaining Greek Jews. The hope was to transport up to twenty individuals weekly from the Greek coast to Turkey.[153] One can see that this route was precisely the one used by Bouena and her compatriots.

When her group arrived in Çesme, Bouena successfully located a Turkish nursemaid for hire in order to care for the infant she had found. From Çesme they continued to Ismir; the entourage boarded a train there and proceeded to Aleppo, Syria.[154] Their arrival is even dated in a verse; they arrived by Hanukah 1943 and celebrated upon their arrival, although they all got rather sick. Bouena thanks the doctors in the clinic who helped care for them.[155]

While in Syria, they were in need of additional medical treatment. Either the water was contaminated or something in the food was unsanitary; in the long run, the entire group suffered considerably. The portions were generous, but something was clearly awry in the kitchen facility set up for the refugees. Bouena writes, tongue in cheek, that "in Aleppo we have a good time. / Even in the bathroom we have company."[156] She adds that while there, "the British bring medicine by the gallon / Because everyone has diarrhea."[157] Ironically enough, Bouena later served as a dietitian and most likely could have isolated the problem that they encountered at this refugee camp.

After the war, there were very few survivors from Salonika. The community of 55,500 Jews was nearly extinguished; 95 percent of them did not survive Auschwitz. Many were subjected to Josef Mengele's experiments. Bouena herself lost all of her family except for the three sisters who had left Greece before the war; Marie emigrated to Marseilles, and Daisy and Rachel settled in Palestine.

The Greek-Jewish returnees found their way to various locales in Greece by plane, by bus, and by foot.[158] The first survivors, a group of 137 Jews who had found refuge either in the city itself or in the nearby hills, appeared at the end of October 1944. A committee was quickly organized on October 28 to register them, whether they were survivors from the hills or from the Polish camps; eventually they numbered 2,000 souls.[159] Their former homes (about 11,000 apartments), 2,300 stores and factories, and other property were all gone; the committee managed to regain about seven public buildings and some homes and offices.[160]

Unfortunately, it was impossible for anyone who had not been in a camp to comprehend the harrowing experience of the internees; there was a lack of compassion toward them, especially on the part of those who had survived by hiding. Former members of the resistance were sometimes suspected of being communists;[161] Bouena herself concealed her affiliation with ELAS for years.[162]

In addition, some Jews had converted while in hiding. Needless to say, the post-war situation was extremely complicated, both psychologically and emotionally; no one was truly capable of dealing with the new reality.

In June 1945, Bouena returned to Greece in two capacities. To the outside world, she was a dietitian working for UNNRA (United Nations Relief and Rehabilitation Administration) and cooking in soup kitchens for displaced persons, but in essence she was an undercover agent working with Jewish authorities in Palestine to set up an underground railroad from Greece to Palestine.[163]

The encounter with the survivors in Siderokastro, the displaced persons camp, was very traumatic for Bouena, but she never wallowed in self-pity. Her brother, Eliaou, sister Regina, paternal aunt, grandmother, and the rest of her family and friends had perished; Bouena committed herself to helping those who survived. In some of the poems, one perceives a sense of "us" versus "them" (non-inmates versus survivor-inmates) that one would not expect from Bouena, for not only does she have the language skills with which to communicate with the survivors, but she, too, is a Salonikan Jew. Bouena, however, was quite unusual among the staff members at the camp.

The Greek survivors were, in general, disappointed and unprepared for the way in which they were received after the liberation of the concentration camps. Some roamed for weeks or months before reaching Greece, only to encounter cruelty from non-Jews—and, to their shock, from Ashkenazi survivors.[164] Interestingly enough, Bouena does not mention an important fact: "The major group to return through Siderokastro was the remnant of the Judenrat, their families, and other prominent hostages who had been interned in the exchange camp at Bergen-Belsen from August 13, 1943, to April 9, 1945."[165] She was concerned with providing proper nutrition, and had her share of difficulties with most of the other staff there.

Bouena was aware of the fact that the combination of the Holocaust experience and the unexpected reception of the survivors by the outside world had its effect; the ambivalent attitude of the survivors can be discerned in the coplas. Bouena reports,

The deportees began to arrive in Salonika in small numbers
With numbers on their arms that the German tattooed on them.
They thought that they would be received with tambourines and trumpets,
But the few who survived and had hidden themselves
Were bitter about what had happened.
The deportees were united together
And they looked at us as [if we were] antisemites.[166]

Rivlin refers to the "anger and tremendous frustration" that the survivors experienced.[167]

This report is very disturbing. Bouena invokes a biblical reference to tambourines and trumpets as a means of greeting the ostensibly triumphant returnees, but one wonders if there was any true sense of triumph on the part of those who survived the camps. Perhaps the fact that they managed to escape Hitler's ovens more than suffices. In the poet's eyes, the survivors are tough and hostile as well as bitter. No one was certain who is against whom and who could be trusted. There was ambivalence on her part as well, for most of the staff working with the displaced persons was neither Jewish nor Sephardi. Despite a sense of miraculousness due to the very fact that these individuals survived, hostile attitudes, whether on the part of Ashkenazim or non-Jews, were difficult to fathom, for Bouena as well as for the other members of the staff.

Many arrived in poor health, often ill with tuberculosis;[168] needless to say, even the so-called healthy ones suffered starvation and deprivation for extended periods of time. The Joint Distribution Committee sent compassionate and helpful representatives. In truth, most of the survivors were afraid to return "home"; when Bouena herself passed through the city en route to Siderokastro, she remarked that it felt like a morgue to her; "The physical as well as human landscape was unrecognizable, bereft of familiar markers and inhabited by strangers. Entire neighborhoods had disappeared and virtually no known faces were to be seen."[169] Be that as it may, the survivors perceived the Joint Distribution Committee as being a stepping-stone to change because of the training course it offered them. After taking this course, a change of attitude on their part became noticeable; they experienced a ray of hope for the first time in years at the prospect of building a new life in Palestine.[170]

After completing her work at the displaced persons' camp, Bouena decided to return to Salonika to see if she could locate any pieces of her past.[171] Although she was not present when her family was deported, she knew that her brother gave some of their belongings to various neighbors and friends for safekeeping as soon as they had to move out of their original home during the Nazi invasion in 1941. Much to her surprise and shock, she discovered some of these treasures in the most unexpected places. One of the most moving verses in the collection pertains to such a discovery in the streets of Salonika. While roaming about, she purchased chestnuts from a street vendor, and noticed that he had wrapped them in paper taken from her own mother's Passover Haggadah. She proceeded to buy all of the pages he had in his possession and was understandably furious with the vendor.[172] Having inadvertently stumbled upon a piece of her former life, tied both to her mother and to her beloved Jewish traditions, she was traumatized. A treasured book was being desecrated for the most mundane purpose;

the disparate pages of the Haggadah surely symbolize for her the haphazard way in which her family and her community were destroyed, and how futile most of the attempts to reclaim anything would be.

Bouena nonetheless sought to reclaim her trousseau and other items that were distributed to Greek neighbors and friends. In her memoirs, she goes into detail about the emotional stress of this search. Possessions took on a new significance to the survivor, and often represented the sole link to a lost heritage. In her poetry, she mentions a silver plate that Sarah Trabout gave her that had been given to her sister Marie for safekeeping:" "I pray that one day she will give it to me. / I want to have it in order to better remember Sarah / Who was a true friend."[173] Bouena chose not to confront her sister about the plate despite its emotional significance for her. Elsewhere she again chose to avoid a confrontation. While in Tel Aviv, she was asked if a certain satin dressing gown was hers, and indeed it was, for her sister Marie brought it from Marseilles for her. However, in order to prevent a quarrel between the couple in possession of the gown, she elected to answer in the negative.[174] Possessions, of utmost importance at times, also become meaningless when compared to larger losses.

As the community was being liquidated, attempts were nonetheless made to provide for the future; it is doubtful that anyone could have foreseen the demise of Salonikan Jewry. Bouena's niece Suzanne gave Eliaou six thousand drachmas for safekeeping. Eliahu bought a bracelet with the cash and gave it to Bouena with the following instructions: it was to be given to their niece at the time of her wedding, but if it were worthless by then, she should receive the monetary equivalent; "And if it is [worth] more, tell her that it is a gift that I am making in honor of her marriage." This was a more than fair means of protecting the value of her cash. Bouena did not see Suzanne until she arrived in Israel; she "gave her the bracelet because the six thousand drachmas were not worth a penny."[175] Eliahu was gone, but his investment was wise and ultimately benefited his niece.

In addition to seeking lost property,[176] Bouena searched for children who had been hidden during the war. Her younger sister Regina had a friend who had married young and gave birth to a boy, who was presumably to be found "with the abandoned babies after the war." Bouena sought him out and located him in the community school, but was startled by his physical appearance, clearly the result of severe malnutrition. Although his mother had not survived the camps, he was fortunate enough to have had an uncle living in Palestine who happily welcomed the boy into his family.[177]

The following verses offer insight into the kind of help extended to Jewish refugees by some non-Jews and religious orders. Many Jewish children were hidden in monasteries and nunneries, and, as mentioned earlier, Bouena approached

Rabbi Koretz with a proposal to save babies precisely by this means.[178] These children's lives were saved, but their postwar identity became extremely problematic. Many of the younger children had no memory of their lives as Jews; some were unable to process the fact that they were actually Jewish and not pious Christians. Bouena was determined to locate a little girl named Sarika Lea. Most likely this was one of the children that she herself had placed in safekeeping before her flight; she expresses appreciation of the humanitarian efforts on the part of the French nuns who saved Jews, including Sarika Lea.[179]

Removing her from the nuns' care was not so simple. Bouena went to the Ville Marie convent to see Sarika, pretending to be her cousin, and located her in the infirmary.[180] In her memoirs, Bouena explains that the nun insisted she buy the girl a pair of shoes, which she did. Although anxious to extricate Sarika, Bouena clearly demonstrated patience, realizing that only time would tell whether Sarika would again feel comfortable as a Jewish girl. In another verse, she informs us that when she took the girl to a restaurant and encouraged her to eat, the child insisted that she must first say grace. Since she had been living in a nunnery for a number of years and had been trained in the basic tenets of Christianity, this was not surprising. No objections were made when she insisted upon crossing herself; Sarika proceeded to eat her meal.[181] A few days later, when the child was well enough to leave the convent, the nuns seemed to notice that she was beginning to flourish. She was sent to Palestine by the Joint Distribution Committee and placed in a kibbutz.[182] Bouena toasts Sarika and the kibbutz, hoping that the arrangement and the transition would be successful.

While on her mission, Bouena met Max Garfinkle, one of the founders of Kibbutz Ein Ha-Shofet. Like Bouena, Max came to Greece with the Palestine Relief Unit in 1945 and had been independently recruited to help set up an underground railroad to Palestine. Bouena and Max were wed at the Monastir Synagogue on July 14, 1946, and then returned to Palestine. Kibbutz life did not suit Bouena, who—after a month that felt like an eternity to her—declared that living there was an untenable option. The couple eventually settled in French-speaking Montreal for the rest of their days.

Bouena's coplas may not rank with those of the literary greats, but they do accurately describe the systematic destruction of one of the most important centers of Sephardi civilization in the Jewish diaspora. Her personal experience and the community's experience are intricately interwoven. The fact that her family had been so involved with the community sharpened her own awareness of the stages in the Nazi plan to remove and destroy all vestiges of Jewish life. Yet Bouena herself never seemed powerless; on the contrary, she helped her fellow Jews through her work with the Red Cross, providing the hungry with food and visiting the young men in forced labor camps. She had the wherewithal to anticipate catastrophe and save some twenty-five babies from certain death. When her attitudes and defiance landed her in prison, her ingenuity enabled her to notify her potential saviors of her whereabouts. After her escape, she continued to defy the Nazis as an active partisan and saved numerous abandoned children, whom she eventually brought to Palestine. Even after the war, she continued by helping the survivors and those who emerged from hiding; she supervised one of the group weddings organized for unmarried returnees of the younger generation in the Matanot La-Evionim building.[183] When the stress of dealing with her own as well as with others' survival abated and she created her own family, this daring woman found the peace of mind with which to record the traumatic events that led to the destruction of her home. It is befitting that she composed all of her verses in Ladino, in an ode to her beloved Salonika.

Ark in Synagogue of the Monastirlis where Bouena was wed; the Monastir (or Monasteriótes) Synagogue is the only one that survived the war.

Wedding photo of Bouena and Max Garfinkle, July 14, 1946. *Courtesy of Ely Garfinkle.*

Komplas de las mizerias Ke izo lo almanes
a Salonique del 1941—1943

1) Es Pesah aij rumores Ke les almanes estan a
la puerta de Salonique; todos aseraron los
magazenes i vengueron presto en Kaza
despoues de ouna ora, se sentia romper
pouertas de magazenes de Koumida i de buveda
el dio Ke mos vouadre de esta llazenoura

2) timprano la mangnana se aje el sileko, ma
agora i este non pouedemos tener savor
porKe salimos de en Kaza a las diez
& politofilaKa (poulisia djoudia) a la pouerta Ke non
mos pouedemos Kreer Ke son djudios
buamos a la saloud de Djelda Sasson

3) Enfrente de mi Kaza trayen Prisonieros
Inglizes a lavorar. Regina les yeva avoua i
pan. oun dia salio fouego Kon la doubara
tememos oun prizoniero
buamos a la saloud de Regina tia Daena
i Reyna Ke lavaron al prizoniero

4) La guerra ningounos ganan, solo madres
yoran i buvdas Kon Kriatouras thikas Ke son
dezmazaladas, la Komunutad lez ayouda
mal! todos me dieron i me daran Ouay
de lo mio Ke me viene a mankar
buvamos a la saloud de Samuel yakar

5) A Salonique aije rumores Ke Hitler se va amourir
ma yo digo Ke pene i Ke non mouera Ke le venga
oun negro mal i Ke non eskape mas a el i sou
deredor moutha dolor de Korason, espero Ke el dic
me va a sentir estas maldiciones Ke lo ethi
buvamos a la saloud de Bessanthi

First page of the second collection of coplas, in Bouena's original
handwriting.

Komplas de las mizerias ke izo lo[s] almanes a Salonique del 1941–1943

Miseries

75. Mousoulini kiere azer ouna Italia fouerte, komo esta aziendo el Alman.
Akavidate makaron. Kien ko[r]re mouthe presto se kaye.
Ya vites kuaolo te akonteseria en Albania.
I si non era el Alman ke vine a Boulgaria,
Ivas a entrar en Gresia kon kadenas por manias.
Bevamos a la saloud de Benvenida.

1. Es Pesah ay romores ke los almanes estan a la pouerta de Salonique.
Todos aseraron los magazines i vingneron preso en kaza.
Despoues de ouna ora,
Se sentia romper pouertas de magazines de koumida i de bivida.
El dio ke moz vouadre de esta hazenoura.

31. El primer dia ke vingneron, los almanes estavan bien rensegnados.
Mos tomaron los tableaus de valor i de grandes pintadores ke loz pinto.
Reyna impeso a gritar. Eliaou le dicho serala, te van a matar.
Bevamos a la saloud de [E]liao[u] ke se los dio i no rezestio.

13. Loz Alvos son fiereros.
Apenas los almanes vinieron,
les vaziaron el magazin.
Por mezes estouvieron inthendo kamiones
I mandandolos en Almagna ke manka de fiero.
Bevamos a la saloud de Rafael Serrero.

CHAPTER 5

Coplas about the Miseries That the Germans Inflicted on Salonika, 1941–1943

Miseries

75. Mussolini wants to create a strong Italy, like the German is doing.
Beware, "Macaroni."[1] He who runs a lot falls quickly.
You saw what would have happened to you in Albania.
And if it had not been [for] the German who came to Bulgaria,
You were going to enter Greece with chains for bracelets.
Let us drink to the health of Benvenida.

1. It is Passover; there are rumors that the Germans are at the entrance
   to Salonika.
Everyone closed their shops and quickly came home.
After an hour, one could hear
The breaking of doors of food and beverage stores.
God spare us from such misery.[2]

31. [On] the first day that they came, the Germans were well informed.
They took from us the valuable paintings that great painters had painted.
Reina began to scream. Eliaou told her: shut up, they are going to kill you.
Let us drink to the health of Eliaou who handed them over and did
   not resist.

13. The Alvos are ironworkers.
As soon as the Germans arrived,
     they [the Germans] emptied out their store.
For months they were filling trucks
And sending them to Germany that lacks iron.
Let us drink to the health of Rafael Serrero.

---

1. *Macaroni* was a slang term meaning "Italian."
2. Literally, "illness."

56. Los almanes tomaron todo.
El pechkador non tiene peche.
El karnesero non tiene carne.
El panadero non tiene pan.
Bevamos a la saloud de Matanoth La-Evionim
Ke da a komer a todas las kriatouras djoudias de la malá.

22. Sarah Trabout and Bouena Sarfatty estan aparejando
La lethe ke la Croix Rouge International les dio
Ke la despartan al réfectoire del Matanoth La-Evionim.
Mr. Arouk[h] vino a dezirles komplas para la devertir.
Se aboltaron en yorando de sentir.
Sarah le dicho: tenemos lavoro de azer aki.
Bevamos a la saloud de Daniel Shaki.

23. Le lethe venia en kachas i enklavadas kon klavos.
Aziamos attention para las avrir.
El padre de Sarah moz akonsejo ke dieramos la kachas i los klavos
I ke mos den komer para los lavoradores ke tenemos a la Rijie.
Bevamos a la saloud de estos lavoradores ke mos bendezieron
Kouando koumieron al refectoire del Matanoth La-Evionim.

27. Mr. Riades ese oun hombre de valor.
Viene cada dia a ver si la lethe eze la major,
Mete el grado[3] a la kaldera.
De la fatha, vemos ke esta bouena.
Bevamos a la saloud de Mr. Riades i la Croix Rouge ke lo empiega.

8. Eliaou Sarfatty tiene mouelino a Lachtira.
Esta abeduvouando mouthos proves ke kieren pan.
Los empregados viejos inda toman el djornal.
Non les abasta kon esta inflation
I Bouena guiza ouna vez el dia; les da a senar.
Bevamos a la saloud de Regina ke ayouda a guizar.

9. Non se ve merendjena ni kalavasa para guizar
Ni mismo tomates ke avia para ar[r]astar.[4]

---

3. According to Güler Orgun, the purpose of the *grado* was to ascertain that the milk had not been skimmed too much (personal communication, March 11, 2011).

4. This is a Portuguese word that means "to lie about" or "to be found in abundance."

56. The Germans took everything.
The fisherman does not have fish.
The butcher does not have meat.
The baker does not have bread.
Let us drink to the health of the "Gifts for the Needy [Organization]"
That feeds all the Jewish children in the neighborhood.

22. Sarah Trabout and Bouena Sarfatty are preparing
The milk that the International Red Cross gave them
So that they distribute it at the refectory[5] of the "Gifts for the Needy."
Mr. Aroukh came to recite complas in order to entertain [them].
They turned around in tears from listening.
Sarah told him: we have work to do here.
Let us drink to the health of Daniel Shaki.

23. The milk came in boxes and nailed closed.
We opened them carefully.
Sarah's father advised us that we should give the boxes and the nails
So that they give us food for the workers who we have at the Regie.[6]
Let us drink to the health of these workers who blessed us
When they ate at the refectory of the "Gifts for the Needy."

27. Mr. Riades is a man of honor.
He comes every day to see if the milk is the best,
Puts the thermometer in the cauldron.
From the look on his face, we see that it is good.
Let us drink to the health of Mr. Riades and the Red Cross that
employs him.

8. Eliaou Sarfatty has a flourmill[7] in Lachtira.
He is helping the many poor who want bread.
The old employees still take their daily wage.
They cannot manage with this inflation
And Bouena cooks once a day; she gives them dinner.
Let us drink to the health of Regina, who helps cook.

9. One does not see any eggplant or courgette[8] for cooking
Nor even tomatoes that used to be found in abundance.[9]

---

5. Dining room, or hall.
6. Jewish Quarter.
7. By the grain silos.
8. Marrow squash.
9. Literally, lying about.

Frouta eze ouna koza de lo pasado.
Solo las bobotas[10] ke la djente se estan ounflando.
Bevamos a la saloud de Haim Toledano.

16. La rezerva de la koumida ke tenemos se esta eskapando.
    Mas djente se mourieron a la Rejie [*sic*] Vardar[11]
    De no tener de koualo senar.
    Dio abasta este perguema.[12]
    Bevamos a la saloud de Simon Amar.

17. Non aye mas savor de la vida
    Kouando los almanes mos yivaron las sias,
    Non tenemoz ande mos asentar ni lougar a respirar.
    Pasensia, haverim, i esto va apasar.
    Bevamos a la saloud de los ke saven esperar.

55. Los almanes mos tomaron el pero i el radio.
    Non sentimos novedades, ni aye kien ke mos vouadre.
    Bevamos a la saloud de los ke tienen koraje.

3. En frente de mi kaza trayen prisonieros inglaizes a lavorar.
   Regina les yeva avoua i pan.
   Oun dia salio fouego; kon la doubara, tomimos oun prisoniero.
   Bevamos a la saloud de Regina, tia Dona i Reyna
       ke lavaron al prizoniero.

19. Los Almanes se posesaron de Salonique.
    A la platia arekojeron los djidios selaniklis
    Y g[y]mnastique los ouvligaron a azer fina ke estavan kansos
    I ke se empesaron a kayer.
    Bevamos a la saloud de Acher Abravanel.

14. Paresemos ounos kodredos enfrente de los almanes.
    La djouventoud se kiere revoltar, ma! La kaye de Salonique eze de asfalt.
    Non aye ni piedras para arrojar.
    Bevamos a la saloud de Avraam Yonatan.

24. Foue a vijitar a loz mansevos
    Ke los almanes tomaron a lavoro forsado.

---

10. David Kunios identified *bobotas* as bread made from corn flour in the early stages of the Occupation. Regular bread was not available, except on the black market, and it soon became a luxury (personal communication, February 25, 2009).

11. One of the "new" neighborhoods in the far western portion of the city (Vardaris) built for the Jews after the fire of 1890. The tobacco company, Regie de tabac, was located there as well.

12. Also spelled *preguema*.

Fruit is a thing of the past.
The people only get stuffed with cornbread.
Let us drink to the health of Haim Toledano.

16. The remaining food that we have is disappearing.
    More people died in the Regie Vardar neighborhood
    From not having anything [to eat] for dinner.
    God grant this plea.
    Let us drink to the health of Simon Amar.

17. There is no more zest for life
    When the Germans took away our chairs,
    We have nowhere to sit nor a place to breathe.
    Patience, friends, and this is going to pass.
    Let us drink to the health of those who know how to hope.

55. The Germans took dogs and radios from us.
    We do not hear news nor is there anyone to protect us.
    Let us drink to the health of those who have courage.

 3. In front of my house they bring English prisoners to work.
    Regina brings them water and bread.
    One day a fire broke out; in the mayhem, we took a prisoner [home].
    Let us drink to the health of Regina, Aunt Dona, and Reina,
        who bathed the prisoner.

19. The Germans took possession of Salonika.
    They gathered the Salonikan Jews at the plaza
    And forced them to do exercises until they were exhausted
    And began to collapse.
    Let us drink to the health of Asher Avravanel.

14. We are like sheep when facing the Germans.
    The youth want to revolt, but! The street of Salonika is of asphalt.
    There are no stones to throw.
    Let us drink to the health of Avraham Yonatan.

24. I went to visit the young men
    Whom the Germans took for forced labor.

De 18 a 28 todo djidio devia yir.
Komo lavorava a la Croix Rouge, tinia carta para entrar.
Loz mansevos estavan koumiendo lahna bouyida kon avoua.
Gosti; non avia ni sal.
Bevamos a la saloud de estos mansevos ke estan soufriendo sin kedar.

25. Kouando vine en kaza de las ergas,[13]
Estava mouerta kansada, de ver estos mansevos soufriendo.
En atornado mi kaza estava yena de madres
A demandar si vidé a sou ijo i komo esta.
A todas les diche ke estan bouenos, ma!
El corazon me douwilyo de ver estos mansevos en dolor.
Bevamos a la saloud de estos mansevos ke estavan sin kolor.

26. El primo ke vide a las ergas foue Salomon Shaki.
Le estava kouriendo sangre de la naris.
Non tenia riza para se alimpiar.
Le di la mia ke non abasto.
Arazgui el volan del vistido i se lo di.
Kontinuyi mi vijita ke el alman me dicho de avansar.
Por segouro ke esta chena nounka me la vo a oulvidar.
Bevamos a la saloud de los ke van a kedar.

29. La segounda veze ke foue a las ergas
Kon mi vezina Bienvenida.
Tiene al ijo ayi.
Trouchemos vestido de moujer i ouna charpa a la kavesa.
Lo kitimos de el kampo de los prizonieros i lo trouchimos a Salonique.
Ma! Malhorozamente en el kamino se mourio.
Rogaremos por el alma del iyo de Bienvenida ke touvo esta sfouerte.

30. Bienvenida eze bivda non tiene a ningounos a la ayoudar
A rempouchar la arabá para yivar al ijo a enterar.
Todos los vizinos le ayoudaron a esta dezmazalada.
Rogamos ke el dio mande pasensia a esta madre amargada.

35. Non mos pouedemos asentar al balkon.
Kon esta kalor la sola koza ke se ve ese padres
Arempouchando arabekas, yevando al ijo

---

13. *Lavoro forsado;* in Greek, *ergasias* is "work," probably mispronounced by the Jews, but it is a reference to forced labor.

Every Jew age eighteen to twenty-eight had to go.
Being a worker for the Red Cross, I had an entrance pass.
The young men were eating cabbage boiled in water.
I tasted; there wasn't even salt.
Let us drink to the health of these young men who are suffering nonstop.

25. When I came home from the labor camp,
I was dead tired after seeing those young men suffering.
Upon my return my house was filled with mothers,
[Each] asking if I saw her son and how he is.
I told them all that they are fine, but!
My heart ached to see these boys in pain.
Let us drink to the health of those young men who had no color.[14]

26. The first one I saw at the work [camps] was Salomon Shaki.
Blood was running down his nose.
He did not have a handkerchief to wipe himself clean.
I gave him mine, which did not suffice.
I tore the flounce of my dress and gave it to him.
I continued my visit since the German told me to move on.
There is no doubt that I will never forget that scene.
Let us drink to the health of those who are going to remain.[15]

29. The second time that I went to the labor [camps]
[Was] with my neighbor Bienvenida.
She has her son there.
We brought women's clothes and a shawl for his head.
We took him out of the prisoners' camp and brought him to Salonika.
But! Unfortunately he died en route.
Let us pray for the soul of Benvenida's son who had this misfortune.

30. Bienvenida is a widow and has no one to help her
To push the cart in order to transport her son to be buried.
All the neighbors helped this unfortunate woman.
We pray that God sends patience to this embittered mother.

35. We cannot sit on the balcony.
In this heat the only thing that one can see is fathers
Pushing wheelbarrows, carrying [their] son[s] to be buried

---

14. In their faces.
15. Survive.

E enterar ke vigneron de las ergas medios muertos.
Souetamos a estos padres sin fouersa saloud i pasensia.

46. Mi fijo vino a viajar el dia ke se deklaro la Guerra.
Deretho al servisio militar, despoues a las ergas
I sin mankar el guetto sin klaridad.[16]
Bevamos a la saloud de los ke non tienen mazal.

4. La guerra ningounos ganan.
Solo madres yoran
I biudas kon kriatouras t[c]hikas ke son dezmazaladas
La komunitad lez ayouda.
Ma! Todos me dieron i me daran.
Guay de lo mio ke me viene a mankar.[17]
Bevamos a la saloud de Samuel Yakar.

34. Paguimos a los almanes petha para trayer la djouderia.
En kaza paresen komo si salieron de ouna grande hazinoura de kama.
Non avia kinino para les dar porke vegneron kon frios.
Souhatamos saloud a estos mansevos keridos.

11. Samueliko, el de la tia Dona,
non savemos koualo se izo.
Soldado de los kouarenta a Veria estava serviendo.
Oye tomimos lettra de la Croix Rouge ke esta prizoniero
I de bouena saloud.
Esperamos ke va a kedar en Italia
asta ke loz almanes se van abaterear.
Bevamos a la saloud de todos los soldados
ke non savemos ande estan.

15. Los djidios de Salonique moz oulvidimos de reir
De kouando el alman paso el bridje.
Kada ouno i ouno se espanta de sou solombra.
Parese komo ouno ke esta kaminando de detrase,
aferando sou hombre.
Ine dizimos: Pasa pounto pasa moundo.
Bevamos a la saloud de Alberto Kamondo.

---

16. Literally, "And not avoiding the ghetto without any clarity."
17. This is from the Italian verb *mancare,* "to lack."

Who returned from the labor [camps] half dead.
We wish these fathers without strength health and patience [well].

46. My son came on a trip on the day that the war was declared.
Straight into military service, then to the labor [camps]
Without missing the ghetto devoid of a ray of light.
Let us drink to the health of those who have no luck.

4. [In] war no one wins.
Only mothers cry
And the community helps unfortunate widows with small children.
But! Everyone gave me and will go on giving me.
Alas! For all of mine that is missing.
Let us drink to the health of Samuel Yakar.

34. We paid the Germans a tax in order to bring the Jewish community home.[18]
They look as if they had just come out of a bedridden illness.
There was no quinine to give them because they came with colds.[19]
We wish health to these beloved young men.

11. Samueliko, the son of Aunt Dona,
we do not know what happened to him.
He was serving as a soldier since the forties[20] in Veria.
Today we got a letter from the Red Cross [stating] that he was a captive
And in good health.
We hope he is going to stay in Italy
until the Germans are going to be sunk.
Let us drink to the health of all the soldiers
whose whereabouts we do not know.

15. We, the Jews of Salonika have forgotten how to laugh
Since the Germans crossed the bridge.
Each and every one of us is afraid of his own shadow.
It seems like someone [who] is walking from behind,
is grabbing your shoulder.
Even so we say: Take a step and get ahead.[21]
Let us drink to the health of Alberto Kamondo.

---

18. Here she refers to the young men from the community who were sent to forced labor.
19. They needed the quinine for the chills.
20. 1940.
21. Phrase suggested by Denah Lida, meaning "one step at a time."

10. Amigos gregos mos kieren ayoudar.
    Se espantan ma! Ine moz vienen avijitar.
    Demandan si kierech ke ayamos algouna koza,
    Ma! Mozotros semos espantozos.
    Bevamos a la saloud de estos amigos
        ke non mankaron de mos enkorajar.

73. Los espagnoles se estan aparejando,
    Ke los almanes los van amandar en espagna.
    Ounos dizen ke se van ayir al Baron de Hirsch.
    Ningounos saven lo ke van adevenir.
    Bevamos a la saloud de los espagnoles i sous avenir.

74. Loz Italianos los van a mandar Athena.
    Se estan espantando de sou solombra a Salonique.
    Kien save lo ke van adevenir?
    Bevamos a la salud de Albert Amir.

18. Marika, la de la nona, se foue Athena.
    Suzane se foue kon eya.
    Esperamos ke se van a salvar i a Suzane bouen mazal.
    Bevamos a la saloud de Alberto ke lo yaman Senegal.

20. Acher Abravanel eskrivio oun artikolo.
    Se paso de ouno al otro komo oun bilietiko.
    Dizia ke mos fouyeramos de Salonique
    Tenemos chanse de bevir;
    Fina ke se paso en negras manos.
    A Acher a Pavlo Mela lo yivaron.
    Non tenemos novedades de el.
    Bevamos a la saloud de Acher Abravanel.

53. Bessantsi se fouyo de Salonique; se foue a Volo.
    Ma! Los almanes savian ande estava.
    Foue aferado i matado.
    Bevamos a la saloud de los ke le ayoudaron a Bessantsi por doz aynos.

10. Greek friends want to help us.
    They are afraid, but! Even so they come to visit us.
    They ask if we need anything,
    But! We are fearful.
    Let us drink to the health of those friends
        who never failed to encourage us.

73. The Spaniards are getting ready,
    Hoping that the Germans are going to send them to Spain.
    Some say that they are going to go to [the] Baron de Hirsch.[22]
    No one knows what is going to happen.
    Let us drink to the health of the Spaniards and their future.

74. The Italians are going to be sent to Athens.
    They are afraid of their own shadow in Salonika.
    Who knows what will happen to them?
    Let us drink to the health of Albert Amir.

18. Marika, the grandmother's maidservant,[23] went to Athens.
    Suzanne went with her.
    We hope that they are going to be saved and good luck to Suzanne.
    Let us drink to the health of Albert, who is called Senegal.

20. Asher Abravanel wrote an article.
    It passed from hand to hand like a note.
    He said that we should flee Salonika
    In order to have a chance to live;
    Until it landed in evil hands.
    And they took Asher to Pablos Melas.[24]
    We have no news of him.
    Let us drink to the health of Asher Abravanel.

53. Besantsi escaped from Salonika; he went to Volo.
    But! The Germans knew where he was.
    He was captured and killed.
    Let us drink to the health of those who helped Besantsi for two years.[25]

---

22. This neighborhood was built on the west side of the city in 1892 to accommodate both homeless Jews after the fire of 1890 and Russian refugees. It was used as a ghetto because it was adjacent to the train station and convenient for organizing deportations.

23. Or caretaker.

24. This was the same prison to which Bouena was taken by the Nazis.

25. He managed to avoid the Germans for two years.

6. Los djidios se empesaron a espantar de avlar Ladino al kaffe de la mar.
Akavidate, dizen, mos poueden arempouchar.
Esperamos ke el dio moz va a vouadrar.
Bevamos a la saloud de Daniel Amar.

36. Todos se espantan de avlar; parese ke aya politofilaka sin brasar.
La sola cosa ke dizen: "boka serada non entra mochka."
Bevamos a la saloud de akejos ke aseran la boka.

59. Los politofilakas expectan [*sic*]²⁶ los trenos para ver si djudios estan
fouyendo.
Ounos kouantos reoucheron de non yir a la flama del Baron de Hirsch.
Bevamos a la saloud de los grego ke ayudaron a djidios a bevir.

2. Temprano la magnana se aze el sileho.²⁷
Ma! Agora i esto non pouedemos tener savor
Porke salimos de en kaza a las diez.
El politofilaka²⁸ a la pouerta
Ke non mos pouedemos kreer ke son djudios.
Bevamos a la saloud de Djelda Sasson.

58. Al ghetto non pouedemos avlar.²⁹
Siempre oun politofilaka para moz espionar,
Dan informationes al alman
Porke lez prometieron ke eyos van a kedar.
Bevamos a la saloud de los ke dizen el dio moz va apiadar.

52. Estamos al getto tremblando de avlar.
Ma! Ine mozotros non kedamos de kantar
Kantigas de novia o de brith mila.
Bevamos a la saloud de Nekama Mallah.

37. Los Modianos son Italianos.
Kierian kazar a la ija, non avia Hahamim.
A doz metros de distansa a la puerta del Baron de Hirsch,

---

26. She meant to write *inspektan*.
27. This should be *selihot*.
28. Here she inserted the Ladino, *poulisia djoudia,* in parentheses.
29. Sometimes "ghetto" appears to be spelled "guetto"—but since her letters U and H are similar, this word is being transcribed as ghetto.

6. The Jews began to fear speaking Ladino at the café by the sea.
   Be careful, they say, they can push us out.
   We hope that God is going to protect us.
   Let us drink to the health of Daniel Amar.

36. Everyone is afraid to talk; there seem to be Jewish police without brass.[30]
    The only thing they say [is]: "Flies don't enter closed mouths."
    Let us drink to the health of those who close their mouths.

59. The Jewish police inspect the trains to see if there are any Jews fleeing.
    Some managed not to go to the flames of Baron de Hirsch.[31]
    Let us drink to the health of the Greeks who helped Jews live.[32]

2. Early in the morning, one recites the pre–Rosh Hashanah prayers[33]
       [of forgiveness].
   But! Now we cannot even enjoy this
   Because we [can only] leave the house at ten AM.
   The Jewish police are at the door
   And we cannot believe that they are Jews.
   Let us drink to the health of Djelda Sasson.

58. In the ghetto we cannot speak.
    [There is] always a Jewish policeman [there] to spy on us,
    Giving information to the Germans
    Because they promised them that they will remain.
    Let us drink to the health of those who say that God will have mercy
       on us.

52. We in the ghetto are terrified to speak.
    But! Even so we don't stop singing
    Wedding or circumcision songs.
    Let us drink to the health of Nehama Mallah.

37. The Modianos are Italian.
    They want to marry off their daughter, [but] there were no rabbis.
    At a distance of two meters from the entrance to Baron de Hirsch,

---

30. That is, without brass decoration on their shoulders.

31. She is using the name of the ghetto from which the deportations set forth as a metaphor for the crematoria.

32. That is, survive.

33. These pre–Rosh Hashanah prayers are recited by the Sephardim early every morning during the month of Elul.

Se izo la houpa. Todos yoraron sin se konsentir.
Bevamos a la saloud del consolo Italiano ke izo possible estos kidouchim.

21. Estamos al gheto; non tenemos pan.
    La sola koza ke dezeamos eze de tener ouna redoma de riki
    I mos emborathar.
    Este modo non vamos a ver mas el Alman
    Ni politofilakas en la sivdad.
    Bevamos a la saloud de Leon Amar.

48. Al getto todos semos auna famia.
    Reyna guiza para todas las famias.
    Kouando non aye bastante karne, Reyna dize ese solo para Regina.
    Bevamos a la saloud de toda la kompagnia.

28. Salonique se froigouo grasias al djidio.
    Lo modernizo; agora estamos al getto
    Komo los ratones a la ratonera.
    Bevamos a la saloud de los ke van akedar
    Ke toparon la salida de esta ratonera.

12. Riketa Yakar se foue Athena aver al ijo
    Ke esta estoudiando al politekhnion.
    Atorno a Salonique djousto para se yir al Baron de Hirsch.
    Bevamos a la saloud de los ke la akonsejaron de non atornar
        a Salonique.

54. Los Avayous se foueron Athena aver a Vital
    Que tenia oun kourchoum a la pierna.
    Vigneron a Salonique para se ir al Baron de Hirsch.
    Bevamos a la saloud de los ke non saven bevir.

47. Al ghetto moramos sech famias en kouatro kamaretas.
    Aye djente dourmiendo en bacho por ande vas kaminando.
    La magnana, para yir al cabinet, asperamos a la sirá.
    Bevamos a la saloud de los ke saven asperar.

72. Estamos al getto [*sic*].
    El solo lougar ke mos dechan yir eze a la kiyila de loz monastirlis.

They made a wedding canopy. Everyone cried without being aware of it.
Let us drink to the health of the Italian consul who made this marriage
possible.

21. We are in the ghetto; we do not have bread.
The only thing that we want is to have a bottle of ouzo
And to get drunk.
This way we won't see the Germans
Or the Jewish police in the city any more.
Let us drink to the health of Leon Amar.

48. In the ghetto we all are one family.
Reina cooks for all the families.
When there is not enough meat, Reina says that it is only for Regina.
Let us drink to the health of the entire group.

28. Salonika was built thanks to the Jews.
It was modernized. Now we are in the ghetto
Like mice in a mousetrap.
Let us drink to the health of those who are going to remain
Who found the exit from this mousetrap.

12. Riketa Yakar went to Athens to see her son
Who is studying at the PolyTechnion.
She returned to Salonika just in time to go to the Baron de Hirsch.[34]
Let us drink to the health of those who had advised her not to return
to Salonika.

54. The Avayous went to Athens to see Vital
Who had a bullet in his leg.
They came to Salonika just [in time] to go to the Baron de Hirsch.
Let us drink to the health of those who do not know how to live.

47. In the ghetto we are six families in four bedrooms.
There are people sleeping on the floor where we walk.
In the morning, in order to get to the bathroom, we wait on line.
Let us drink to the health of those who know how to wait.

72. We are in the ghetto.
The only place that we are allowed to go is to the Monastir Synagogue.[35]

---

34. That is, to be transferred to the ghetto.
35. Because this building was used by the Red Cross, it was not destroyed during
the war (Messinas, *The Synagogues of Salonika,* 96–97).

Todos yorando i arogando ke el dio mos pardone si tenemos pekados.
Bevamos a la saloud de Samuel Toledano.

Deportation

49. Albala se izo presidente de la komunitad.
Save el alman i tambien arovar.
Eze mas antisemith de eyos.
Non mos va a deshar ni kaveyos.
Bevamos a la saloud de los kavalieros.

50. El solo ke kedo a la komunitad de los mouestros eze Alfonse Levy.
Mos da koraje sin pensar de sou avenir.
Bevamos a la saloud de Yoseph Amir.

Hasson

65. Hasson se izo el patron de la komunitad.
Le parese ke aki va a kedar.
Por segouro ke va aver algouno ke se va avenger.
Le parese ke siempre loz almanes la van arezgatar.
Bevamos a la saloud de Samuel Kattan.

7. Papanaoum se izo amigo kon Hasson.
Todos dizian ke tiene este antisemit kon oun djidio?
Estan aziendo endjountos los planos por la deportation del los djidios,
I tomar todos los bienes de loz desmazalados.
Esperamos ke non van aparvenir,
Porke Salonique eze siudad de nese.
Bevamos a la saloud de akeyos ke kreyen ke vamos a bevir.

69. Sarah Trabout se kazo kon el ermano de Hasson.
El padre atheto porke se espanto.
Hasson le dicho: Ho este kazamiento se va azer
O tous ijos van a desparaser.

La houpa se izo kon flores i ouna limouzina
Pasearon a los novios a las kayes del Baron de Hirsch.
Sarah yorando ke non keria sentir mezzo el nombre de el novio.

Everyone crying and begging God to forgive us if we have sins.
Let us drink to the health of Samuel Toledano.

Deportation

49. Albala became president of the community.
He knows German and also how to steal.
He is a greater antisemite than they.
He is not even going to leave a hair [on our heads].
Let us drink to the health of the gentlemen.

50. The only one who was left in the community on our side is Alfonse Levy.[36]
He gives us courage without thinking of his own fate.
Let us drink to the health of Joseph Amir.

Hasson

65. Hasson seized control of the community.[37]
And he thinks he is going to stay.
Surely there is going to be someone to take revenge.
It seems to him that the Germans are always going to rescue him.
Let us drink to the health of Samuel Kattan.

7. Papanaoum became friends with Hasson.
Everyone said: What is this antisemite doing with a Jew?
They are making the plans together for the deportation of the Jews
And to take all the belongings of these unfortunates.
We hope that they are not going to succeed
Because Salonika is a city of miracles.
Let us drink to the health of those who believe that we are going to live.

69. Sarah Trabout married Hasson's brother.
Her father agreed because he was intimidated.
Hasson told him: Either this wedding is going to take place
Or your children are going to disappear.

The huppah was made with flowers
And a limousine took the couple for a ride to the streets of the
    Baron de Hirsch.
Sarah crying that she didn't want to hear mention of the groom's name.

---

36. She refers to the community leadership.
37. His role is analyzed in chapter 4; he assumed that by appropriating the community for himself, he would also be guaranteed special rights.

Hasson los kijo mandar en oun kampo de privilijiados.
Sarah refouzo; se kijo yir kon sou famia.
Bevamos a la saloud de Sarah
    ke arogamos ke este biva i sana.

71. La ermana de Hasson es empregada de la komounitad.
Save todos los sekretos de la djouderia.
Se loz dio a Hasson para sou koulevreria.
El tiempo de la deportation
Se intho de oro ke el ermano arovo.
Hasson la mando kon los privilijiados i a Salonique atorno.
Estouvo djousgada.
Malhorozamente non avia testimognos para la kondanar.
Todos se mourieron al krematorio del Alman.

57. Del Baron de Hirsch venian a tomar lethe de la Rejie [*sic*] Vardar.
El dia ke non vigneron foue el louyto a Salonique.
La preparation de la deportation empeso de ayi.
Bouena Sarfatty kon el ayoudo de la Croix Rouge Internationale.
El direktor se yama Rene Burkard sin se espantar.
Hasson la aharvo a lougar de la ayoudar.
Bevamos a la saloud de Bouena ke la yaman Jeanne d'Ark.

Koretz

39. Koretz eze el primo grand Rabino estragnere.
Los Saltielim lo troucheron.
Agora al ghetto estan komo piojo entre koustoura.
Esta modo vendieron la djouderia.
Bevamos a la saloud de los Segouras.

40. Los ke se opozaron a trayer a Koretz
Por grand rabino foueron inkarmados.
Touvieron difikultad para el brith mila de los keridos.
Bevamos a la saloud de Alber Tsimino.

Hasson wanted to send them to the camp for the privileged.
Sarah refused; she chose to go with her family.
Let us drink to the health of Sarah
    whom we pray should be alive and well.

71. Hasson's sister is an employee of the community.
    She knows all the secrets of the Jewish community.
    She gave them to Hasson for his snakelike[38] business.
    At the time of the deportation,
    She stuffed herself with gold that her brother stole.
    Hasson sent her with the privileged and she returned to Salonika.
    She was judged.
    Unfortunately, there were no witnesses to condemn her.
    Everyone had died in the German crematorium.

57. They came from Baron de Hirsch to get milk from the Regie Vardar.
    The day they did not come was a day of mourning for Salonika.
    The preparation for the deportation began from there.
    Bouena Sarfatty [came] with the help of the International Red Cross.
    The director is named René Burkhardt without being afraid.
    Hasson hit her instead of helping her.[39]
    Let us drink to the health of Bouena, whom they call Joan of Arc.

Koretz

39. Koretz is the first foreign chief rabbi.
    The Saltiels brought him.
    Now in the ghetto they are like lice in a seam.
    This is the way they sold [out] the Jewish community.
    Let us drink to the health of the Segouras.

40. Those who opposed bringing Koretz
    As chief rabbi were unfortunate.
    They had difficulty with the circumcision of their loved ones.
    Let us drink to the health of Albert Tsimino.

---

38. That is, lowdown.

39. This anecdote is documented in her memoirs and discussed in chapter 4;
Hasson beat and tortured her in the presence of Kurt Waldheim because she came to
distribute the milk when the ghetto had been sealed.

41. Koretz se izo soudito grego; no le kierian dar souditansa.
    Dio el Bet Ahaim[40] para poueder parvenir.
    Avrieron las mearaotte en sou presensia.
    Kon los eskeletos, toparon djoyas i objectos presiozos.
    Se loz yevo a sou kaza ke izo ouna kamareta mouziom.
    Kouando avia algouno ke avlava i avria la boka,[41]
    Le dava oun kandelar i la aser[r]ava.
    Bevamos a la saloud de Michel Amar.

43. Los Almanes tomaron a los djovenes a las ergas.
    La malaria los estava koumiendo.
    Solo los ijos de los amigos de Koretz non se foueron.
    Les dio papel ke lavoran para el.
    Bevamos a la saloud de Avraam Apoel.

38. Koretz mos vendió, a todo la djouderia
    Para se salvar el i su familia i toda su kompagnia.
    Mos dicho ke el viene de venir de la Europa
    I todos los djidios komen bien i non la bobota.
    Bevamos a la saloud de Daniel Serotta.

44. El grand rabino Koretz mos vindio a los almans.
    Le parisio ke semos kriatouras djougando a kach, kach.[42]
    A la kiyila de los Monastirlis vino a avlar.
    Lo empesaron a ak[h]arvar; lo kierian despedasar.
    Los politofilakas los rezgataron.
    Bevamos a la saloud de loz amargados.

45. Los Kalderon arepoucharon a Koretz.
    El politofilaka yamaron al alman.
    Los tomaron en prizion i nounka se soupo koualo devigneron.
    Bevamos a la saloud de los Kalderon prisionieros.

61. Los almanes mos sero la fabrika de matza
    I Pessah non tenemos koualo machkar.

---

40. In Hebrew, literally, "the home of the living"—a euphemism for the cemetery.
41. About to divulge the truth.
42. *Kaç*, in Turkish, means "run" or "escape," and *al* means "take." In the game *alcachi*, an object is suddenly dropped into the hand of a child who must flee before being caught (Michael Molho, *Traditions and Customs*, 125–26). It is also quite possible that she was referring to the same game, hide and seek, but in its French form, *cache cache*, as suggested by Güler Orgun (personal communication, March 16, 2011).

41. Koretz became a Greek subject; they did not want to give him
    citizenship.
    He gave [them] the cemetery in order to succeed.
    They opened the tombs in his presence.
    With the skeletons, they found jewels and precious objects.
    He took them to his home where he made a room into a museum.
    When there was someone who spoke up and opened his mouth,
    He gave him a candelabrum[43] and shut him up.
    Let us drink to the health of Michel Amar.

43. The Germans took the young men to the labor [camps].
    Malaria was consuming them.
    Only the sons of the friends of Koretz did not go.
    He gave them papers [stating] that they are working for him.
    Let us drink to the health of Avraham Apoel.

38. Koretz sold us out, the whole Jewish community,
    In order to save himself, his family, and his entourage.
    He told us that he just came from Europe
    And all the Jews are eating well and not just cornbread.
    Let us drink to the health of Daniel Serotta.

44. The chief rabbi Koretz sold us out to the Germans.
    It appeared to him that we are children playing a game of hide and seek.
    He came to speak at the Synagogue of the Monastirlis.[44]
    They began to beat him; they wanted to tear him apart.
    The [Jewish] police saved him.
    Let us drink to the health of the embittered.

45. The Calderons repudiated Koretz.
    The Jewish police called the Germans.
    They took them to prison and it was never known what happened to them.
    Let us drink to the health of the imprisoned Calderons.

61. The Germans closed our matsah factory
    And we have nothing to chew for Passover.

---

43. As a bribe.
44. Those from Monastir (as Selaniklis were from Salonika), which is Bitola
in Macedonia today. It is either the Monastir Synagogue or the Synagogue of the
Monastirlis.

El Rabay Koretz moz dicho ke komamos pan.
Bevamos a la saloud de los ke se van apasar de pan.

42. La komunitad mitio avizo.
Koremos aver koualo eze el kontenido.
Koretz ordeno ke komomas Pessah fijon.
Bevamos a la saloud de Mochon.

51. Hitler se va areventar ine[45] djidios a Salonique va akedar.
Mos vamos a reir de el kouando
Va a tener oun estremeser negro e krouel.
Bevamos a la saloud de Albert Havouel.

5. A Salonique aye rumores ke Hitler se va a m[o]u[e]rir,
Ma yo digo: Ke pene i ke non mouera.
Ke le venga oun negro mal
I ke non eskape mas a el i sou deredor moutha dolor de korason.
Espero ke el Dio me va a sentir estas malditiones ke le et[c]hi.
Bevamos a la saloud de Bessanthi.

64. Hitler mos kiere mandar a viajar para moz matar.
Non mos kiere iliminar a Salonique
Porke tenemos amigos i vizinos ke van aver.
Bevamos a la saloud de Ichoua Haver.

32. Foue ouna grande dezgrasia kouando los almanes tomaron
A los mansevos sin pathas las piedrieron en Koritza.
Los amigos arempoucharon la arabá
Fina la pouerta del Baron de Hirsch
Ke van apozar antes ke los manden a Pologna sin piadad.
Bevamos a la saloud de estos mansevos ke non poueden manear.

33. Rachel, la de la tia Ezmeralda, tenia kanser.
Para la abachar de la eskalera foue oun estremeser.
Los almanes arempouchavan.
Rachel gritava; esta chena nounka me la vo a oulvidar.
Bevamos a la saloud de los ke kedaron i ke lo van akontar.

---

45. In Turkish this is *yine.*

Rabbi Koretz told us to eat bread.
Let us drink to the health of those who are going to "pass over" the bread.

42. The community posted an announcement.
We ran to see what are its contents.
Koretz ordered us to eat beans on Passover.
Let us drink to the health of Mochon.

51. Hitler is going to drop dead and still the Jews are going to remain in
Salonika.
We are going to laugh at him when
He is going to have a black and cruel shuddering [experience].
Let us drink to the health of Albert Havouel.

5. There are rumors in Salonika that Hitler is going to die,
But I say: Let him suffer and not die.
May a great misfortune befall him and those around him
And may they not be spared[46] great heartache.
I hope that God will hear these curses that I cast upon him.
Let us drink to the health of Besantsi.

64. Hitler wants to force us to travel in order to kill us.
He does not want to eliminate us in Salonika
Because we have friends and neighbors who are going to see.
Let us drink to the health of Ichoua Haver.

32. It was a great disgrace when the Germans took
The young men who lost their legs in Koritza.
Their friends pushed the cart
Up to the entrance of the Baron de Hirsch.
Where they were going to stay before they send them to Poland
mercilessly.
Let us drink to the health of these fellows who could not move.

33. Rachel, the maidservant of Aunt Ezmeralda, had cancer.
It was torture to get her down the stairs.
The Germans pushed.
Rachel screamed; I am never going to forget this scene.
Let us drink to the health of those who remained and who are going
to recount the tale.

---

46. Literally, escape.

70. Sarah me dio oun plato de plata.
    Marie mi ermana lo tiene.
    Rogo ke oun dia me lo va a dar.
    Lo kiere tener para mas me a kodrar de Sarah
    Ke foue ouan amiga sensera.
    Espero ke Sarah esta en Gan Eden.

63. Yom Kipour se etha *michibira*[47] al governo.
    Agagno ethimos al patron de estas tierras.
    Bevamos a la saloud de la liberation.

Flight

66. Despues ke Hasson me aharvo, me dethedi de me fouyer.
    Demandi ayoudo a Georgette Modiano ke atheto i me lo dio.
    Ande Madame Soula me mando en Verria a las plateaus Ebes.
    El marido esta en Ejypto; era konsolo a Salonique de Albania.
    Malhorozamente preso me mando
        porke kieria tomar a sou amiga.
    En atornando de Veria al hotubus
    Vide el transporto de djidios del ghetto del Sien i Soukouenta i ouno
    Para loz mandar a Pologna.
    El treno non avia ventanas, oun bourako de vezes en kouando.

    Apenas abachi del hotobus vide oun djornalista
        ke era Politofilaka.
    El nombre es Bensasson, el ermano de Alice.
    Me miro i me suivio para ver ande vo a yir.
    Me entri a la Stoa Karasso.
    Este modo lo piedri; vine ande Georgette temblando.
    Me demando ke me akontisio.
    Le diche todo bueno; se passo.
    Me kedi doz nothes ande Georgette
    I me mando ande el Dr Scouros ke estouve kinze dias.
    Todos mon [sic] bouenos para mi, tambien Afro[48]
        ke nounka la vo oulvidar.
    Ma! Komo se empesaron a espantar,
    Daniel Modiano me arkilo ouna kamareta kon moutho oro.
    Oun dia Daniel me dicho ke tiene pasaporto Italiano.

---

47. This is the Hebrew word for a blessing made publicly in the synagogue for the health or safety of the ill, soldiers, the government, and the like.

48. She was the daughter of a Dr. Scouros, also mentioned in copla 76.

70. Sarah gave me a silver plate.
    My sister Marie has it.
    I pray that one day she will give it to me.
    I want to have it in order to better remember Sarah
    Who was a true friend.
    I hope that Sarah is in heaven.

63. On Yom Kippur they make a blessing for the government.
    Today we blessed the owner[49] of these lands.
    Let us drink to the health of the liberation.

Flight

66. After Hasson hit me, I decided to flee.
    I asked Georgette Modiano for help, who agreed and gave it to me.
    She sent me to Madame Soula in Veria at the plateaus of Ebes.
    Her husband is in Egypt; he was the Albanian consul in Salonika.
    Unfortunately she soon sent me away
        because she wanted to take in her girlfriend.
    On returning from Veria on the bus
    I saw the transport of Jews of Ghetto 151[50]
    [Organized] to send them to Poland.
    The train had no windows, sometimes a hole.

    As soon as I descended from the bus I saw a journalist
        who was with the Jewish police.
    His name is Bensasson, Alice's brother.
    He looked at me and followed me to see where I was going.
    I entered the Stoa Karasso.[51]
    In this way I lost him. I arrived at Georgette's trembling.
    She asked me what had happened.
    I told her everything is fine; it passed.
    I stayed two nights at Georgette's
    And she sent me to Dr. Scouros where I remained for fifteen days.
    Everyone was good to me as well as Afro
        whom I never will forget.
    But! Since they began to fear [for themselves],
    Daniel Modiano rented me a room for a large sum of gold.
    One day Daniel told me that he has an Italian passport [for me].

---

49. Or lord.
50. One of the smaller ghettos north of the Baron de Hirsch ghetto.
    51. *Stoa* is an arcade; today the Stoa Karasso is one of the smaller markets, in which trinkets are sold.

Tou nombre eze Flora Tivoli, nasida en Livorno Italia
I te vaz a yir Athena kon el treno Italiano.
Bevamos a la saloud de Daniel Modiano.

67. A Veria avia Soupe Populaire para las kriatouras.
Madame Soula era la prezidente.
Me yevava mouthas vezes a ayoudar.
La prima veze isi el signo de la croix. Ma! Arevez.
Grasias a ouna dama me yevo al bureau i me lo ambezo.
La sola koza eze:
"Non te espantes; yo kiero bien a los djidios."
Bevamos a la saloud de esta dama ke foue a Verria
Despoues de la Guerra i non la topi.

60. Daniel Modiano se okupo de kitar djidios del Baron de Hirsch.
El konsulo Italiano lez dio passaporto falso para poueder fouyir.
Bevamos a la saloud de Daniel i las otoridads Italianas de Salonique.

68. Me foue con Daniel Modiano a tomar el treno de los Italianos.
Tomi el brasso de Daniel, tremblando i pedandome.
Solo kouando entri al treno me sourti.
Bevamos a la saloud de Daniel ke foue oun angel para mi.

76. Los almanes tomaron a loz Italianos prizonieros al Akropol.
Metieron bandiera; "la croix garnie" esta flotando.
Mozotros mos estamos dezesperando.
Moz vouadramos komo los ratones a loz bourakos.
Ounos kouantos djidios foueron aferados a Haydari.
Loz mandaron [kon] oun treno; [los] mandaron a Polonya.
El resto loz mataron.
Bevamos a la saloud del Dr Scouros, Afro e toda sou famia.

77. Estamos Athena.
Salimos a merkar sena; vemos amigos o konosidos.

Your name is Flora Tivoli, born in Livorno, Italy,
And you are going to go to Athens on the Italian train.
Let us drink to the health of Daniel Modiano.

67. In Veria there was a soup kitchen for the children.
Madame Soula was the president.
She took me there many times to help.
The first time I made the sign of the cross. But! Backwards.
Thanks to a woman [who] took me to the office and taught me.
The only thing is:[52]
"Do not fear; I like the Jews."
Let us drink to the health of this woman [for whom] I went to Veria
After the war and did not find her.

60. Daniel Modiano took care of smuggling Jews out of the Baron de Hirsch.
The Italian consul gave them false passports to enable them to flee.
Let us drink to the health of Daniel and the Italian authorities in
     Salonika.

68. I went with Daniel Modiano to take the Italians' train.
I took Daniel's arm, trembling and farting.
Only once I entered the train did I relieve myself.
Let us drink to the health of Daniel, who was an angel for me.

76. The Germans took the Italians as prisoners to the Acropolis.
They raised the flag; the garnet cross[53] is waving.
We are becoming desperate.
We hide ourselves like rats in holes.
A few Jews were caught at Haidari.[54]
They were sent by train; they were sent to Poland.
The rest were killed.
Let us drink to the health of Dr. Scouros, Afro, and all of his family.

77. We are in Athens.
We go out to buy dinner; we see friends or acquaintances.

---

52. She probably meant, "the only thing this woman told me was."

53. The assumption is that Bouena thought the swastika looked like a garnet cross.

54. Mark Mazower describes the camp that was set up in September 1943, "If there was one place in Greece where the use of terror was refined and exploited to the full it was in the SS-run camp at Haidari, several kilometers outside Athens. In part a transit camp where Italian soldiers, Jews and others were held before they were sent north out of the country, Haidari also housed prisoners awaiting interrogation at SS headquarters, as well as hundreds of hostages who were selected for mass executions" (*Inside Hitler's Greece,* 226).

Non dizimos ni shalom ni bouenos dias.
Non savemos si eze pouro djidio
O politofilaka del Alman.
Bevamos a la saloud de los ke toman prekotion.

78. Maurice Nico i yo a Evia mos fouyimos.
Madame Tsakousti moz ayoudo.
Apenas arevimos a Evia arkilimos ouna ahir
Kon oun kavayo, oun azno i ouna moula por vezinos
Sin kontar las mochkas ke venian.
Bevamos a la saloud de Madame Stakousti i toda su famia.

79. Kamino media ora para lavar la kolada.
Komo non se bien espremer,
El avoua me kaye endriva.
Me asento al sol para me sekar porke non tengo koualo trokar.
Bevamos a la saloud de David Yakar.

80. Arkilimos oun vapor de pechkadores a Tourkia.
Mos fouemos; a Thesme abachemos.
Mos paresio ke eze a Gan Eden ke venimos.
Bevamos a la saloud de Maurice i Nico.

81. Hanouka kouarenta e tres: Estamos a Halepo [Siria].
Oun resfouyido se fouyo del campo.
A la atornada, troucho ouna redoma de vino.
Bevimos; Ma! Era tosko.[55]
Kantemos i moz izimos hazenos.
Al otro dia al hopital moz topimos.
Bevamos a la saloud de los doctores de la clinik ke moz ayoudaron.

82. Moz yevaron a Palestina.
Komo non teniamos permi a Haiffa,
Non moz decharon abachar.
Yo touvo mazal; Ma! Otras a Gaza laz yevaron.
Aye oun Hamsi ke non se pouede rezestir.
La arena entrava en los ojos.
Non aye bastante tendas para avrigar.
Bevamos a la saloud de akeyos ke saven gritar.

83. Albert Alchek mos resevio kon korason.
Mos dio koraje i a mouchos avrigo.

---

55. Probably from *tosigo,* "poison."

We say neither hello nor good day [to them].
We do not know if this [person] is a loyal Jew
Or a German collaborator.
Let us drink to the health of those who take precautions.

78. Maurice, Nico, and I fled to Evvia.
Mme. Tsakousti helped us.
As soon as we arrived in Evvia we rented a stable
With a horse, an ass and a mule for neighbors
Not counting the flies that came.
Let us drink to the health of Mme. Stakousti and her whole family.

79. I walk a half hour in order to wash the laundry.
Since I do not know how to wring the water properly,
The water drenches me.
I sit in the sun to dry myself because I have no change of clothing.
Let us drink to the health of David Yakar.

80. We rented a fishing [steam] boat to Turkey.
We set forth; we debarked at Çesme.
We felt as if we had come to heaven.
Let us drink to the health of Maurice and Nico.

81. Hanukah 1943: We are in Aleppo, Syria.
A refugee escaped from the camp.
On the way back, he brought a bottle of wine.
We drank [it], but! It was lousy.
We sang and we became ill.
The next day we found ourselves in the hospital.
Let us drink to the health of the doctors from the clinic, who helped us.

82. They took us to Palestine.
Since we did not have a permit for Haifa,
They did not allow us to disembark.
I was lucky, but! Others were taken to Gaza.
There is an eastern [hot] wind that no one can withstand.
The sand went into the eyes.
There are not enough tents to provide shelter.
Let us drink to the health of those who know how to shout.

83. Albert Alchek received us warmly.
He gave us courage and gave shelter to many.

Lez bouchko lavoro i mos amostro oualo eze el amor.
Bevamos a la saloud de este pedagogue.

84. En Halepo tenemos vida de alegría;
Mezmo al kabinet tenemos kompagnia.
Bevamos a la saloud de los resfouyidos ke tienen daeria [*sic*].

85. A Halepo loz Inglezes trayen kon bidon la melezina
Porke todos tienen daeria.
Por segouro ke eze la koumida.
Los platos estan bien enchidos fina ariva.
Bevamos a la saloud de los ke se akavidan.

Komplas ke Eskrevi del 1945 al 1947

86. Foue Athena; vide a Tilde Cohen.
Me konte komo se vouadraron esta famia.
Al palasio del rey foueron bouenas resividos
Bevamos a la saloud de las prezensias ke salvaron esta famia.

90. Los deportados empesaron a venir a Salonique en tsikos nombres
Kon noumeros al braso ke al aman les enfiko.
Les parisio ke loz van aresevir kon tambour i trompeta,
Ma! Los pokos ke bivieron i se eskoundieron
Estavan amargados de lo pasado.
Loz deportados formaron union
I a mozotros moz miraban komo antisimith.
Tomavan lo ke kierian de la Join.
Savian pelear i arojar[56] el kouchak.
Es solo kouando se foueron a Palestina kon la *akshara*[57]
Se kiere lavorar para azer noueva vida.
Vigneron mouthos kon tuberculose.
El Joint los miro de korason.
Bevamos a la salud de estos amargados.

---

56. Nehama spells it *arrožár,* "to throw with arrogance."
57. This is a Hebrew term, *hakhshara,* an agricultural training course for potential immigrants to Palestine.

He found them jobs and showed us what love is.
Let us drink to the health of this pedagogue.

84. In Aleppo we have a good time;
    Even in the bathroom we have company.
    Let us drink to the health of the refugees who have diarrhea.

85. In Aleppo, the British bring medicine by the gallon
    Because everyone has diarrhea.
    For sure it is [because of] the food.
    The plates are filled to the top.
    Let us drink to the health of those who are careful.

Coplas I Wrote between 1945 and 1947

86. I went to Athens; I saw Tilde Cohen.
    She told me how this family hid itself.
    They were well received in the palace of the king.
    Let us drink to the health of the principality[58] that saved this family.

90. The deportees began to arrive in Salonika in small numbers
    With numbers on their arms that the German tattooed on them.
    They thought that they would be received with tambourines and
        trumpets,
    But! The few who survived and had hidden themselves
    Were bitter about what had happened.
    The deportees were united together
    And they looked at us as [if we were] antisemites.
    They took what they wanted from the Joint.[59]
    They knew how to fight and to throw the belt.[60]
    It is only when they went to Palestine after a training course [that]
    It is necessary to work in order to make a new life.
    Many came with tuberculosis.
    The Joint took care of them compassionately.
    Let us drink to the health of these embittered [souls].

---

58. Possibly "princedom."

59. This was the American Jewish Joint Distribution Committee, established in 1914. After the war, it offered emergency aid and attempted to address educational and cultural needs of the survivors, hoping to reinstate a sense of community and a return to normality.

60. This may connote starting a fight.

88. Las religiozas Fransezas foueren umanitarias.
  Ocuadraron djidios en sous komunitad sin se espantar.
  La tsiketika Sarika Lea salvaron.
  Bevamos a la saloud de los religiozas
    del konvento de nouestra sivdad.

89. Despoues de la Guerra foue aver a Sarika al konvento.
  La madre Superieur[e]a me dicho esta a l'imfermiri ke [h]kazina.
  La vide, le yevi bombones
  Que era la prima vez ke via la souer le dicho ke gostara.
  Despoues de ounos kouantos dias, tomi a Sarika.
  El join la mando a Palestina.
  Bevamos a la saloud de Sarika e la kiboutz ke la abriga.

98. Yivia a Sarika Lea al restaurant.
  Le diche ke koumiera.
  Me respondio ke eye non pouede komer sin azer la orasion.
  Le diche ke iziera i eskapo en aziendo
    el signo de la Croix i empose a senar.
  Bevamos a la saloud de Daniel, pariente.

91. Foui a Zvestokori al sanatorio a ver a Sarika.[61]
  Vino del laguer kon tuberkuloza.
  Estava a la kama kon moutha kaentoura.
  Me izo pena de verla. Sarika, non te oulvidi.
  Espero ke *refoua chelema*[62] presto te va a venir.
  Bevamos a la saloud de Sarika i el Dio ke te deche bevir.

92. Isaac Arouk[h] tenia ouna protejada.
  Oun dia a la ventana del laguer
  Vido prisionieros ke vingneron a lavorar.
  La nigna empeso a gritar: "Mr. Arouk[h]!"
  Isaac dicho: "Kien me yama?"
  "Misseure, aki." La nigna le arondjo oun pan.
  Tenian bastante al pavion de las operadas.
  Mr. Arouk[h] nounka se olvido ke este pan lo salvo.

93. Samy Yakar se salvo de loz almanes.
  Ma! El tiempo de la revolution kijo yir a ver a sou amiga.

---

61. This was another Sarika, probably a peer of hers.
62. A Hebrew expression for a speedy recovery from an illness.

88. The religious French nuns were humanitarians.
    They hid Jews in their nunneries without fearing [for themselves].
    They saved little Sarika Lea.
    Let us drink to the health of the religious women
        from the convent of our city.

89. After the war I went to see Sarika in the convent.
    The Mother Superior told me that she is ill in the infirmary.
    I saw her, brought her sweets
    Which was the first time that the sister told her she could taste them.
    A few days later, I took Sarika.
    The Joint sent her to Palestine.
    Let us drink to the health of Sarika and the kibbutz that shelters her.

98. I took Sarika Lea to a restaurant.
    I told her that she should eat.
    She replied that she cannot eat without saying [making] a prayer.
    I told her that she should do it and she finished making
        the sign of the cross and began to eat.
    Let us drink to the health of Daniel, a relative.

91. I went to Asvestochori[63] to the sanitorium to see Sarika.
    She returned from the concentration camp with tuberculosis.
    She was in bed with a high fever.
    It pained me to see her. Sarika, I did not forget you.
    I hope that a speedy recovery will come to you soon.
    Let us drink to the health of Sarika and may God let you live.

92. Isaac Aroukh had a protégée.
    One day at the window of the concentration camp
    He saw prisoners who came to work.
    The girl began to scream: "Mr. Aroukh!"
    Isaac said: "Who is calling me?"
    "Sir, here." The girl shoved him a loaf of bread.
    They had enough at the pavilion of the women who were operated upon.
    Mr. Aroukh never forgot that this bread saved him.

93. Sammy Yakar escaped from the Germans.
    But! At the time of the revolution he wanted to go see his girlfriend.

---

63. This village, in Greek, Asvestos, literally, a "village of calcium," is located about 10 km from the center of town, and offers the driest climate around, making it an ideal place for a sanitarium (David Kounio, personal communication, February 1, 2011).

Oun kourchoum a la kavesa le vino.
Al pounto mourio a los venti i dos.
El proverbo dize: "Kien se vouadro, sou madre non lo yoro."
Foue Athena despoues de la Guerra,
Kontrato kon la UNRRA[64] para ayoudar los desplasados.
Foue al *Beth Hahaim* a ver la tomba de Samuel ke estava enthida de
   photographias.
Miri a mi deredor; vide ouna nigna ke era sou amiga.
Mi madre dizia: "Kien se vouadro, sou madre non lo yoro."

94. Foue a Salonique despoues de la Guerra kon la UNRRA.
En kada kaleja en envierno venden kastagnas; merki ounas kouantas.
Me las mitio en oun papel ke era la agada de mi madre.
Merki todos los papeles ke el vendedor tinia.
Le diche: "Esto izitech los livros de la djouderia?"

95. Regina mi ermanika tenia una amiga.
Se kazo mouy tskika.
El tiempo de la deportation pario oun ijo.
Lo mitieron a las kriatouras abandonadas despoues de la guerra.
Lo foue a verlo.
Estava a la eskola komunala del Sien i soukouenta i ouno.
Me espanti de verlo.
Tenia ouna kavesa grande i oun pouerpo eskeleto.
El join lo mando a Palestina ande el ermano de la madre
Ke estouvo bien mirado.
Bevamos a la saloud de los ke se salvaron.

96. Vengo de ambezar ke Georgette Modiano atorno a Salonique.
La foui a ver tres vezes i non la topi.
Regreti de kitar Salonique sin ver a Georgette.
Le eskrivi doz vezes. La prima lettra non me respondio.
A la segounda la mandi "recommandé."
Me atornaron la lettra ke el adresso non ese boueno.
Espero ke Georgette esta sana i alegre.

97. La souerte de Daniel Modiano foue ouna trajedia.
Estava en Italia en oun hotel al Lac Superiere.

---

64. United Nations Relief and Rehabilitation Administration, established
November 9, 1943, to repatriate and support war refugees.

A bullet hit his head.

He died on the spot at [the age of] twenty-two.

The proverb says: "He who protected himself, his mother didn't have to cry for him."

I went to Athens after the war,

Contracted with the UNRRA to help the displaced persons.

I went to the cemetery to see Samuel's grave that was full of photographs.

I looked around me; I saw a girl who was his girlfriend.

My mother said: "He who protected himself, his mother didn't have to cry for him."

94. I went to Salonika after the war with the UN Relief Association.

On every street in the winter they sell chestnuts; I bought a few.

They were given to me in paper that was my mother's Haggadah.[65]

I bought all the papers that the vendor had.

I told him: "Is this what you did this to the books from the Jewish quarter?"

95. My little sister Regina had a friend.

She married very young.

At the time of the deportation she gave birth to a boy.

They placed him with the abandoned children after the war.

I went to see him.

He was in the community school in [District] 151.

I was shocked to see him.

He had a large head and a skeletal[66] body.

The Joint sent him to Palestine to stay with his mother's brother

Where he was looked after well.

Let us drink to the health of those who were saved.

96. I just learned that Georgette Modiano returned to Salonika.

I went to see her three times and did not find her.

I regretted leaving Salonika without seeing Georgette.

I wrote her twice. She didn't answer the first letter.

The second one I sent it registered.

They returned the letter to me because the address was no good.

I hope that Georgette is well and happy.

97. The fate of Daniel Modiano was a tragedy.

He was in Italy in a hotel on Lake Superior.

---

65. The booklet containing the Hebrew text for Passover Seder.
66. Emaciated.

Los almanes vigneron, mataron a el i a su kompagnia.
Los katavres foueron ethados al lac.
Esto izo el Alman mas Negro de pharo i Aman.

99. Foue a Tel Aviv.
Moche, el marido de Stella, me amostro ouna robe de chambre de satin.
Me demando si era mia; le respondi no.
Non kieria ke se peleara kon sou moujer.
La roba Marie me la troucho de Marsilia.
Este modo me desfizieron "todo tsivit i karaboya"[67] todo lo ke tenia.
Si mi madre la via iva a dezir:
"Lo ke kedo del ladron, se lo yevo el endevino."

87. Suzane me souvrina tenia sech mille drachmas.
Se loz dio a vouadrar a Eliaou
Porke el kougnado se las estava koumiendo.
Eliaou merko ouna mania.
Me la dio ami e me dicho despouese ke se va a kazar dasela.
Si non tiene valor dale las paras
I si ese mas dile ke ese regalo ke le ago a sou kazamiento.
Suzan se fouyo kon sou marido apenas se kazo.
A Tel Aviv la vide i le di la mania
Porke los sech milles drakmes non valia ni oun penez.
Bevamos a la saloud de Rafel.

100. Non foue fathile para mi de me akodrar i eskrevir de lo pasado
Kozas ke me kiero oulvidar.
Remersio Linda i Ely ke me enkorajaron
A ke se enteresaron a la estoria de Salonique.

---

67. This expression is based on two Turkish words; see the glossary for their literal meanings.

The Germans came, killed him and his coterie.
The cadavers were thrown into the lake.
This was done [by] the German more evil than Pharoah and Haman.

99. I went to Tel Aviv.
Moshe, Stella's husband, showed me a satin dressing gown.
He asked if it was mine; I replied: No.
I did not want him to quarrel with his wife.
Marie had brought me this robe from Marseilles.
In this way they squandered all that I owned.
Had my mother seen it she would have said:
"What was left over from the thief, the fortuneteller took away."

87. Suzanne, my niece, had six thousand drachmas.
She gave them to Eliaou for safekeeping
Because her brother-in-law was spending them.
Eliaou bought a bracelet.
He gave it to me and told me that later when she is going to get
    married, give it to her.
If it has no value, give her the monetary equivalent
And if it is [worth] more, tell her that it is a gift that I am making in
    honor of her marriage.
Suzanne escaped with her husband right after she married.
In Tel Aviv I saw her and gave her the bracelet
Because the six thousand drachmas were not worth a penny.
Let us drink to the health of Rafael.

100. It was not easy for me to remember and to write of the past
Things that I want to forget.
I thank Linda and Ely who encouraged me
And who were interested in the history of Salonika.

GLOSSARY

Bouena made frequent use of words from languages other than Ladino. Each glossary entry indicates the language from which the word comes: Arabic = A; French = F; German = G; Greek = GR; Hebrew = H; I = Italian; Portuguese = P; Turkish = T. Altogether the glossary includes the following numbers of words from each language: Arabic, one; French, fifty-two; German, one; Greek, four; Hebrew, ninety-six; Italian, two; Portuguese, two; Turkish, seventy-one.

Order: Bouena's spelling, sometimes followed by / indicating proper spelling; word of origin in parentheses, followed by verses in which it appeared.

A la garçon: F, like the boys

Afekoumin (afikoman): H, piece of middle matsah of three broken off and often hidden during the Passover Seder

Afsakadji: H, Turkish ending with Hebrew word for someone who engages in prolonged fasts or breaks (*hafsakot*) from eating

Agada (haggadah): H, book read at Passover Seder

Ahir: T, stable or barn

Akshara (hakhshara): H, agricultural training program in preparation for going to Palestine

Alechek/ališik (alişik): T, relation

Amalek: H, biblical archenemy of Jewish people who attacked them

Aman (Haman): H, the archvillain who planned to destroy Persian Jewry as related in the Scroll of Esther read on Purim

Ambér: T, amber seed that releases an odor

Antari (entari): T, sleeveless dress of smooth fabric, in striped or floral material that crossed and buttoned on the left side

Apouliterio (apolitirio): GR, certificate of discharge from the army

Après-midi: F, afternoon (get-together)

Arabá: T, cart

Ar[r]astar: P, to lie about, to have in abundance

Arbaa ve es(t)rim: H, twenty-four

Asara be-Tevet: H, tenth of the Hebrew month of Tevet, a minor fast day

Askerier: T, the military

Askierlik/askyerlik (askerlik): T, military service

Atelier: F, workshop

Avdela (havdalah): H, blessings at end of the Sabbath separating it from the rest of the week

Aziendo bazaar (hazer bazar): T, to bargain, to ask the price of

Azlaka (hatslaha): H, success; abundance

Bachilaki: GR, hopscotch

Bachiste/bašistén (badesten): T, covered bazaar

Bakír: T, worthless copper coin

Balabaya (baal bayit): H, head of household

Bar mitzvah: H, ceremony for boys at age thirteen

Basheste (bashistén): F, old section of market

Baston (baton): F, walking stick

Bedel: T, military exemption tax

Benadan (benadam): H, man (good person)

Bera(k)ha: H, blessing

Berseau: F, cradle

Besiman Tov: H, may it be a sign of good fortune

Bet [H]aha[y]im: H, literally "house of the living," euphemism for graveyard, cemetery

Beth Din: H, rabbinical court

Bey: T, Turkish title of honor or rule

Bikour Holim: H, literally "visitation of the sick"; society that cares for the ill

Birchim (ibrishim): T, silk threads

Bozadji: T, vendor of fermented millet drink (*boza*)

Brasar: F, to braze, to decorate with brass

Brith, Brit Mila: H, circumcision ceremony

Bourako (buráko): P, hole

Bureau: F, office

Chamach (shamash): H, beadle

Chapeau: F, hat

Charpa (sharpa): F, scarf

Chechit (sheshit): T, choice, variety

Chekalim (shekalim): H, currency of Zionist associations

Chevouette (Shavuot): H, harvest festival in spring

Chofar (shofar): H, ram's horn blown on the High Holidays

Čivít (tsivit): T, literally "indigo" or "laundering powder"; the expression "to make everything tsivit with karabóya" means to waste or squander

Clisa (kilise): T, church

Croix: F, cross

Croix Garnie: Garnet Cross

Croix Rouge: F, Red Cross

Depo (dépôt): F, storage, warehouse

Dernier krie (cri): F, the last word, utmost refinement (of fashion)

Despanser (dispensaire): F, clinic

Deventual: T, full body-length apron

Dib(o)uk: H, demon, name of famous Yiddish play by S. Ansky in 1914

Dinim: H, laws

Dondurmadjes: T, ice-cream seller

D(o)ubara: T, racket, mayhem

Eloennou che ba chamaim (Eloheinu sheba shamayim): H, God who is in heaven

Ergas/ergasias: GR, forced labor camp, work camp

Estragnere (étranger): F, foreign

Fenél (fener): T, lantern

Feredjé: T, part of ladies costume sometimes a kerchief and sometimes an overall put on when going out

Fez: T, Turkish traditional headpiece

Fillet/filet: F, mesh

Gan Eden: H, Garden of Eden, heaven

Getres: F, spats

G[h]etto (giotto): I, iron foundry, herein a restricted area for Jews

Gilé (gilet): F, waistcoat

Greve: F, strike; en grève: on strike

G[y]mnastique: F, gymnastics, exercises

Ha[h]kahim: H, wise men, rabbis

Halisa: H, release of widow without children from marriage to brother-in-law

Hamsi (hamsin): A, hot eastern wind

Han(o)ukia: H, candelabrum lit on Hanukkah

Hassid: H, member of ultra-Orthodox sect of Judaism

Hatan Torah i Berechit (Bereshit): H, honor (like a groom or hattan) of being called to (read) Torah given on Simhat Torah

Haver: H, member, friend

Hazan: H, cantor

Hen: H, favor, beauty (from the expression "to find favor")

Hevra: H, social company

Houpa (huppah): H, bridal canopy

Hourt(o)um: T, hose

Hût (ud): T, oud

Ichbeteredjis: T, middlemen

Jupe-culotte: F, divided skirt, culotte

Kach (laç): T, run or escape

Kacher (kasher): H, kosher

Kadich (kaddish): H, Aramaic prayer in memory of the deceased

Kameotte (kameyot): H, amulets

Kaparas (kapparot): H, sacrifices

Karabóya: T, lit. sulfate of iron or black dye. *See* čivít.

Karnet (carnet de bal): F, dance program, card

Kartie[r] (quartier): F, quarter

K[e]iyila/ot (kehilla): H, congregation, community

Kepazelik: T, degradation, ignominy

Keren Hakayemet: H, Zionist association

Keren Hayisod: H, Zionist organization

Ketouba (ketubah): H, marriage contract

Kib[o]utzim (kibbutz, sing.): H, collective communal society

Kidouch (kiddush): H, prayer over wine on the Sabbath and holidays

Kiduchim: H, marriage ceremony

Kieristidjis: T, lumber merchants

Ki(e)ra: T, rent

Kirim: T, fur coat

Koanim (cohanim): H, priests

Kokma (hokhma): H, wisdom

Komardjes: T, sports fans

Kombinezon (combinaison): F, slip

Konak: T, estate

Korban: H, sacrifice

Korsage: F, corsage

Kote maravi (kotel maaravi): H, Western Wall in Jerusalem

Kouchak, kušác (kuşak): T, lit. belt

Koundouria/kundúrya (kundura): T, footwear

Koundouriero/kunduriero: T, shoemaker

Kourch(o)um: T, bullet

Kouti/kutí (kutu): T, box

Koyar: T, detachable collar

Kúkla: T, doll

Kulibera (kulube): T, hut dweller (hut)

Lac Superiere: F, Lake Superior

Lachon (lashon): H, lit. tongue or language, meaning Hebrew

Lag(u)er: G, (concentration) camp

Le chana aba be-Jeruchalaim (li-shana ha-baa be Yerushalayim): H, "Next year in Jerusalem," traditionally said at the end of the Passover Seder

Lehaim: H, to life (salud)

Lingère: F, linen maker

Lo(u)rginon: F, pince-nez

Loula(lulav): H, 3 species including the main palm branch with willow and myrtle branches used on Sukkot with a fourth component

Mab(o)ul: H, flood

Machguia (mashgiah): H, ritual supervisor

Machia (mashiah): H, messiah

Magazin (magasin): F, store

Maguin David (magen David): H, Star of David

Malá (mahalle): T, neighborhood, quarter

Ma(a)minim: H, self-reference to believers in Sabbatai Zevi and his 1666 conversion to Islam (otherwise known as Dönme)

Mankar (mancare): I, to be lacking, missing, to overlook or fail

Mariage blanc: F, marriage of convenience

Maskaralik: T, disgrace

Mekanes (makam): T, Turkish classical music, system based on melody types

Mishtrabá (mashrapa): T, mug

Matanot La Evionim: H, (Society of) Gifts for the Needy

Matza (matsah): H, unleavened bread

Mazal: H, luck, good fortune

Mearaotte (mearot): H, caves, tombs

Meguila (megilla): H, scroll, one of five read in public on different occasions

Mer(o)uba: H, literally "square," or scribe-like Hebrew writing

Michibira (me-she-berakh): H, prayer in public for welfare of

Mingnan (minyan): H, quorum of ten male worshippers

Minha: H, afternoon prayers

Misseure (monsieur): F, sir

Mitsvot: H, term for the four species used on the holiday of Sukkot

Mizouzotte (mezuzot): H, sign on the doorpost

Mochav (moshav): H, farming cooperative with private homes

Moel (mohel): H, ritual circumciser

Moraotte (meoraot): H, incidents

Mosandara/musandará: T, attic

Mouchamadjis: T, linoleum sellers

Mouchteri /muŝterí (muşteri): T

Nes[e]: H, miracle

Obogó (bogmak): T, bundle

Officier: F, officer

Pansement: F, dressing of wound

Papion (papillon): F, butterfly, bowtie

Paradis: F, bird of paradise

Parás: T, money

Parchemenes (parchemin): F, parchment

Parnasa: H, livelihood

Parohet: H, Torah cover

Pasoukes (pesukim; pasuk, sing.): H, verse from the Bible

Pavion (pavillon): F, pavilion

Permi (permis): F, permit

Pinkas: H, registry, membership (book)

Pliser (plissure): F, pleats

Politofilaka: GR, citizens' police

Polo: F, knitted cap

Recommandé: F, registered (mail)

Réfectoire: F, refectory, dining room or hall

Refoua chelema (refuah shelayma): H, wish for a speedy recovery

Regie: F, administration or management

Robe de chamber: F, dressing gown

Saleptsi (salepchi): T, salep vendor

Satin: F, satin

Sefer-tasin (sefer tasi): T, lunch pail, number of pots of exactly the same dimension, superposed and held by a handle

Seliho(t): H, prayers of forgiveness recited before Rosh Hashanah

Shabat agadol (Shabbat Ha-Gadol): H, important Sabbath preceding Passover

Shalom: H, hello

Sharkí: T, slow oriental tune

Signor de Rabotay: H, Lord of Our Fathers

Sirá: T, line

Soeur: F, sister, nun

Sotlathi/sotlatsi (sutlach): T, rice (and milk) pudding

Sougritadjas: T, insurance agents

Souka (sukkah): H, booth built during the Feast of Tabernacles

Soupe Populaire: F, soup kitchen

Soy(e): T, lineage, line of descendants

Tableau: F, painting

Talmide hakamim: H, learned scholars (literally "students of the wise")

Tanid (taanit): H

Tasin: T

Tefila (tefillah): H, prayer

Tembel: T, idler, lazybones

Tevila: H, ritual immersion

T(h)ora: H, the Five Books of Moses

Tiskou lechanim rabotte (tizku li shanim rabot): H, you should merit a long life

Toutoun (tutún): T, tobacco

Tsai (çay): T, tea

Tsalguin (čalgí): T, orchestra

Tsametsi: T, market

Tsanta/čánta (çanta): T, trunk

Tsarchi/tsatchi: T, marketplace

Tsavaha (tsavaa): H, will

Tsitsik (chichek): T, flower

Tu Bishvat: H, the fifteenth day of the Hebrew month of Shevat

Vagon-lit/wagon-lit: F, sleeper

Voile: F, veil

Volan/volant: F, gathered flounce of dress

Yadrán (yerdan): T, string (of pearls or the like)

Yagourthis: T, yogurt sellers

Yousourin (yisurin): H, pains, travails

Zarzavá (zebzevat): T, vegetables

Ze a kise chel Eliaou Anavi (ze ha-kise shel Eliyahu Hanavi): H, this is Elijah the Prophet's chair

Zembíl: T, basket

Zi(y)ara: T, visit to grave of family member or saint

NOTES

Preface

1. Her birth name was actually Linda, but when she was an infant it was changed to Bouena after her recuperation from an illness; such name changes reflect a Sephardi custom intended to deceive the angel of death. There is also some confusion as to her precise birth year: Bouena stated that it was 1918, but numerous relatives were certain that this was a miscalculation and that she was born in 1916 (Ely Garfinkle, personal communication, July 3, 2010).

2. Apparently, Moises went to his granary outside the city despite the fact that the area was quarantined due to the threat of the plague; while there, her father contracted this unidentified contagious disease and died upon his return home (Ely Garfinkle, personal communication, July 3, 2010).

3. Approximately 12,898 Jewish men were conscripted in Greece at this time; the majority of the 50th Regiment, nicknamed "the Cohen Regiment" of Thessaloniki, was Jewish. See Constantopoulou and Veremis, *Documents on the History of the Greek Jews,* 34 and note 23.

4. See Garfinkle, "The Memoirs of Bouena Garfinkle." In the mid-1970s, her son, Ely (who was named after Eliaou), arranged for a friend of his, Veronika Kisfalvi of Montreal, to record her memoirs as she related them; Vera calculated that this took about a year to complete (Veronika Kisfalvi, e-mail message to author, November 8, 2010). For a complete analysis of her memoirs, see Levine Melammed, "The Memoirs of a Partisan from Salonika," 151–73.

5. Garfinkle, "The Memoirs of Bouena Garfinkle," 8.

6. See Dublon-Knebel, *German Foreign Office Documents,* 24–25.

7. The first roundup was carried out on the Sabbath, henceforth known as the "Black Sabbath." Its purpose was to humiliate thousands of men who were left standing in the sun for hours without any head covering, surrounded by armed soldiers who abused them as they dehydrated. The men subsequently suffered even more terribly once they were mobilized. Freedom for seven thousand of them was purchased in October for a small fortune, some 2.5 billion drachmas, amassed with the help of outside contributions. See Yakuel, "On the Path to Destruction," 277–82; Mazower, *Inside Hitler's Greece,* 238–39; and Rivlin, *Encyclopaedia,* 272–76. The latter states that 6,500 men, and not the "exaggerated" figure of 10,000, were assembled on that Sabbath.

8. Along with the majority of the community, the Sarfattys were forced to leave their home and move into one of the three areas designated to become ghettos; they found a residence on Sigrou Street.

9. In another version, the deputy for one district did not appear, and Bouena was asked to investigate this (eulogy by Ely Garfinkle, in "Lives Lived," *The Globe and Mail,* October 3, 1997).

10. The original homestead was on the corner of Tsimiski and Agias (Saint) Sofia Streets, but when they needed to be in a house with a bomb shelter they moved to

Mitropoleos Street in April 1941. When the ghettos were formed, the family moved to the aforementioned residence on Sigrou Street near the Synagogue of the Monastirlis.

11. This was most likely the Monastir Synagogue, although Bouena does not specify.

12. See Mazower, *Salonica, City of Ghosts,* 397.

13. Daniel gave her food and grain to help her in the initial weeks of flight. The poems describe Modiano's demise. However, there is an interesting document that concerns him—a report by the German war administration counselor Merten to the German consulate in Salonika dated April 26, 1943. A train transporting soldiers on furlough contained eighteen Jews as well; according to the Italian consul, they were Italian citizens. Merten personally examined their papers and permitted thirteen to leave but detained Modiano, accusing him "of receiving gold from Greek Jews who wanted to prevent the seizure of their property by the German authorities" (See Dublon-Knebel, *German Foreign Office Documents,* 128–29).

14. This is confirmed in a letter from the Veterans Appeal Board of Canada, July 3, 1990, which summarizes some of her activities and states, "There is sufficient evidence to warrant a finding that the appellant was part of the Greek underground and thus does meet the service requirement of the War Veterans Allowance Act."

15. This was the EDES, or Greek Democratic Organization, composed of royalists and led by General Napoleon Zarvos. There were Jews from Salonika who joined the EDES. It is difficult to find precise numbers regarding Jewish members, but Yosef Ben estimates that there were at least a thousand Jewish participants in the two groups, namely, the loyalists and the communists (Ben, *Greek Jewry in the Holocaust,* 124–25).

16. This was the ELAS, the activist arm of the National Liberation Army (EAM) and, according to Yosef Ben, the more important of the two groups. Its members included workers and farmers as well as members of the intelligentsia and the middle class who had belonged to political parties ranging from communist to socialist and to professional unions; all were anti-royalist (Ben, *Greek Jewry in the Holocaust,* 124). The Jews of Athens were located closer to the hills and joined the ELAS; one report mentions that three hundred of the six hundred Jewish members of the EAM died in action (ibid., 125, and Mazower, *Inside Hitler's Greece,* 297–321). Apparently, some members of the EAM offered to help Jews flee Salonika and even approached Rabbi Koretz to extend their help, but were refused (Kerem, "Efforts to Rescue," 88).

17. This mission and a number of others are not mentioned in Bouena's memoirs, but they appear in her poetry as well as in the list of her partisan activities compiled by her son.

18. Maritsa used a route well known to those arranging to flee Greece, usually with the aid of partisans: from the shores of Attica (a region comprising Athens and its surroundings) by sea to the island of Evvia; from there via fishing boats or other vessels to Çesme on the Turkish coast. In August 1943 the British consulate in Ankara received instructions from London to grant entrance permits to every Jew who reached Turkey (Kerem, "Efforts to Rescue," 83).

19. Mazower points to two options: fleeing to the hills or leaving Greece by "travelling to the coast at Evvoia, from where *caizues* (fishing boats) took them to Turkey. Help did not always come without a price," as they were often forced to hand over their money and possessions, but "they were rarely denounced, despite the rewards offered by the SS" (Mazower, *Inside Hitler's Greece,* 261).

20. Judith Tydor Baumel mentions the roles that women played in dealing with survivors: they were relief workers for UNRRA, the Joint Distribution Committee, and the Religious Emergency Council (formed by the British chief rabbi); social workers; nurses; and emissaries from Palestine (Baumel, *Double Jeopardy*, 31).

21. The first survivors, a group of 137 Jews who had found refuge either in the city itself or in the nearby hills, entered Salonika at the end of October 1944. On October 28, a committee was quickly organized to register the survivors from the hills and the Polish camps who ultimately numbered 2,000. Their homes (about 11,000 apartments), 2,300 stores and factories, and other property were all gone. The committee managed to regain about seven public buildings and some homes and offices. For details, see Rivlin, *Encyclopaedia*, 289.

22. Garfinkle, "The Memoirs of Bouena Garfinkle," 114.

23. Ibid., 157.

24. When she fled Salonika, her brother had given her a pouch with valuables; in order to survive, she sold these items one at a time. Unknown to Bouena, Eliaou had hidden gold coins in the heels of her shoes. Because she had only one pair of shoes throughout the war, the shoes actually survived the war and accompanied her to Palestine. Ely Garfinkle still has these Turkish coins in his possession (personal communication, July 3, 2010).

25. Garfinkle, "The Memoirs of Bouena Garfinkle," 166.

26. Ibid., 170.

27. Ibid., 173.

28. Ibid., 170.

29. Ibid., 143.

30. Ibid., 188.

31. See Cohen, "Judeo-Spanish Song," tapes 4, 5, 13, 14, and 20–23; "Three Canadian Sephardic Women"; and "Selanikli Humour in Montreal."

32. See Havassy, "The Ladino Song."

33. Bouena recorded close to three hundred proverbs dealing with the Nazi period; nearly five hundred proverbs cursing the Germans; and over a hundred general proverbs in Ladino. One suspects that this might not be all she wrote and recorded.

34. Ladino, or Judeo-Spanish, developed directly from medieval Spanish; the exiles continued to communicate in the language of their birthplace despite relocation to a new diaspora. Ladino can be written in Roman as well as in Hebrew (usually Rashi script) letters, and often includes words or expressions that reflect the new environment of the exile. While modern Spanish developed on Iberian soil, Ladino preserved fifteenth-century grammatical and linguistic styles in the diaspora.

35. See Refael, *Un grito en el silencio*, 68–69; Ely Garfinkle, e-mail message to author, September 16, 2009.

Introduction

1. Salonika will be spelled with a K because this is the form advocated by the *Selaniklis,* the term used by the residents of the Greek city, Thessaloniki, to refer to themselves.

2. This term first appears in the Bible, in 2 Samuel 20:19, and is translated as "mother and city in Israel" or "mother-city in Israel" (rather than Judaism).

3. This translation appears in the English edition of the 1553 Ferrara publication (Usque, *Consolation for the Tribulations of Israel*, 211).

4. According to a survey from a Turkish paper, in 1906 there were 47,312 Jews (or 54 percent of the population), 31,070 Turks, 15,012 Greeks, and 3,697 Bulgarians living in the city. Other figures are higher and claim that the Jewish population even rose to 75,000. See Michael Molho, "A History of the Jews of Salonika," 21–22.

5. See Benbassa and Rodrigue, *Sephardi Jewry*, 81.

6. The number of European residents in the city grew from one hundred in 1768 to ten thousand in the 1890s (Mazower, *Salonica, City of Ghosts*, 217). Regarding the infiltration of European fashion, see ibid., 223.

7. Kerem, "The Europeanization of the Sephardic Community," 68.

8. Mazower, *Salonica, City of Ghosts*, 267.

9. Marcus, "The Beginning of the Haskalah," 70–77.

10. This is yet another term loosely based on the Hebrew reference to a "mother-city" in Israel.

11. Rena Molho, "Education in the Jewish Community," 267.

12. Messinas, *The Synagogues*, 47–48.

13. Mazower, *Salonica, City of Ghosts*, 218.

14. Bowman, *The Agony of Greek Jews*, 18.

15. See Colonas, "The Contribution of the Jewish Community," 171. There were Jewish refugees in the city from the end of the nineteenth century and pursuant to pogroms in Russian in the early 1900s. See Naar, "From the 'Jerusalem of the Balkans,'" 440.

16. See Rena Molho, "Jewish Working-Class Neighborhoods," 178–85. "Moreover, by locating the new neighborhoods in the hitherto undeveloped suburbs, it changed the face of the city" (185).

17. Mazower points to the spread of poverty by the end of the century, explaining that although in 1831, the poor numbered 30,000, by 1913 their numbers had reached 150,000 (*Salonica, City of Ghosts*, 235).

18. In the modern period, "the metropolis of Israel" (note 10, above, and Rena Molho, "Education in the Jewish Community," 259) appears alongside the traditional term of endearment: "Salonika, for example, served as the mother city for the Macedonian Jewish communities located in Veroia, Kavalla, Serres and Drama . . . Salonika's traders and industries extended to Kavalla, Serres and Veroia" (Plaut, *Greek Jewry*, 26).

19. Lewkowicz, *The Jewish Community*, 93.

20. Mazower, *Salonica, City of Ghosts*, 264–65.

21. Rozen, *The Last Ottoman Century*, 1:155.

22. It is not clear whether the conscription policy went into effect immediately in 1909 or in a few years' time; it eventually did affect immigration (Naar, "From the 'Jerusalem of the Balkans,'" 444). As a matter of fact, Naar notes that after 1916, the youth "fled in droves" (454).

23. It should be noted that in 1908 there were between eight and ten thousand workers in the tobacco industry; most of them were Jewish girls (Hadar, "Aspects of Jewish

Family Life," 191). In the great tobacco strike of 1914, Jewish women tobacco workers were quite active (Rozen, *The Last Ottoman Century,* 1:172).

24. Rena Molho, "Popular Antisemitism and State Policy," 254, 259.

25. A pogrom that week included numerous incidents of rape and vandalism of stores and homes. Various consuls protested; the king and queen were sympathetic but the local authorities dealt poorly with the violent situation. The first blood libel in the city occurred in 1913; additional occurrences seemed to have been prevented by the government. See Rena Molho, "Popular Antisemitism and State Policy," 256–59.

26. Rozen, *The Last Ottoman Century,* 1:168.

27. Rena Molho, "The Jewish Community of Salonika," 394.

28. Rena Molho refers to the nonthreatening image of Greek nationalism, especially when compared to the Western model. She explains, "the Greek state introduced a new political reality vis-à-vis the Jews according to which the sovereign state was not threatened by the different minorities within it, while it embraced them as equal members" ("The Jewish Community of Salonika," 399).

29. For details, see Mazower, *Salonica, City of Ghosts,* 275–81.

30. Ibid., 280–81.

31. Fleming, *Greece,* 71.

32. Mazower, *Salonica, City of Ghosts,* 282–85. Officials came from Athens, Crete, and the Peloponnese. The census conducted listed 61,439 Jews among the 157,889 residents of the city.

33. Bowman characterizes this period as one of "Central European economic and imperial expansion" in which "Salonika was the greatest prize." Apparently, "both before and during World War I the Habsburg Empire was concerned lest Salonika become the exclusive Mediterranean entrepôt for one of the competing nationalist groups in the Balkans" (*The Agony of Greek Jews,* 24–25).

34. For details concerning these developments, see Fleming, *Greece,* 74; and Mazower, *Salonica, City of Ghosts,* 290–91.

35. The city, whose narrow streets housed wooden buildings closely lined up, was a firetrap; in addition, its ability to fight fires was abysmal. This fire began in the heat of the summer when there was reluctance to deplete the water supplies; thus, the decision was made to bomb any structure in the path of the fire in order to prevent its spread. Some claimed arson, but the theory cannot be proved. See Plaut, *Greek Jewry,* 76–78; and Michael Molho, "A History of the Jews of Salonika," 23–24.

36. See Rena Molho, "Jewish Working-Class Neighborhoods," 173–94, especially 186.

37. According to Mazower's calculations, there were 9,500 buildings destroyed and seventy thousand homeless individuals (*Salonica, City of Ghosts,* 300). Fleming refers to the destruction of 8,000 buildings, six hundred Torah scrolls, eight schools, libraries, and the chief rabbinate as well as the displacement of forty to fifty thousand Jews (*Greece,* 78).

38. See Rozen, *The Last Ottoman Century,* 1:174; and Plaut, *Greek Jewry,* 33.

39. Rozen, *The Last Ottoman Century,* 1:175.

40. See Mazower, *Salonica, City of Ghosts,* 300–304. Some three to four thousand Jews with savings were able to leave for Paris (Rena Molho, "Jewish Working-Class Neighborhoods," 190).

41. Undesirable areas were chosen such as the Anghelaki quarter (Rena Molho, "Jewish Working-Class Neighborhoods," 189). Another cause of emigration was the switch by the government to direct taxation instead of the traditional Turkish non-intrusive method (Plaut, *Greek Jewry*, 33).

42. Continuity was disrupted in many areas of life. The main site for recreation had traditionally been the synagogue; previous favorite locales for walks and relaxation were located by the sea and were no longer accessible.

43. For details, see Mazower, *Salonica, City of Ghosts*, 310–40.

44. Fleming, *Greece*, 88.

45. Ibid., 85.

46. Rena Molho, "Popular Antisemitism," 262.

47. "As long as Jews were a majority group in Salonika, they were able to muster enough opposition to the Sunday-closing laws throughout the northern provinces. A new period began with the resettlement of refugees from Asia Minor in Salonika" (Plaut, *Greek Jewry*, 40).

48. I thank Shmuel Refael for informing me of this nickname.

49. Benbassa and Rodrigue, *Sephardi Jewry*, 100.

50. Mazower, *Salonica, City of Ghosts*, 377.

51. Plaut found estimates claiming that during the course of fourteen years (1918–32), 75 percent of the communal property was lost (*Greek Jewry*, 35).

52. Some two thousand rioters attacked this quarter, set it afire, and beat the residents as the police watched. Michael Molho estimated that thousands of these souls moved to Tel Aviv as a result ("A History of the Jews of Salonika," 25). Lewkowicz believes that this triggered immigration to Palestine, France, and North and South America (*The Jewish Community*, 48). The trial that followed was a travesty, for it included claims of Jewish provocation and the acquittal of those arrested (Mazower, *Salonica, City of Ghosts*, 385–86).

53. This analysis is presented in Benbassa and Rodrigue, *Sephardi Jewry*, 142–43.

54. Rena Molho, "Jewish Working-Class Neighborhoods," 190.

55. Naar's study of Ellis Island passenger lists reveals that in the three years prior to the fire, there was substantial emigration to the United States, which peaked between 1915 and 1916 ("From the 'Jerusalem of the Balkans,'" 448). By 1924, U.S. government restrictions forced the émigrés to seek refuge elsewhere, so they went to Palestine, Latin American, France, and Italy (ibid., 456).

56. For example, the Allatini family owned a brick factory as well as a flourmill with the Modianos—who, together with the Fernandez family, owned the Olympos distillery.

57. For a fairly comprehensive discussion of immigration patterns, see Hadar, "Aspects of Family Life," 275–85; 302–14.

58. Rena Molho, "Judeo-Spanish Plays," 141.

59. Haviv, "Local Community Projects," 216.

60. See Ussishkin, "Community Activity," 211–14. The Hirsch Hospital provided without charge forty-eight beds, and another twelve for birthing mothers; there were a hundred children in the orphanages.

61. Benbassa and Rodrigue refer to them as the "Franco Elite," which included the Allatini, Fernandez, Modiano, Morpurgo, Saias, and Torres families (*Sephardi Jewry*, 81).

62. For a description of the Allatini palace, see Mazower, *Salonica, City of Ghosts*, 223.

63. See Kerem, "The Europeanization of the Sephardic Community," 60–69.

64. For details, see Benbassa and Rodrigue, *Sephardi Jewry*, 101.

65. See Bunis, *Voices from Jewish Salonika*, 61–78, regarding these trends.

66. Rena Molho, "Education in the Jewish Community," 259–69.

67. Rozen, *The Last Ottoman Century*, 1:160.

68. This park is mentioned in the verses.

69. Romero, *Entre dos (o más) fuegos*, 456–61. This organization was a fairly powerful socialist faction.

70. Mazower, *Salonica, City of Ghosts*, 371, 372, quotation on 374.

71. Hadar, "Aspects of Family Life," 191, 211; and Mazower, *Salonica, City of Ghosts*, 364.

72. There were also Jewish prostitutes and wet nurses (Mazower, *Salonica, City of Ghosts*, 363, 365–66).

73. Kerem, "The Europeanization of the Sephardic Community," 64–65. Benveniste also mentions seamstresses and embroiderers, who usually worked from their homes (*The Jews of Salonika in Recent Times*, 67–68).

74. Mazower calls the *modistra* or dressmaker "the icon of new femininity in the interwar city," who was "called into being by female spending power" (*Salonica, City of Ghosts*, 364).

75. Vervenioti, "Left-Wing Women," 105. "Thousands of girls joined the resistance —defying rural conventions for the first time, and ignoring or persuading their parents—and became politically active" (Mazower, *Inside Hitler's Greece*, 186).

76. Ibid., 279–80. He refers to this as a time when they had experienced an unusual degree of power, but only fleetingly.

77. Bunis discusses these developments in *Voices from Jewish Salonika*, 23–25, and the influence of Hebrew and Aramaic is mentioned on 67–71. He also analyzes Salonikan Judezmo, and points to uses that characterize it on 71–98. Some of the linguistic changes accompanying modernization have appeared in the discussion above regarding Ladino newspapers.

78. See Benveniste, *The Jews of Salonika in Recent Times*, 126. Examples of words that changed are *kal* instead of *kahal* for "congregation" or *biri* for the *brit* (circumcision) "blessing." Examples of Spanish forms for Hebrew words are *balabaya* for "homeowner," in Hebrew, *baal bayit* or *tani* instead of *taanit*, or "fast."

79. Bunis constructed categories in which French was frequently used—including words dealing with cuisine and entertainment, fashion and cosmetics, music, health care and hygiene, commerce, municipal zoning, modern inventions, and abstract matters (*Voices from Jewish Salonika*, 100). The majority of Bouena's French terms fits into these categories.

80. The Greeks sought to advance their language; in 1931, the government forbade the teaching of Judezmo/Judeo-Spanish or French in Jewish schools. The Alliance Israélite Universelle, which had schools in Salonika as early as 1873, considered Ladino to be antiquated; the Zionists favored Hebrew; the elite preferred French; and the workers and communists stood by the traditional Ladino. These divisions reflect the political and economic divisions of society as well as the repercussions of the pressures of modernity. See Mazower, *Salonica, City of Ghosts*, 376–78.

81. See bibliography for full reference.

82. One also finds *complas* or *conflas*. There seems to have been a Hispanic medieval tradition that preceded them; see Refael, *I Will Tell a Poem*, 19, for a theory on this topic.

83. For a discussion of their development, see ibid., 17–25.

84. Weich-Shahak, "Coplas," 41.

85. Romero, *Coplas sefardies*, 16.

86. The genre became known as "coplas de felek." For examples from Salonika, see Refael, *I Will Tell a Poem*, 37–41; a discussion of their similarity to the Hebrew *piyyut* appears on 31–32.

87. Ibid., 32–33. Romero also contends that the copla authors' writings reflected a respectable level of knowledge and that they were cultured individuals who were writing their poems for the less cultured (*Coplas sefardies*, 21–22).

88. Moshe Attias mentions this in "The Salonikan Romancero," 205, and bemoans the fate of this genre, explaining that because the younger generation was imitating the Europeans, they did not bother to continue this tradition.

89. Romero listed 262 items as having appeared in print between 1700 and 1941. See *Bibliografía analítica de ediciones de coplas sefardies*.

90. See Refael, *I Will Tell a Poem*, 37–41.

91. Refael is of the opinion that this is a rare instance of documentation in lyrical form; he explains that the poet modeled her work on the traditional copla, yet simultaneously renovated as she wrote (*Un grito en el silencio*, 67, 68, 71).

92. Ibid., 69.

93. The first number refers to the collection; the second refers to the number of the particular copla.

94. See the glossary for specific lists.

95. Refael, by contrast, chose to adjust her spelling to a more unified form that conforms to other poems included in his collection. One can compare his orthography to that of the original by referring to *Un grito en el silencio*, 293–95, and to verses 1–15 in the second collection, below.

96. Weissler, *Voices of the Matriarchs*, x.

97. See Refael, "The Holocaust in the Poetry of Bouena Sarfatty of Salonika" and *Un grito en el silencio*, 65–76; and Havassy, "The Ladino Song."

98. Refael, *Un grito en el silencio*, 71, 75.

99. In his discussion concerning Sephardi Holocaust survivors (in Israel), Refael points to the fact that they did not begin to discuss their experiences openly until the 1970s; this is the same decade in which Bouena began to record her memoirs. There is no doubt that the overwhelming number of Ashkenazi survivors in Israel overpowered and almost eradicated the Greek experience from the collective memory. The fifth president of Israel, Yitzhak Navon (1978–83), was one of the main forces behind creating an awareness of the Sephardi trauma in the Israeli public; for example, he fostered the founding of a choir of survivors. In the following decade, one perceives the beginning of exposure to and awareness of the history of these communities during the Holocaust. See *Un grito en el silencio*, 31–32 and note 37.

100. One suspects that she recorded the coplas while or after the different images flooded her memory; some of the verses comprise miniature units that are directly related to one another.

101. Roskies, *The Literature of Destruction*, 9.

102. She mentions this often (Garfinkle, "The Memoirs of Bouena Garfinkle," 25, 46–47, 48, 68, 72, 76–77, 128–29, 171, 276).

103. See Weissler, *Voices of the Matriarchs*, 45, for a discussion of these concepts.

104. Ibid., 515.

105. Ibid., 255.

106. Alan Mintz offers an in-depth analysis of responses to catastrophe and the critical issues involved. His list of critical issues cover the amount of time that has passed between the event and the response, the writer's relationship to the event, his focus, language, attitudes toward "the enemy," and how the lost world is imagined (*Hurban*, 2).

107. See samples of her handwriting from each collection in chapters 3 and 5. Refael analyzed some of her poems in his book on Holocaust poetry and admitted that there were words and phrases that he found to be illegible (*Un grito en el silencio*, 73–74).

108. This has been a process of years, which included returning to the difficult passages time and again, and frequent consultation with native Ladino speakers.

109. See the index of community members' names.

110. Here I accepted the interpretation of Mme. Güler Orgun of Istanbul.

111. Bouena was remiss in numbering her larger collection. She skipped from 24 to 27, 30 to 36, and 51 to 58—and omitted 290–300 and 375–78. She also numbered some verses twice (119, 186, 209, 250, 276, and 288). As a result, the total number of coplas in the collection is 413, 18 fewer than the number that appears in her list, namely 431.

1. Bouena's Ode to Salonika

1. For an analysis of dissonance at the end of the nineteenth century and the first known Ladino memoir by a printer/rebel/musician/journalist, which is "a barometer of Jewish inclusion and isolation, of symbiosis and marginalization," see Halevi, *A Jewish Voice* (quotation on xxxviii).

2. For a discussion of this genre, see Bunis, *Voices from Jewish Salonika*, 174.

3. These are Besantsi and Abravanel, who will appear again in the discussion of Ladino publications at the end of this chapter as well as in the second collection of coplas, in which their fate is discussed.

4. It is rather difficult to determine which synagogue she meant, as this was obviously a shortened name. According to Messinas, *The Synagogues*, the following synagogues might be the "Midrash": Midrash Estrumza (60); Midrash Botton and Neta Na'aman (62); Midrash Katan (67–68); Midrash Han Joseph Benveniste (68); Midrash Biti (68–69); Midrash Solomon Sabbethai (71); Midrash Varsano (72); Midrash Pinto (76); Midrash Carasso (83); Midrash Beit Yaakov (86); Midrash Beit Isaac (87); Midrash Or Ahaim (91); Midrash Bello and Marmoles (92); Midrash Beit Avraham (92–93); Midrash Bezez, Broutho, and Angel (93); Midrash Barouh Beraha (93–94); Midrash Solomon Hassid and Ahavat Olam (94). One would guess perhaps they belonged to the Midrash Botton or Gerush Sepharad Synagogue, relocated on Ptolemeon Street after the fire of 1917. There are Sarfattys listed as members of the Aragonese, Gerush Sefarad, and New Sicilian congregations—and some who were guests and later joined the Etz Hayim and Shalom synagogues as well. Ironically enough, there is a photo of the Sarfatty synagogue in *Salonique*, 183. For a list of synagogues in 1941, see Messinas, *The Synagogues*, 139–41; for those in 1919, 142–45.

5. The dowry itself is a monetary sum that represents the rest of the bride's possessions.

6. Hadar, "Aspects of Jewish Family Life," 231.

7. These women tended to hide in or seek the protection of their kitchens.

8. "May it be a good sign" in Hebrew.

9. Funds were collected from inheritance taxes, from a 1 percent dowry tax, from contributions, as well as from organized fundraising events. See Hadar, "Aspects of Jewish Family Life," 232. It is interesting to note that in other Sephardi communities in earlier periods, there were also *dotar* organizations whose sole function was to provide dowries for female orphans and for girls without financial means. In Holland, the Sacred Society for Granting Dowries for Orphaned and Poor Brides was established in 1613; two years later, the Venetian society Hebra de casas hophâos was established. See Bodian, "The 'Portuguese' Dowry Societies," 30–61; Horowitz, "The Dowering of Brides," 347–71; and Orfali, "The Portuguese Dowry Society," 143–56.

10. The irony is that *hermandad* means "brotherhood" (rather than sisterhood, in this case). In New York, there was a Salonikan mutual aid society established in 1917 called Ermandad Salonikiota de Amerika. They received appeals from home and sent funds to the Azilo de Lokos (insane asylum), Bikur Holim, and Matanot La-Evionim after the fire of 1917, after the Campbell riots in 1931, and during World War II. In 1922, they reorganized into a larger, more comprehensive society called Ermandad Sefardit de Amerika. See Papo, *Sephardim in Twentieth Century America,* 308–10; and Naar, "From the 'Jerusalem of the Balkans,'" 467–69.

11. Holocaust survivor René Molho refers to this as "a kind of economic caste system" in her description of how her friend was enamored of a girl from a poor family who was wonderful, but that there was no possibility that the two could be joined in matrimony (*They Say Diamonds Don't Burn,* 4).

12. Young Hebrews Association.

13. Italian fedora.

14. Gifts for the Needy Association. In the 1920s and 1930s, this was a popular choice of locale for wedding celebrations as well as balls.

15. See copla 412.

16. *Ashugar* is the trousseau. See Garfinkle, "The Memoirs of Bouena Garfinkle," 102.

17. There is a special dowry chest made of wood called the *forcel* that is arched or curved. The wealthy added decorations such as Stars of David and Hebrew printing with gold and silver backgrounds to theirs; the poor used wooden boxes (Hadar, "Aspects of Jewish Family Life," 229). Educated girls also put books in their chests (234).

18. See coplas 276 and 267, for example.

19. Michael Molho, "A History of the Jews of Salonika," 25.

20. See copla 422.

21. For songs dealing with these items, see Garfinkle, "The Memoirs of Bouena Garfinkle," 169.

22. See copla 165.

23. Bunis informs us that this ceremony was known as the *lavadura de la lana* (the washing of the wool), which took place on the thirty-third day during the period of forty-nine days of the counting of the Omer, the period between Passover and Shavuot. It was timed to occur with the first shearing of the sheep, and because the courtyards were large, between twelve and fifteen women from the neighborhood joined together in the washing; other women, relatives and friends, were also invited: "This date coincides with the festival honoring R. Simeon Bar Yohay, which puts an end to the period of mourning decreed by the rabbinical academy following the death of 33 of its students,

in commemoration of which the Jews did not shave or cut their nails." This explanation from *Voices from Jewish Salonika,* 154–55n90, appeared in the Ladino publication *Aksyón* in 1938. See also Attias, "Marriage Customs," 29.

24. See copla 316.

25. See copla 250b.

26. Attias, "Marriage Customs," 29. Here he describes a special washing day that took place after the groom examined the bride's trousseau. This was apparently an occasion for singing galore—sometimes in the presence of paid singers.

27. Michael Molho, *Traditions and Customs,* 10.

28. According to Attias, "Marriage Customs," 30, this was the day after the all-night *almosama* party for the bride.

29. Bunis refers to the day of the *alvorada,* literally "the day of dawning," when the family gathered for a display of the trousseau; presumably this celebration took place around this time. See *Voices from Jewish Salonika,* 145–46.

30. Attias, "Marriage Customs," 30. The wealthier families hired musicians who played the drums, violin, and the oud. Uninvited female musicians such as Bona la Tanyedora frequently appeared as well.

31. See copla 246.

32. The *korban* was part of the feast that was considered to be a sacrifice; wealthy families slaughtered a sheep, and meat was always distributed to the poor. This tradition exists in Islam as well.

33. These details can be found in Attias, "Marriage Customs," 30.

34. See copla 166.

35. See copla 45.

36. See copla 256. Bouena refers to eight days, but the celebration lasted one week.

37. This topic is discussed in more detail in chapter 4.

38. This is the aforementioned Gifts for the Needy Association, established in 1911, which played a pivotal role in helping the less fortunate members of the Jewish community cope with the endless stream of misfortunes they encountered in the twentieth century. See Hadar, "Aspects of Jewish Family Life," 261. After the war, as returnees emerged from the mountains and from hiding, there were both group and individual weddings. According to Lewkowicz, 196 weddings took place in 1945 and 1946. The group weddings were held at the Matanot La-Evionim building, where Michael Molho officiated. See Lewkowicz, *The Jewish Community of Salonika,* 198–99. Although Lewkowicz claims that there were 39 group weddings between 1945 and 1947, the community registers list only 2 in April 1946; the first included 19 couples, and the second was arranged for 18 (Erika Perahia, director of the Jewish Museum of Thessaloniki, e-mail message to author, August 18, 2011). This information is now available in the computerized archives of the Jewish Museum. I counted only 14 in the April 7 photo from the museum, but it is quite possible that not all the brides posed for the photographs.

39. This synagogue was built on Sigrou Street after the fire of 1917. Because the Red Cross had used it during the war, it was not destroyed, although it needed repair. It is used for special occasions today. See Messinas, *The Synagogues,* 96–97.

40. It was at this time that she attempted to locate her trousseau and did indeed find it. See chapter 4.

41. Men have not fulfilled the commandment to procreate until they have one son and one daughter; women have no such directive.

42. See copla 85.

43. See copla 220.

44. Michael Molho alludes to naming ceremonies for girls as *fadamientos* (*Traditions and Customs*, 66–68). The original ceremony was the *hadas*, observed in medieval Spain following all births, but was continued only by the Sephardi Jews while in Spain as well as in the Sephardi diaspora. For more details regarding the medieval *hadas*, see Levine Melammed, "Noticias sobre los ritos," 235–43.

45. See copla 318.

46. This was an atonement ritual.

47. See copla 326.

48. See copla 371 and the accompanying note explaining this practice.

49. In Ashkenaz in particular, women had become involved in this ceremony and were bringing the child directly to the mohel, that is to say, entering the men's area of the synagogue and taking part in public. Different rabbis reacted differently: some objected to this on the basis of modesty; others felt they could not control the situation; yet others suggested allowing the women to bring the baby from the home to the portal of the synagogue and then having a male carry him to the ritual circumciser, who was located in the midst of the men. See Grossman, *Pious and Rebellious*, 185–86 and 190, regarding women circumcisers; a more detailed discussion of women's roles in the ceremony is presented in Baumgarten, *Mothers and Children*, 65–77.

50. See copla 273.

51. See copla 342. In copla 407, Bouena discusses the type of food served at different occasions. Small slices were served at evening parties; at weddings, there were pastries or fine tortes; preserves appeared on the table at engagement parties; and "at a circumcision, almond balls."

52. See copla 177.

53. See copla 176.

54. See coplas 334, 84, and 180.

55. See copla 84.

56. See copla 372.

57. Bouena called him an *afsakadji*, the Turkish reference to a person who makes *afsakod* (*hafsakot* in Hebrew)—namely, interruptions. His tradition was to fast for eight days, presumably from sunrise until sunset, beginning with the traditional fast day, the tenth of the Hebrew month of Tevet (although fasting was not done on the Sabbath). Bunis refers to this phenomenon but states the fasts were six weeks (except for the Sabbath day), beginning with the reading of the book of Exodus until the end of the following month of Shevat. Bouena's grandfather began about a week earlier. Bunis includes additional details, such as how they immersed themselves in ritual baths, went home, wept, sat on the ground while barefoot, put ashes on their foreheads, and wore sackcloth like mourners (*Voices from Jewish Salonika*, 140, 152n57).

58. See copla 129.

59. See copla 42. Ely Garfinkle shared information with me that shows how sharing and inheriting worked in this family, and not only for the boys. There was an antique gold bracelet that Bouena's grandfather had copied so that the girls would not be jealous. No one knew who was in possession of the original. Among the male descendants, there was a ring with an antique stone that was considered to be the family crest and had been worn by the patriarch of the family. The custom was that the first-born male

got the ring; thus, Ely inherited it when he reached the age of twenty-one. He assumed that her brother, Elie, gave his sister the ring, which she then gave to his namesake. Ely passed on his own ring to his eldest son when he turned twenty-one and made copies for himself and his other children, who each received a copy at the age of twenty-one (e-mail message to author, February 6, 2011).

60. See copla 399.

61. Interestingly enough, only two verses deal with funerals or burials; they have been placed at the end of the section. One describes the pain and anguish at funerals, and the other describes the passing of a woman who was 110 years old. See coplas 48 and 86.

62. See copla 101. This description is similar to that in copla 13, in which the father returned home and then tossed out a copla.

63. See copla 80.

64. See copla 112.

65. Malcolm Chase and Christopher Shaw suggest, "Perhaps as a species we are given to nostalgia, for each adult carries the memory of an age when the experience of time was different" (Chase and Shaw, "The Dimensions of Nostalgia," 4).

66. Rabbi Michael Molho was known to have had an impressive library.

67. See copla 73.

68. For information on Jewish libraries, particularly private ones, see Beit-Arié, "The Private Nature," 91–103; Kaplan, "The Libraries of Three Sephardi Rabbis in Early Modern Western Europe," ibid., 225–260; and Gutwirth and Dolader, "Twenty-Six Libraries from Fifteenth-Century Spain," 27–53. In the Huesca archives, a list was found regarding twenty-six private libraries in Jaca that contained more than eight hundred books. See also Assaf, "Time of the Book and the Book," 292–316.

69. See copla 151.

70. See copla 183. Bouena did not mention the name of the cantor who sang there; four names of cantors who served this congregation in 1919 appear in Messinas, *The Synagogues,* along with details concerning the Italian architecture (84–86).

71. See copla 387. Baroness Clara de Hirsch, widow of Baron Maurice de Hirsch, donated the bulk of the funds for building this hospital; it was sold to the government in 1951 and was renamed Hippocratio (Ippokráteio) Hospital.

72. The social, political, and economic repercussions of the fire are discussed in greater detail in chapter 2, which treats modernity and tradition.

73. See copla 287.

74. See coplas 145 and 146.

75. This was a true act of loving kindness, based on the teachings of the Torah that emphasize one's duty to care for widows and orphans.

76. Moise Allatini, who was exposed to "occidental culture while studying medicine in Italy, was the first benefactor to address the reorganisation of the educational system. Allatini gained the support of a small group of progressive Jews imbued with western ideas because of their occupations" (Rena Molho, *Salonica and Istanbul,* 128). He established a school fund, Hessed Olam, in 1856. In 1873, a school was established in his name, and the orphanage was established in 1908. See Rena Molho, *Salonica and Istanbul,* 94.

77. See Rena Molho, *Salonica and Istanbul,* 131, for a chart of the Jewish schools in the city in 1912, of which there were twenty-eight.

78. See copla 2. Mazower points out that after 1908, "a vigorous workers' movement, led chiefly by Jewish and Bulgarian intellectuals, exploded into life" (*Salonica, City of*

Ghosts, 267). He also refers to the tobacco workers' strike in April 1936, which presented a front of twenty-five thousand workers (357).

79. See copla 71.

80. See copla 130.

81. See copla 231.

82. See copla 116.

83. See copla 170.

84. See copla 169.

85. See Garfinkle, "The Memoirs of Bouena Garfinkle," 61. Bona is mentioned in copla 27. I also found reference to "an invitation written by Bona," in which Bouena describes an ambiguous invitation to a home that was going to be so crowded that she thought it might be preferable not to attend the event.

86. See Nehama, *Dictionnaire du judéo-espagnol*, 541. The entry "tañadéra" discusses the fact that women like Bona were always present at family occasions: circumcisions, *presyados* (trousseau parties), *fiançailles* (engagement parties), *viólas* (the night before brit), *noces* (nocturnal parties), Purim parties, *threnes* (lamentations), and funerals. Their repertoire was vast and included ballads, *epithalames* (nuptial songs), *aubades* (songs for dawn), serenades, and *quolibets egrillards* (naughty jeers). He then writes this of the legendary Bona: "Animatrice inégalée, elle était de tous les événements de famille. Alerte, intuitive en diable, enjouée ou lugubre, suivant le cas, elle était douée d'un flair remarquable et d'un veritable don d'ubiquité, et elle apportait, avec un à-propos surprenant l'entrain ou la gravité qui convenaient. La gaudrille ou la complainte déchirante jaillisaient de ses lèvres, de son attitude avec un naturel fascinant. Les saccades et les trilles de son tambourin plein de vie formaient orchestre, fanfare, clarion ou carillon de glas." Apparently, she often played with the aforementioned Tramuz, and the two frequently argued "over their fee for their required, or sometimes unrequired, services" (Michael Molho, *Traditions and Customs*, 64).

87. Moshe Attias wrote that she was perceived as one of the "Last Mohicans" of this profession ("The Salonikan Romancero," 205). She used a Basque drum, which connected them to Spain, and she was the life of the party and beloved by all. She might appear uninvited, bringing laughter and mirth wherever she went; the women received her lovingly. She rarely performed for the men (Michael Molho, "Birth and Childhood among the Jews of Salonica," 263–64). She is also mentioned in Havassy, "The Ladino Song," 121n223; in Bunis, *Voices from Jewish Salonika*, 170–71; and elsewhere—as she was so well known.

88. See copla 195.

89. Michael Molho writes about Ben Sanchi, an energetic and principled man who mastered ten spoken languages and was a fervent Zionist. He was brave and devoted and demanded respect and rights for the Salonikan Jews, publishing pieces that criticized antisemites. He was oblivious to costs, whether financial or personal, and published propaganda in order to improve communal institutions and obtain equal rights for all Jews, regardless of their financial status ("Spaniolit Journalism in Salonika," 104).

90. See copla 279.

2. Tradition versus Modernity and Historical Developments

1. "Tradition is the enactment and dramatization of continuity: it is the thread which binds our separate lives to the broad canvas of history" (Chase and Shaw, "The Dimensions of Nostalgia," 11).

2. See copla 81.

3. Her sense of nostalgia is completely understandable. As Chase and Shaw point out, "Nostalgia is experienced when some elements of the present are felt to be defective and when there is no public sense of redeemability through a belief in progress" ("The Dimensions of Nostalgia," 15).

4. One cannot deny that there were secular Jews in Salonika—Jews who intermarried or who were not concerned with tradition—but a discussion of the secular Jews is beyond the scope of this book.

5. This pastime was often enjoyed while sitting on balconies.

6. Jacques Stroumsa refers to the "Tour Blanche," which "even today dominates the sea promenade of Salonika (the Boulevard Nikis)," whose upper levels had been rented to youth groups such as the Maccabi (*Violinist in Auschwitz,* 29).

7. Outside Israel, the festival of Sukkot is observed for seven days followed by two additional days, Shemini Azteret and Simhat Torah.

8. There are medieval precedents of women initiating such observances, but those found thus far concern women in Ashkenazi congregations.

9. See copla 72.

10. Yehuda Hatsvi, e-mail message to author, October 5, 2010.

11. See Attias, "Purim in Salonika," 56–57, for detailed descriptions of the Jewish market and its metamorphosis before Purim, and 57–58 for a discussion of the gallows. Purim traditions were carefully observed by all; for a similar description of the sugar figures and trays, see Handeli, *A Greek Jew from Salonica Remembers,* 20.

12. The *mishloah manot,* or sending of at least three portions (of food), is one of the commandments to fulfill on Purim, along with giving money to charity and coins to the children.

13. See Handeli, *A Greek Jew from Salonica Remembers,* 23, for a description of the wooden hammers.

14. The origin of this custom is often mistakenly attributed to Saragossa in Aragon, Spain.

15. For evidence that this is an Italian tradition and not a Spanish one originating in the community of Saragossa, see Attias, "Purim Holiday," 167. Even Bouena confused the two, most likely because of the similar pronunciation of Syracosa and Saragossa.

16. Hadar, "Aspects of Jewish Family Life," 116.

17. The woman who was crowned "queen of the neighborhood" was in charge of washing! See copla 21.

18. This Turkish ouzo, or arak, is made from the remains on the bottom of the *plamento,* a four-hundred-liter barrel. Most famous was the Nahmias raki, supposedly made from a "secret" recipe brought by members of the family who were exiled from the island of Majorca. The company flourished until 1921, when the Greek government passed restrictive laws. See "Economic Life in Salonika," 238.

19. See copla 150, in which Bouena mentions a massacre on this day. There is a tendency to attribute the dates of all of the Jewish catastrophes to the Ninth of Av or thereabouts; either Bouena was not so strong on Jewish history or the community incorporated such events as the Expulsion from Spain and various pogroms as part of this national day of mourning.

20. See copla 48.

21. See copla 230.

22. See copla 388.

23. See copla 113.

24. See copla 345.

25. This is a reference to the *conbibador* or *conbibadora*, who announced the wedding information.

26. See copla 397.

27. See copla 82.

28. Michael Molho, "A History of the Jews of Salonika," 22.

29. For the sake of review, some developments mentioned in the introduction will be noted again.

30. Lewkowicz writes, "Zionism and Zionist organizations became part of an intracommunal struggle in which Zionists fought against the 'assimilationists' by introducing Hebrew and a new way of secular Jewish education" (*The Jewish Community of Salonika*, 45).

31. It should be noted that not all repercussions were negative. Construction thrived in the city as new schools, hospital, orphanages, and other buildings appeared. Vassilis Colonas points out that the Jews were "freed of the legal restrictions previously imposed by Ottoman law" and shopping arcades, department stores, and factories were built by Jewish investors ("The Contribution of the Jewish Community," 166, 168–70).

32. Naar also discusses these developments as precipitating emigration in "From the 'Jerusalem of the Balkans,'" 448–54.

33. See, for example, the discussion in Hadar, "Aspects of Jewish Family Life," 101–103.

34. Rozen, *The Last Ottoman Century*, 1:175

35. Although the poor had no choice in the matter, many of the wealthier and more educated members of the community began to emigrate.

36. For basic information on this man and the movement, see Scholem, *Sabbatai Sevi.*

37. See copla 67.

38. See copla 358.

39. Dublon-Knebel, *German Foreign Office Documents*, 159n435. For more details, see Kallis, "The Jewish Community of Salonica under Siege," 34–56.

40. See coplas 350 and 351. The fate of this family is recorded elsewhere; apparently they moved to Athens. Isaac was arrested by the Germans, sent to Auschwitz, and worked in the Canada Commando. He later encountered his family at the camp; his supervisor promised to send his teenage sons to work forces and to save his wife, but not his mother. Ultimately his forty-year-old wife was considered to be too old to save (Matsas, *The Illusion of Safety*, 230–31).

41. See copla 139.

42. See copla 154.

43. See copla 140.

44. This situation became more aggravated as time passed and by no means improved during the pre–World War II period. See, for example, Hekimoglou, "Jewish Pauperism in Salonika," 195–205.

45. See copla 344.

46. Kallis, "The Jewish Community of Salonica under Siege," 37.

47. See copla 421.

48. See copla 10.

49. Uziel, "The History of the Zionist Movement," 114. For more details, see Shalem, "The Workers' Moshav 'Tsur Moshe,'" 351.

50. Women's crafts in Salonika, in particular those of the seamstresses and the embroiderers, were sought out by non-Jewish women (Michael Molho, "A History of the Jews of Salonika," 25).

51. See copla 322. See also Hadar, "Aspects of Jewish Family Life," 293–96, regarding fictitious marriages and engagements in order to obtain permits to Palestine.

52. See copla 327.

53. See copla 8.

54. See coplas 262 and 6.

55. Yedi Kule is Turkish for Heptapyrgion, or Fortress of Seven Towers. In Greece, this is the Heptapyrgion citadel in Salonika, where Eliaou was apparently stationed at one time. See coplas 398 and 425.

56. See copla 173.

57. See copla 186a.

58. Mazower points out that hundreds of Jewish young men fought in the Greek army (*Salonica, City of Ghosts,* 391).

4. "The Miseries That the Germans Inflicted on Salonika"

1. The EDES, or the Greek Democratic Organization, was composed of royalists led by General Napoleon Zarvos. There were Jews from Salonika who joined the EDES. It is difficult to find precise numbers regarding Jewish members, but there are estimates that the two groups, the loyalists and the communists, had a sum total of at least one thousand Jewish participants (Ben, *Greek Jewry in the Holocaust,* 124–25).

2. The ELAS (National Popular Liberation Army) was the activist military arm of the National Liberation Army (EAM) and, according to Ben, was the most important partisan group. Its members included workers and farmers as well as members of the intelligentsia and the middle class, who had belonged to political parties ranging from Communist to Socialist and had belonged to professional unions; all were anti-Royalist (*Greek Jewry in the Holocaust,* 124). The Jews of Athens were geographically closer to the hills, so joined the ELAS; one report mentions that three hundred of the six hundred Jewish members of the EAM died in action. See ibid., 125; and Mazower, *Inside Hitler's Greece,* 297–321.

3. See Refael, *Un grito en el silencio,* 73.

4. See Lévy, *And the World Stood Silent,* 21. Only a few poems in this collection are reminiscent of Bouena's style, in that specific places and events appear. For example, poems by Yehuda Haim Aaron HaCohen Perahia mention an encounter with Michael Molho; see "After the Catastrophe in Salonika," 162–65; the fact that the British have liberated Athens is also noted in "A Little Hope," 151–55.

5. For details, see Mazower, *Inside Hitler's Greece,* 15–22.

6. Releasing them was an unusual step for the Germans; see Bowman, *The Agony of Greek Jews,* 41.

7. See copla 1. Bowman writes that very few actually witnessed their entrance, perhaps solely due to fear, for they immediately confiscated Jewish homes (*The Agony of Greek Jews,* 48).

8. See Mazower, *Inside Hitler's Greece,* 237–38.

9. Their original home was on Mitropoleos Street; they had to move to the ghetto and found a place on Sigrou Street. See photos in the preface.

10. See copla 13.

11. See copla 56. Mazower discusses the resultant famine throughout the entire country (*Inside Hitler's Greece*, 23–52).

12. Because they viewed themselves as being in competition with the Italians, they attempted to move as quickly as possible. During 1941 and 1943, there were 250,000 deaths (Mazower, *Inside Hitler's Greece*, 26, 41). Bowman writes, "Famine was apparently a by-product of the German rape of Greece, as opposed to the official Nazi occupation policy implemented elsewhere (especially Poland)" (*The Agony of Greek Jews*, 44–45).

13. This association has been mentioned numerous times in the discussion of prewar Salonika.

14. Yacoel, "The Memoir of Yomtov Yacoel," 28. "The basement office of *Matanoth* on Mizrachi Street became the meeting place for all those who cared about Jewish philanthropies and about the Jewish affairs of the city in general" (ibid., 28–29). Elsewhere, Bowman writes that they served five thousand meals each day to Jewish children and fresh milk to more than fifteen hundred infants (*The Agony of Greek Jews*, 49). When this organization was closed, the leaders reopened it under the cover of the Allatini Orphanage and with the cooperation of the Hellenic Red Cross (ibid., 49–50).

15. "The only substantial outside support came from the Greek Red Cross initially, and from the International Red Cross later on" (Bowman, *The Agony of Greek Jews*, 28).

16. See copla 23.

17. See copla 22. Bouena mentions a Mr. Aroukh, who would come to entertain the girls by reciting coplas, which they enjoyed thoroughly—but Sarah had to remind him that they were actually engaged in work. Isaac Aroukh must have survived somehow because Bouena tells the story of an incident at the lager; presumably he lived to tell the tale. One of his protégées who was coming to work noticed him and called out his name. She had bread, which she pushed through the window because "they had enough at the pavilion of the operated women." She might have been a victim of Dr. Mengele. At any rate, Mr. Aroukh believed that this bread saved his life. See copla 92.

18. See copla 27.

19. Bouena was most likely not aware of the degree to which the Greeks were aiding the Germans, for the governor general of Macedonia, Vassilis Simonides, organized a special service to dispose of the Jewish property (YDIP). "The largest single act of plunder took place in October 1942 when the Germans released Jewish men from forced labor in return for a massive payment from the Jewish community. . . . The YDIP played an important part in the destruction of Jewish Salonika, giving an official Greek stamp of approval to the mass plunder of Jewish property. . . . The distribution of Jewish assets gave the German and the Greek-collaborationist authorities a very useful way of rewarding collaborators and buying loyalty" (Apostolou, "The Exception of Salonika," 180).

20. Mazower, *Inside Hitler's Greece*, 85. Bowman writes, "To the consternation of the occupiers, Greeks would cheer the appearance of the British POWs" (*The Agony of Greek Jews*, 45).

21. See copla 3.

22. Five days later, Consul Zamboni heard that after paying considerable sums, the wealthy Italian Jews had slipped into the Italian occupied area, and later that week, he seemed certain that close to twelve hundred wealthy Jews were now in the Italian zone (Carpi, *Italian Diplomatic Documents*, 40–41).

23. See copla 19. A more detailed description appears in Yacoel, "The Memoir of Yomtov Yacoel," 36–40.

24. Apostolou claims, "The incident not only typified the wanton brutality with which the German armed forces participated in the persecution of Jews; it also underlined the completeness of German control and the helpless isolation of the Jews." Although the governor general did not initiate this act, "he not only raised no objection, but appears to have implemented it without seeking the approval of his superiors in Athens; similarly, he appears not to have informed them of the public abuse of the Jewish men" ("The Exception of Salonika," 177–78). Matsas notes that "some Christians showed approval, but the great majority remained silent. There was no protest from the various unions in Salonika. The University officially ignored the indignities forced upon its fellow citizens" (*The Illusion of Safety*, 35).

25. It is quite possible that her choice of words was influenced by the post-Holocaust image comparing the victims to sheep being brought to the slaughter.

26. These images appear in copla 14.

27. Corroboration of Bouena's reports and more details about the community's organization can be found in Yacoel, "The Memoir of Yomtov Yacoel," 41–62.

28. See copla 24.

29. See Mazower, *Inside Hitler's Greece*, 239.

30. See copla 25.

31. See copla 26.

32. René Molho writes, "Jews are sent to clear the swamps around Larissa, which are a source of mosquitos and malaria. The conditions are harsh; the workers slave away and are undernourished. They come down with malaria. The sickest are returned to Salonika" (*They Say Diamonds Don't Burn*, 9).

33. See copla 29.

34. See copla 30.

35. Carpi, *Italian Diplomatic Documents*, 40n86.

36. Mazower, *Salonica, City of Ghosts*, 397–98, 418. In the analysis of the role of the chief rabbi, there is further discussion of this event.

37. See copla 15.

38. See copla 10. However, the Greeks in Salonika were very quiet in public. The governor general objects to nothing and provides assistance to the Germans. "No senior Greek political figure in the city was thus prepared to forfeit his support [of chief Wehrmacht administrator Max Merten] and waste valuable political capital by speaking out on behalf of the Jews" (Mazower, *Salonica, City of Ghosts*, 410–11).

39. See Kerem, "Efforts to Rescue," 82.

40. Stroumsa stresses the fact that his "Greek Orthodox friends in Salonica had attempted several times to persuade me to join the Greek Liberation Army, E.A.M./A.G.M. But I had not wanted to follow their advice, simply for the reason that I did not want to abandon my wife and my parents, to whom I was so greatly attached" (*Violinist in Auschwitz*, 43). All of them were killed in the camps, but he could not have foreseen this.

41. See Mazower, *Inside Hitler's Greece*, 258. According to Matsas, in 1943 "the resistance organization EAM pleaded with the Jews of Salonika, asking them not to follow German orders and to leave the city." The university branch "directed Jewish students to partisan territories," managing to recruit 250 of them. The escape was difficult and dangerous, but since most were veterans of the war in Albania, they managed to escape. (*The Illusion of Safety*, 271).

42. Carpi, "The Jews of Greece," 118. Apostolou also discusses the discrepancy in scholarship regarding Greek-Christian reactions to events. He is well aware of the contrast between the assistance Jews received in southern Greece and what they did and did not receive in Salonika. He points to Mazower's argument that antisemitism cannot explain the discrepancy in the fates of the different communities, and emphasizes the fact that this topic has not been studied properly, possibly because of its sensitive nature; the proclivity seems to be to generalize regarding the generosity of Orthodox Greeks and their hospitality. The bottom line is, in his opinion, that Salonika was the exception, for most Greeks had little to no contact with Jews. He cites Stroumsa's testimony in the French edition of his book that not only was there a language or accent problem, but that most of the families would never have agreed to hide the Jews (Stroumsa, *Tu choisiras la vie*, 136) ("The Exception of Salonika," 166–68, 188n23).

43. Ben, *Greek Jewry in the Holocaust*, 44–45. An in-depth discussion of the objective obstacles to fleeing Salonika appears on 205–206.

44. See copla 73; Ben, *Greek Jewry in the Holocaust*, 96–97.

45. Carpi, *Italian Diplomatic Documents*, 30.

46. By May the Italian Consulate was no longer selecting bona fide Italian citizens but tried to grant citizen certificates to Greek Jews (Fleming, *Greece*, 124). Mazower writes that even as late as mid-July, 320 Jews were granted protection by the consul as they boarded a train for Athens (*Salonica, City of Ghosts*, 407).

47. Carpi, *Italian Diplomatic Documents*, 26.

48. See copla 74.

49. See copla 20.

50. See copla 53. Besantsi and Abravanel are mentioned as having been talented journalists in the collection of verses about Salonika. See coplas 9, 88, 188, 278, 279, and 307.

51. Bouena believes that he was captured and murdered in Volos. Michael Molho writes of Mentech Bensantsi, who was arrested in Crete rather than Volos and taken to a concentration camp in Larissa (which is not far from Volos), then to Salonika, and finally sent to Auschwitz (*In Memoriam*, 68).

52. See copla 2.

53. See copla 58. The Jewish police will be discussed in detail.

54. Carpi, "A New Approach," 271–72. Mazower corroborates this and adds, "Aware of their opposition to the deportations, hundreds of Jews fled to the Italian zone, with the courageous assistance of Italian diplomats and soldiers. The Germans had closed down all the other consulates in Salonika in November 1942 so Zamboni, the Italian consul, found himself in a position of unique importance" (*Inside Hitler's Greece*, 244–45). The last group was freed as the result of negotiations with Hasson; see the discussion below.

55. See copla 37; Carpi, "A New Approach," 270, 275n31. Apparently Castruccio, who also attempted to save some Jews at the very end, is often given credit for his predecessor's actions.

56. See copla 28.

57. See copla 47. Bouena salutes those who had patience and "knew how to wait" in these stressful times.

58. Yacoel describes the demographical transfers from the perspective of the community administration; see "The Memoir of Yomtov Yacoel," 99–102, 109–110.

59. See copla 72. Each synagogue was built by Jews according to their birthplace. Monastir is the Ottoman name for Bitola prior to 1913. This Sephardi community also suffered during the war, but as the result of the Bulgarian policy toward non-Bulgarian subjects residing in annexed territories. On March 11, 1943, the Jews of Monastir (or Monastirlis) were deported together with the other Macedonian Jews; most were sent to Treblinka.

60. See copla 32.

61. See Rivlin, *Encyclopaedia*, 292.

62. His first appointment was as aide to Shabtai Saltiel, the head of the community, but he was then placed under arrest for part of 1942 until March when he received his new post. See Dublon-Knebel, *German Foreign Office Documents*, 30n100.

63. See Yacoel, "The Memoir of Yomtov Yacoel," 111, 118; he mentions the higher figure of 250. Carpi quotes the consul's report of 200 (*Italian Diplomatic Documents*, 45). Bowman corroborates this figure, explaining that Jacques Albala organized these young men, some of whom were sons of "prominent Jews" who had made special arrangements for their sons (*The Agony of Greek Jews*, 66–67).

64. His reputation at Bergen-Belsen was equally negative. There he also was in a position to punish inmates of the Star Camp, also known as the Albala Camp, and his corrupt methods there were well known. See Reilly, *Belsen*, 15; Lattek, "Bergen-Belsen," 50; and numerous passages in Koretz, *Diary of a Youth*.

65. See copla 49.

66. This is copla 59. She notes that some flights were successful, and there were those who received aid from Greeks and avoided the camps altogether. At the end of the verse, Bouena toasts these Greeks "who helped the Jews live."

67. Albala "was persona non grata in the Jewish community for having terrorized the community, among other excesses" (Bowman, *The Agony of Greek Jews*, 62).

68. Ben, *Greek Jewry in the Holocaust*, 207. He is described as "the cynical instigator, guide and advisor to the German camp commandants and left behind him a sad memory of a tyrannical inquisitor and torturer" (Matarasso, "And Yet Not All of Them Died," 158).

69. See copla 65.

70. The president of the tribunal trying Hasson after the war was quoted as saying that this was one of the things he'd heard about the defendant; see Mazower, *Salonica, City of Ghosts*, 401 and 466n22, regarding the Special War Crimes Court Martial.

71. Bowman, *The Agony of Greek Jews*, 232.

72. See copla 69.

73. Ben, *Greek Jewry in the Holocaust*, 207.

74. René Molho, *They Say Diamonds Don't Burn*, 6. She adds that the younger brother was sent to Auschwitz and "in less than a month, he is killed by the other prisoners."

75. This incident is mentioned briefly in the preface.

76. Burkhardt and his wife were delegates of the CICR which "acted in the most humanitarian ways, pushing the quality of their aid to the limits of German patience . . . made sure that the Jewish community received its fair share of aid"; his wife "did not restrict Jewish mothers from her institutions" (Bowman, *The Agony of Greek Jews*, 180–83).

77. Yacoel describes the changes in this quarter as of March 6, including double sentries and instructions to the Jews not to be outside after 10:00 AM; see "The Memoir

of Yomtov Yacoel," 118–19. Kounio also writes about the camp at Baron de Hirsch in *A Liter of Soup*, 3–6.

78. See copla 57. At the close of the verse, she toasts herself and adds, "whom they called Joan of Arc" after her name. Bouena saw numerous Nazi officers in the vicinity and distinctly remembered one with whom Hasson was consorting in her presence. Years later, while watching television with her son in the 1970s, she recognized him—Kurt Waldheim, who by that time was serving as Secretary General of the United Nations (1972–81), much to Bouena's horror. At that time, her claim seemed farfetched. When he later sought to head the Austrian government in 1986, his role as a Nazi was revealed; it was confirmed that he had served as an ordinance officer in Salonika from 1942–43. A similar story is recorded by Yeshua Matsas of Yanina, who was the deliveryman for gold and jewelry collected from the Jews of Larissa. There he was hit on the head twice by a German officer whom he recognized later as a candidate for president of Austria; he was apparently the first person to recognize the former Nazi officer (*The Illusion of Safety*, 315–17).

79. Garfinkle, "The Memoirs of Bouena Garfinkle," 12–13.

80. See copla 7.

81. See copla 71.

82. Carpi, "A New Approach," 276.

83. Molho and Nehama, *The Destruction of Greek Jewry*, 91.

84. Carpi, "A New Approach," 276–77.

85. "After the capitulation of the Badoglio government, most of these Jews (who had escaped from Greece)—with Hasson at the head of the line—fled in boats to southern Italy, a region already liberated by the Allies, where the Jews reported Hasson's crimes to British Intelligence, who after extensive delays delivered him into the hand of the Free Greek authorities in Cairo" (Carpi, "A New Approach," 279n41).

86. These facts are well known and are corroborated in Matsas, *The Illusion of Safety*, 407–408. Bowman points out that this "major postwar trial against Jewish collaborators, in particular those who actively supported the German persecution and deportation of the Jews, was the only major such postwar trial initiated by Jews in Europe" ("Salonikan Memories," 22).

87. Final lines of copla 71. Nevertheless, there were survivors there who "told tale after tale of how they had been interrogated, tortured and tricked into giving up their valuables" (Mazower, *Salonica, City of Ghosts*, 406).

88. Garfinkle, "The Memoirs of Bouena Garfinkle," 178–81. For some reason, probably because the experience was so traumatic for her, Bouena thought that the trial lasted five days. Aside from this one detail, the rest of her report is corroborated by Rivlin, *Encyclopaedia*, 292. Albala was sentenced to fifteen years.

89. According to Bowman, after the chief rabbi declined to shake the queen of Greece's hands, the revisionists, anxious to challenge the Mizrahi Zionists, "took the opportunity to demand that a modern western rabbi be engaged to replace him after his retirement" ("Salonikan Memories," 7). He cites a fellow student from Berlin who characterized most East European students at the Hochschule as intelligent yeshiva students who were politically unsophisticated. "They had little understanding of the nature of the Nazi movement or its designs against the Jews" (*The Agony of Greek Jews*, 63).

90. Ibid., 63–64.

91. Fleming plainly states this: "Koretz had been unpopular with the community from the outset, as he was a non-Sephardic, German modern Orthodox rabbi and perceived as an outsider" (*Greece,* 118).

92. See copla 40. According to Cecil Roth, he was "the least successful of all religious leaders in the long history of Salonikan Jewry, and very rapidly was in conflict with most communal leaders, particularly the Zionists." The community was not interested in prolonging his services after 1937, but the governor general of the city in the Metaxas reign supported him and "demanded that his term be extended. It is through the interference of the Greek dictatorial government that Dr. Koretz remained the Chief Rabbi against the will of Salonika Jewry" ("The Last Days of Jewish Salonica," 49–55).

93. One might suppose that communication would be entirely dependent upon him, but there were a quite a few members of the community who were fluent in German.

94. Rozen, "Jews and Greeks Remember Their Past," 111.

95. René Molho, *They Say Diamonds Don't Burn,* 7, 10.

96. See copla 38.

97. Kerem, "Efforts to Rescue," 88.

98. See copla 43.

99. The original cemetery encompassed 500,000 square meters, but was whittled down to 380,000 in 1920. While its location was originally considered to be outside the city parameters, as Salonika grew, its location became more central and desirable. The Greek government coveted precisely this spot, intending to build a university there; the community entered difficult negotiations with the Greeks in both 1933 and 1936. The Salonikan Jews felt that its destruction during the Nazi era occurred because of pressure by Governor General Simonides, rather than by the Germans (Rivlin, *Encyclopaedia,* 246–47, 275–76). Regarding Simonides and other collaborators, see Apostolou, "The Exception of Salonika," 165–96. At first an unreasonable transfer of half a million graves was demanded and when the community did not act upon this demand, "the Greek technical services were ordered to take over the massive demolition of the cemetery" (Rena Molho, *Salonica and Istanbul,* 63–64). Yacoel offers an insider's perspective in "In the Anteroom to Hell," 71–77. For a brief history of the cemetery, see Michael Molho, *El cementerio judío de Salónica.*

100. See copla 41. It seems as though Bouena was being dramatic, or perhaps recording what she believed to have happened. However, the fact is that in October, the community was ordered to make a huge payment; it was clear that the Germans intended to obtain the cemetery's land. Although the sum demanded was lowered substantially, the cemetery remained on the Nazis' list. After its confiscation, vandals desecrated the site in November; plans were being made to build a municipal park and university in its stead. In December, workers broke headstones, scattered bones, and stole marble for personal use. This event was extremely traumatic, needless to say.

101. Fleming, *Greece,* 118. Fleming includes a quotation from the Eichmann trial (session 47) in which the rabbi is considered to be a traitor because of "criminal cowardice" (241n54).

102. See copla 39.

103. See reports in Dublon-Knebel, *German Foreign Office Documents,* 29–32. In April, in a conversation with the prime minister of Greece, he "pleaded that the 2,000

year-old community not be liquidated" (32). Perhaps the rabbi believed that the Jews were going to Krakow. "Conceivably, in order to avoid jeopardizing the fiction of resettlement in Krakow, which was being circulated among the Jews of Salonika, the transports to Auschwitz were kept secret from the representatives of the Foreign Office in Greece as well" (45).

104. Handeli, *A Greek Jew,* 44–46.

105. He condemns the rabbi for his use of these students for nefarious purposes and for his selfishness; by being efficient and following orders, his family received special privileges ("The History of the Jews of Saloniki," 264).

106. Bowman writes that there "was little overt action initially by the Germans to create suspicion of their more deadly intent" (*The Agony of Greek Jews,* 232). He also writes that "Rabbi Koretz cajoled the community to follow the German orders; he encouraged the youth to marry; he offered larger quotas for forced labor. Every move in hindsight was the wrong one, and the tensions within the panicked community exacerbated the bad feelings between the Sephardi masses and their unpopular Ashkenazi Chief Rabbi" ("Salonikan Memories," 18).

107. Mazower, *Salonica, City of Ghosts,* 400.

108. Garfinkle, "Tale of a Ghetto Conspirator," 10.

109. She was by no means alone. Matarasso writes that "he screamed, demanded and threatened everybody" ("And Yet Not All of Them Died," 149). He cites a communiqué from March 5: "We recommend to our coreligionists to remain calm and prudent, not to panic and not to trust shameless rumors" (150).

110. See copla 44. One of the entries in Molho's *In Memoriam* is entitled "Aggression contre Koretz" (99–100).

111. See copla 45.

112. See copla 61.

113. Conflicting dates for this meeting appear in the records, so it is unclear as to whether it was in March or April 1943, but either way, it was at a date that was far too late to have changed anything.

114. Oddly enough, the fact that there was a daughter as well is rarely mentioned, but perhaps because she was so young, she was not noticed; Lili was born in 1939 and her older brother, Arieh, was born in 1928.

115. "It was only upon their return to Salonika that Koretz's family realized that their father had been branded a traitor and Nazi collaborator. Scored as arrogant and power-hungry, he was charged with hiding the bitter truth about the fate that awaited the Jews in order to further his own interests. He was blamed for too readily acquiescing to the Germans' demand that he provide a detailed list of the Jewish population in the city, thereby enabling them to pursue their plans more efficiently. He was accused of betraying the community out of selfish motives and bringing about the loss of many lives that might otherwise have been spared. These charges, taken together, have created the image that is etched on the Jewish historical memory" (Rozen, "Jews and Greeks Remember Their Past," 117). A survivor stated in an interview that no one talked to Mrs. Koretz or her son when they returned from Bergen-Belsen (Lewkowicz, "After the War We Were All Together," 264). The family came to Palestine illegally in December 1946; in 1992, Arieh self-published a translation of the Greek diary he kept. See *Diary of a Youth* and *Bergen-Belsen.*

116. See Bowman's report regarding a letter from Rabbi Molho to Koretz's widow in *The Agony of Greek Jews,* 261n26.

117. He studied at the Hochschule fur Wissenschaft des Judentums and the Orientalischen Institut in Berlin as well.

118. David (Andreas) Kounio, personal communication, May 31, 2011.

119. He was not aware of the fact that Mrs. Koretz was imprisoned for four days upon her return to Salonika and the children were left to fend for themselves. They moved in with the professor who was living in the home to which they were moved in 1941. See her witness testimony, recorded and transcribed at the Tel Aviv branch of Yad Vashem together with that of her son Arieh, a lawyer, on January 11, 1976; file no. 3527/304.

120. Garfinkle, "The Memoirs of Bouena Garfinkle," 144–145.

121. Bowman, *The Agony of Greek Jews*, 228.

122. *Sephardi Jewry*, 167. They also briefly compare the situation to that confronted in Athens, pointing out that the personalities of the respective rabbis were quite different and that in Salonika, there was "an open chain of command within the Jewish community whose very existence helped the process of spoliation and deportation" (171).

123. "After the War We Were All Together," 264.

124. Rozen, "Jews and Greeks Remember Their Past," 111–12.

125. Ibid., 121–23. Rozen lists the early recorders of history as Molho, Emmanuel, and Recanati. She writes that in order for Israelis to dissociate themselves from the shame of the victims and "to vindicate Greek collective consciousness for not having done enough to prevent the deportations," there was no alternative but to blame Koretz (130).

126. Ibid., 144.

127. Isaac Samuel Immanuel wrote a good portion of the first volume of *Zikhron Saloniki*. His lengthy discussion of the role of Koretz is found in "The History of the Jews of Saloniki," 261–64.

128. Lewkowicz, "After the War We Were All Together," 255.

129. See also Matarasso, "And Yet Not All of Them Died," 193, regarding the encouraging of young couples to wed.

130. See copla 51.

131. See copla 5.

132. Mazower, *Salonica, City of Ghosts*, 397.

133. Bouena sought a means of informing the outside world as to her whereabouts. She hoped that by appealing to the ego of her German guard, she might succeed in having her inadvertently provide a helpful clue. She informed the guard where she could find expert tailors and the bait was taken. The very appearance of the Nazi in the shop conveyed the message precisely as Bouena had intended (Garfinkle, "The Memoirs of Bouena Garfinkle," 15). The partisans dressed in Nazi uniforms in order to infiltrate the prison. This escape is mentioned in the preface as well.

134. After the war, Bouena heard that Georgette returned to Salonika, but she was not successful at locating her and regretted this dearly (see copla 96).

135. This information is found in the first part of copla 66.

136. See copla 67.

137. "Numerous memoirs illustrate . . . how difficult it was for city boys and girls to adjust to rough life in the mountains, especially after the weakening famines of the previous winters" (Bowman, *The Agony of Greek Jews*, 166).

138. It is interesting to note the discrepancy regarding the motivation of the consul. For Bouena, it was a humanitarian act. However, the author of a recent study on fascism contends that these individuals were saved solely due to political and economic considerations, not humanitarian. See Rodogno, *Fascism's European Empire*, 391–92.

139. See copla 66, comprising more than twenty lines. The verse begins with her decision to flee after being struck by Hasson. For some reason, in her poetry she did not write about her incarceration in prison; yet in her memoirs this plays a significant role. Not only did Bouena use her ingenuity while in jail to alert her comrades as to her whereabouts, but she managed to exploit her female guard. However, after the war, Bouena sought out the partisan who saved her, only to discover that the guard had tracked him down and murdered him.

140. Carpi discusses two means of escape from Salonika that were arranged by the Italian consulate: granting citizenship rights and underground smuggling. The smuggled individuals were led to the Italian-occupied zone "regardless of their nationality." There were officers "in charge of the movements of the Italian military trains which traveled from the German zone to the Italian zone. . . . This operation must have been carried out with the knowledge of both consuls, and in certain cases with their participation as well" ("A New Approach," 284–85).

141. See copla 68.

142. "Le cas de Mademoiselle Buena Sarfatty est par trop éloquent: Cette jeune fille qui ète au service de la Croiz Rouge Suisse, reçut du Consulat d'Italie de faux papiers d'identité au nom de Maria Tivoli, italienne originaire de Livourne. Le jour du départ de tous les Juifs sujets italiens et des 'assimilés,' pour Athènes, Mme Tivoli, *alias* Mlle Buena Sarfatty, en voile noir, passa devant le contrôle des Cerbères de la Gestapo. Le traître Hasson, attaché au service de cette organisation maudite, reconnut Mademoiselle Sarfatty qu'il avait impudemment giflée au camp du Baron Hirsch, quelques jours auparavant, mais intimidé par la presence du Consul, il n'osa rien révéler" (Michael Molho, *In Memoriam,* 141).

143. See copla 60. According to Dublon-Knebel, he was forbidden to leave, "accused of receiving gold from Greek Jews who wanted to prevent seizure of their property by the German authorities" (*German Foreign Office Documents,* 129). His wife remained with him, although their children were sent to Athens.

144. Once again, Bouena is precise about the details. Carpi relates the identical story, assuming that they were naïve to have thought that once on Italian soil, they were safe, and states that "their complacency proved to be their downfall." A week after the capitulation of Italy, an SS unit arrived and guarded the hotel until September 22 when they spent two nights butchering three generations of four of the most eminent Italian Jewish families ("A New Approach," 286–87).

145. See copla 97. Other Sephardi poets drew parallels between Hitler and Torquemada and other enemies of the Jewish people. See Lévy, *And the World Stood Silent,* 42–43.

146. Nico (sometimes spelled Nikko) was a dear friend of hers from Salonika.

147. Garfinkle, "The Memoirs of Bouena Garfinkle," 31.

148. Those who fled successfully usually managed to do so thanks to the aid of the partisans: from the shores of Attica (the area surrounding Athens) by sea to the island of Evvia, and from there in fishing boats or other vessels to Çesme on the Turkish coast (Kerem, "Efforts to Rescue," 83).

149. See copla 80.

150. Mazower, *Inside Hitler's Greece,* 258.

151. According to Bowman, the "attitude of the Resistance toward the Jews was magnanimous. Anyone who spoke Greek was considered a Greek" (*The Agony of Greek Jews,* 147).

152. Mazower points to two options for flight: fleeing to the hills, or leaving Greece by "travelling to the coast at Evvoia, from where *caizues* (fishing boats) took them to Turkey. Help did not always come without a price," as they were often forced to hand over their money and possessions, but "they were rarely denounced, despite the rewards offered by the SS" (*Inside Hitler's Greece*, 261). Bouena's group was accompanied by a Greek priest, whom she assumed was a partisan. However, after they arrived in Palestine, he was dressed as a military physician ("The Memoirs of Bouena Garfinkle," 86).

153. A detailed account of these developments is found in Friling, "Between Friendly and Hostile Neutrality," 309–423, especially 407–11. Various boatloads, including those carrying children are mentioned; one wonders if one of them contained Bouena and her charges.

154. It was reported that the "Greek consul in Izmir, who related to the Jews as he did to all other Greeks, was also involved and was organizing their transfer to Aleppo. From there, the refugees would require entrance visas to Palestine" (ibid., 410). See also Bowman, *The Agony of Greek Jews*, 199–202.

155. See copla 81.

156. See copla 84. She toasts the health of these suffering refugees.

157. See copla 85. Bouena points out that the plates were "filled to the top."

158. See Lewkowicz, "After the War We Were All Together," 247, for figures and details. Some had been participants in the death march that was intercepted by the Russians.

159. Bowman divides those who avoided deportations into three groups: some five hundred youth fighting in the partisans, families who escaped and his in mountains and villages; foreign citizens ("Salonikan Memories," 18–19).

160. For details see Rivlin, *Encyclopaedia*, 289.

161. Bowman discusses the unfortunate fate of some Jews who, after the war, were subjected to anti-Semitism and were also perceived as communists (*The Agony of Greek Jews*, 218). Fleming alludes to the "resentment and impassivity of Greek Christians who thought they were gone forever and had laid claim to their property. When asked to return the property, some Christians went so far as to express regret that not all the Jews had been killed. All of the survivors were depressed and stunned by the magnitude of the destruction" (*Greece*, 168).

162. In "Tale of a Ghetto Conspirator" she was careful not to mention this affiliation.

163. Baumel mentions the roles that women played in dealing with survivors, as relief workers for UNRRA, the Joint Distribution Committee, and the Religious Emergency Council (formed by the British Chief Rabbi), or as social workers, nurses, and emissaries from Palestine (*Double Jeopardy*, 31).

164. Survivors from Thrace and Macedonia crossed the southern border. Rivlin writes about this unexpected reception, noting the tensions with Greeks who had plundered Jewish property and the problems for Jewish institutions regarding restitutions and inheritance procedure. The Jewish aid that was offered, both from Palestine as well as from international groups, was insufficient in every way, particularly emotionally ("The Return from the Inferno," 38–40).

165. Bowman, *The Agony of Greek Jews*, 227. Matarasso confirms this information, stating that in September 1945, those liberated from Bergen-Belsen arrived there ("And Yet Not All of Them Died," 164).

166. See copla 90.

167. Rivlin, "The Return from the Inferno," 39.

168. See copla 91. There Bouena mentions traveling to a sanatorium in Zvestokori to see a friend named Sarika who had "returned from the war with tuberculosis. She was in bed with a high fever."

169. Fleming, *Greece,* 168.

170. See copla 90, an unusually long verse. The Joint Distribution Committee started helping in April 1945, and tried to help them reclaim property that was previously theirs. One representative estimated that there were twelve hundred survivors under the age of seventeen in Athens and six to seven thousand more in the rest of Greece. Despite participating in the preparatory program, there was often a long wait (Rivlin, "The Return from the Inferno," 41–43). The survivors who remained in Greece encountered an additional hardship, the cruel and bloody civil war from 1946 to 1949.

171. Some of her experiences at this juncture have been presented in the preface.

172. This is copla 94. She seems to have been so stunned by the occurrence that even in the writing of the copla she neglected to toast anyone.

173. See copla 70.

174. See copla 99 for the original phrasing; the final lines contain a saying about thieves and fortunetellers.

175. See copla 87.

176. This was a sore point for many returnees and the majority was not successful, with or without the aid of agencies. The Jewish Committee tried to discover which homes were "sold" during the deportations and which stores might be restored to their owners or their owners' descendants (Rivlin, "The Return from the Inferno," 41–43). Regarding property, see also Fleming, *Greece,* 174–78; Plaut, *Greek Jewry,* 79–88; and Mazower, *Salonica, City of Ghosts,* 420–25.

177. See copla 95. Bouena describes him as having had "a large head and a skeletal [emaciated] body."

178. The general policy was to send surviving children to Israel, although some who had lived with Christian families and had no memories of their past were reluctant to leave.

179. See copla 88. There she toasts the "religious women from the convent in our city." She and the members of her group approached parents of newborns and warned them that there was danger ahead, emphasizing the fact that the lives of babies would surely be at risk. The girls engaged in their activities after sundown, removing their badges and dressing like Greek girls in order to get past the police. They wrapped the babies like packages and then deposited them at convents or monasteries. Bouena hid nearby in order to observe and ascertain that the sisters or nurses found the "packages." Because she could not return to the ghetto at night, she would stay overnight with Christian friends. Bouena "succeeded in 'abandoning' 25 babies" ("Tale of a Ghetto Conspirator," 10).

180. See copla 89.

181. See copla 98.

182. See copla 89.

183. Bouena was photographed on April 7, 1946, at the first group wedding for couples, which she helped organize. See fig. 1.2.

BIBLIOGRAPHY

Apostolou, Andrew. "'The Exception of Salonika': Bystanders and Collaborators in Northern Greece." *Holocaust and Genocide Studies* 14, no. 2 (2000): 165–96.

Assaf, Simcha. "Time of the Book and the Book." [In Hebrew.] *Rishumot* 1 (1917): 292–316.

Attias, Moshe. "Marriage Customs in Salonica." [In Hebrew.] *Edoth* 1 (1946): 28–35.

———. "Purim Holiday." In *Salonique,* 157–67.

———. "The Salonikan Romancero." In *Salonique,* 200–205.

———. "Purim in Salonika." [In Hebrew.] *Guinzach Saloniki* 1 (1961): 55–73.

Baumel, Judith Tydor. *Double Jeopardy: Gender and the Holocaust.* London: Vallentine Mitchell, 1998.

Baumgarten, Elisheva. *Mothers and Children: Jewish Family Life in Medieval Europe.* Princeton, N.J.: Princeton University Press, 2004.

Beit-Arié, Malachi. "The Private Nature of the Hebrew Medieval Book Production and Consumption." [In Hebrew.] In Kaplan and Sluhovsky, *Libraries and Book Collections,* 91–103.

Ben, Yosef. *Greek Jewry in the Holocaust and the Resistance, 1941–1944* [in Hebrew]. Tel-Aviv: Ahdut and the Institute of the Saloniki Jewry Research Center, 1985.

Benbassa, Esther, and Aron Rodrigue. *Sephardi Jewry: A History of the Judeo-Spanish Community, 14th–20th Centuries.* Berkeley: University of California Press, 2000.

Benveniste, David. *The Jews of Salonika in Recent Times* [in Hebrew]. Jerusalem: Kiryat Sefer, 1973.

Bodian, Miriam. "The 'Portuguese' Dowry Societies in Venice and Amsterdam: A Case Study within the Marrano Diaspora." *Italia* 6 (1987): 30–61.

Bowman, Steven B. *The Agony of Greek Jews, 1940–1945.* Stanford, Calif.: Stanford University Press, 2009.

———. "Salonikan Memories." In Bowman, *The Holocaust in Salonika,* 1–22.

Bowman, Steven B., ed. *The Holocaust in Salonika: Eyewitness Accounts.* N.p.: Sephardic House, 2002.

Bunis, David M. *Voices from Jewish Salonika.* Jerusalem: Misgav Yerushalayim, 1999.

Carpi, Daniel. "A New Approach to Some Episodes in the History of the Jews in Salonika during the Holocaust." In Rozen, *The Last Ottoman Century and Beyond,* 2:259–89.

———. "The Jews of Greece during the Holocaust Period (1941–43)." [In Hebrew.] In *Then and Now: Annual Lectures on the Jews of Greece,* ed. Zvi Ankori, 107–35. Tel Aviv: Tel Aviv University, 1984.

Carpi, Daniel, ed. *Italian Diplomatic Documents on the History of the Holocaust in Greece (1941–1943).* Tel Aviv: The Diaspora Research Institute, Tel Aviv University, 1999.

Chase, Malcolm, and Christopher Shaw. "The Dimensions of Nostalgia." In *The Imagined Past: History and Nostalgia*, ed. Shaw and Chase, 1–17. Manchester: Manchester University Press, 1989.

Cohen, Judith R. "Judeo-Spanish Song in the Sephardic Communities of Montreal and Toronto." Ph.D. diss., Université de Montréal, 1989.

———. "Selanikli Humour in Montreal: The Repertoire of Bouena Sarfatty Garfinkle." In *Judeo-Espaniol: Proceedings of the 4th International Conference on the Judeo-Spanish Language*, ed. Rena Molho, Hilary Pomeroy, and Elena Romero, 220–42. Thessaloniki: Ets Ahaim Foundation, 2011.

———. "Three Canadian Sephardic Women and their Transplanted Repertoires: From Salonica, Larache and Sarajevo to Montreal and Kahnawáke." In *Folk Music, Traditional Music, Ethnomusicology: Canadian Perspectives, Past and Present Folk Music*, ed. Anna Hoefnagels and Gordon Smith, 150–62. Cambridge: Cambridge Scholars Press, 2007.

Colonas, Vassilis. "The Contribution of the Jewish Community to the Modernization of Salonika at the End of the Nineteenth Century." In Rozen, *The Last Ottoman Century and Beyond*, 2:165–72.

Constantopoulou, Photini, and Thanos Veremis, eds. *Documents on the History of the Greek Jews: Records from the Historical Archives of the Ministry of Foreign Affairs*. Athens: Kastaniotis Editions, 1999.

Díaz-Mas, Paloma. *Sephardim: The Jews from Spain*. Chicago: University of Chicago Press, 1992.

Dublon-Knebel, Irith. *German Foreign Office Documents on the Holocaust in Greece (1937–1944)*. Tel Aviv: Tel Aviv University, 2007.

"Economic Life in Salonika." In *Salonique*, 233–48.

Felman, Shoshana, and Dori Laub. *Testimony: Crises of Witnessing in Literature, Psychoanalysis, and History*. New York: Routledge, 1992.

Fleming, K. E. *Greece: A Jewish History*. Princeton, N.J.: Princeton University Press, 2008.

Friling, Tuvia. "Between Friendly and Hostile Neutrality: Turkey and the Jews during World War II." In Rozen, *The Last Ottoman Century*, 2:309–423.

Garfinkle, Bouena Sarfatty. "The Memoirs of Bouena Garfinkle." Unpublished typescript, 1975.

Garfinkle, Buena [*sic*]. "Tale of a Ghetto Conspirator." *The Pioneer Woman* (April 1947): 10–11.

Grossman, Avraham. *Pious and Rebellious: Jewish Women in Medieval Europe*. Waltham, Mass.: Brandeis University Press, 2004.

Gutwirth, Eliezer, and M. A. Motis Dolader. "Twenty-Six Libraries from Fifteenth-Century Spain." *The Library*, 6th ser., 18 (1996): 27–53.

Hadar, Gila. "Aspects of Jewish Family Life in Salonika, 1900–1943." [In Hebrew.] Ph.D. diss., University of Haifa, 2003.

Halevi, Sa'adi ben Besalel. *A Jewish Voice from Ottoman Salonica: The Ladino Memoir of Sa'adi Besalel a-Levi,* ed. Aron Rodrigue and Sarah Abrevaya Stein, trans. Isaac Jerusalmi. Stanford, Calif.: Stanford University Press, 2012.

Handeli, Ya'acov. *A Greek Jew From Salonica Remembers,* trans. Martin Kett. New York: Herzl Press, 1993.

Hassán, I. M. "Un género castizo sefardí: Las coplas." In *Los sefardíes: Cultura y literatura,* ed. Paloma Díaz Más, 103–23. San Sebastián: Universidad del País Vasco, 1987.

Havassy, Rivka. "The Ladino Song in the Twentieth Century: A Study of the Collections of Emily Sene and Bouena Sarfatty-Garfinkle." [In Hebrew.] Ph.D. diss., Bar-Ilan University, 2006.

———. "'Si mosós no las vamos a recoger . . . ': The Songbooks of Emily Sene and Bouena Sarfatty-Garfinkle." In *Los sefardíes ante los retos del mundo contemporáneo: identidad y mentalidades,* ed. Paloma Díaz-Maz and María Sánchez Pérez, 247–56. Madrid: CSIS, 2010.

Haviv, Gavriel. "Local Community Projects and Various Charity Institutions." [In Hebrew.] In *Salonique,* 215–19.

Hekimoglou, Evanghelos. "Jewish Pauperism in Salonika, 1940–1941." In Rozen, *The Last Ottoman Century and Beyond,* 2:195–205.

Horowitz, Elliott. "The Dowering of Brides in the Ghetto of Venice: Between Tradition and Change, Ideas and Reality." [In Hebrew.] *Tarbiz* 56 (1987): 347–71.

Immanuel, Isaac Samuel. "The History of the Jews of Saloniki." In Recanati, *Zikhron Saloniki,* 1:3–272.

Kallis, Aristotle A. "The Jewish Community of Salonica under Siege: The Antisemitic Violence of the Summer of 1931." *Holocaust and Genocide Studies* 20, no. 1 (2006): 34–56.

Kaplan, Yosef, and Moshe Sluhovsky, eds. *Libraries and Book Collections* [in Hebrew]. Jerusalem: Shazar Center, 2006.

Kazis, Y. S., trans. *Los amores de Yangulas* [in Ladino, Hebrew font in Rashi script]. 2 vols. Salonika: Idisiyon del "Shamar," 1927.

Kerem, Itzhak. "Efforts to Rescue the Jews of Greece during the Second World War." [In Hebrew.] *Pe'amim* 27 (1986): 77–109.

———. "The Europeanization of the Sephardic Community of Salonika." In *From Iberia to Diaspora: Studies in Sephardic History and Culture,* ed. Yedida K. Stillman and Norman A. Stillman, 58–74. Leiden: Brill, 1999.

Koliopulos, John S., "Brigandage and Irredentism in Nineteenth-Century Greece." *European History Quarterly* 19 (1989): 193–228.

Koretz, Arieh. *Bergen-Belsen: Tagebuch eines Jugendlichen.* Göttingen: Wallstein, 2011.

———. *Diary of a Youth: Bergen Belsen 11.7.44–30.3.45* [in Hebrew]. N.p.: n.p., 1992.

Kounio Amariglio, Erika. *From Thessaloniki to Auschwitz and Back: Memories of a Survivor from Thessaloniki.* London: Vallentine Mitchell, 2000.

Kounio, Heinz Salvator. *A Liter of Soup and Sixty Grams of Bread.* N.p.: Sephardic House, 2003.

Lattek, Christine. "Bergen-Belsen: From 'Privileged' Camp to Death Camp." In *Belsen in History and Memory*, ed. Jo Reilly, David Cesarani, Tony Kushner, and Colin Richmond, 37–71. New York: Frank Cass, 1997.

Levine Melammed, Renée. "The Memoirs of a Partisan from Salonika." *Nashim* 7 (2004): 151–73.

———. "Noticias sobre los ritos de los nacimientos y de la pureza de las judeo-conversas castellanas del siglo XVI." *El Olivo* 13, nos. 29–30 (1989): 235–43.

Lévy, Isaac Jack. *And the World Stood Silent: Sephardic Poetry of the Holocaust.* Urbana and Chicago: University of Illinois Press, 1989.

Lewkowicz, Bea. "After the War We Were All Together: Jewish Memories of Postwar Thessaloniki." In Mazower, *After the War Was Over*, 247–72.

———. *The Jewish Community of Salonika: History, Memory, Identity.* London: Vallentine Mitchell, 2006.

Marcus, Shimon. "The Beginning of the Haskalah and Upgrading the Educational System in Salonika." [In Hebrew.] In *Salonique*, 67–73.

Matarasso, Isaac Aaron. "'And Yet Not All of Them Died . . . ': The Destruction of Salonika's Greek Jews during the German Occupation." In Bowman, *The Holocaust in Salonika*, 125–235.

Matsas, Michael. *The Illusion of Safety: The Story of the Greek Jews During World War II.* New York: Pella, 1997.

Mazower, Mark. *Inside Hitler's Greece: The Experience of Occupation, 1941–1944.* New Haven, Conn.: Yale University Press, 2001.

———. "Policing the Anti-Communist State in Greece, 1922–1974." In *The Policing of Politics in the Twentieth Century: Historical Perspectives*, ed. Mark Mazower, 129–50. Providence, R.I.: Berghahn, 1997.

———. *Salonica, City of Ghosts: Christians, Muslims and Jews, 1430–1950.* New York: Alfred A. Knopf, 2005.

Mazower, Mark, ed. *After the War Was Over: Reconstructing the Family, Nation, and State in Greece, 1943–1960.* Princeton, N.J.: Princeton University Press, 2000.

Messinas, Elias V. *The Synagogues of Salonika and Veroia.* Athens: Gavrielides Editions, 1997.

Mintz, Alan. *Hurban: Responses to Catastrophe in Hebrew Literature.* New York: Columbia University Press, 1974.

Molho, Michael. "Birth and Childhood among the Jews of Salonica." [In Hebrew.] *Edoth* 2 (1947): 255–69.

———. *El cementerio judío de Salónica.* Madrid: Instituto Arias Montano, 1949.

———. "A History of the Jews of Salonika." In *Salonique*, 5–37.

———. *In Memoriam: Hommage aux Victimes Juives des Nazis en Grèce.* Thessaloniki: Revue Hellinismos Abroad, 1973.

———. "Spaniolit Journalism in Salonika." In *Salonique*, 103–108.

———. *Traditions and Customs of the Sephardic Jews of Salonica.* New York: Foundation for the Advancement of Sephardic Studies and Culture, 2006.

Molho, Michael, and Yosef Nehama. *The Destruction of Greek Jewry, 1941–1944* [in Hebrew]. Jerusalem: Yad Vashem, 1965.

Molho, Rena. "Education in the Jewish Community of Thessaloniki in the Beginning of the Twentieth Century." *Balkan Studies* 34 (1993): 259–69.

———. "The Jewish Community of Salonika and Its Incorporation into the Greek State 1912–19." *Middle Eastern Studies* 24 (1988): 391–403.

———. "Jewish Working-Class Neighborhoods Established in Salonika Following the 1890 and 1917 Fires." In Rozen, *The Last Ottoman Century and Beyond*, 2:173–94.

———. "Judeo-Spanish Plays on the Themes of Tradition and Change in the Early Twentieth Century." *Proceedings of the Twelfth British Conference on Judeo-Spanish Studies (2001): Sephardic Language, Literature and History*, ed. Hilary Pomeroy and Michael Alpert, 141–48. Leiden: Brill, 2004.

———. "Popular Antisemitism and State Policy in Salonika during the City's Annexation to Greece." *JSS* 50 (1988): 253–64.

———. *Salonica and Istanbul: Social, Political and Cultural Aspects of Jewish Life.* Istanbul: Isis Press, 2005.

Molho, René. *They Say Diamonds Don't Burn: The Holocaust Experiences of René Molho of Salonika, Greece.* Berkeley, Calif.: Judah L. Magnes Museum, 1994.

Naar, Devin E. "From the 'Jerusalem of the Balkans' to the *Goldene Medina:* Jewish Immigration from Salonika to the United States." *American Jewish History* 93, no. 4 (2007): 435–73.

Nehama, Joseph. *Dictionnaire du judéo-espagnol.* Madrid: Instituto Arias Montano, 1977.

Norich, Anita. "Jewish Literatures and Feminist Criticism: An Introduction to Gender and Text." In *Gender and Text in Modern Hebrew and Yiddish Literature*, ed. Naomi B. Sokoloff, Anne Lapidus Lerner, and Anita Norich, 1–15. New York: JTS, 1992.

Ofer, Dalia, and Lenore J. Weitzman, eds. *Women in the Holocaust.* New Haven, Conn.: Yale University Press, 1998.

Orfali, Moises. "The Portuguese Dowry Society in Livorno and the Marrano Diaspora." *Studia Rosenthalia* 35 (2001): 143–56.

Papo, Joseph M. *Sephardim in Twentieth Century America: In Search of Unity.* San Jose, Calif.: Pelé Yoetz, 1987.

Perez, Avner, and Gladys Pimienta, eds. *Diksionario Amplio Djudeo-espanyol-Ebreo.* Maale Adumim, Israel: Instituto Maale Adumim, 2008.

Plaut, Joshua Eli. *Greek Jewry in the Twentieth Century, 1913–1983.* Madison, N.J.: Fairleigh Dickinson University Press, 1996.

Recanati, Auri. *Jewish Community of Salonika 1943.* Jerusalem: Erez, 2000.

Recanati, David A., ed. *Zikhron Saloniki: Grandeza i Destruyicion de Yeruchalayim del Balkan (= A Memorial to Saloniki)* [in Hebrew]. 2 vols. Tel Aviv: The Committee for Publishing the Book of the Community of Saloniki, 1971, 1985.

Refael, Shmuel. *Un grito en el silencio: La poesía sobre el Holocausto en lengua sefardí: Estudio y antología*. Barcelona: Tirocinio, 2008.

———. "The Holocaust in the Poetry of Bouena Sarfatty of Salonika." [In Hebrew.] *The Languages and Literatures of the Spanish and Oriental Jews*, ed. Jacob Bentulilla, David Bunis and Ephraim Hazan, 128–41. Jerusalem: Misgav Yerushalayim, 2009.

———. *I Will Tell a Poem: A Study of the Judeo-Spanish (Ladino) Coplas* [in Hebrew]. Jerusalem: Carmel, 2004.

Reilly, Joanne. *Belsen: The Liberation of a Concentration Camp*. London: Routledge, 1998.

Rivlin, Bracha. *Encyclopaedia of Jewish Communities: Greece* [in Hebrew]. Jerusalem: Yad Vashem, 1998.

———. "The Return from the Inferno." [In Hebrew.] *Massuah* 3 (1995): 38–46.

Rodogno, David. *Fascism's European Empire*. Cambridge: Cambridge University Press, 2006.

Romero, Elena. *Bibliografía analítica de ediciones de coplas sefardíes*. Madrid: Consejo Superior de Investigationes Científicas, 1992.

———. "Las Coplas sefardíes: Categorías e estado de la cuestión." In *Actas de las Jornadas de Estudios Sefardíes*, ed. Antonio Viudas Camarassa, 69–80. Cáceres: Universidad de Extremadura, 1981.

———. *Coplas sefardies: Primera selección*. Cordoba: Ediciones el Almendro, 1988.

———. *Entre dos (o más) fuegos: Fuentes poéticas para la historia de los sefardíes de los Balcanes*. Madrid: Consejo Superior de Investigaciones Científicas, 2008.

Roskies, David. *Against the Apocalypse: Responses to Catastrophe in Modern Jewish Culture*. Cambridge, Mass: Harvard University Press, 1984.

———. *The Jewish Search for a Usable Past*. Bloomington: Indiana University Press, 1999.

———. *The Literature of Destruction: Jewish Responses to Catastrophe*. Philadelphia: JPS, 1988.

Roth, Cecil. "The Last Days of Jewish Salonica." *Commentary* 5 (1950): 49–55.

Rozen, Minna. "Jews and Greeks Remember Their Past: The Political Career of Tzevi Koretz (1933–43)." *Jewish Social Studies* 12, no. 1 (2005): 111–66.

———. *The Last Ottoman Century and Beyond: The Jews in Turkey and the Balkans, 1808–1945*, vol. 1. Tel Aviv: Tel Aviv University, 2005.

Rozen, Minna, ed. *The Last Ottoman Century and Beyond: The Jews in Turkey and the Balkans, 1808–1945*, vol. 2. Tel Aviv: Tel Aviv University, 2002.

Salonique, Ville-Mère en Israël [in Hebrew]. Jerusalem and Tel Aviv: Centre de Recherches sur le Judaïsme de Salonique, 1967.

Scholem, Gershom. *Sabbatai Sevi.* Princeton, N.J.: Princeton University Press, 1976.

Sciaky, Leon. *Farewell to Salonica.* New York: Current Books, 1946.

Shalem, Haim. "The Workers' Moshav 'Tsur Moshe.'" [In Hebrew.] In *Salonique,* 351.

Sokoloff, Naomi, Anne Lapidus Lerner, and Anita Norich, eds. *Gender and Text in Modern Hebrew and Yiddish Literature.* New York: JTS, 1992.

Stein, Sarah Abrevaya. *Making Jews Modern: The Yiddish and Ladino Press in the Russian and Ottoman Empires.* Bloomington: Indiana University Press, 2004.

Stroumsa, Jacques. *Tu choisiras la vie: Violiniste à Auschwitz.* Paris: Édicions du Cerf, 1998.

———. *Violinist in Auschwitz: From Salonica to Jerusalem, 1913–1967.* Hartung-Gorre Verlag Konstanz, 1996.

Usque, Samuel. *Consolation for the Tribulations of Israel,* trans. Martin A. Cohen. Philadelphia: JPS, 1965.

Ussishkin, Moshe. "Community Activity in the Realms of Housing, Education and Social Aid at the Threshold of World War Two." In *Salonique,* 211–14.

Uziel, Joseph. "The History of the Zionist Movement." In *Salonique,* 109–15.

Vervenioti, Tassoula. "Left-Wing Women between Politics and Family." In Mazower, *After the War Was Over,* 105–21.

Weich-Shahak, Susana. "Coplas: A Judeo-Spanish Educational Genre." *Journal of Jewish Music and Liturgy* 21 (1998–99): 41–50.

———. "Stylistic Features of the Sephardi Coplas." *Hispano-Jewish Civilization after 1492,* ed. Michel Abitbol, Yom-Tov Assis and Galit Hassan-Rokem, 101–24. Jerusalem: Misgav Yerushalayim, 1997.

Weissler, Chava. *Voices of the Matriarchs.* Boston: Beacon Press, 1998.

Yacoel, Yomtov. "In the Anteroom to Hell: Memoir." In Bowman, *The Holocaust in Salonika,* 25–121.

Yakuel, Yom-Tov. "On the Path to Destruction." In *Salonique,* 275–90.

INDEX OF COMMUNITY MEMBERS'
NAMES THAT APPEAR IN THE COPLAS

Families

INDEX

For community members' names appearing in the coplas, see the separate index.
Page numbers in italics represent illustrations.

tobacco workers, 1, 34; girls as, 11, 29, 83, 264n23; organizing and striking, 4, 117, 273n78
Trabout, Sarah, x, 183, 190–91, 208, 217, 231, 233, 239
traditional dress, 14, 71, 91, 93, 145, 147, 151, 157. *See also* fez
trousseau, 21–25, 30, 36, 59, 63, 65, 67, 71, 270n16, 271n26, 271n29, 274n86; Bouena's, xii, 208, 271n40
Tsur Moshe moshav, 50, 51, 165
Turkey, xii, 6, 49; Donmëh, return to, 47, 169, 169n179; flight to, 204, 205, 243, 262nn18–19, 287n152; Greek consul in, 287n154; Greeks in, 47

UNRRA, 12, 206, 249, 263n20, 287n163

Vardar, Regie, 3, 6, 99, 152n149, 171, 191, 217, 218n11, 219, 233
Venizelos, Eleutherios, 5, 6, 7, 23, 47, 49, 172, 173, 173n185; street, 35, 71, 121
Veria, xii, 201, 223, 239, 241

Waldheim, Kurt, 233n39, 282n78
weddings, 18, 21, 22, 23, 24, 25, 26, 41, 45, 52, 61, 65, 67, 69, 71, 73, 97, 99, 111, 147, 148n144, 208, 270n14, 272n51; Bouena's, xi, xii, *212;* group, xv, *27,* 210, 271n38, 288n183; inviters to, 46, 276n25; during WWII, 180, 188, 227, 229, 231

White Tower, 39, 40, 131, 131n120, 145, 159, 175, 175n189, 275n6
widows, x, 28, 30, 32, 73, 77, 78n31, 79, 165, 185, 186, 196, 198, 221, 223, 273n71, 273n75
women's roles, 11, 13, 15, 16, 20, 21, 23, 29, 30, 36, 39, 41, 43, 46, 50, 87, 97, 122–25, 135, 139, 141, 169, 267n72, 275n17; in ceremonies, 28, 39, 75, 135, 137, 272n49, 275n8; as cultural transmitters, 12, 13, 36; as musicians, 125, 274n86; as volunteers, 184; in wedding preparations, 24, 25, 30, 36, 71, 148n144, 270n23; during WWII, x, 159, 185, 196, 222, 263n20, 267n75, 287n163. *See also* Bona la Tanyedora; dressmaking; baths: ritual bath; widows
World War I, 5, 8, 10, 47, 265n33

Yangoula, 173, 173n184
Yedi Kule prison, 51, *52,* 131n120, 159, 159n163, 277n55
Yom Kippur, 39, 44, 133, 135, 175, 239
Young Turk Revolution, 3, 7; influence on Jews, 46

Zamboni, Guelfo, 188, 202, 278n22, 280n54, 285n128
Zionism, 7, 46, 50, 165, 276n30; and establishing school, 34; and groups, 4, 7, 10, 50, 165, 169; and socializing, 63
Zionist fundraising, 41, 50, 167, 169

RENÉE LEVINE MELAMMED (BA, Smith College; MA, PhD, Brandeis University) is Professor of Jewish History at the Schechter Institute in Jerusalem and the academic editor of the gender and Jewish women's studies journal *Nashim* (IUP). Her first book, *Heretics or Daughters of Israel? The Crypto-Jewish Women of Castile,* received two National Jewish Book Awards. She has also authored *A Question of Identity: Iberian Conversos in Historical Perspective* and numerous articles in English, Hebrew, French, and Spanish; and edited a Hebrew collection of essays, *"Lift Up Your Voice": Women's Voices and Feminist Interpretation in Jewish Studies.*

www.ingramcontent.com/pod-product-compliance
Lightning Source LLC
Chambersburg PA
CBHW070402100426
42812CB00005B/1602